Power and Community in World Politics

Bruce M. Russett

YALE UNIVERSITY

W. H. FREEMAN AND COMPANY
San Francisco

Library of Congress Cataloging in Publication Data

Russett, Bruce M
    Power and community in world politics.

    Includes bibliographical references.
    1. International relations. I. Title.
JX1391.R87   327   73-13590
ISBN 0-7167-0782-9
ISBN 0-7167-0781-0 (pbk.)

Printed in the United States of America

1 2 3 4 5 6 7 8 9

for Meg and Lu

Above all things may you be young and glad.
And even if it is Sunday may you be wrong.
For when men are always right they are no
longer young.

e. e. cummings

Contents

Preface

The "peace research" movement has represented an attempt to apply rigorous and frequently quantitative analytical techniques to questions of war and peace, drawing on the theories and methods of all the social sciences. The movement has changed greatly over the past fifteen or so years. At the beginning of that period, a handful of innovators were trying, with the examples of Quincy Wright and Lewis Frye Richardson before them, to apply rigorous techniques of theorizing and data analysis. They were greatly hampered by the lack both of adequate data for analysis and of the financial assistance necessary to support their projects and to gather a "critical mass" of scholars. And only a few members of the handful came from academic backgrounds where they had been properly trained in scientific method and quantitative techniques. On the whole, progress took on the nature of a bootstrap operation. Men such as Karl Deutsch, Harold Guetzkow, Robert North, and the *Conflict Resolution* group at the University of Michigan were pioneers, and often pioneers in territory that was not barren, but, indeed, rather well populated by hostile tribes.

During the course of the 1960s this situation changed drastically. Each of the men or groups just mentioned established major research projects, often with substantial financial assistance from the federal government, particularly the National Science Foundation. They trained new scholars at their universities, and indeed those they trained in turn trained others, for a third generation of researchers. These were joined by others, from different intellectual traditions. By the beginning of the 1970s a number of major data archives were accessible to scholars anywhere; enormous improvements in the sophistication of computers, and of users of computers, made possible much more searching examinations of the data; "classical" data analysis had been supplemented, and sometimes replaced, by simulation; theories had been refined and often expressed formally; and virtually every major American university had several faculty members actively engaged in scientific analysis on problems of peace and war. Moreover, the movement had spread abroad, especially to Britain and Scandinavia. Particularly notable was the group that grew up at the Peace Research Institute in Oslo, bringing a set of theoretical perspectives derived more strongly from sociology and providing a point of view that did not always coincide with that held by most North Americans. It seemed that a peace research community was safely established—and indeed it began to take on some of the characteristics of an "establishment."

But it was not solidly established. For one thing, many of us probably exaggerated, perhaps in understandable enthusiasm, the power of our new theories and methods. In having to struggle to build the movement, we often failed to communicate, or even fully to recognize, the very limited nature of our achievements, based as they were on only a few short years of research by what never numbered more than about a hundred active, producing scholars. We had not solved the problem of why wars happen any more than medical researchers had solved the problem of the causes of cancer; at best we had some partial answers to some very limited questions, and some promising leads. We had failed (not very surprisingly, considering the complexity of the phenomena) to develop a coherent overarching theory; this made teaching difficult and often left students confused and put off. Some reaction to the oversell began to set in—not least among a few of the former enthusiasts.

Probably more important was a realization that we had been asking a narrower set of questions than we had fully realized. Most American "peace researchers" were never simpleminded cheerleaders for "our" side in the Cold War; indeed we can take pride, in retrospect, in being more open-minded than many of our contemporaries. Yet I think we failed seriously to consider, in the rigorous ways which we championed, some critical hypotheses about the roots of that conflict. We were not, on the whole, very sensitive to theories of imperialism or to the need for testing alternative explanations of that phenomenon, such as those stressing economic versus ideological determinants. And though we *were* sensitive to the problem of inequalities among peoples and nations of the world as a root of war, and of the need to narrow those inequalities, we were not very imaginative in seeking alternative explanations for the causes of those inequalities.

Our difficulties were compounded by changes in the world environment. Widespread revulsion against United States foreign policy, both within the United States and abroad, compelled a new set of inquiries for which we were not entirely prepared. Our failure to carry these out rapidly and searchingly enough left the field to others. Although it was essential to have new minds and perspectives join the inquiry, not all the joiners shared a concern for testable theories and evidence. (Many *did*, however.) Some already knew the answers, and thought of research as a means of demonstrating rather than discovering. Research groups broke up, funds grew scarce, and many researchers shifted to other interests—most notably to problems of domestic rather than international political and social conflict. Although we have continued to add to our knowledge, I think the "peace research" movement is no stronger *now* than it was at the end of the 1960s—though I believe the shakeup which has forced us to reexamine some of our assumptions will work to the long-run health of the movement.

From a personal standpoint, I believe that the basic commitment to a social science of peace research, composed of a respect for evidence, the development of rigorous, formal theory, and an openness to the theories, data, methods, and findings of other sciences, was and remains right. But I recognize that not all elements of that formula are always appropriate, and that we do not always apply them even when they are.

Nor do all the questions we asked several years ago still seem the important ones. Some of the pieces in this volume have a slightly quaint air about them. Not surprisingly, this is most noticeable in the more applied papers, notably Chapter 6 ("The Asia Rimland as a 'Region' for Containing China"). The concern for containing China, in light of the industrial and military weaknesses of China, a revised view of Chinese intentions, and the rise of Japanese capabilities, is clearly passé. Methodologically and theoretically, Chapter 2 ("A Macroscopic View of International Politics") expresses a conviction I now hold a little less firmly. Initially written in January 1968 (though not published until four years later), it accurately summed up the thrust of my work at that time, and that of a number of other scholars. It represented an emphasis on the distribution of bonds, links, patterns of interaction, and transactions among states; on alliance formation and cohesion, integration, clusters of states that may form, scatter, and re-form to build or to weaken major coalitions. This was a "macroscopic," "systemic," "environment of international politics" mode of analysis that concentrated on characteristics of whole international or national systems. With international systems, questions of polarity, stability, and power concentration over the entire globe, and also in regional subsystems, were important. Additionally, much attention was given to regional integration and to pairwise or "dyadic" relationships among nation states. Cross-national research using aggregate data on nation-states fed into this work, and also provided the basic information employed in comparative research on the international behavior of various types of national systems.

I do think this approach has proved valuable, and I have not abandoned it. At the same time, and in part because of its successes, its omissions are also apparent. In my more recent work I have become more interested in subnational political system determinants of foreign policy, and sufficiently more interested in ideological influences to want to compare them systematically with economic influences. Even in dyadic relationships, it is obvious that we must be more concerned with problems of dependence and the structures of national and international systems that create or reinforce dependence. And other scholars are pointing out the limitations of a perspective that focuses on national actors at the expense of ignoring transnational ones.[1]

---

[1]Although hardly the only such argument, perhaps the most comprehensive is made by Robert O. Keohane and J. S. Nye, in their introduction and conclusion to the special issue of *International Organization*, 25, 3 (summer 1971), pp. 329–49 and 721–48, on "Transnational Relations and World Politics."

SOME REFLECTIONS

This volume brings together a number of papers written over the past twelve years. It does not include any of my papers on comparative politics or on methodology nor, with two partial exceptions, does it include articles subsequently incorporated in substantial part into the text of my other books.[2] All but the introduction and one and a half of the papers[3] have been previously published, though they do not include those materials published in the most readily accessible journals of political science—*World Politics* and the *American Political Science Review*. The purpose, nevertheless, is not simply to bring together in a convenient spot various fugitive pieces, but to bring together a set of papers that have a coherence and common focus or common foci. Thus what is here is most of my article-length writings on international politics, with the above exceptions and excepting a few which, though on international politics, are not importantly related to this main body. What is here is interwoven around the themes of macroanalysis of international politics and of war avoidance and international cooperation. Together they say some things—particularly about futures, about power and its limits, and about integration—that are not otherwise available. The materials stem from a concern with how social science can contribute to better policy, and specifically from a conviction about the limitations of a power-oriented view of world politics and a concern with the conditions for peaceful cooperation among nations.

In putting these together I have confined my editing to minimal details in some previously published materials. Essentially I have only eliminated redundancies such as methodological discussions which were the same in more than one piece, removed some anachronisms or revised references to events as "recent" that are no longer recent, and updated a few footnotes. In the latter case, I have completed references to some materials that were only "forthcoming" at the time the original articles were written, but have not tried to add new material. In a handful of instances I have revised or clarified dated material, but not so as to make myself look like an inspired prophet. Some of the oldest materials (notably Chapter 10, "Cause, Surprise, and No

---

[2]One of those partial exceptions is Chapter 2, "A Macroscopic View of International Politics," about half of which was included in the final chapter of my *No Clear and Present Danger: A Skeptical View of the United States Entry into World War II* (New York: Harper and Row, 1972). Despite the duplication it is essential to have it here for its function of tying together many pieces of research I carried out over the preceding decade. Without it the integration I have attempted here would be nearly impossible. The other exception is Chapter 13, "Pearl Harbor: Deterrence Theory and Decision Theory." A somewhat updated version, stressing historical and policy considerations, also appeared in *No Clear and Present Danger*. In that incarnation, however, I omitted much of the theoretical material in the original version as reprinted here; that theoretical material was a further and necessary development of the theory specified in "The Calculus of Deterrence," here Chapter 12. Without the Pearl Harbor material "Calculus" is incomplete.

[3]Chapter 15, "The Instruments of Influence and the Limits of Power," and part of Chapter 9, "The Rich Fifth and the Poor Half."

Escape") look a little gray around the fringes. Some of the policy recommendations in that piece have been made obsolescent by technological developments like the hot line, and other theoretical and methodological points have been overtaken by recent research. But I think that most of it still remains relevant, and I have left it pretty much alone rather than selectively cut it in a way that would inevitably destroy its integrity.

Methodologically, the pieces in this volume are eclectic. Many use quantitative data and mathematical techniques such as correlation, factor analysis, or simple contingency tables. At least one (Chapter 7, "Is There a Long-Run Trend toward Concentration in the International System?") attempts a rigorous empirical test of several deductive hypotheses derived from statistical theory. Others, such as Chapter 12 ("The Calculus of Deterrence"), test a variety of hypotheses proposed by me and other theorists, but without the strict deductive origin. Yet others, such as Chapters 4–6 (about regions and regionalism) and Chapter 17 ("An Empirical Typology of International Military Alliances") are analyses stimulated by various hypotheses, but with an important inductive component. Others use some quantitative data without any tests of association whatever, or like Chapter 13 ("Pearl Harbor: Deterrence Theory and Decision Theory") and Chapter 10 ("Cause, Surprise, and No Escape") solely employ case study materials. Still others are speculative, attempts at synthesis rather than new research, or even, like Chapter 14 ("A Countercombatant Deterrent?"), in large part normative.

The first chapter ("International Behavior Research: Case Studies and Cumulation") explicitly sets forth the argument that the study of international politics must not be limited to the practitioners of any single, narrow set of methods. Some important questions easily lend themselves to mathematical model building or to rigorous empirical testing. For others the task is not so obvious or straightforward, but it can be done, without seriously compromising the utility of the results, by someone determined to do so. I suspect that these instances are *much* more common than is believed by many scholars and policy makers suspicious of quantitative research. Nevertheless there are also cases, many of them, where scientific methods are not readily applicable, or can only illuminate some corners of a very large problem. If those problems seem important, either from a normative perspective or because they seem to hold the key to broader scientific generalization, then of course there is no excuse for not attacking them with whatever tools do seem applicable. It is simply a matter of recognizing that a good carpenter carries a diverse kit of tools, not just a hammer.

ACKNOWLEDGMENTS

Over the twelve-year span represented by the material in this volume I have accumulated more intellectual debts than I can possibly acknowledge, and some of which I am surely not even aware. But I would be greatly remiss if I

failed to mention at least those present and former colleagues who contributed, in easily traceable ways I remember well, to two or more of the
papers: Karl Deutsch, Paul Hammond, Betty Hanson, J. David Singer, and
John Sullivan. Karl Deutsch also made a special contribution. In my first
year as a graduate student I caught the highly contagious enthusiasm for the
scientific study of world politics with which he infected so many of us in his
first year on Yale's faculty.

Over much of the time my research has been generously supported by the
National Science Foundation, through Grants GS-614 and GS-2365, and by
ARPA, Behavioral Sciences, through Contract N0014-67-A-0097-0007 admin-
istered by the Office of Naval Research. The access to these funds, which allowed me to ask the questions I considered important in ways I thought
appropriate, is something I do not take for granted. Yale University, in addition to placing me in the midst of some of the world's most stimulating students and colleagues, supported some of the research and helped provide
money for my leaves. Two years of leave—one at the Mental Health Research
Institute of the University of Michigan and one at the University of Brussels,
supported by Guggenheim and Fulbright-Hays awards, made much reflection
possible. My family and friends may not remember the debts I owe them,
but I do.

London   *Bruce M. Russett*
August 1973

Introduction

DETERRENCE, INTEGRATION, AND COMMUNICATION

The common theoretical concern that flows through most of the following papers addresses the conditions under which nations can act cooperatively. On the most basic level this means war avoidance through deterrence: even during times of conflict, the leaders of nations are aware of their mutual interests in not fighting, or at least in limiting whatever violence does occur. At another level, where nations are bound by positive ties that supersede simple fear of mutual destruction, it means maintenance of peace through integration. At a yet higher level it means the peaceful pursuit of mutual goals that can only be reached through agreement on coordinated action. Communication—the sending and receiving of information about each other's preferences and capabilities—lies at the heart of any effort for the resolution of power conflicts.

International politics, as a form of social life, involves a mixture of conflicts and cooperation. In all our relations, even with friends and family, there is competition as well as cooperation. Usually the competitive elements are kept under control because of the primary importance of maintaining the cooperative relationship, at the cost, occasionally, of giving in to a friend's or relative's interest when two immediate self-interests conflict. Moreover, with someone we love and with whom we share a sense of identity, it is sometimes a pleasure rather than a sacrifice to give up something for the other person. In international politics, however, there is little affection or sense of shared identity, and the need for maintaining a cooperative relationship is usually less obvious or immediate. Thus in our thinking about it we tend much more to emphasize the elements of competition, but we should remember that both competitive and cooperative elements are still there, and that any effort to achieve our own goals must include some of each. This applies even to war or threatened war, as in arms races.

One standard analytical example is that of "the prisoners' dilemma," which we shall take up in the next paragraph, although that is only one subset out of a variety of non-zero-sum games.[1] And as is discussed in the final chapter of this volume, ideas derived from the theory of collective goods in economics have a great deal to say about these problems. We cannot review all the material compiled on these topics, but a selective and introductory examination will serve to point out some of the themes of this book.

Let us consider a few non-zero situations, and explore some conditions that may facilitate cooperative solutions. Briefly recall the basic example characterizing the prisoners' dilemma. Two people are arrested and held incommunicado after an armed robbery and murder. Each is questioned separately and presented with this choice by the police official: "I'm pretty sure that you two were responsible for the killing, but I don't have quite enough evidence to prove it. If you will quit cooperating with the other prisoner, confess first, and testify against the other prisoner, I will see that you are set free without any penalty, though he will be sentenced to life imprisonment. On the other hand, I am making the same proposal to him, so if he confesses first you will be the one to spend a life in prison, and he will go free. If you both stop cooperating with each other and confess simultaneously, we will have a little mercy, but we will still sentence you both to 20 years in prison for armed robbery. Should you both be stubborn we cannot convict you for a major crime, and I can only punish each of you for a smaller crime in your past life, carrying a one year prison term. If you want to take a chance that your fellow prisoner will keep quiet, go ahead. But if he doesn't—and you know what sort of criminal he is—you will do very badly. Think it over."

Each prisoner thus has a choice of two strategies, which we may describe as cooperating with his fellow prisoner by refusing to confess, or defecting from that cooperation by confessing. Either of these may be combined with either act by the other prisoner, giving four possible outcomes. Labelling these from the point of view of the first prisoner, these outcomes are R for reward, where both cooperate with each other by not confessing; P for the punishment they both receive if they both defect and confess simultaneously; T for the temptation the first feels to defect and confess while the other does not; and the condition where the other prisoner defects, but our first prisoner does not, leaving him with a payoff S as a sucker. The prisoners' dilemma differs from games with other payoff structures in that the relative size of the payoffs (as measured here by length of prison term) for each player is: $T > R > P > S$.

Although by no means universal, this structure is common enough in international politics, especially in settings of arms races and crisis behavior, to

---

[1] See especially Anatol Rapoport and Albert Chammah, *Prisoners' Dilemma* (Ann Arbor: University of Michigan Press, 1965), and Anatol Rapoport, *Two-Person Game Theory: The Essential Ideas* (Ann Arbor: University of Michigan Press, 1966).

deserve close attention. In an arms race, for example, the worst outcome usually is thought to be for the other side to have a manifestly more effective capability than one's own; this is especially true when the possibility of a credible first strike capability is at issue. To be at the mercy of such a force is the S outcome; to have it would be T. To abstain from an arms race and so to be able to divert resources to domestic needs is presumably quite a good outcome (R). In a highly competitive and ideologically charged situation perhaps it is less desirable than being able to wipe out your opponent, but good enough to be clearly better than an arms race carried on at substantial expense with enough vigor to prevent either side from achieving a clear advantage (P).

The relative payoffs thus are just the same as for the hapless prisoners who are asked to confess. Given the conditions laid down for the prisoners' dilemma—that the *relative* payoffs are as described, that there is no communication, and that this is a one-shot, single-play situation—the "rational" choice for each prisoner acting by himself is to defect by confessing. That assures him of the better outcome for either eventuality of the other's behavior. If the second prisoner also confesses, our first gets P, which is bad but at least better than S; if the second does not confess, then our first gets T, which is even better than R. There is no effective incentive to cooperate by not confessing; hence both prisoners end up with quite a bad outcome (P), though not the very worst that might have happened to either if one cooperated while the other defected (S).

Does this mean, because we have pictured the relative payoff structure as the same, that two nations in an arms race are therefore condemned to the risk and waste of interminable expensive arms competition? In 1950 that seemed to be the case. President Truman's scientific advisers told him that they thought they could build a powerful new bomb, hundreds of times more powerful than the atomic bomb—this was to be the H-bomb. It would be an awesome weapon, and any war in which it was used surely would leave millions dead. It would probably be best for mankind, and for the United States itself, if the bomb were never built. But the Russians had all the same basic scientific knowledge that the Americans had, and neither power would contemplate allowing the other to have such a fearsome weapon unless it had it too. It seemed better to go ahead and build it if the Russians could be expected to build it also, for even though building an H-bomb would leave both countries exposed to its dangers, that was considered better than being at the mercy of the Russians without a counter. Lacking any prospect of an enforceable agreement that neither would build H-bombs, both sides felt themselves forced to build a weapon they might have preferred not to have exist.[2]

Yet that is not always the outcome, for unlike the prisoners, national governments find it sometimes possible to communicate and to commit themselves to pursue the strategies of joint cooperation. A formal agreement, perhaps a treaty, if combined with inspection to verify whether the agreement was

---

[2] See Warner Schilling, "The H-Bomb Decision: How to Decide without Actually Choosing," *Political Science Quarterly*, 76, 1 (March 1961), pp. 24–46.

being kept, would provide the instrument for commitment. It takes a long time to build and deploy modern weapons in sufficient quantity to be militarily decisive, unlike the act of defection in prison, which requires only a moment. With good inspection techniques one nation can expect to detect betrayal before it becomes effective; thus, at worst, it would end with a P payoff rather than S. That inspection may be agreed upon and mutually executed (with inspectors permitted to roam about each others' countries) or merely unilaterally executed by mutually tolerated means (observation satellites and perhaps spies). But only if each has reliable information about others' activities—facilities for communicating capability—do they have a means for verifying the other's commitment.

Not all arms race situations fit the prisoners' dilemma model, though communication is still a critical element in the ability to achieve cooperation. The previous example assumed that a situation of strategic parity offered a reasonably good solution—the second best of four for each of the two parties. Probably a different situation applied to the American-Soviet rivalry during the 1950s and perhaps early 1960s. The Russians were in a position of strategic inferiority: they could not credibly threaten a first strike against the United States except in response to the most dire provocation against their position in Eastern Europe. Although they had sufficient military means to deter any unprovoked American attack they dared not do anything that might endanger the American global position so much that the United States government would consider it appropriate to use nuclear weapons.

For the Russians, the payoffs seem to have retained the structure characteristic of the prisoners' dilemma. Their best outcome would have been even the mild form of T represented by a *parity* that would result if the Russians merely closed the gap while the Americans abstained from adding more weapons. The worst possible outcome was S, with the Americans able to widen their already existing superiority. In the middle, the punishment, P, of accepting an extremely expensive race merely to keep their existing inferiority from getting worse was better than S, but the rewards, R, of staying in the same relative position without exacerbating the race were still preferable. Thus, $T > R > P > S$. But this was not the way, nor the mirror image of the way, the Americans saw things. Like the Russians, they saw a relative deterioration in the existing arms balance, S, as their worst outcome, but a temptation, T, of spending heavily to *widen* their superiority had little attraction for them. They were satisfied with the status quo of the existing arms balance, R. Second best was maintaining their existing superiority with a new construction program matched, on a ratio basis, by that of the Russians, P. The temptation to seek an improvement in their relative situation came in as third best because it promised to be so expensive. S was both least preferred and highly unlikely, given the high quality of American intelligence about Russian armaments, especially by means of the U-2 overflights. (Officials in the American executive branch with access to secret information were never very worried about the so-called "missile gap" that became such a public issue in 1960.) Assuming this is a reasonably accurate picture of most American officials' preferences, then $R > P > T > S$.

Therefore, the Americans preferred the rewards of "cooperation" to all other outcomes, though they were quite prepared, as second best, to administer punishment to the Russians (and of course to themselves) if Moscow refused to cooperate. Since the Russians naturally preferred R to P, the two countries could get to R if the Americans could publicly *demonstrate* that (1) they were fully aware of Russian missile-building efforts and the Russians could not push the S payoff upon them without their knowledge, and (2) the American payoff structure was indeed as described; that is, that they were prepared to go to great lengths to match new Russian missile building with enough of their own to maintain superiority. They had to show that their political system was strong enough to undertake such a project—that American taxpayers would support it with very high expenditures—and that their economy was strong enough to carry the burden. There would be some point at which the economy could no longer bear the burden; then S (at least the limited form of S, the counterpart of the limited form of T, or parity, experienced by the Russians), would become preferable to P. But given the much larger American economy and the domestic political atmosphere of the Cold War, there was no need to approach that level. Thus R—that is, a limited form of R representing a moderation of new construction to keep the existing relative balance, not a reduction of forces on both sides—was attainable.

Ultimately, of course, the Russians did catch up to parity, in effect because the Americans permitted them to do so. By the mid-1960s the relative numbers of weapons on both sides meant far less than it had; even with numerical inferiority the Russians were strong enough to provide certain retaliation at a level of damage that could hardly make any American first strike seem worthwhile in Washington. Under those circumstances it made little difference whether the Russians had only a third of the American number of missiles, or about as many. At least it no longer made enough difference to make worthwhile the great new expenditures the United States would have required to maintained the old ratio. Thus the situation changed, and a new set of outcomes was accepted, because the *payoff structure changed.* For the United States, S became a much more acceptable outcome, perhaps even preferable to R and thus best of all—so long as S was defined as rough parity but *not* marked inferiority for the United States. The change in the payoff structure, coupled with each side's capabilities for acquisition of information, produced an "agreement" on mutual parity that has proved very stable.[3]

---

[3] The failure to go beyond parity at a rather high level of spending to an actual balanced *reduction* in capabilities on both sides requires a quite different set of explanations, attending to inertia, bureaucratic pressures, and "military-industrial complex" explanations focussing on the unpalatability, to powerful forces within both nations, of reduced arms spending. And we must note that the beneficent effects of communication depended on the fact that under the technology of the time parity meant that neither side had a first strike capability. Had parity meant that each side's forces were highly vulnerable, knowledge of the fact would have been most *de*stabilizing.

A very important way in which undesirable outcomes for both players may be avoided, therefore, is through changes in the payoff matrix. In international politics this is probably most likely to occur because of technological or economic developments that make formerly preferred outcomes more costly, or formerly feared ones less so. (Those are frequent concerns of this book.) But the payoff structure may vary from what it seems because of people's *valuations* of the outcomes. For our prisoners, for example, the situation would be vastly different if one or both of them held some principle of "honor among thieves," with a prickly conscience that made it painful to betray the other man. Suppose that these were both in fact innocent men, and moral ones at that. One might well *prefer* to accept a long prison term himself rather than condemn the other, unjustly, to an even longer term. It would be still easier for one prisoner to do the "moral" thing and not defect if he were reasonably certain that the other prisoner felt much the same way. Under these circumstances he would not only avoid what would be for him the worst payoff (pangs of conscience with T), but he would get what would be for him the highest payoff when both refused to defect.

In international politics it is often easy to dismiss thoughts about the effect of morality, since only a relatively small number of people are prepared to say, "Better me dead than both of us" when considering deterrence of a nation conceived of as an enemy. But such considerations should not be ignored. Many Americans and Russians would at least shrink from delivering a nuclear first strike even if they thought they could do it with little cost in lives or dollars to themselves; President Kennedy is said to have refused military advisers' pleas to launch a surprise attack on the Cuban missile sites in part because he thought it would be wrong to do so.[4] In this book we shall consider how bonds among peoples are built up, in part through communication, so as to create at least a limited sense of mutual identification, which brings "conscience" to bear. And we shall also consider (especially in Chapter 14, "A Countercombatant Deterrent?") some rather complex interactions between technological considerations and the emergence of stronger moral inhibitions against killing civilians through aerial attack.

These considerations introduce an element beyond the immediate strategic situation, the fact that one's actions in the "game" have consequences not only for the payoffs specified in this "game," but for those of other quite different "games" as well. It is a logical next step, then, to consider what happens if a situation like prisoners' dilemma occurs in the context of later relationships that can be anticipated. Suppose one of our prisoners (let us call him Leon) is a member of a very tough gang, one that considers the betrayal of one of its members to be an extremely grievous offense. The other prisoner, Dick, knows that if he confesses and Leon does not, he, Dick, will go free—but that Leon's

[4] Graham Allison, *Essence of Decision: Explaining the Cuban Missile Crisis* (Boston: Little, Brown, 1971), p. 203.

gang will assassinate him. Dick's payoff structure is very different from what merely counting the years of the various possible prison terms would suggest; T drops from Dick's most preferred outcome to his least preferred. Or imagine that they are in normal times business partners, and that the sentences originally expressed in years are instead expressed only in days. After serving a possible short term in prison each partner will return to the firm and the two will want to get along in their mutual self-interest; a betrayal for small stakes would jeopardize their entire relationship.

So too among nation-states, each may observe a sworn commitment even when in the immediate short run it might seem in its interest to defect from such a commitment, and each may observe it for deep reasons of self-interest that have nothing to do with ethics or morality. International law is of course violated frequently, but in normal day-to-day procedure, such as that concerning transportation, communication, respect for the persons of ambassadors, and movement of travellers between nations, governments far more often observe the accepted legal principles. Especially if their acts are readily observable to others (again, ties for handling communication and information between nations are crucial), they pass up the immediate benefits of seizing a valuable cargo or person because they cannot afford the reprisals and disruption of future traffic that would surely follow.

Assume that the prisoners' dilemma occurs repeatedly for the same individuals, and under conditions where the players do not expect the sequence to end forthwith. Many experimental psychologists and others, led by Anatol Rapoport and his colleagues, have done just this under laboratory conditions. Their experience now includes that of thousands of players, of 50 to several hundred plays by the same individuals. There is a typical sequence that many players adopt. At the beginning they often play cooperatively, with each partner being rewarded. After a short while, however, one partner becomes tempted to defect. But his partner will usually retaliate after being betrayed once or twice, so both take the punishment outcome. Each may thereafter make efforts to reestablish cooperation, but without means for overt communication this is a difficult business, and a would-be cooperator may well continue to receive the sucker's penalty. He may interpret this as betrayal, and may himself return to defection. In international politics too, it may be very hard to shift into cooperative behavior. The first initiatives may not be perceived as cooperation at all, or if perceived as such they may be interpreted as weakness and thus be exploited. After a good deal of trial and error, however, many players do in fact succeed in cooperating consistently again, but it may take a long, painful time before a favorable pattern is established.

Under these conditions, each play is eventually seen not as an end in itself, but as a means of communicating one's intentions to the other with the hope of achieving the payoffs of joint cooperation on later plays. In this way it resembles the ongoing politics among nations, where cooperation does breed expectations of cooperation, and defection breeds continuing fears of the double cross. Ultimately, over many plays, it does become *possible* to *develop* trust. After a while the players become increasingly confident that they know how each other will behave.

Substantively for international politics, we must be aware of the need to limit the negative payoffs that might arise from any one or few interactions, especially in the early and middle-term of a relationship. If the negative payoffs become too great, the long-term sequence may never be completed because of the elimination of one or both parties; thus the players never reach the late state of possible consistent cooperation. The payoff structure is not something inexorably handed down by the fates, requiring political leaders always to adapt their behavior to it.

SOME INTERWOVEN CONCERNS

There are a number of sources of instability in long-term repetition of non-zero-sum situations; similarly an initially unstable situation can become stablized. We have already referred to the effects of *technological change* in varying the payoff structure, and of changes in participants' *valuations* of the outcomes. Another is the *difference in valuation* of a particular outcome among various political leaders *within a particular nation*, or differences between the leaders and much of the public. This may be compounded by differences in the "discount rate" each attaches to future events. A political leader rarely expects to be in office indefinitely, but he is likely to worry about being returned in the next election. The temptation the political leader feels to take short-term gains or avoid short-term losses, even at the cost of probably greater long-term losses to the country at large, may be very strong, especially if the probability of long-term losses is not widely understood by the public. He cares, in a way not felt by others, about preserving his own power and prerogatives now.[5] We shall consider this problem repeatedly, most notably in Chapter 13, which examines Japanese government decision making leading up to the Pearl Harbor attack.

We shall be concerned about structuring various actors' perceptions of available payoffs in many chapters. It is considered as a general problem in Chapters 12, 15, and 19 ("The Calculus of Deterrence," "The Instruments of Influence and the Limits of Power," and "Collective Goods and International Organization"). Chapter 10 ("Cause, Surprise, and No Escape") deals, like Chapter 13 on Pearl Harbor, specifically with the points at which decisions make war more and more nearly inevitable through a successive closing off of alternatives, and the need to avoid presenting an opponent with a set of options all of which are highly unpalatable. Chapter 10 also considers how opponents can communicate reassuring information, about their lack of

---

[5] The best statement of this point of view that I have seen is by Daniel Ellsberg, "The Quagmire Myth and the Stalemate Machine," *Public Policy*, 19, 2 (spring 1971), pp. 217–74. Of course, a political leader's concern for his own self-interest need not be nearly so cynical, or so conscious, as I have implied, but less conscious motives may have the same effects.

hostile intent, or hostile capability, to each other. Chapter 11 ("The Complexities of Ballistic Missile Defense") asks what the acquisition of a particular weapons system would communicate both to enemies and to allies, and Chapter 14 ("A Countercombatant Deterrent?") considers the consequences of communicating a change in intent rooted in a different American evaluation of the payoffs from current deterrent policy. Part II taken as a whole, and especially Chapters 12–14, offers a detailed examination of deterrence as a means of war avoidance.

Changes in the valuations of the payoffs may occur over the course of an extensive game. How are trust or "conscience" actually developed? How can deterrence change over the long run to a situation of "integration?" Deterrence and integration are substantively related; war avoidance shades into questions of the maintenance of peace, and from there to the cooperative pursuit of mutual goals that neither party can reach by itself. Some aspects of this are touched upon in Chapters 4 through 6, dealing with regional cooperation in general and with Asia in particular. Means of communication take on even greater importance. Chapter 6 ("The Asia Rimland as a 'Region' for Containing China") suggests that the long term prospects for cooperation are best among states that share substantial trade and institutional bonds, common political orientation, and basic social and cultural similarities. Some of the theoretical considerations about the causes and consequences of bonds between nations are developed more fully in the concluding chapters of the book ("Transactions, Community, and International Political Integration" and "Collective Goods and International Organization").

Such bonds also play a different sort of role in deterrence, when the problem of deterring an attack on a third party is at issue. Chapter 12 ("The Calculus of Deterrence") shows that the stronger trade and various other communication bonds between major and minor powers are, the more likely it is that the major power will go to war to defend the minor one. (When I wrote that paper in 1963 I thought it therefore a good idea to enhance the credibility of American deterrence by strengthening America's interdependence with its allies; I am no longer so sure—on those grounds, at least.) Chapter 16 ("Components of an Operational Theory of International Alliance Formation") juxtaposes the point of view that stresses the role of community ties in determining alliance partnerships against that which emphasizes only calculations of power and interest. The following chapter ("An Empirical Typology of International Military Alliances") examines some aspects empirically. It shows that alliances oriented to power or interest are fairly good at providing deterrence despite the findings of Chapter 12, but that, fully in conformity with Chapter 12, in alliances characterized by community bonds the members are likely to fight side by side.

Near the beginning of this introduction we spoke of a sense of shared identity, where one comes to see the other person's welfare as an aspect of one's own; "conscience" is usually most effective in governing our behavior toward those we know well. A great density and diversity of contacts between individuals, and indeed between nations, is required to develop this kind of relationship; the contacts must be seen as, on the whole, mutually rewarding to both partners.

But such bonds among nations develop very slowly, at a glacial pace, as shown in Chapters 2 and 5 ("A Macroscopic View of International Politics" and " 'Regional' Trading Patterns, 1938–1963"). Peace through homogeneity certainly is neither very near (see especially Chapter 9, "The Rich Fifth and the Poor Half") nor on many grounds even desirable. Furthermore, there are certain exclusive and zero-sum aspects of integration and cooperation (see Chapter 18), so that to some extent a high level of integration between some nations makes it more difficult for those same nations also to be integrated with others. It is important to focus integration efforts on those relationships where, for reasons of power considerations, the potential rewards or dangers are greatest. These questions must be addressed because our world is already one of enormously greater interdependencies than ever before (see Chapter 3, "Indicators for American's Linkages with the Changing World Environment," and especially Chapter 8, "The Ecology of Future International Politics") and will become even more so in the near future (Chapter 9, "The Rich Fifth and the Poor Half").

The experience of common action to achieve mutually desired goals seems to be especially beneficial in building community ties. The famous "Robbers' Cave" experiment, performed by several psychologists in a boys' camp, bears heavily on this. The boys were divided into two rival groups and antagonisms were deliberately fostered. After the two groups had become sufficiently hostile the leaders then tried to see how the tensions might be reduced. They tried bringing the groups together for enjoyable events, but that did little good. Then they created situations where the two groups *had to cooperate* with each other in order to obtain something both wanted. After at first reluctantly taking part in the latter activities, the boys developed a new spirit and antagonisms eased. For international politics, this suggests the importance of major cooperative action by hostile governments, an importance that goes far beyond the immediate goal sought by such action. Possibly joint activities in space might have some of the necessary effect, or joint activities to control global pollution. Perhaps even concerted, long-term effort to explore ways to develop trust and avoid the prisoners' dilemma would itself, as an effort, generate trust and mutual identification in addition to the specific effect of whatever concrete steps were undertaken.[6]

In concluding, let us note a few of the other circumstances which have been found to affect the frequency with which players, under experimental conditions, choose cooperative rather than competitive strategies, and suggest their

---

[6] Muzafer Sherif, et al., *Intergroup Conflict and Cooperation: The Robbers' Cave Experiment* (Norman: University of Oklahoma Press, 1961). This is also the theme of Vincent Rock, *A Strategy of Interdependence* (New York: Scribner's, 1964).

possible relevance for international politics. Of course it is a long jump from the laboratory to the world of the national leader, but the findings about variations in experimental procedures are nonetheless stimulating. They are important too because of an inherent difficulty in any analysis of the "real world" of international politics—we can only examine what *has been done;* if we want to generate preferred *futures* we will have to look at behavior under other conditions and try to make analogies where appropriate.[7]

1. Two-person games are more likely to be played competitively than are similar games with three or more players. This suggests that cooperation may be harder to achieve in a bipolar world than in a balance-of-power system, perhaps because it is easier to compare one's own achievements with those of a single other player, and thus perceive him as an opponent. This is relevant to the discussion of concentration and polarity in Chapter 7 ("Is There a Long-Run Trend toward Concentration in the International System?").

2. Personality characteristics seem to make a difference. Individuals scoring high on the well-known California *F* (for Fascist) scale are likely to play competitive strategies in prisoners' dilemma. It matters who our leaders are.

3. Experimental evidence clearly supports the point made earlier that competitive strategies are more common where there is no means of communication between the players. Many kinds of information need to be communicated: activities, reasons for those activities, intentions, and preferences (i.e., payoff structures) are relevant in varying degrees. An essential component seems to be that any prior announcement of cooperative behavior be *honest.* If one player uses the opportunity to deceive his opposite, the result is often a longer run of reciprocal or mutual defection than happens when no communication is permitted. If the game is to be repeated, one must not abuse the hot line.

4. It makes a difference how the game is described by the experimenter in discussing it with the players before they begin. He can present it largely as a situation where the aim is for each player to do the best he can regardless of what happens to the other players, as a game where the aim is to do better than the other, or as a game where the important thing is for both to do well. Not surprisingly, the cooperative strategy is played least often by players for whom "do better than the other fellow" predominates in the pregame orientation. The game description becomes a self-fulfilling prophecy. Thus the terms of reference, even if given rather subtly by the experimenter, do matter seriously even though the numbers assigned to various payoffs are the same in each case. And thus it may very much matter what preconceptions people bring to the analysis of international politics. Those who have been taught, informally or in school, to think of the world as "red in tooth and claw" where the overriding

---

[7] These and other relevant findings are reported regularly in several journals: *Behavioral Science; Journal of Conflict Resolution;* and *Simulation and Games.*

goal is to maximize the national interest of one's own state relative to that of others will behave differently in their selection of policy preferences. They will be less ready and able to play cooperative strategies. (This consideration is also mentioned in Chapter 19 here, "Collective Goods and International Organization.") This is a fundamental argument that has been made against excessively cold-blooded "strategic thinking" about Cold War problems. One side alone cannot make all conflicts go away; yet if we insist on seeing the world as a constant struggle, we will indeed make it more nearly so.

1
International Behavior Research: Case Studies and Cumulation

The best chef knows all dishes casually, and a few intimately.
MARIANNE

RESEARCH STRATEGIES AND CLEAVAGES

It is now a tiresome cliché, and one with a good many unpleasant associations, that there are critical methodological and philosophical gulfs within the collectivity of scholars and practitioners of international politics. Certainly there are many different *foci* of attention, such as the five sets of variables identified by Rosenau for comparing the sources of foreign policy (systemic, societal, governmental, role, and idiosyncratic),[1] or Singer's labels for international linkages (structure, interaction, and behavior),[2] and numerous *methods* for examining each focus (for example, interviewing, survey research, and content analysis). Furthermore, each of the major methods can be further subdivided for the taxonomist's pleasure (for example, thematic versus symbolic content analysis and computerized versus manual content analysis), and the proponents of one approach will dispute violently over one method as compared with another. These disputes and divisions are expected and essential for the progress of understanding in a field as diverse as international

Reprinted from *Approaches to the Study of Political Science,* Michael Haas and Henry Kariel, editors (San Francisco: Chandler Publishing Company, 1970).

[1] James N. Rosenau, "Pre-Theories and Theories of Foreign Policy," in *Approaches to International and Comparative Politics,* R. Barry Farrell, editor (Evanston: Northwestern University Press, 1966), pp. 27–92.

[2] J. David Singer, "The Global System and Its Subsystems: A Developmental View," in *Linkage Politics: Essays on the Convergence between National and International Systems,* James N. Rosenau, editor (New York: The Free Press, 1969).

relations, and especially one where our experience with large-scale research has yet to produce compelling results. No effort can or should be made to resolve all methodological conflicts or to impose a uniform research strategy.

While most professionals engaging in the analysis of international relations would doubtless agree with the necessity to maintain a pluralistic research community, many would nevertheless contend that certain *particular* cleavages in the collectivity are so deep and fundamental as to threaten the future of the enterprise. There are a few major characterizations which seem to cut the body squarely in two, and which seem to delineate groups that have little in common with one another. One of these cleavages is between the scholars concerned with theory building and the practitioners, with not too many individuals possessing the skills and experience to talk knowledgeably and credibly on either side. But with the growth of midcareer programs which send policy professionals to academic campuses for interchange and with the great increase in the number of scholars who either serve as part-time consultants or who spend full-time periods of service in government agencies, this gap, while still productive of misunderstandings and even complete communication failures, is on the whole a manageable and tolerable one.

Much more serious is another cleavage which in part intersects with the first but also partially coincides with it—the gap between those who self-consciously think of themselves as social scientists, especially those who employ quantitative research methods, and those whose self-image and analytical style is more closely associated with historical analysis and the intensive study of particular cases. A case in this sense may be either a particular region or country, or a particular event, such as a decision or crisis. This cleavage intersects with the first because many scholars can be found on both sides, though in part of its course it runs along with the first because hardly any policy makers have firsthand experience with quantitative research or the background to understand it when presented with its full technical paraphernalia. Where cleavages coincide, the maintenance and stability of a system are endangered.

Furthermore, the communication failures become complicated by other sociological and psychological mechanisms. Quantitatively oriented scholars exude self-confidence and sometimes even arrogance—they look at the substantial development of their section of the discipline, which has grown up almost entirely within only the past decade, compare it with the similar but now much more extensive development of quantitative orientations in psychology and economics, and feel they are riding the wave of the future. For now they write for each other, train their graduate students at a number of the more prestigious universities, ignore their nonquantitative academic colleagues, and make little effort to convey to policy makers those of their findings which, if properly packaged, might be of considerable value. And a good many nonquantitative scholars sense both the arrogance, and behind the arrogance, a threat to their own influence. They are unsympathetic with the methods, cannot read the reports, see little of relevance in the findings, and sometimes deliberately close off potential channels of communication that do exist.

The consequences of protracted guerrilla warfare for the growth of a social system are seldom favorable, and it is clear that policy makers and scholars, both quantitatively and traditionally oriented, have suffered from their battles. They in fact do have a good deal to say to each other, and neither of their research approaches is complete without the other. Specifically, the so-called nomothetic-idiographic dilemma is an artificial one; neither the case study nor the general kind of systematic analysis I shall call correlational study can alone provide the basis for reliable and valid generalizations about international politics. I intend to suggest in this essay the *value of both types* and how the two must *complement* each other in critical ways.

THE USES AND AGGREGATION OF CASE STUDIES

Case studies abound in the literature of international politics. They are in fact far more numerous than are synthetic or broadly comparative examinations, and any list of their contributions to the study of foreign policy making, alliance formation, crisis behavior, and other areas would be incomplete and superficial. How can we explain the persistent popularity of this approach?

We are all aware that a case study cannot by itself establish propositions about uniformities in behavior. Practitioners of the approach, as well as its critics, agree about the idiosyncrasies of particular cases and the impossibility of deriving either deterministic or rigorously stated probabilistic laws from a single case. I shall show later how the case study nevertheless does have important value for the *scientist*; and despite its problems, there is no doubt in the mind of the *policy maker* that a case study has great utility to him. What is it, then, that he expects to learn from the intensive analysis of a single event, such as the Cuban missile crisis of 1962 or the Quemoy crisis of 1958?

The policy maker is likely to be concerned with a relatively small class of events, with a few cases that resemble the Quemoy or Cuba crisis, but in which the consequences are major. His Monday morning quarterback role is especially important under these circumstances; he is anxious to learn what *mistakes* were made—what was done wrong or left undone—so as not to repeat the error next time. Important lessons can, for example, be derived from communication or intelligence failures, whether human or technical.[3] Mistakes in judgment, in tactics, or in strategy also will be looked for avidly. For the policy maker it is important to know *who made the mistakes* so that the miscreant can either be corrected or prevented from having another opportunity. Who had a set of perspectives that turned out to be inappropriate? Who was unduly influenced by particular narrow interests within the nation? Who used the crisis for personal self-seeking?

For low-level decisions, of the kind that have many counterparts and can

---

[3] For example, Roberta Wohlstetter, *Pearl Harbor: Warning and Decision* (Stanford: Stanford University Press, 1962).

be delegated to subordinate levels in the decision-making process simply because comparable decisions are presented fairly often, it is fairly easy to tell what was a mistake and what was not. But such evaluations become harder to make the closer one comes to sweeping and unique decision nodes. Even if the mistake is clearly identified, it may be hard to know what to do about it. Appropriate action can be taken against the perpetrator, but to apply the lessons of the mistake to further decisions is not so easy. It can be done only after deciding what other decisions fall within that general class, where a sufficient number of the relevant variables are similar. We may think we know the lesson of Munich, but the lesson of Sarajevo is the opposite. Which applies to Southeast Asia? About all that can be done solely from case experience is to use it to sensitize one to future situations that may be similar. But from the single case it is impossible to know *how often* such events are likely to occur, or under what particular *kinds of conditions* they may arise.

All the gains that may accrue from an intensive case study are relatively short-run accessions. With personnel turnover and changing conditions the lessons of earlier cases will be forgotten or thought not applicable and later ones will take precedence. The value of discrete cases for the cumulative building of information about experience is nil. We need controls, by observing many cases and accounting for the relevant varying factors, in order to establish causal relationships. But this does not mean that one case study has no value when rigorously combined with other cases or integrated with the findings from other modes of analysis. Case studies have at least four uses in building cumulated knowledge:

1. They can stimulate the production of *hypotheses* about possible regularities. This is essentially the sensitization function referred to above. It is important to note both that most hypotheses later investigated with correlational techniques are *originally generated* from case study material, and that such generation is merely a *beginning*, not an end point, in the scientific process.[4]

2. Case studies can test in a different and more appropriate context the *inferences* made from suggestive but not fully appropriate correlational analyses. For example, there are now several cross-sectional (synchronic) studies, based on the examination of nearly 100 countries, which show a clear negative relationship between level of economic development and the frequency or magnitude, or frequency and magnitude, of internal violence.[5] Rich countries evidence much less internal violence than poor

[4] This function of case studies is of great value to the policy maker as well as to the scientist in expanding his intuitive base. For a useful essay, see James W. Fesler, "The Case Method in Political Science," in *Essays on the Case Method in Public Administration*, Edwin A. Bock, et al., editors (Brussels: International Institute of Administrative Sciences, 1962), pp. 65–88.

[5] See Ivo Feierabend and Rosalind Feierabend, "Aggressive Behavior within Polities, 1948–1962: A Cross-National Study," *Journal of Conflict Resolution*, X (September 1966), 249–71; Bruce M. Russett, *Trends in World Politics* (New York: Macmillan, 1965), Chapter VIII; Robert S. McNamara, speech to American Society of Newspaper Editors, Montreal, May 18, 1966.

or middle-income ones. Yet generalizing from such cross-sectional studies to scientific or policy statements about what may happen over time is full of obvious pitfalls. What we have is an interesting hypothesis that economic development, eventually at least, will produce more stable regimes in countries that are now poor. But the hazards of generalization demand an effort to move from the simulated "time" analysis implied by looking at several levels or "stages" of development to some actual time (longitudinal, diachronic) analyses of historical cases. Is there a discernible regularity in the relation between development and violence in eighteenth- and nineteenth-century England, for instance?[6] A single finding of such a regularity would not verify a probabilistic hypothesis, nor would the absence of the regularity refute it. Repeated case studies, however, provide the new data base required for verification or rejection, and may, as tendencies emerge while the cases are being compiled, suggest important refinements.

3. Similarly, if the correlational pattern relating two variables, say violence and stability, is satisfactorily established, the case study provides an often unsurpassable means for pursuing a far more critical question, namely, What is the *causal* relationship between the two variables?

First of all, one looks at the *temporal* sequence. It might be that above the middle levels of development an improvement in economic conditions produces, through greater satisfaction, a decrease in the stimulus to violence. Or on the contrary, a decline in the frequency of violence may promote stable social and political conditions that make economic growth and controlled change possible. Whereas there are now available some statistical techniques employing correlational analysis for the investigation of causal propositions, those techniques are at best approximate procedures for eliminating certain possibilities without confirming the others, and at worst depend upon such restrictive assumptions about the data that they cannot even validly eliminate possible explanations.[7] Only a set of carefully dissected case studies can in the end do this job satisfactorily.

Second, case studies may be employed to *eliminate spurious* correlations. Again, the association between violence and development may be real enough but not necessarily causal in either direction; both may be the product of some third variable, or they may interact in a very

---

[6] For a preliminary effort, see Charles L. Taylor, "The Rise of Political Activity among British Working Men, 1790–1850," paper presented to the annual meeting of the American Political Science Association, New York, September 1966.

[7] See Herbert Simon, *Models of Man* (New York: Wiley, 1957), Chapters I–III; Hubert M. Blalock, *Causal Inferences in Nonexperimental Research* (Chapel Hill: University of North Carolina Press, 1964), and "Causal Inferences, Closed Populations, and Measures of Association," *American Political Science Review*, LXI (March 1967), 130–5; Hayward Alker, "Causal Inferences in Political Research," in *Mathematical Applications in Political Science*, Joseph L. Bernd, editor (Dallas: Southern Methodist University Press, 1966), II, 7–43.

complicated manner. Some of these findings too may be checked if one has a good deal of high quality cross-sectional data on a variety of potentially relevant variables, but the case study approach is surer and more direct.

4. Finally, case studies are essential to the refinement and qualification even of a hypothesis strongly supported by high correlations. *Deviant-case analysis* here can provide an understanding of those instances that do not fit the general pattern of association.[8] Only by probing into the particular circumstances of the different behavior can one begin to distinguish limits of the empirical domain to which the hypothesis may be expected to apply. Most generalizations are more powerful when so restricted than as universal statements. Deviant-case analysis obviously requires first knowing what pattern the case deviates from.

All these uses of case studies, however, assume further correlational analyses at a later state. Without iteratively shifting back and forth, without later correlational analyses building upon the hypotheses suggested, or supported by the case studies, one is only a little better off than without any case studies at all.[9] A sequence of steps something like the following is essential:

a. The original case studies. All work on a particular class of phenomena, whether wars, democratic political systems, or whatever, begins with descriptive studies by those who are interested in a particular problem, with a dissection of the individual political system or an intensive study of the events in the conflict.

b. From the information provided by a variety of such case studies a taxonomy can then be constructed, consisting of a standard set of categories that attempt to identify the important variables and suggest hypotheses about their functional relationships. This taxonomic stage is crucial to the next step in the analysis. Though it may be done in conjunction with further analysis, it is a valuable step in itself, and even if

---

[8] For a more extended discussion, see especially Patricia Kendall and Katherine Wolf, "The Two Purposes of Deviant Case Analysis," in *The Language of Social Research*, Paul Lazarsfeld and Morris Rosenberg, editors (Glencoe: The Free Press, 1955).

[9] In one prominent political science department regarded as behavioral, case studies have been declared unacceptable as dissertation topics. However, the rule has not been enforced when the role of the case study in theory building is carefully identified in the prospectus.

I am aware that no two cases are ever completely *identical*, and thus that all comparisons require careful controls to determine whether they are sufficiently similar to make the comparison profitable. Much of the art in political science lies in a good sense for penetrating behind verbal or other differences to identify similar cases where comparison will be productive, and in avoiding the verbal and other traps that misleadingly suggest relevant similarities. But I do assume that none of us rejects entirely the possibility of making such comparisons.

done alone it is not to be deprecated as "mere description," as some quantitatively oriented scholars are occasionally prone to do.[10]

c. From the large number of cases, as classified by taxonomic procedures, it is then possible and necessary to move to *correlational analysis.* The hypotheses suggested by the individual case studies and taxonomy need to be tested systematically by rigorous techniques to determine the probabilities with which particular bivariate relationships will hold, the nature (such as linear or curvilinear) of the relationships, and their sensitivity to the effects of third variables. One moves from the original suggestion that two variables may be related to a detailed probabilistic statement. This statement may be extremely complex and based upon a very sophisticated manipulation of the material in what is simply referred to as "correlational" study. The satisfactory analysis of this material is seldom if ever a matter of simply performing one or two routine computations, but a *repetitive* process of sequentially performing similar but varying computations exploring various related but differentiable hypotheses until, figuratively speaking, the ground is littered with discarded hypotheses (and less figuratively, littered with discarded computer printouts.)[11]

d. Once certain refined and carefully checked statements have been produced, however, it will be necessary eventually to *return to a case study approach.* The statistical manipulations will reach a point where there still remain plausible alternative hypotheses that cannot be discarded on the basis of the material at hand. The data may be too contaminated by error, coded according to too gross a set of categories, or, despite great efforts to compile a large sample of cases, may in the end be based on too few instances to permit sufficiently refined multivariate analyses for discarding hypotheses. In particular, the multivariate analysis of data where the nation-state is the unit of analysis quickly begins to press against the

---

[10] Arthur F. Wright, "On the Uses of Generalization in the Study of Chinese History," in *Generalization in the Writing of History*, Louis Gottschalk, editor (Chicago: University of Chicago Press, 1963), p. 36, makes a distinction between "labelling" (or taxonomic) generalizations and "regularity" (correlational) generalizations. For a discussion of how some historians are coming to grips with the problems considered here, see—of the other essays in the Gottschalk volume—those by Walter P. Metzger, Louis Gottschalk, Roy Nichols, William Aydelotte, and David Potter. Another useful reference on the comparative method in history is William H. Sewell, Jr., "Marc Bloch and the Logic of Comparative History," *History and Theory*, VI, 2 (1967), 208–18. See also Michael Haas, "Comparative Analysis," *Western Political Quarterly*, XV (June 1962), 244–303.

[11] Factor-analytic studies come to mind here. There are several major decisions in any factor analysis—how to treat communalities, whether to normalize the data, how many factors to rotate, what kind of rotation to perform—that can change the final results. The analyst must decide which technical alternatives are compatible with his theoretical purposes and, of those that pass this test, try enough to be sure the results are not seriously affected by different technical decisions. A comparison of the factor analysis results with those obtainable by other related techniques, such as nonmetric procedures or clustering techniques, may also be necessary. The principle of proceeding by strong inference to a single crucial experiment is a worthy ideal but often is not practicable.

limitations inherent in the fact that there are, by the most generous definition of the term, only about 130 sovereign states in the current world.[12] Thus, using the taxonomy either as originally compiled or, more likely, as refined on the basis of the correlational studies, analysis shifts back to the identification and scrutiny of a particular case in order to winnow out some of the remaining alternative hypotheses and to suggest new ones.

e. But if one has, through a case study, raised the level of sophistication from what was produced by the correlational analysis, the process is still far from complete. If it is established that in this instance the temporal sequence was from A to B and not vice versa, one still needs to know how often—always, usually, rarely?—this happens, and further case studies, eventually feeding into second stage correlational analyses, are essential.

The crucial point is that *both kinds of studies are critical to the development of scientific knowledge* either for its own sake or as reliable advice to the policy maker; neither one alone is satisfactory. Some scholars may prefer to work solely with one approach or the other. One may be better suited for a particular person's temperament, or he may have such a comparative advantage in the skills of one approach over the other that it is not productive for him to attempt both. Other analysts will find it easier to shift back and forth and may enjoy doing so. In any case, a recognition of the basic symbiosis between the two is essential to the long-run health of the research process.

Some of this may seem obvious, and other parts may be excessively vague and general. There are, however, plenty of illustrations from international politics research in recent years that show the limitations of both approaches when pursued separately. There are instances both of urgent needs for new case studies and of extant case studies that must now be brought together. There are even instances of case studies that employ a good many of the techniques of modern quantitative social science but that were undertaken prematurely, without first order taxonomic and especially correlational analysis, and are hence of little or even negative value in the cumulative process. We will draw examples from the deterrence and escalation literature and from studies of political integration. The deterrence literature well illustrates the need for a judicious combination of the case study and correlational approaches, and research on international integration provides an excellent example of some quantitative case studies that were inadequately based upon theoretical and correlational materials, and whose policy conclusions were therefore rendered questionable.

---

[12] The need for intensive case studies would in fact be a great deal less pressing if our universe were sufficiently large to permit much more reliable inferences from sophisticated multivariate analysis; but that need would not be eliminated, as indicated by the continuing role of depth interviews concomitant with survey research.

CASE STUDIES OF POLITICAL INTEGRATION

The study of international political integration has been plagued with poorly articulated case studies. Though a great many writers are ostensibly concerned with the topic, it seems as though each has a different definition of integration and is concerned with a different set of dependent and independent variables. While many of these variables could be recoded to provide the basis for a correlational study looking for general patterns, the effort required would be substantial. To date the most notable effort at employing a common analytical framework in undertaking case studies specifically as inputs to a correlational analysis remains the 1957 Princeton study directed by Karl Deutsch.[13] This project produced some very important tentative generalizations about necessary and helpful conditions for sucessful integrative efforts, but it also left largely unexamined some of Deutsch's most stimulating hypotheses, such as those about transactions and communications flows.

For example, in several of his later works Deutsch has developed a null model baseline for measuring an "expected" level of transactions in the absence of political, geographic, or other influences which would cause a nation to "prefer" transactions with a particular partner in excess of what its size alone would predict. The deviation of actual trade from this expected volume, expressed as an index of relative advantage (RA) is taken as an indication of possible political relevance for integration.[14] Although Deutsch and others have made fairly plausible deductive arguments about why greater-than-expected transaction levels should be conducive to integration, there have so far been few rigorous correlational analyses, and at best a very few case studies, which move in the direction of establishing the proposition.[15] Thus predictive studies, which would infer the likelihood of continued or further political integration on the basis of actual deviations from expected trade patterns, become extremely hazardous.

The hazards are well illustrated in a recent case study of the prospects for political integration in Western Europe.[16] Examination of the indices of relative acceptance within the region shows an increase throughout the early years following World War II, but, by 1957, a leveling off onto a plateau, with few notable changes in either direction since then. What has happened is that both the actual and the expected volumes of commerce have themselves grown enormously over the same period, so that trade among the countries of the

---

[13] Karl W. Deutsch, et al., *Political Community and the North Atlantic Area* (Princeton: Princeton University Press, 1957).

[14] Richard Savage and Karl W. Deutsch, "A Statistical Model of the Gross Analysis of Transaction Flows," *Econometrica*, XXVIII (July 1960), 551–72. Contrary to some assertions, Deutsch does not crudely argue that such deviations indicate the presence of integration, but merely that they indicate the presence of influences favorable to it.

[15] Amitai Etzioni, *Political Unification* (New York: Holt, Rinehart and Winston, 1965) compares four cases with stimulating results, but the coding procedures are not fully replicable.

[16] Karl W. Deutsch, Lewis J. Edinger, Roy Macridis, and Richard L. Merritt, *France, Germany, and the Western Alliance* (New York: Scribner's, 1967).

Six is four times what it was at the end of the 1950s. This growth is masked in the RA analysis because of a great expansion in the Six's total foreign trade (not just with each other), their consequent increased weight in all world markets, and the deliberate use of the RA model to control for such "size" effects. Nevertheless, the result is that for the typical country of the Six, the proportion of its national income that is derived from or spent on trade with the other members of the Common Market is more than *twice* what it was in 1957. Hence the conclusions drawn depend entirely upon which of the alternative analytical models one prefers. I have argued elsewhere that it is not the null model deviations that make most of the difference for political integration, but indeed the size of the impact that trade makes, relative to the domestic economy.[17] If one accepts the latter argument, then Western Europe has made great strides in developing the bases for a highly integrated political system.

In the end the analyst is reduced to weighing the relative plausibility of the arguments in which different conclusions are deduced from different premises. There have been no tests, performed on a variety of countries where the dependent variable of political integration is rigorously measured, to say which— high RAs or high ratio of trade to income—is more often associated with successful integration. Until such studies of the relationships between relevant independent variables and past integration are performed, case studies undertaken for *predictive* purposes raise a great many unintended questions.

Similarly, Deutsch makes other conclusions in his study of Western Europe which depend upon a choice between two alternative theoretical models with little empirical evidence as to which is the more powerful. For example, one table shows that the percentage of a national sample in France and West Germany with "good feelings" toward the other country rose from 11 percent in each to 30 percent and 37 percent respectively. These figures are juxtaposed against figures that show, for the same countries at the same time, an increase only from 6 to 21 percent and from 5 to 20 percent in the proportion who said they would trust the other nation in case of war. From these figures Deutsch draws the baleful consequence of a growing "trust gap."[18] But it is not clear why we should prefer the trust gap interpretation, rather than one that stressed simply the growth in trust or its faster proportionate growth than the growth of mere liking. Again, evidence on which of the two variables has been more closely related to political integration in past cases is almost entirely lacking. Thus, while the Deutsch study was in many respects well executed, and doubtless the need for predictive studies cannot always be postponed in favor of more basic research, the ultimate value of the study remains in some doubt. A clearly articulated set of hypotheses, to which further case studies could contribute, is needed.

---

[17] Bruce M. Russett, *International Regions and the International Systems*, (Chicago: Rand McNally, 1967), Chapter VIII. For related doubts about this conclusion see Ronald Inglehart, "An End to European Integration?" *American Political Science Review*, LXI (March 1967), 102.

[18] Deutsch, Edinger, et al., op. cit., p. 249.

If the variant of political integration in which one is interested happens to be the growth of supranational institutions, there are of course not many past cases which can be offered as candidates for intensive study. A number of writers have urged that conditions in underdeveloped countries are for these purposes sufficiently different from those in developed areas that generalizations about integrative processes cannot be transferred from one to the other.[19] If this conclusion is correct, then one is virtually limited, in finding a basis for predicting whether a full political union will develop from the EEC, to those instances in which two previously independent nations joined or split apart in North America or Western Europe in the twentieth century. Even stretching the definitions, I can think only of Newfoundland-Canada and Yugoslavia as successes, and England-Ireland and Norway-Sweden as splits. Perhaps the universe could be expanded somewhat by going back into the nineteenth century or by adding unions formed of areas that had not previously been sovereign (for example, post-1918 Czechoslovakia), but even so the limits are easy enough to see.

The existence of such limits, however, does not necessarily indicate that the task is hopeless. Virtually all hypotheses of any interest about international integration specify not merely a casual relation between two variables, but also a specific mechanism or mechanisms by which the effect is produced. Where there are too few potential cases to produce an adequate basis for correctional procedures, or where such case studies would be far too expensive and time consuming to replicate, one can look at the specific mechanism and shift levels of analysis. For example, Ernst Haas's famous study of the European Coal and Steel Community specified some hypotheses about spillover that could be tested on subgroups and individuals within various ECSC agencies.[20] Or in my own study of Anglo-American relations, in which the dependent variable of integration or responsiveness was extremely difficult to measure at the national level, I shifted at one point to an analysis of the behavior of particular legislators differentiated according to the number and strength of their personal or constituency ties with the other country. I then was able to determine the amount of behavioral difference that possessing such ties made, and could with a little more confidence return to inferences about the probable effect on national decisions of a decline in such ties at the aggregate level.[21] Often, in fact, the theoretical structure appropriate to an analysis may require correlational and case studies at a lower level even if the material at the aggregate level is plentiful and not too ambiguous.

---

[19] For example, J. S. Nye, *Pan-Africanism and East African Integration* (Cambridge: Harvard University Press, 1965).

[20] Ernst Haas, *The Uniting of Europe* (Stanford: Stanford University Press, 1957).

[21] Bruce M. Russett, *Community and Contention: Britain and America in the Twentieth Century* (Cambridge: M.I.T. Press, 1963), Chapter 10. Leon Lindberg and Stuart Scheingold have done an interesting job of specifying the coding procedures for measuring the dependent variable of political integration. See their *Europe's Would-be Polity: Patterns of Change in the European Community* (Englewood Cliffs: Prentice-Hall, 1970), and also the work being done by Donald J. Puchala, cited in Chapter 18 of this volume.

Another aspect of the international integration literature that demands new case studies, with a view to eventual correlation analysis of those case studies, is the problem of sequence. Even where it is possible to identify certain regularities, such as the association at one time period between trade patterns and the existence of intergovernmental institutions, it is not possible with a snapshot to see which causes which or even, temporally, which leads which. Furthermore, the pace of movements in both such variables is normally so glacial that it is virtually impossible even with a ten-year interval to be very firm in causal inferences. Intensive examination of developments in particular geographically or politically defined areas, with frequent snapshots over a very substantial time span and particular attention to the political consequences, is required.

DETERRENCE AND ESCALATION

Some of my own experiences in strategic analysis indicate both the opportunities and the need for a synthesis of the case study and correlational approaches.[22] Based largely upon individual case studies of international crises, generalizations about what factors contribute to the success of deterrent threats abound in the strategic literature. It has been alleged that successful deterrence requires overall strategic superiority or at least parity or local military superiority, that the area to be defended must be of demonstrable intrinsic value, and that democracies where dissent is visible are less able effectively to demonstrate commitment; a variety of other propositions have been expressed either as laws or hypotheses. In a correlational study of seventeen instances of attempted deterrence between 1930 and 1961 I was able to show that the empirical evidence provides little support for any of these simple statements, and instead suggested, on the basis of further correlational evidence, that successful deterrence, or a decision to fight if deterrence failed, depends largely upon the strength and number of various ties between the would-be deterrer and the party he is attempting to protect.

Such a correlational study did not, however, demonstrate that deterrence succeeded or war resulted *because* of these bonds. To make such a demonstration requires not just the associational evidence, but a detailed look at the perceptions and decision-making process of officials in the government of the potential attacker and defender. Only if they perceived those ties and took them into account would the hypothesis be supported. In order to find evidence of such perceptions and calculations, I later looked in depth at a particular historical instance, the Japanese decision to attack Pearl Harbor in addition to escalating military acitivity within Southeast Asia. This evidence, however, does not close the matter. In the first place, the Japanese decided to attack *despite* the hypothesized perceptions and calculations; while this finding was not inconsistent with the basic formulation of the original model, some re-

---

[22] See Chapters 12 and 13 in this volume.

finement was necessary. More important, the single case still does not establish the *probability* of such behavior or its interaction with other variables. Since few of us would subscribe to a completely deterministic model of human behavior, the need for gauging the probabilities demands a series of further case studies in which the relevant variables are measured rigorously by common definitions. From these further case studies can then come the second stage correlational analysis.

To be useful, however, case studies have to be done in such a way that they can eventually be analyzed within a common framework, with the same variables, measured in the same way and studied in each. It is often helpful if such studies are undertaken *from the beginning* within such a framework, where the student of each case is consciously asking the same questions as is every other analyst, and where by a painstaking repetitive process of sharpening and refinement the coding and data-gathering procedures are made fully comparable. Few examples of such large-scale projects can now be found in international relations or political science. Perhaps the best in a related field is the set of country studies being undertaken by the Yale Economic Growth Center in response to a widespread dissatisfaction among economists with the quality and comparability of national income accounts in developing countries. Very great resources are going into the compilation of fresh data by standardized categories, which eventually can be subjected to rigorous cross-national analysis.[23]

It is seldom essential, however, for such studies to be done originally within a common set of questions and definitions. A great number of valuable correlational analyses have been performed by a secondary coding of case studies originally undertaken for very different reasons. Here all the assets of good traditional case studies are of great value: the virtues of great detail, so that a wide variety of unanticipated questions can in fact be answered from the data by reordering the original information, and careful documentation, so that even where the case study does not itself contain the necessary information, the secondary analyst has good clues as to where he can himself dig it out from the primary materials with a minimum of wasted excavation. In fact, it is probably just as well for many correlational analyses to be done on preexisting case study material. Given the primitive state of most international relations theory, a standardized descriptive framework might produce premature closure on a restricted and erroneous set of questions. But eventually the need for a common analytical model does arise. Further case studies cannot be undertaken to check on inferences from the correlational analysis unless the hypotheses are carefully articulated.

---

[23] In international relations the most important efforts are still at an earlier stage. James N. Rosenau has been coordinating a group of comparative foreign policy studies around his set of categories for levels of analysis and gross characteristics of nations; the studies appeared in his *Linkage Politics*, op. cit. A second comparative study, sponsored by the SSRC, is Robert W. Cox and Harold K. Jacobson, et al., *The Anatomy of Influence: Decision Making in International Organization* (New Haven: Yale University Press, 1973).

Certainly it is not exclusively the literature of international integration that is marked by disconnected analytical case studies and premature predictive case studies. One of the most obvious others is the effort to generalize about the stability or war proneness of bipolar and multipolar international systems. Extremely few historical examples have been studied in depth, but this has not inhabited a good many authors from making rather sweeping generalizations based on a combination of deductive inference[24] and analogizing from historical instances. The available evidence on historical systems is rarely coded rigorously, and it is used in a fashion that is hardly more than anecdotal.

The situation becomes even worse with attempts to generalize from past cases to the contemporary international system. Such serious differences exist between both the abstract models and the available historical instances on the one hand, and the contemporary system on the other, that it becomes extremely difficult to decide whether the appropriate variables have been controlled and a "good" analogy produced, or whether the differences are critical. Desperately needed at this point are some correlational studies with a large number of cases, coded for a variety of variables that different theories regard as potentially relevant, with sophisticated multivariate quantitative analysis. Note the latter emphasis: I am specifically not implying that it will be enough simply to compare systems by the number of major actors and the number of war casualties in a bivarate correlation, though that is the necessary beginning. Technology, weapons systems, alliance aggregation, relative size and number of powers, the time elapsed since other wars, and many other variables will have to be taken into account. In this respect the current work of Michael Haas, Singer and Small, and Denton promises ultimately to be very important.[25]

It should be entirely clear from the preceding discussion that, though I have suggested a dichotomy between case studies and correlational studies, a case study can be systematic and may make use of a great many correlational materials from lower levels of analysis. The very intensive analyses to which the 1914 crisis has been subjected by the Stanford group illustrate well the degree to which sophisticated computerized content and aggregate data analysis can be employed. At the same time, the Stanford group has not limited its attention to the events of 1914, and has looked also, though so far less intensively, at the Bosnian crisis of 1908, the Cuban missile crisis, the deteriora-

---

[24] The major essays, of varying quality, probably are Morton A. Kaplan, *System and Process in International Politics* (New York: Wiley, 1957), Part I; Karl W. Deutsch and J. David Singer, "Multipolar Power Systems and International Stability," *World Politics*, XVI (April 1964); Kenneth Waltz, "The Stability of a Bipolar World," *Daedalus*, XCIII (summer 1964), 881–909, and Richard N. Rosecrance, "Bipolarity, Multipolarity, and the Future," *Journal of Conflict Resolution*, X (September 1966), 314–27.

[25] Michael Haas, "International Subsystems: Stability and Polarity," *American Political Science Review*, LXIV (March 1970); J. David Singer and Melvin Small, "Alliance Aggregation and the Onset of War," in *Quantitative International Politics*, J. David Singer, editor, op. cit., pp. 247–86; Frank Denton, "Some Regularities in International Conflict Behavior," *Background*, X (February 1966), 283–318.

tion of Sino-Soviet relations, and others.[26] Even a nonquantitative examination of other cases quickly brings home the limitations of a case study approach taken in isolation. At least one noted writer on the 1914 events virtually attributes the outbreak of war to the military pressures produced by the war and mobilization plans prepared by the antagonists.[27] Comparative analysis shows, however, that essentially the same plans existed in three previous crises during which general war did not break out. One can quickly find instruction in the difference between necessary and sufficient conditions.

The World War I study and the case studies of the other crises, quantitative and nonquantitative, illustrate an area where the need for integrating the many case studies is especially apparent. There must be innumerable classified studies on the "lessons learned" in many of the crises in which the United States has been involved since World War II. Just a moment's reflection will bring to mind a great number of published studies—many of each set of events and using the full spectrum of analytical techniques—that have been done on the escalation and de-escalation for the two Berlin confrontations, the Korean War, the Indochina conflicts in 1954 and more recently, the Quemoy-Matsu crisis, the Cuban missile and Bay of Pigs affairs, and others. With all these intensive studies, combined with substantial speculation and deductive theorizing about escalation sequences, we have the basis for a very complex and sophisticated set of coding rules that could put those case studies within a common framework and begin to extract evidence for the support or disconfirmation of general hypotheses.

One could begin by trying to construct an empirical "escalation ladder," in which the goal would be to discover exactly which steps usually follow others— what is the "normal" sequence of events, up and down—so as better to single out the significance of deviations. Is "skipping a rung" more likely to result in further or more rapid escalation; or, as a demonstrative step, does it have important deterrent value in preventing counterescalation? Or, more satisfactorily, *when* and *for what steps* does "skipping" produce such results? And even more basic, is it even possible to construct such a ladder? Do sufficient

---

[26] The Stanford Studies on Conflict and Integration of the 1914 events are largely scattered in a great number of book chapters and journal articles, but much now appears in Ole R. Holsti, *Crisis, Escalation, War* (Montreal: McGill-Queen's University Press, 1972) or will appear in a forthcoming volume by Nazli Choucri and Robert C. North. Materials by this group relevant to other interactons include Ole R. Holsti, "External Conflict and International Cohesion: The Sino-Soviet Case," in *The General Inquirer*, Philip J. Stone, editor (Cambridge: M.I.T. Press, 1966), pp. 343–58; Holsti, Brody, and North, "Measuring Affect and Action in International Reaction Models: Empirical Materials from the 1962 Cuban Crisis," *Peace Research Society Papers*, II (1965), 170–89; P. Terry Hopmann, "International Conflict and Cohesion in the Communist System," *International Studies Quarterly*, XI (September 1967), 212–36; and M. George Zaninovich, "Pattern Analysis of Variables within the International System: The Sino-Soviet Example," *Journal of Conflict Resolution*, VI (September 1962), 253–68.

[27] Barbara Tuchman, *The Guns of August* (New York: Macmillan, 1962), Chapters II–VI. I am indebted to Richard A. Brody for the example.

uniformities exist to make it possible to say that, usually at least, a given sequence is followed? Or is the meaning of certain steps sufficiently different in threat—for instance, under some conditions troop movements may represent a higher stage of escalation than mobilization, and under others vice versa— that two or three intersecting ladders need to be constructed for distinct dimensions? Factor analysis, cluster analysis, or other inductive techniques, perhaps especially those which can operate merely on ordinal rather than interval data, should be of high potential use in sorting out the regularities in this large body of data.[28]

AN OPPORTUNITY FOR SYNTHESIS

The deterrence literature illustrates in especially poignant form the current doldrums of international politics research. It is no secret that strategic analysis has relied heavily, though hardly exclusively, on the case study method. Nor is it any secret that many scholars in the field feel a certain malaise, a sense that the accomplishments of the past few years do not equal the contributions made during the "golden age" when such scholars as Kahn, Kissinger, Schelling, and Wohlstetter were most visible. Even if their assessment is correct, it by no means reflects on the intellectual quality of the men who continue to produce in the area. Partly it is a result of the shift of resources and concern to the Vietnam war. In part too it is the price of success: acceptance of the theory and policy consequences stemming from the principle of invulnerable second strike forces has meant a revolution in military-political doctrine and practice, a tough act to follow in short order. But the need for some fresh approaches, both methodological and conceptual, is becoming apparent.[29]

The need is forced in part by behavioral questions about deterrence that the original approach could not answer. It also stems from changes in the international environment within which the major powers operate. The strategic analysis community addressed itself largely to a bipolar world; that bipolarity has weakened greatly, though we are unsure how to describe the new one. Also, the analysts of strategy, perhaps in part because of their bipolar focus, concentrated too heavily on a perception of the international political process as dominated by conflict. Despite Schelling's contributions toward an understanding of the mixed-motive situation, I think this is the most telling indictment made by the critics of "strategic thinking."[30] To temper this emphasis

---

[28] A major study of great promise for producing an empirically based taxonomy of escalations is Richard Barringer, *The Condition of Conflict: A Configural Analysis* (Cambridge: Center for International Studies, M.I.T., ACDA/WEC-98, Draft Technical Report, 1967).

[29] My thinking on this has been notably influenced by Roy E. Licklider, *The Private Nuclear Strategists* (Columbus: Ohio State University Press, 1972).

[30] The principal critiques, containing a variety of trenchant, irrelevant, and mistaken points, are Anatol Rapoport, *Strategy and Conscience* (Ann Arbor: University of Michigan Press, 1964), and Phillip Green, *Deadly Logic* (Columbus: Ohio State University Press, 1966).

on conflict, a broader attention to conflict resolution and cooperation is required. This leads to what I see as an escape from the present sense of letdown—an integration of the strategic field with an avowedly social-scientific search for the causes of war. It would be directed to historical as well as to contemporary information and would be less bound by the culture of the 1950s and the 1960s than the strategic field has been.

The chances for such an integration exist precisely because a parallel reassessment is appearing among some of those most firmly committed to a quantitative or systematic approach. A number of international relations scholars have remarked that they too sense a new mood among their colleagues, a felt need for the digestion and evaluation of the scientific achievements of the past decade. There is no doubt that reputations have risen and fallen sharply in the study of international relations; most of the major lights of the past decade are now in eclipse. Some approaches have faded because it turned out to be virtually impossible to put data into their imaginative theoretical systems; others (especially some simulations) are being looked at askance from a doubt whether their expensively accumulated data have enough to say about the "real" world. Still others have been more nearly institutional failures, where the resources necessary to build a self-nurturing organization proved lacking.

This new mood stems less from a change in intellectual convictions than from an evolution of the terrain being surveyed. It is not a matter of questioning the scientific enterprise *qua* science, but only a matter of doubts about particular techniques and procedures—a process that is in fact a requisite for a science. In 1960 the discipline had hardly anything to show in the way of research achievements other than case studies. Now we have a substantial amount of theory expressed or expressible in formal symbolic terms and a large number of empirical studies using a spectrum of quantitative methods running from simple political arithmetic to the most complex multivariate statistical procedures for manipulating both numerical and verbal data. Some of the latter procedures will turn out to be overly complex for the relatively crude data to which they are applied; but despite the doubts all of us have about everyone else's manipulations, it is too early to rule out any path yet taken as merely leading to a cul de sac.

Thus it is important for the so-called traditional scholars to recognize the diversity achieved and the consequent inability to dismiss the entire enterprise as misguided or irrelevant. It can no longer be ridiculed as simply the product of a couple of simulations and the counting of postcards.[31] The variety is such that the traditional scholar could surely gain insight from applying some of the new techniques to any problem that interests him. On the other hand, both the data and the hypothesis-generating potential of the traditional materials will

---

[31] As evidence I would offer my own rather approximate survey of the academic political science and international relations journals published in the United States during 1966. About 30 percent of the articles either made use of mathematical formulations or had the equivalent of at least two tables. I recognize, however, that this survey of *publications* almost certainly exaggerates the number of quantitative *practitioners*.

for the foreseeable future be essential (if occasionally exasperating) for those who seek to build a science. Precisely because of the quantitative advances, this need becomes apparent. But successful use of the case study approach will require much careful winnowing of old material and designing research for new efforts.

PART I

The Environment
of World Politics

2
A Macroscopic View
of International Politics

THE ENVIRONMENT OF POLITICS

The thrust of this chapter is simple and direct: it expresses my growing conviction that political research, and especially research on international politics, has too much neglected the *environment* of politics. That is, we have often failed to study the role of social, economic, and technological factors in providing the *menu* for political choice. Relatively speaking, too much effort has gone into examining the ways in which choices are made, the political process itself, rather than into asking, in a rigorous and systematic way, what possible choices were in fact available and why those possibilities and not some others were available.

It is this emphasis on looking at the wider environment within which political decision makers act that I mean by the title, a macroscopic view. A microscope is of course an instrument for looking in great detail at a tiny portion of tissue or other material, ignoring the whole of a large organism or system for the sake of a painstaking examination of the structure or processes of one element. The term "macroscope" is meant to refer to just the opposite kind of tool, one for examining, in a gross way, the entire system or at least large portions of it. The fine detail available from the microscope is lost, but compensation comes from an image of the interrelationships of the parts. I

Reprinted from *The Analysis of International Politics*, James N. Rosenau, Vincent Davis, and Maurice East, editors (New York: The Free Press, 1972).

deliberately use the word macroscope in place of telescope as the opposite for microscope. A telescope is of course used for making distant objects appear close, for bringing out the detail of distant objects that one cannot approach physically. In this sense its function is not so different from that of the microscope. Like the latter it implies a relatively narrow view; one chooses to focus upon a particular star rather than on the entire galaxy that is visible to the naked eye in the night sky. So what I will be referring to is more nearly analogous to a wide-angle lens for a camera than to a telephoto lens.

The other aspect of this approach that I would emphasize here, as preface, is the interdisciplinary implication. To investigate these environmental questions political scientists have had to seek out a great deal of information from other sciences, physical as well as social. Because we are interested in social, economic, and technological factors, however, does not mean that we must become amateur sociologists, economists, or engineers so as to do original research in those disciplines. If we did we would certainly do it badly. But we have had to learn enough to understand their major findings, and to use their data. We have to know what the major nonpolitical trends are or may be so that we can develop some sense of how they may widen or limit the range of political choice.

DATA BASES FOR TAXONOMY AND HYPOTHESIS TESTING

I will try to justify this view in greater detail below, with comments that will be deliberately sweeping and provocative. First let me sketch very briefly some developments in theory and research on international politics in the past few years, identifying the rise of what has been called a quantitative, or behavioral, or self-consciously social-scientific study of international politics. This scientific mode is crucial to the rigorous, as compared with the merely stimulating, use of the macroscopic model. Some of the theoretical and conceptual breakthroughs necessary for the emergence of such an approach are apparent in some articles and a few books of the middle and late 1950s, with the primary impetus traceable directly to the work of Quincy Wright just before World War II. But it was not until about 1963 that major research results, the really quantitative books with findings, appeared in sufficient number as to mark the emergence of a science.[1] First came the development of taxonomies and

---

[1] Quincy Wright, *A Study of War* (Chicago: University of Chicago Press, 1942, 2 vols.). Some later empirical contributions whose importance is now apparent are the content analysis studies of Ithiel Pool, Daniel Lerner, and Harold Lasswell: *Symbols of Internationalism* (Stanford: Stanford University Press, 1951), *Symbols of Democracy* (Stanford: Stanford University Press, 1952), and *The Prestige Papers* (Stanford: Stanford University Press, 1952); William Buchanan and Hadley Cantril, *How Nations See Each Other* (Urbana: University of Illinois Press, 1953); Karl W. Deutsch, *Nationalism and Social Communication* (Cambridge: M.I.T. Press, 1953); Karl Deutsch and Lewis Edinger, *Germany Rejoins the Powers* (Stanford: Stanford University Press, 1959); and Lewis F. Richardson, *Arms and Insecurity* (Pittsburgh:

explicit models, sometimes using simple mathematics, but largely limited in application to a few case studies or pilot efforts. Then came a more widespread effort at hypothesis testing as contrasted with description, however careful and rigorous. And finally, by the mid-1960s, we saw the deliberate search for large-scale data bases, with many comparable observations for many variables.

This tends to become a "historical sociology" approach, with roots in the work of Weber or, if one is searching for a legitimator, perhaps even Aristotle. The approach makes use of a wide variety of data on the components of international systems, both present and historical systems. Such large data bases are essential for systematic comparison and hypothesis testing about the behavior of nations. They are also essential for continuing the taxonomic efforts. This classificatory or mapping exercise in fact establishes the operational definitions of many of our variables. The original classifications of nations, or of foreign policy influences, or of behavior patterns, were based largely on deductive theory and impressionistic evidence. Now, however, we can check and supplement these classifications with inductively based taxonomies from examining these large data bases to find the patterns of similarity and cleavage. Thus nations can be categorized in terms of similar patterns of attributes or interdependence. On many grounds, for instance, Japan can be grouped with the Western European nations. a fact that could have been suspected but not satisfactorily established without a great deal of information. Furthermore, we can now go beyond the taxonomies to look for the *relationships* between the boxes, or variables, so identified.

These developments impose no restrictions on *where*—that is, at what level of analysis—to develop powerful hypotheses. Many studies, for one example, have focused on the personality characteristics or life experiences of *decision makers*. Much of the most interesting theory of the 1950s applied to this level, and led to a number of important cross-national elite studies. Second, we are just now beginning to see important studies of the patterns of *interactions* among nations. Charles McClelland, for instance, is compiling a complete mapping of governments' verbal and physical acts toward other governments in the current international system, and has begun to publish some very important analyses of recent patterns that show unsupported ways in which the

---

Boxwood Press, 1960) and *Statistics of Deadly Quarrels* (Pittsburgh: Boxwood Press, 1960). In 1963 were published Harold Guetzkow, et al., *Simulation in International Relations* (Englewood Cliffs: Prentice-Hall); Robert North, et al., *Content Analysis: A Handbook with Applications for the Study of International Crisis* (Evanston: Northwestern University Press), and my *Community and Contention: Britain and America in the Twentieth Century* (Cambridge: M.I.T. Press), although the first two are essentially how-to-do-it volumes discussing the techniques behind the important substantive articles published elsewhere. The ten-year gap between *A Study of War* and the publications of Pool, Lerner, Lasswell, Buchanan, Cantril, and Deutsch may well mark the damage done to the nascent science of international politics by the intellectual as well as material disruption wrought by World War II and its aftermath, when almost all scholars were pressed into applied work. On the other hand, the enormously enhanced funding recently available for research is largely due to war and cold war.

sequence of events in crises is different from that in "normal" times.[2] Other
analyses have been concerned with comparative foreign policies, in the sense
of how differences in *national* characteristics affect national policies. These may
be relatively small differences, such as between parliamentary and presidential
systems, or changes in the structure of particular countries over time. The
large-scale comparisons, however, require larger data bases and more gross,
more aggregated national characteristics. Thus it is possible to investigate
what difference being economically developed, or democratic, or European
makes for behavior. Finally, at this same level of aggregation are the patterns
of *linkages* among nations. Included here are the studies of trade ties, bonds
of communication, and frequency of membership in international organizations. Such studies lead on to comparisons of *international systems*, defined by
a combination of the pattern of linkages plus certain characteristics of the
states being linked. Thus a comparison of bipolar with multipolar systems depends on measures of the relative size of the major nations making up the
systems, and the linkages among states that signify the bonds of alliance.

In my own work I have largely concentrated on the gross, aggregated
characteristics of states and their linkages for explaining nations' behavior.
I started out with that approach largely as a matter of hunch, and since then
have retained it because of the good predictive (or retrodictive) power that
in fact seems to be available with it, for very many kinds of problems. Study
at lower levels of analysis is critical for quite a large number of situations and
issues, however, and it is not at all true that effort should be *confined* to the
aggregated level. In fact, some real limits to the utility of aggregate data
analysis are becoming very clear, and the rapid progress of the macroscopic
approach actually brings us nearer to those limits. So all the returns are
certainly not in.

THE MENU OF CHOICE IN FOREIGN POLICY

Whatever its utility, the basic characteristic of this approach is in asking what
are the *limits* of political choice, and here I return to my opening comments
about the environment of politics. What determines the choices available to
(or perceived by) national decision makers? What are the limits *within which*
personality differences, or different role conceptions, or alternative styles of
bargaining and negotiation, can affect choice? This distinction between the
process of selection among alternatives ("competition for scarce resources";
"the sharing of values") and the set of choices offered is perhaps crucial to an
understanding of the recent United States foreign policy dilemma. If you walk
into a restaurant, what you order of course depends on how hungry you are,

---

[2] Charles A. McClelland, "Access to Berlin: The Quantity and Variety of Events, 1948–63,"
in *Quantitative International Politics: Insights and Evidence*, J. David Singer, editor (New York:
The Free Press, 1968) is a preliminary study of these data. See also McClelland and Gary A.
Hogard, "Conflict Patterns in the Interaction Among Nations," in *International Politics and
Foreign Policy*, James N. Rosenau, editor (New York: The Free Press, 1969, 2nd edition).

what your tastes are, and how much money you have. It also depends on what the menu offers. Dinner at a pizza palace offering dozens of varieties of pizza is not likely to be very satisfactory if you don't happen to like pizza.

Not many people are very happy about the menu that has been provided to us in Southeast Asia. Neither escalation nor withdrawal, in any of their possible permutations, nor continuing to slog on somewhere in between, looked like a very attractive policy. There *is* no "good" solution to the predicament, only a selection of bad options, some of which are less bad than others. Now of course there are some differences among Americans on just what the possible range of choice offered really is. Or rather, there are different perceptions of what the consequences of selecting various options would be. The right-wing or hawk opposition to current policy sees more opportunities for the use of military force than the government probably sees. The hawks do think that a wider and more intense application of violence could bring a meaningful military victory. The left-wing or dove viewpoint, on the other hand, stresses the irrelevance of events in Southeast Asia to American vital interests. They maintain that an American withdrawal in South Vietnam and Communist victory would not seriously endanger other Asian nations' security or, even if there should be a domino effect, that even all of Southeast Asia is not so critical to the distant and powerful United States as to be worth the price we are paying.

The American government, presumably somewhere in between these dissenting views, for some time expressed what was really a rather broad United States consensus. It maintained that neither the alleged alternative put forth by the right, nor that of the left, was a real one; that each would have undesired consequences that its protagonists did not anticipate. More recently perspectives, both of some people in government and in wide segments of the populace at large, have changed. But strong opposition to the war did not spread far beyond intellectual circles before 1968, a fact the latter tend to forget. And even in the middle of 1968 the range of realistic choice, as generally perceived, was not wide. While Gallup poll respondents had become as likely to refer to themselves as doves as hawks, few favored a unilateral American withdrawal from South Vietnam.[3] Though many would have preferred a somewhat different policy by their government, most had in mind matters of style and emphasis rather than a drastic shift. They still saw their nation as distressingly bound by previous acts to a short and not very varied menu.

THE POWER OF MACROSCOPIC PREDICTION

I suggested that the aggregate macroscopic view could be shown to have a good deal of power for predicting policy, that it works well in a great number of instances. This is so because both perceptions and policy are quite stable for most nations, as I will now try to demonstrate. My initial example will be from

---

[3] American Institute of Public Opinion press release, April 30, 1968.

the work Hayward Alker and I have done, individually and together, on voting behavior in the United Nations.[4] First, we found that a very wide variety of *particular* issues and roll calls—about the Congo, Korea, Chinese representation, disarmament, South Africa, West New Guinea, and many others—are in fact usually concerned with one of the *major broad* issues of contemporary world politics. Three great cleavages or "superissues"—the Cold War, colonialism, and the role of the United Nations organization itself—account for about 60 percent of the variance in roll call voting. This in itself was a surprising regularity, and provided a basis for an empirical typology of issues. And I think most observers would agree that these are truly the issues around which the entire globe (as contrasted with more parochial regional disputes) currently does divide.

From there it was easy and appropriate to try to predict the voting behavior of particular nations on these superissues. For instance, Alker found that on Cold War issues he could predict most of the variation in voting position (75 percent of the variance) by knowing only a few basic facts. Simply categorizing the various states according to regional or caucusing groups would do that well, as would knowing a few facts about the military and economic bonds among nations (their alliance commitments and their receipt of trade and aid from the United States and the Soviet Union.) This too was surprising, to us as well as to others. We had been given many predictions that nothing resembling this level of regularity would emerge; that delegates' voting decisions depended too heavily on the vagaries of instructions from home, or upon volatile interests of the delegations, or interdelegation bargaining, or upon what nation's representative happened to be sitting next to a delegate on a particular day. Furthermore, we found that we could "predict" more than 80 percent of the variance in states' voting by knowing their *past* voting behavior. Even data on positions taken ten years earlier provided that kind of predictive power.

Votes on smaller, more parochial, and more transient issues are of course more difficult to predict. But on these three continuing and salient cleavages we could do very well at the aggregate, macroscopic level without knowing anything about changing conditions or decision processes *within* individual governments. Changes of personnel in the delegations; changes in the leadership of the home governments; alternation of parties; all had little effect. Even changes of regime or governmental structure, as caused by coups or palace revolutions, made little difference to the leaders' perceptions of choice in the United Nations, or at least to their actual choices of behavior.[5] In all but a

---

[4] Hayward R. Alker, "Dimensions of Conflict in the General Assembly," *American Political Science Review*, 58, 3 (September 1964), pp. 642–57; Alker and Russett, *World Politics in the General Assembly* (New Haven: Yale University Press, 1965); and Russett, *International Regions and the International System* (Chicago: Rand McNally, 1967), Chapters 4 and 5. See also R. J. Rummel, "Some Empirical Findings on Nations and Their Behavior," *World Politics*, 21, 2 (1969), pp. 226–41.

[5] Cf. also David H. Blake, *Leadership Succession and Foreign Policy* (Ph.D. dissertation, Rutgers University, 1968).

literal handful of cases it took a virtual social revolution, with an impact on the level of that occuring in Iran with the overthrow of the Mossadegh regime or Guatemala and Arbenz in the 1950s, to produce a very marked shift. Furthermore, we can specify what we mean by a marked shift. Cuba's change of polarity from Batista to Castro was by far the greatest national flip-flop between the late 1950s and the early 1970s. On a scale of Cold War issues, Guatemala and Iran shifted their UN voting by an amount that is roughly one-third of Cuba's change, and there are but six other states that moved by even a fifth as much as Cuba did (not necessarily in the same direction).[6] In most instances one could "map" the political differences and concurrences of nations in a very stable way.

Similarly, in my recent work on regional groupings[7] I found that I could predict about 80 percent of the variance in patterns of membership in the world's more than 150 international organizations, or patterns of trading relationships, or UN voting behavior, or social and cultural similarities, by knowing what any *one* of those patterns looked like. Finally, knowing international organization memberships ten years previously, or trading patterns ten years previously, allowed one to predict between 85 and 95 percent of the variance in the later period. In the case of trade, one could even predict more than three-quarters of the 1963 variance from the 1938 pattern, despite World War II, the Cold War, and decolonization. Thus these influences, and we include here the very important regional and other bonds of community among nations, change at a glacial pace in this international system. The stabilities of our world are, on examination, very impressive.

Finding these continuities contrasts very sharply with the task of day-to-day journalism and impressionism. The journalist's job is to tell us how today is different from yesterday, and to do so in a sufficiently vivid manner to attract and hold our attention. When writing about Anglo-American relations, for instance, a good journalist like Drew Middleton changes his evaluation constantly. He looks not at the system level but at political events, personalities, and personnel changes in decision-making positions. Anglo-American relations are good one day following a meeting of chiefs-of-state, and bad the next day as a consequence of a new disagreement. It is precisely against this participant's-eye view that I am reacting, trying to back up and gain perspective both on how the relations between two states fit into the global pattern of relationships and how they perform over a much longer time span. The journalist's view is, at best, like confusing the business cycle with the long-term secular trend in the economy. And at that it is not likely to be analogous to a concentration on the depression and inflation ends of the business cycle, but only on the numerous rather mild fluctuations in between.

It is of course true that the macroscopic kind of approach is not *very* good for explaining why the United States acted as it did during a specific period of

---

[6] Russett, *International Regions*, pp. 90–91.
[7] Ibid., Chapters 6–11. Also Chapter 5 of this volume.

stress like the Suez crisis of 1956—though it is not bad even for that—but it *is* quite good for explaining why, after 1957, the drift of British alliance (NATO) policy was one way and the movement of France's leaders was in another direction.[8] The basic underlying bonds of the relationship with America were very much stronger in one case than in the other, as revealed by macroscopic analysis. And a more detailed, microscopic examination shows that the British elite, after overcoming their bitterness at American inconstancy, drew the lesson that Britain could never again afford to take a critical policy decision in conflict with the United States position; their dependence on this country was too great. The French, on the contrary, concluded that they could not again afford always to depend on the support of a United States that had independent interests; thus they must prepare the basis for action that might be independent of or even in major conflict with America.

Note, incidentally, that neither of these countries' directions since 1956 can be traced to the idiosyncrasies of single parties or decision makers. Britain's decision for dependence was made by a Conservative government and was then carried out, to the point of virtual obsequiousness, by a Labour government. France's review of its commitments was begun well before De Gaulle took office. Alliances and alignments of various sorts thus are rooted in long-term influences and in environmental factors over which politics does have some control, but only over the passage of substantial periods of time. This sounds like a very general affirmation, but in fact the data are there to document it.

Such a perspective on the stabilities of world politics has crucial policy implications. Too often observers and policy makers take alarm at every coup or change of government. The Chicken Little syndrome (The sky is falling! Run and tell the President!) is widespread. But if important policy reversals in these countries are rare, expensive attempts to affect the composition of the next governing coalition in Boonistan are at best unnecessary, and more likely a dangerous waste of resources that will ultimately weaken the United States both abroad and domestically. Many roots of an interventionist foreign policy lie in the faulty intellectual understanding that is unaware of the gross stabilities.

POLITICAL VARIABLES AS PREDICTORS OF POLITICAL OUTPUTS

Such constancy reminds us again of the limits of politics, of the degree to which future choices are controlled by past choices, and of the restricted degree to which the available menu is set by political choice in any case. Differences among types of political systems, for example, are *poor* predictors, on the aggregate level, of most variations in the outputs of economic and

---

[8] Cf. Russett, *Community and Contention*, op. cit., and Chapter 12 of this volume.

social systems. Some examples, drawn from within the United States as well as from cross-national studies are:

1. Type of *political* system (authoritarian versus competitive) is often only a moderately good predictor of international political behavior. In the UN General Assembly, type of political system explained only about a quarter of the variance of voting on East-West issues, and was essentially unrelated to voting on North-South issues. With some economic and cultural attributes, on the other hand, one could account for as much as half of the voting variance.[9]

2. Political system *outputs*, such as public spending in various functional categories, can on one level be very well explained by such *environmental* characteristics of a system as its level of income, degree of urbanization, racial composition, and average level of educational attainment. This has been effectively demonstrated by comparing budgetary data on cities and on American state governments. But the outputs are very *poorly* predicted by political system characteristics such as governmental structure, relative party strength, or electoral competition.[10]

3. On another level, however, these system outputs can be equally explained by knowing what the proportionate expenditures were in the *past*. A simple model predicting that the relative allocation in the future will be the same as it has been gives extremely good results.[11] In this sense the irrelevance of politics to *change* stems from the strength of political organizations to maintain themselves against the competing claims of other organizations in a bargaining situation. This constancy has been found in American cities, at the level of the federal budget, and even apparently in the national budget of the Soviet Union, where current spending on ballistic missile defense can be seen as largely the bureaucratic inertia of previous purchase of antiaircraft equipment.[12]

These conclusions at the aggregate level are of course controversial. It is still appropriate to maintain that other variables, more sophisticated indicators, or more interesting multivariate models will produce better results,

---

[9] Alker and Russett, op. cit., Chapter 11.

[10] Thomas R. Dye, *Politics, Economics, and the Public: Policy Outcomes in the American States* (Chicago: Rand McNally, 1967); John Patrick Crecine, *Governmental Problem Solving: A Computer Simulation of Municipal Budgeting* (Chicago: Rand McNally, 1969); and a forthcoming study by Stephen V. Stephens of Johns Hopkins University.

[11] Crecine, op. cit., and Otto A. Davis, M. A. H. Dempster, and Aaron Wildavsky, "A Theory of the Budgetary Process," *American Political Science Review*, 60, 3 (September 1966), pp. 529–47.

[12] On the latter, see Graham T. Allison, *Conceptual Models and the Cuban Missile Crisis* (Boston: Little, Brown, 1971). It should be noted that Allison makes a strong case for knowing, especially in the analysis of crisis situations, about bureaucratic politics as well as system-level variables.

in the sense of higher explanatory power for the political variables. But the results so far are intriguing, and perhaps help to meet an accusation that is frequently made against certain kinds of political scientists—that they are not interested in politics. Being interested in political outcomes does not necessarily require being interested in the political process.

A LIMITED DEFENSE OF INDUCTION

Many of these findings have been obtained from testing, on large data bases, some relatively simple hypotheses about the interrelation of political and environmental variables. Others nevertheless should not be dressed up with the appearance of hypothesis testing, but have been obtained essentially from taxonomic or other inductive efforts. Inductive uses of various techniques, such as multiple regression, factor analysis and multidimensional scaling, "casual modeling," and "curve fitting," have proved extremely valuable at the macroscopic level. Their productivity in research to date provides a powerful defense of induction, or "fishing expeditions," at that level and at this stage in the growth of the science.

Now certainly even the inductive political fisherman needs some theory to guide him. You have to know what pools and streams to fish in, how to select tackle, and how to manipulate the tackle. Some inchoate theory must specify what the most promising variables for the inductive exercise are to be, and you had better understand the kind of functional relationships that your procedures are seeking. It is hardly worthwhile to use statistical procedures that search for additive relationships among variables if an adequate theoretical system specifies multiplicative relationships. If revolutionary potential is a curvilinear function of income you will not discover it by using only a linear regression model. And surely you need the ability to formulate a set of alternative hypotheses so as tentatively to "explain" the results. Only with that much theory can you then go on to understand more about the relationships, to formulate further and more explicit hypotheses about what the causal mechanism is and under what circumstances it applies. Doing political analysis without it is like fishing with a bent pin in a laundry tub, and likely in the long run to be about as profitable.

But induction per se has been much maligned. Whatever the approach, the aim is to arrive at nonobvious propositions. Our natural science colleagues may now be more heavily deductive than we, but that is in part made possible by past inductive successes which are now part of their knowledge (e.g., much of the work of Galileo, Newton, and especially Kepler). Because our international politics discipline is so sorely lacking in good, deductive, formal, rigorous theory, we often are forced to be rather heavily inductive, and can often achieve substantial payoffs despite the handicap of weak theory. And since we are in any case speaking in terms of probabilistic hypotheses, the deviant cases are subject to careful microscopic examination. We first need the macroscopic studies to identify the deviant cases as such, but in no sense can we dispense with detailed analysis.

Yet there is one critical limit to the kind of knowledge we derive from induction, and it concerns the difference between prediction and explanation. Inductively discovered patterns can be used for substantial periods of time to predict political behavior. If we know empirically that *A* is associated with *B*, we may derive important policy benefits from predicting changes in *B* as a result of changes in *A*, without knowing *why*. But however exciting and important the discovery of high aggregate correlations may be, prediction without "understanding" is vulnerable to system changes; when we do not understand why two variables are related our predictions are vulnerable to shifts in the relationship. Historic determinants of alliance formation may not hold in the nuclear era; where power considerations once brought nations together in military pacts, nuclear proliferation now is associated with the *absence* of formal alliances. (In all the years since completion of the 42-nation western security system in 1955, no other nations have aligned themselves with either the United States or any major Western European state.) Or, in the nineteenth century the degree of alliance aggregation in the international system was negatively correlated with the magnitude and severity of war, suggesting a causal relationship in that greater predictability of national behavior implied by the alliances kept the system more stable and less war prone. A prediction from this observation into the twentieth century, however, would have gone badly astray, since after 1900, with the increasing rigidity of European power relationships, alliance formation became positively associated with the outbreak of war.[13] A failure to explore the *political* mechanisms beneath the correlation would have led to an eventual failure of prediction.

Similarly, the high degree of association discussed previously between environmental variables and political ones could be very deceptive in future international politics. Since 1945 the international system has been remarkably stable in the continued dominance of two superpowers (one significantly stronger than the other) with a substantial gap between them and the other major states. The relative gap between superpowers and others may have narrowed slightly in recent years, and together with Russian consolidation of an invulnerable second strike nuclear force the system has changed somewhat, modestly in the direction of greater multipolarity. But these changes are very moderate when compared with the kind of dramatic system change that has in the past resulted from great war or from revolution in a major state. They are also moderate compared with the kind of system change one can imagine from a technological breakthrough that made cheap nuclear weapons available to all. Only new theory, not the continued extrapolation of inductively derived

[13] David Singer and Melvin Small, "Alliance Aggregation and the Onset of War, 1815–1945," in Singer, editor, op. cit.

patterns, could tell us which past regularities would hold and which would be shattered in the new system. Some of the old constraints on political choice would surely be broken.

In this respect our present understanding of international politics is perhaps comparable to the understanding of American voting behavior reached by the early survey analyses. They established that certain demographic character-istics, such as religion, income, and occupation, were highly correlated with partisan choice.[14] These correlations were fairly stable over time, but enough individuals, typically less than 20 percent, changed their votes and so could reverse the outcome of the preceding election. Induction and knowing the gross correlations were not enough to know the dynamic elements—who would change, and whether the changes would be enough to make a major shift in the state of the system. Yet it is hard to imagine these later questions being studied in the absence of the earlier inductive findings. In many respects, then, this paper is more of a retrospect than a prospect. It expresses a certain amount of satisfaction with where we have been, but tells us less surely where we should go next.

Wherever we go, it is important to press ahead both on the empirical front and on that of abstract theory. The advocates of a purely deductivist social science often point to modern economics as proving the power of deductive theory. To a degree they are right. But deductive theory building has charac-terized much work in economics for a century or more, with but limited ac-complishments for much of the time; the greatest successes of economics date only from World War II. No more than 30 years ago did the data necessary to test or apply macroeconomic theory become available to scholars and planners. Only then was the Keynesian revolution solidified, and the op-portunity for proper theoretical refinement presented.

Some find it tempting to reject not only induction but even the necessity to put deductively derived propositions to the test. The later Greek philo-sophers have been described as

> led away by their intellectual triumphs into the conceit that it ought to be possible to think out the whole structure of the natural world from a few axioms. Recourse to experiment was in their view a sign of an inferior mind, a view which was no doubt reinforced by the fact that in Greece most of the manual work was done by the helots, an inferior class, so that the manual work of an experiment would be well below the dignity of a philosopher.[15]

This mistake, the author observes, was fatal to Greek science. He further

---

[14] Paul Lazarsfeld, Bernard Berelson, and Hazel Gaudet, *The People's Choice* (New York: Columbia University Press, 1944) and Bernard Berelson, Paul Lazarsfeld, and William McPhee, *Voting* (Chicago: University of Chicago Press, 1954).

[15] R. V. Jones, "Science, Technology, and Civilization," *Bulletin of the Institute of Physics and the Physical Society* (April 1962), p. 97. See also Chapter 8 in this volume on the need for imagination, data, and rigor.

characterizes the mandarin civil servants of China: "As they stewed in their own intellectual juice, their imagination was not given the jolting stimuli that arise only from contact with the new experience gained from experiment."

Even when deductive theory is tested and not refuted, one still must raise probing questions about the theory. Careless testing, on inadequate data or small samples, can mean that a variety of deductively derived systems will "work" if no demands are made that the initial premises be politically relevant. Thus the ideal position—that only the deductions, not the premises, need be plausible—cannot be widely accepted in a social science with serious data problems.[16]

IRREVERSIBLE CHOICES

As children of modern psychology we all are well aware of the limitations on our personal choice as individuals—limitations of genetic endowment, of environment, and of experience. Without accepting a rigidly deterministic model of human action, we nevertheless comprehend the severe restrictions within which our *private* choice is able to move. But I think we perceive less clearly what are the bounds on the *public* choice exercised by leaders of nations, we too often fail to consider their real options, either as might be seen by an objective observer or as seen by the decision maker himself.[17]

If it is true that political choice is severely circumscribed, we must focus special attention on a particular kind of choice node, on those decisions which sharply restrict the menu of future options. Often choices are not irreversible, and one may at least approximate, at a later point, an option that was rejected earlier. For this kind of situation the adage about *any* decision being better than *no* decision, or a paralysis of will, is especially appropriate. But this happens less often than we may like to think. In too many circumstances the model of the decision tree is all too relevant; as we proceed from one node to another previous options become irrecoverable. Japanese leaders in 1941 found that successive choices cost them so many alternatives that in the end the decision to fight the United States, in a war they did not really expect to win, seemed unavoidable.[18] The American decision to develop atomic weapons brought technical knowledge that cannot be unlearned, immensely complicating disarmament efforts. The Red Army, whose incursion into Central

---

[16] See the appendix on mathematical arms race models by Peter A. Busch in my *What Price Vigilance?* (New Haven: Yale University Press, 1970).

[17] For a similar perspective see Harold and Margaret Sprout, *An Ecological Paradigm for the Study of International Politics* (Princeton: Center of International Studies, Research Monograph No. 30, 1968). The renewed attention to spatial variables in macroscopic analyses also owes much to the Sprouts' long work on the subject.

[18] Chapter 13 of this volume. There was *finally* a general consensus, among Japanese of many political persuasions, on this step. Robert North and his Stanford associates seem to be reaching a similar judgment about the German decision for war in 1914.

Europe for the defeat of Hitler we applauded, became less welcome in a changed international system. The decision to fight a "limited" war now may be at the expense of later economic growth, with the consequence that a nation's material power base is forever smaller than it might have been had armaments not taken the place of capital investment.

This is an especially serious problem in international politics because we know so little about the articulated consequences of our decisions. Neither the best theorist nor the most confident man of action can really know what the ramifications of an act will be. And the danger is compounded by the *speed* with which decisions are forced upon leaders before even whatever inadequate analytical tools we have can be brought to bear on the choice. Scientific and technological advances that bring the entire world within reach of instantaneous communication, or any target on the globe within 30 minutes of destruction, can leave little time for reflection. When population natural increase rates are two percent a year, total population doubles in thirty years. A world whose population has once reached three billion will never again be the natural, uncrowded environment that our ancestors knew. The further environmental consequences of a jump from three billion to six billion on earth are far different from those of a jump from three million to six million. There are also unimagined consequences of the *level* of power available to change our environment. One manifestation is the potential destructiveness of nuclear warfare, but another ostensibly more constructive manifestation is in the changes that modern industrial processes and urban living patterns are inflicting on the environment. Scientists warn us about an "ecological crisis" from pollutants that could quite literally make the globe uninhabitable.

Hence the old virtues of any decision being better than none become transmuted. The avoidance of a decision that would work irreversible changes looks attractive if there is some chance that our science can, given time, help us better to evaluate the consequences of decision.

Japan's 1941 policy is a good example of how hard it may be to recognize critical decision nodes when they do appear. America's incremental creep into the Vietnam quagmire is another. Regrettably, there is no automatic warning signal to flash before the decision maker. Until our science becomes better developed, perhaps all one can do to identify such nodes before they are passed is always to have someone ask explicitly, "What will it cost if this decision turns out badly? How, if at all, could we turn back?" This scepticism might help prevent seduction by alternatives that seem to carry fairly high probabilities of favorable outcomes, and high benefits if they work, but disastrous costs should they fail. The acquisition of very expensive weapons systems (because their costs will foreclose other military or civilian options) is an especially relevant class, as is the procurement of systems with very greatly enhanced capabilities. So, in this world, is a superpower's decision actually to use military force. And so, perhaps unfortunately, would be a decision to implement a major disarmament measure. In the last case, however, our foreign policy making system is well supplied with cautionary voices; for the others the devil's advocate has too often been reticent or unwelcome.[19]

Karl Marx showed us some economic foundations of politics. However flawed the glass through which he saw his vision, the image it projects remains a vibrant one. To give that view perspective, we must equally see the social and technological bases of choice. Politics, it sometimes seems, has become the arena for avoiding cataclysm. Political gladiators can destroy far more readily than they can create; their task is one of avoiding error. But they are human, and in repeated encounters ultimately they do blunder. In the spirit of Marx, it may be more fruitful to ask what shapes the arena than what determines each stroke of their blunt swords.

These final comments may perhaps suggest some needs, and also suggest how the many elements of new and traditional political theory must be combined. To make wise political choices in an era of rapid technological and social change requires a great variety of pieces of information.

1. We must know our own values. Here, in defining what we want to achieve, remains the central role of traditional normative political philosophy.

2. We also must know the consequences of various alternative actions. This must be specified in an involved and complex way, using such modern theoretical perspectives as general systems theory.

3. In the role of political engineers, we must know too about the processes of our own American political system and how it works, so as to be able to use and strengthen those elements that will support the action we desire.

4. Finally, we must discover the environmental constraints, what choices are actually available, what the options really are. The farther ahead we can see the greater is likely to be our choice.

---

[19] If this sounds like an argument for always trying to avoid any possibility of the worst outcome, I do not mean it to be. It can be argued that American involvement in Vietnam stemmed from such a strategy—an attempt to prevent the very bad consequences, however unlikely, of the domino effect. If so, the strategy's proponents ignored the risks of an outcome very nearly as bad, and more probable—the quagmire.

3
Indicators for America's Linkages with the Changing World Environment

Writing a paper on indicators relevant to the study of international politics is, in some serious degree, an inversion of the proper priorities. Relative to our human or mechanical information-processing facilities, we well may already have too much information in some areas. Particularly in crisis, the State Department and other government agencies become information bottlenecks, forcing personnel to take steps, whether arbitrary or nearly random, to *reduce* the flow of information that they pass up to higher levels.[1] Thus, the process of selection by which a decision maker's data inputs are restricted and biased becomes of critical interest, and demands the creation of better theory to specify what is relevant and what trivial. Ideally, we should start with formal and well-articulated theory, moving only then to data collection to test critical hypotheses or to provide essential predictors.

SOME GENERAL CRITERIA OF SELECTION

But, currently, ingenuity in specifying possible measures substantially outruns the state of international theory, which is only by exception either formal or well articulated. Although I have my own theories of international politics,

Reprinted from *The Annals of the American Academy of Political and Social Science*, 388 (March 1970).
[1] An interesting description of this as a general phenomenon is Anthony Downs, *Inside Bureaucracy* (Boston: Little, Brown, 1967).

and am familiar with those of other scholars, all are woefully incomplete. And several efforts, both governmental and academic (for example, in the State Department and at the Inter-university Consortium for Political Research), are underway to gather and collate vast bodies of information. Hence, in the spirit of sweeping the horizon to take in most of the major landmarks, I will be obliged to list a wide variety of possible indicators without being able to say here just exactly what the analyst should do with them. In many cases, uses for the indicators will appear, in far more varied form than now can be listed, once they are available to stimulate the imagination of theorists. Certainly most, or even the most important, of the uses of national income accounting measures were not envisioned at the time when the system was initially devised.

The major problem is far less one of identifying possible indicators of variables that one would like to measure than a problem of deciding, among a virtual infinity of potential *indicators*, which ones can serve as measures of *variables* that are theoretically important. Just because there is unavoidable slippage between the analytical concept or variable and the empirical indicator, it is often useful, where possible, to employ several indicators, each of which may tap different aspects of the underlying variable of interest.

At the same time, this does *not* mean that I will simply list an enormous number of possible indicators purely as a stimulus to induction, or engage in specifications for a data bank without any idea of what would be done with that data bank. International relations theory is far enough advanced at least to identify *which variables* would be interesting and relevant to important questions of American foreign policy, if not always to specify in exactly *what ways* the variables will be important: that is, we can hypothesize, often with a high degree of confidence, about a relationship between two variables without necessarily being able to say just what the strength of that relationship is (how much *variance* in one is accounted for by the other, the squared correlation coefficient); the nature of the relationship (how much of a *change* in one will be necessary to produce a given amount of change in the other, the regression coefficient); or even the existence or direction of causality (Does one *produce* a change in the other? If so, which is which? Or are changes in both the result of a third variable?). This kind and degree of specification can come only through extensive research, precisely the kind of research that will be stimulated by the existence of an "indicator bank." So the following list will be derived implicitly from what I consider to be the most important (potentially powerful) theories of international relations, even though the theories often do not tell us precisely what the effect of changes in some of the variables will be.

The list will, in addition, deliberately err on the side of inclusiveness; I will try to list most of what would be relevant at the deliberate cost of including some things that will not prove to bear any substantial relationship to variables we consider important, and at the cost of a rather high degree of redundancy. I assume that I am charged with providing a reasonably complete menu, ensuring, so far as possible, that nothing that might be tasty will be overlooked, and leaving it to the consumer to choose from the menu in accordance with his tastes, appetite, and pocketbook. Furthermore, no data-gathering scheme will be static. Just as new variables of interest will be suggested as a project moves from the programmatic to the concrete, the low utility of others will become apparent and they can be dropped. There is no reason to think that in embarking on such a project, one is accepting a commitment to an infinitely expanding universe. And it should, of course, be remembered that, in principle, a social indicators project for the world environment is not a subset of a social indicators project for the United States, but quite the *opposite*. Hence I will, perhaps, be forgiven for seeming ambitious.

Fewer Units

Even with these caveats and with some reduction of indicators, the task will be larger than practicable for the foreseeable future. Several possibilities for further reduction do exist. Both the number of variables and the number of observations can be reduced by systematic procedures. First, the number of observations, or units on which data are necessary, can often be sharply reduced by careful use of random and stratified sampling procedures. This will be especially necessary for certain attitudinal variables—like those obtained by survey research or content analysis on affective and cognitive structures of mass, and of elite, decision makers—that will be discussed below. If certain kinds of data on the attributes, behavior, or value orientations of the world's nations are needed, and it is too expensive to gather such data for all 140 or more independent states and "major" colonies, then random sampling can be employed to select, say, 20 percent of those units. If the same units were studied over time, one would have a panel that could monitor changes over time and could, within specifiable limits, be generalized to the entire international system.

Random sampling is most useful, however, only where one has little additional theory or information that specifies some units as more important than others. In any study, either of the international environment *per se* or of America's linkages with it, it is clear that some units *are* far more "important," because of their size, power, or critical positive or negative interactions with the United States. A random sample that failed to include our most important allies and enemies, and perhaps the largest neutrals, would be of very limited use indeed. Hence any such system would probably have to include, at least, the Soviet Union, Mainland China, the United Kingdom, France, West Germany, Japan, and India.

Several other states, including Canada, Brazil, and Italy, might also be included in the above "musts." More likely, however, they and others of lesser moment could be taken into account by a stratified sample specified by theory and policy interest. One would want to be sure, for instance, that some Middle Eastern state or states were represented in the sample, and a randomly chosen sample might not include any. Thus, one could divide the world into several geographical or sociocultural regions, as seemed most relevant for most theoretical purposes. Very possibly, they would be Western Europe and North America as well as Australia and New Zealand, Latin America, North Africa and the Middle East, Sub-Saharan Africa, Communist countries, and non-Communist Asia.[2] With a proportionate number of states selected from each area, or with an appropriate weighing scheme, one could then properly generalize from this sample to the world. One could *not*, however, generalize to the particular regions or groupings. It is very unlikely that enough states from any one area would be included to permit reliable statements about the area.

Another possible use of stratified sampling, replacing or perhaps supplementing the regional one, would be to control for levels of economic development. Sampling procedures designed to include a number of developed, developing, and underdeveloped states could strengthen the bases for generalization. Furthermore, if the number of categories were kept small (say two or three), it might still be feasible to generalize from the subsample to all states in the category.[3]

Fewer Variables

For reducing the number of variables to a manageable proportion, other techniques are required. Of special relevance are various computerized procedures for reducing a great body of intercorrelated variables to a few common dimensions, dimensions for which marker variables or composite indices can be constructed to give a fairly reliable measure of each variable within sets of highly intercorrelated variables. For instance, it is well established that a great number of measures of economic development are highly intercorrelated, both across nations and across regions within nations. The intercorrelations are so high that, frequently, three-quarters or more of the variance in one variable can be predicted merely by knowing the other variable. For many (though certainly not all) purposes, these variables are highly interchangeable; by collecting data for one or two, where the data are relatively accessible or known to be of particularly high quality, the researcher can do without direct measures of the other. Or, if one is less interested in a particular variable—such as gross national product (GNP) per capita—than in some more general phenomenon (such as "economic development"), one may prefer to gather data on several, but hardly all, of the relevant components and construct from them, by systematic procedures, a composite index (perhaps GNP per capita plus literacy

[2] For the origin and suggested membership of these groupings, see Bruce M. Russett, *International Regions and the International System* (Chicago: Rand McNally, 1967); and W. Curtis Lamb and Bruce M. Russett, "International Politics in the Emerging Regions," *Peace Research Society (International) Papers*, 12 (1970).

[3] There are a variety of criteria or categories available for such stratified sampling. See, for instance, the five-level scheme in Bruce M. Russett, et al., *World Handbook of Political and Social Indicators* (New Haven: Yale University Press, 1964), pp. 293–303.

plus urbanization, possibly weighted according to some specified formula) that can serve as an overall measure. In doing so, one still avoids collecting data on a wide variety of indices, but, by using the composite, avoids allowing error or other idiosyncratic variation in a particular variable to influence the index unduly.

The utilities of such a procedure are applicable to both the specification of attributes of nations and to specification of aspects of relations between nations. Rudolph Rummel, for instance, has found that 236 variables on international variation in certain attributes can be rather completely described by only fifteen uncorrelated summary dimensions. Similarly, he has found that approximately the same number of dimensions will serve to reduce 94 variables on relations (positive or negative linkages of behavior).[4] Rummel has made some systematic comparisons of his results with those of other scholars. His dimensions could be used for data reduction or, if that is somewhat premature, either his basic approach or other kinds of pattern analysis could be applied at a later stage after some new data became available.

The problem of data availability is one which I have not faced in detail in this chapter. At this point, it would seem more useful to suggest what we think we may need than merely to say what we can do with what is already available. And though I am fairly familiar with what government agencies and other private scholars have in the way of data, I have not made a special or systematic evaluation of these resources. But it is possible, at the risk of some inaccuracies, to indicate, very roughly, a scale of relative availability of indicators. Hence, everything, either individually or by major categories, will be coded with one of the following numbers:

(1) Data are now available for each variable across most or all major political units. The data for a particular distribution will have been gathered into a single source, though by no means can all of the variables marked with this number be found in a single data bank.

(2) The data are available now for most major political units, but scattered, and would have to be processed or gathered together, perhaps at "substantial expense."

(3) Data are not now available, even scattered, for many countries, but are sufficiently derivative from available material to be feasible with a "reasonable" budget.

(4) Interesting data are now available for only a few (less than ten) countries and would require a "large" data-gathering investment ($1,000 or more per variable per country—sampling is almost unavoidable here).

---

[4] See especially his articles, "Some Dimensions in the Foreign Behavior of Nations," *Journal of Peace Research*, 3, 1966, pp. 201–24; "Some Attributes and Behavioral Patterns of Nations," *Journal of Peace Research*, 2, 1967, pp. 196–206; and "Indicators of Cross-National and International Patterns," *American Political Science Review*, 68, 1 (March 1969), pp. 127–47. See also D. V. McGranahan, et al., *Contents and Measurement of Socioeconomic Development* (Geneva: United Nations Research Institute for Social Development, 1970).

UNITED STATES LINKAGES WITH THE
WORLD ENVIRONMENT

Several different cuts, in addition to the substantive ones, need to be made in this data universe. First, we must distinguish between *stocks* and *flows*—what has accumulated and is available at any given moment in time, and transfers during a particular time period. The transfers may be measured either as a given amount (for example, dollar aid for economic development) or a proportionate change from a previous period. Some flows can be calculated merely by knowing the stock at two points in time. One-way flows, in cases where there is reciprocation, require direct measurement.

Second, we must distinguish between total linkages and dyadic or pairwise linkages. Thus, it is important to know the United States overall balance of payments, but for many purposes, we must also know whether it is in surplus or deficit with particular areas or nations. The latter represents a substantially greater demand on information-gathering facilities than does the former; in instances where I think that dyadic data may be significantly less available (and I mean here something more than just multiplying the recording costs of the total linkage by 140 nations to get all the dyadic links) I have so coded the listings (for example, 2D).

Finally, almost all of these indicators need to be matched with equivalent domestic indicators for comparison. It is important to know, not just the level of American foreign trade overall, or with a particular country, but the proportionate impact that trade makes on the entire GNP; not just the number of American residents abroad, but also their proportion of the total population. Sometimes it is hard to identify the appropriate domestic index to serve as a denominator, but it is, nevertheless, important to find one.

The role of the United States in the United Nations, and possibly the North Atlantic Treaty Organization (other international organizations are much less important in this respect), constitutes a special case of the dyadic relations. In addition to interactions with other states in the *arena* of the United Nations, it is necessary to consider its interactions with the United Nations itself. Thus, it would be necessary to record United States political initiatives in the United Nations, and the proportion of successful initiatives, by superissue (class 3).

Almost all of the above could be broken down into further subcategories, but this should indicate the range of information needed. Insofar as possible, the initial data collection should proceed by highly disaggregated categories. Small categories can later be collapsed into theoretically meaningful units with sufficient empirical content, but inclusive categories cannot be disaggregated, if theory requires, without going back to the original data. Furthermore, it is essential, when discussing America's linkages to the world, to control for the links that apply to various strata and geographic and cultural segments of American society. The United States is by no means a homogenous mass. If people in the eastern states become more closely linked with Europe and those in California with Asia at the same time that the American population is shifting westward, the effects will hardly be the same as a uniform increase would produce.

Table 3-1
Indicators of U.S.-International Linkages

A. Economy

A-I: Stock	*A-II: Flow*
Investment holdings: U.S.-owned firms abroad (1), and foreign firms in U.S. (1, 2D).† Raw material needs from abroad: demand minus annual domestic supply (2).	Trade (exports and imports) in goods (1). Receipts from and payments for shipping (1, 2D), investment (1, 2D), and tourism (1, 2D).

B. Political cooperation

B-I: Stock	*B-II: Flow*
Troops based abroad, plus dependents (2). Membership in intergovernmental organizations, probably subdivided by function, e.g., economic, technical, explicitly political (1). Embassy and other political personnel, e.g., AID: U.S. abroad (1), and foreign within U.S. (2). Attitudinal indicators (see *E* and *F*, next page) (4).	Visits by heads of state and foreign ministers (2) Aid for economic development (1), military uses (1), disaster relief (1), other uses (1). Treaties concluded, perhaps subdivided by functional purposes (3). Executive agreements, by function (2). "Distances" between U.S. voting position in the UN and the positions of other states, by major issue dimensions (3).

C. Political conflict

C-I: Stock	*C-II: Flow*
Weapons, by major categories (1). Military personnel (1) Military expenditures (1). Bases abroad, including undersea (1). Attitudinal indicators (see *E* and *F* below) (4).	Violent conflict: duration and troops involved (1). Number killed in violent conflict: military and civilian (1) Diplomatic protests (1). Expulsions of diplomatic personnel (1). Threats expressed by "top" government officials (1) Antiforeign demonstrations and riots (1). Military shows of force (1).

---

† Arabic numerals in parentheses at the end of entries refer to the availability of data, as described in the text. Data for which dyadic relationships may pose difficulties are designated with the letter **D**.

D. Communications

D-I: Stock	D-II: Flow
English language speakers abroad, and foreign language speakers in U.S. (2).	Migrants: total, and professional personnel (1).
English language teachers abroad, and foreign language teachers in U.S. (2).	Short-term travellers, including tourists (1).
Residents abroad, and foreigners living in U.S. (2).	Business travellers, including conferees (1 or 2).
Citizens who have been abroad (2), and foreigners who have been in U.S. (4), by age, occupation, length of stay.	First class mail (1).
Regular foreign broadcast listeners (4?).	Books and magazines, or fourth class mail (1).
News agencies: offices and correspondents (1).	Telegrams and radiograms (1).
Nongovernmental organizations of which U.S. organizations are members, by function (1), including international corporations (2).	Telephone calls (1).
	Radio broadcasts, e.g., by USIA (1).
	Television broadcasts and listeners (2).
	Motion picture films and viewers (2).
	Translation of books, etc. (1).
	Students: U.S. abroad, and foreign in U.S. (1).
	Faculty members: U.S. abroad, and foreign in U.S.—brain drain and gain (1).

E. Attitudinal, of mass

E-I: Stock	E-II: Flow
Popular images: U.S. images of various foreign people, and foreign images of Americans, controlled as to socioeconomic status (4).	Rates of change in E-I indicators.
Popular images: U.S. images of foreign governments, and foreign images of U.S., controlled (4).	
Popular "trust": U.S. trust of foreign governments in stress situations, and foreign trust of U.S., controlled (4).	
Popular attitudes on major issues, including, but not limited to, UN super-issues in international politics (4).*	

F. Attitudinal, of elite

F-I: Stock	F-II: Flow
Same variables as in E-I.	Rates of change in F-I indicators.

* See Hayward Alker and Bruce M. Russett, *World Politics in the General Assembly* (New Haven: Yale University Press, 1965), for definition of the major issues. The Cold War, colonialism or intervention in Africa, supranationalism, and Palestine would be the most important.

THE WORLD ENVIRONMENT

The world environment needs to be examined from four different perspectives, involving at least two distinct levels of analysis, the so-called system level and the national level. The system concern stresses the patterns of relationships between nations. Partly this is a matter of the structure of the system: whether it is bipolar or multipolar, with cohesive blocs or shifting, fluid alignments. These aspects are tapped mainly by examining the *linkages* among nations—who is tied to whom, how firmly, and by what links or bonds. Another aspect of the system focus concerns the *distribution* of goods and other attainments throughout the system: whether the distribution is egalitarian or unequal, and whether the distribution of one attainment, say, power, is similar to, or quite different from, that of another, say, wealth.[5]

To identify different levels of analysis does not always imply that entirely different data are needed. For the data on distributions must be compiled from information on the achievements and other *attributes* of particular *nations*, data which are important in their own right. And, finally, a concern with the nation-state level must be addressed to people's attitudes and value aspirations. We shall primarily discuss the nation-state needs first, emphasizing the system focus at the end. But even while considering the nation-level indicator, one needs to remember that it, too, should often be disaggregated to deal with the interaction of subgroups within nations. For instance, insofar as we go beyond aggregate measure of mass attitudes to data on particular elite decision makers or sets of decision makers, we penetrate beneath the nation-state level.

National Attribute Data on Politics and Its Social Environment

Information on a variety of characteristics of nations, and specifically national governments, is required. Many of these are *environmental* data, concerned with the level and characteristics of economic development in a country, its provision of health facilities, the kind and extent of communications facilities, the level of educational attainment reached by the populace, and the distribution of resources among various strata and subgroups within the nation.[6] Some physical data on pollution have become highly relevant, for example, comparative levels of pesticide concentration in human tissues (class 4). Sociocultural data on the characteristics and diversity of the populace also form a part of this.

---

[5] Special emphasis on this can be seen in Johan Galtung, "A Structural Theory of Aggression," *Journal of Peace Research*, 2, 1964, pp. 95–119.

[6] For an example of work on the quality of life, see Michael Haas, "Toward the Study of Biopolitics: A Cross-National Analysis of Mortality Rates," *Behavioral Science*, 14, 4 (July 1969), pp. 257–80.

In addition, a variety of *political* variables are critical. Some of these involve judgments about the gross characteristics of national political systems (for example, authoritarian, competitive, and the like; but more, and more useful, are specific data on political events (the frequency and intensity of different manifestations of overt conflict and, equally important, the use of orderly processes of decision, conflict resolution, and change (for example, elections, orderly governmental succession); the concentration or diffusion of power in the system and its manifestations in various party and unofficial structures; and governmental output—the purposes and extent of governmental activity in the system. Table 3-2 lists the variables which have been collected, on a comparable basis, by Charles L. Taylor and Michael C. Hudson of the Yale World Data Analysis Program for the second edition of *World Handbook of Political and Social Indicators.* Indicators for circa 1965, and usually for earlier post-World War II years, can be classed as class 1. Data must be available, however, for points, and as change rates, covering the future, and also some base line data from historical periods earlier in the twentieth century, perhaps even before that. Where appropriate, they must also be aggregated for the various world regions.

Table 3-2
List of Variables from World Handbook of Political and Social Indicators

---

Political structure and performance

Year of consolidation of modernizing leadership
Year of current constitution
Year of independence
Education expenditure (total, dollars per capita, and as percentage of GNP)
Defense expenditure (total, dollars per capita, and as percentage of GNP)
Internal security forces (total, per thousand square kilometers, and per thousand working-age inhabitants)
Military manpower (total, per thousand square kilometers, and per thousand working-age inhabitants)
Party fractionalization, based on seats and on popular votes
Press freedom index
Voter turnout as percentage of population over 19, and as percentage of electorate

---

Civil order and government stability

Major regular governmental power transfers
Governmental power adjustments
Major renewals of governmental power
Major irregular governmental power transfers
Riots
Demonstrations
Armed attacks
Deaths from domestic violence
Governmental sanctions
Foreign interventions

(Continued)

Table 3-2

List of Variables from World Handbook of Political and Social Indicators (*Continued*)

Political environment

Percentage of population in cities over 100,000
Concentration of population
School enrollment ratios
Students in higher education per million inhabitants
Changes in literacy
Literacy
Educational stock
Foreign and domestic letter mail per capita
Telephones per thousand population
Radio and television receivers per thousand inhabitants
Newspaper circulation per thousand inhabitants
Crude birth and death rates
Infant mortality rates
Protein and calories per capita per diem
Physicians per million population
Income distribution
Land distribution
Ethnic and linguistic fractionalization
Christian communities as percentage of population
Islamic community as percentage of population

Size and economic development

Population and population growth rate
Area and population density
Agricultural area and density
GNP and growth rates
GNP per capita and growth rates
Scientific manpower and journals
Energy consumption (total, per capita, and growth rates)
Distribution of male labor force—percentage in mining and manufacturing
Distribution of male labor force—percentage in agriculture
Percentage of economically active male population engaged in professional and technical
  occupations
Agricultural and industrial shares of GDP
Gross fixed domestic capital formation as a percentage of GNP

External relations

Air fares (in dollars) to New York and Moscow
Memberships in international organizations
Diplomats sent abroad and received
Number of diplomatic missions received from U.S. and USSR
Concentration of export commodities
Concentration of export-receiving countries
Foreign trade as percentage of GNP
Foreign mail as percentage of total mail

Source: Charles L. Taylor and Michael C. Hudson, *World Handbook of Political and Social Indicators*, 2nd edition (New Haven: Yale University Press, 1972).

The Worldwide Distributions of Value Achievement

The environmental variables suggested above, and listed in more detail in Table 3-2, also need to be processed in such a way that their worldwide distribution becomes apparent. Where appropriate, the national totals must be combined for various regional aggregates, but more is involved. We need gross indices of whether the distribution has become more or less equal. In addition to the mean and the worldwide total for a given variable, like income, the standard deviation and other indices of equality, such as the Gini index, are required. These can then be compared across variables and over time to see if particularly unstable conditions are emerging. It would be impractical and wasteful to try to map global distributions for all the variables listed in Table 3-2, but certain representative items should be measured. The Lasswell and Kaplan value inventory provides a useful set of categories for indicating the possible scope:[7]

Wealth	GNP per capita, energy consumption per capita
Enlightenment	Literacy, radios, and newspapers
Well-being	Physicians, infant mortality rates
Skill	Students in higher education, and professional and technical personnel
Power	Military forces, military expenditures, GNP, population
Respect	
Rectitude	
Affection	

The last three (and power) are what Lasswell and Kaplan call "deference" values. In international politics, they are not gauged by simple aggregate indices as are the first five, for they concern attitudes rather than attributes. Nor can they be tapped by direct measures of the units concerned, because what matters is the degree of respect, and the like, accorded to a unit by others. Some combination of survey research and content analysis is required. Survey research could tap mass attitudes in at least the major non-Communist nations, and content analysis of speeches by heads of state, United Nations delegates, or elite newspapers would indicate official or influential attitudes. A variety of theories suggest that when an individual or nation ranks high on achievement of certain "objective" values, but remains fairly low on deference values like affection or respect, the situation is very unstable, and the individual or nation may resort to violence in order to redress the imbalance. A relatively

---

[7] Harold Lasswell and Abraham Kaplan, *Power and Society* (New Haven: Yale University Press, 1950).

equal distribution of power in the world, but an unequal distribution of respect, might point to such a potential disruption. Note, moreover, that the utility of such measures is *not* limited to this section on distributions. The data for basic national units would also be highly valuable in connection with the information on attribute data and, for that matter, the material on international linkages below. I did not include it elsewhere, however, and mention it only briefly here, because the costs of obtaining the information appear prohibitive. It clearly falls into class 4, and material regarding quite a large number of pairs of nations would be required. Possibly, a pilot effort could be addressed to American deference toward other nations and vice versa.

For intranational politics, some measure of governments' command of deference values vis-à-vis their own populations could be gleaned from more accessible domestic event data: for example, the frequency of antigovernment demonstrations, or the need of the government to resort to repressive acts of arrest or censorship.

Value Aspirations

We need to know, not just what people or nations have, but what they want. All peoples do not share the same goals, nor are goals uniform within any given nation. They can be identified only through extensive survey research or content analysis. Although some preliminary efforts have been made, they are, so far, very incomplete and unreliable; further research on a scale big enough to be valuable would clearly fall into class 4.[8] For some purposes, it would be enough to monitor the major regions of the world, inasmuch as a detailed nation-by-nation focus is clearly impossible. Some further inferences about the salience of those values important in international politics can be obtained rather cheaply (class 3) from data on delegations' activities in the United Nations. As suggested earlier, it is fairly easy to infer preferences from voting positions on the major issue-dimensions in the General Assembly; to these can be added measures of the relative salience of issues to particular governments. Salience measures can be derived from data on frequency of speech-making, introduction or amendment of resolutions, and regularity of voting at all by the delegations. One finds, for instance, that certain Afro-Asian nations find colonialism issues much more salient to their interests than are cold war issues, but that quite the opposite prevails for other nations—nations whose voting positions on the East-West spectrum are indistinguishable from the first.

A running computer content analysis of United Nations debates would prob-

---

[8] For a content analysis of children's readers in 41 countries, see David McClelland, *The Achieving Society* (Princeton, N.J.: D. Van Nostrand, 1960), and for a survey research project addressed to only four nations, see *International Studies in Values in Politics*, recently undertaken by Philip E. Jacob and his associates at the University of Pennsylvania and in Poland, India, and Yugoslavia.

ably be the most productive strategy for dealing with this set of variables. It would be relatively expensive, but would provide data, on a wide spectrum of values, for the governments of all nations. This need not, and should not, be limited to the United Nations issue dimensions. To the degree that one is interested in divergences between government and opposition or popular attitudes, of course, this approach would be of limited use. Data on, for example, the ethnic, educational, and career characteristics of decision makers, especially as they diverge from those of the general population, could assist inferences here.

Linkages of a World Society

Data are necessary for at least three distinct types of measures.

1. *Level.* First, we need data on the overall world level of such linkages. For this, *all* of the items in the United States linkages section of this chapter are appropriate, and reasonably complete and reliable data could probably be gathered.

2. Data on the spread of global communications, for instance, are critical to an assessment of the pervasiveness of a world society. This involves a combination of the earlier identified communications linkage indicators with the appropriate attribute information, such as data on the number of literates and city dwellers. In addition, data on the level of particular countries' total involvement are necessary. This is obviously more difficult than the preceding item, but, again, it could be done for many variables and countries.

3. Knowing the level for each country, we then need data on countries' patterns of linkages. Many, or even all, of the linkages of the United States with particular countries, as discussed above, would be fully appropriate for the linkages of *all* nations with one another, providing a complete mapping of the network. Obviously, all such data are not available, and cannot be made available within the scope of any imaginable project. As a bare minimum, the following would provide a rough indication of the spectrum of worldwide linkages:

   International organization memberships (1)

   Trade in goods (1)

   United Nations superissue distances (3)

   Conflict data (especially, but not exclusively, overt violent conflict) (2)[9]

---

[9] Conflict and cooperative data have been gathered by Rudolph Rummel, and Charles A. McClelland in McClelland's World Event Interaction Survey at the University of Southern California. They are now available from the Inter-university Consortum for Political Research, Ann Arbor, Michigan, 48106.

Additional network data on treaties (2) and on the exchange of diplomatic personnel (2) would form important, if somewhat less pressing, needs.

We require information on whether a nation's linkages are few or many, and then on whether they are concentrated or diffuse. A simple fourfold classification is appropriate.

1. Some nations may have many ties, ones that are highly diffuse. We may call these the cosmopolitan countries, and typical examples would be the United Kingdom—with many links to Europe and also to Commonwealth countries in Asia and Africa—and the United States—with many ties to Europe and Latin America, and a fair number also to Asia and Africa. Other countries with this kind of pattern and a substantial, if somewhat lower, total number of linkages are Japan, Australia, Israel, and Egypt. These diffused linkages build a pattern of interdependencies and cross-pressures between regional groupings and help to mitigate the divisive effects of

2. "Communal" countries, which have a relatively high number, but heavily concentrated pattern, of linkages. Such linkages may contribute importantly to international bonds and the growth of regional groupings, but without the first type of country, too, they weaken the global fabric. Typical of these states are those of Eastern Europe and of Latin America.

3. There are also many countries which we may, perhaps, label insular. These are countries whose ties are diffused, but, in any case, not numerous. Many of the new African countries fit this description.

4. Finally there are the isolates, with very few ties, and those heavily concentrated. East Germany and Communist China are the most extreme cases. They belong only to groupings of Communist countries, not to broader regional or global groupings, and are not even tied into all the Communist groups.

Most countries, of course, fall somewhere near the middle of one or both dimensions, and are not pure types; nevertheless, their role in the international system does depend heavily on just what the mixture is. We must, then, be especially concerned with overlapping bonds of various sorts among nations. The United States, for instance, might be rated as a cosmopolitan country, except that its otherwise diffuse linkages almost totally ignore China and, to some degree, Eastern Europe.

Inferences about the polar structure of the international system require a combination of information that includes both a global overview of the pattern of bonds, as described above, and information on national power bases. The pattern data come from the attribute material, and tell us how many "regional" groups (not necessarily in the sense of fully contiguous geographic regions) there are in the world, their cohesion (number of bonds within each group), and their degree of separateness from other groups. The power base data indicate the strength of the group for global action, and are necessary because the mere existence of a regional grouping does not make it a "pole" of significance in the international system. Relevant power base indicators—all but one are class 1—include:

> Population
> GNP
> Energy production
> Central government expenditures and revenues (2)
> Military expenditures
> Military personnel

The problem of producing precise measures of national power has not been solved either analytically or empirically. The above are not all of equal importance, and some may be redundant, but they should include most of the important elements.

One other critical aspect of the study of global linkages in the worldwide political environment concerns the speed and cost of transportation, including the transportation of messages (communication), men, goods, and destructive capabilities. What is the extent to which one nation can affect another at a distance? It seems unlikely that the decline in power is linearly related to distance. But precisely what is the function, and how is it affected by topography, by technological change, and by the state of a given nation's resources at any particular time? It has been contended, for example, that because of the accessibility of ocean transport, and the primitive state of transportation in North Vietnam, the United States can transport men and equipment to the war zone in Southeast Asia more cheaply than can China.[10] Such factors are critical to modifying the power base data for adequate descriptions of influence, but very hard to obtain (class 4). A distinction between global powers (superpowers) and regional powers who are, nevertheless, able to exercise great control over a substantial local population may be worthwhile. How rapidly is conflict becoming more global, and what is the differential between the rate at which major powers have improved their ability to strike at small powers anywhere, and that at which small powers have strengthened their capacities to hit each other over distance?

Finally, some attention must also be given to nongovernmental links, especially to those bonds which cannot be identified with particular nations. One

---

[10] See Albert Wohlstetter, "Theory and Opposed Systems Design," *Journal of Conflict Resolution*, 12, 3 (September 1968), pp. 302–31.

obvious example is that of nongovernmental organizations (class 1), including cross-national associational bonds among labor unions, business and trade organizations, religious groups, student groups, and the like. International commercial corporations form a related category (class 3?).

In conclusion, I am impressed both by the magnitude of the data effort implied by this outline, and by the amount of data already extant in various holdings around the country. Perhaps we need, more than new data-gathering efforts, a serious attempt to bring together, clean, make comparable, and distribute to active researchers the information that already exists, or that can be manufactured rather easily. I certainly doubt that our discipline is, or soon will be, sufficiently collectivized to supervise the central gathering of massive new data resources. Nor is the climate of the government or foundations especially auspicious for great new ventures of such magnitude. But if we had a good inventory and distribution service for what now exists, individual scholars could fill in gaps more efficiently, using and encouraging others to use testable models of international phenomena. A central service could then select some particular variables, for their substantive or theoretical interest and, in the absence of other scholars' activity, for special collection.

4

Global Patterns of Diplomatic Exchange, 1963–1964

IN COLLABORATION WITH W. Curtis Lamb

DIPLOMATIC LINKAGES

As the bipolarity of power in the international system has diffused in the direction of greater multipolarity, and as many prominent theorists of international politics have come to advocate reinforcing such a trend toward a multipolar "balance of power," theoretical and substantive interest in the linkages among nations has also grown. In abstract models with two or a few actors, the system may be characterized largely in terms of the relative power bases of the actors: whether, for example, if there are three states, they are all of more or less equal strength, or whether one or two are very much larger than the other(s). Even in a many-state system this simple perspective might be sufficient, provided there was a large enough size differential between, say, two major contending elephants and the mice who comprised all the remaining fauna. Such a perspective has sometimes been applied, though not altogether accurately even then, to the international system of the first postwar decade.

But in most of the real international systems of any interest to us, information on the size or power bases of the component nations must be supplemented by information on the distribution of bonds among those states. Thus we are concerned with patterns of interaction, transaction, and institutionalization, with alliance formation and cohesion, with the clusters of states that

Reprinted from *Journal of Peace Research*, 1, 1969. Written in collaboration with W. Curtis Lamb.

may form, scatter, and re-form to build and weaken major coalitions. A pole is not a single state, but a group of nations joined by linkages of varying types and strengths; and the ability of a pole to generate allegiances can be weakened as easily by inadequate or misguided attention to its bonds as by military failures or an eroding power base. As one theorist has put it, perhaps over-stating, "Of all the factors that make for the power of a nation, the most important, however unstable, is the quality of diplomacy."[1]

Clusters of nations may be delineated according to a wide variety of criteria and operational indicators. In a recent volume, one of the present authors examined the relationships among a number of such variables generally con-sidered relevant to delineating groups of nations. The exercise showed cluster-ings of nations as determined separately by such criteria as cultural similarity, behavior in international politics, commercial exchange, common membership in international organizations, and geographic proximity. It also explored somewhat the interactions among these different influences, including changes over time, the degree to which the knowledge of nations' clustering by one criterion could be used to predict their grouping by another, and the relation-ship of the clusterings to patterns of violent conflict.[2] The relation of this approach to the delineation of "subsystems" was discussed and attention was given to the common use of terms like system or subsystem to identify groups of interacting units. It was noted that in the rigorous usage found in general systems theory, a variety of empirical tests, each looking for different types of interactions, would have to agree before a cluster of states or other units could properly be identified as a system.[3] This is similar to the conception, in the theoretical literature on regionalism, that one may find "all-purpose" regions where the tests of proximity, interaction, homogeneity, etc., all con-verge on the same basic set of units.

Such convergence is in fact rarely observed in international reality, but the effort to establish groupings by different criteria, and to look for areas of agree-ment between criteria, has been of some use. It is in effect a mapping or taxo-nomic exercise in the spirit of Linnaeus, searching for groups which may for many purposes be described as *actors* in international politics. These groups of nations constitute actors between the level of the nation-state and that of the entire global system.

Some see this elaboration of middle range regional actors as a hopeful sign that the keen edge of national power politics may be dulled in regional inter-

[1] Hans J. Morgenthau: *Politics among Nations* (New York: Alfred A. Knopf, 1965), 4th edition, p. 139.

[2] Bruce M. Russett: *International Regions and the International System* (Chicago: Rand McNally, 1967).

[3] O. R. Young: "The Impact of General Systems Theory on Political Science," *General Systems: Yearbook of the Society for General Systems Research*, 9 (1964), p. 239. Another of Young's articles is also relevant, though it does not use rigorous system identification pro-cedures. See his "Political Discontinuities in the International System," *World Politics*, 20, 3 (1968), pp. 369–92.

actions.[4] Others, more conscious of the false hopes that can be pinned on even the most ad hoc of regional alliances, have urged prudence.[5] When one's purposes are carefully specified, it may indeed be useful to speak of NATO, or the Afro-Asian group, or even the now-fissioning "Communist bloc" as an actor. And to the degree that different criteria do agree on the identification of a particular set of states as a group or cluster, confidence in the importance and general utility of the "actor" perspective on such a group is increased.

The regional actor perspective is relevant to international relations in two senses: the regional actor as participant in global politics, mentioned above; and the region as a relatively autonomous political subsystem. While this latter focus is of less relevance to the monumental issues of nuclear war, large-scale ideological confrontation, and grand alliances, it is now being recognized that there are a number of international events (particularly in the developing world) best understood by analysis at the regional level: e.g., border wars, small-scale interventionism, local competitions for prestige and regional markets. Regarding regional actors in global politics, the kind of material presented here confronts issues that generations of thinkers have considered. In the much younger study of regions as international subsystems, this kind of analysis might well provide foundation parameters. Each of the underdeveloped regions of Southern Asia, the Middle East, Southeast Asia, and Africa has now received attention from a capable analyst of regional politics.[6] The theoretical implications of this regional systems analysis have not yet been set out in detail, however, nor has much data been brought to bear on the issues which have emerged. The kind of international events best analyzed from this perspective depends on the number and type of different attributes and interactions that cluster around any given regional group.

Whether or not one finds the prescriptive formulations about regional actors mentioned above attractive, an empirical base for analysis is essential: hence the search not only for such easily specified groups of nations as those belonging to particular military alliances or caucusing groups, but for the inductive identification of other groups by general criteria.

In this chapter we add, to the sets of groupings already identified in *International Regions and the International System*, the groups of states that emerge from patterns of international diplomatic exchange. We draw upon the data compiled by Steven J. Brams and generously made available by him, data on

---

[4] Haas's early statement is in this vein. Cf. Ernst Haas: "Regionalism, Functionalism and Universal International Organization," *World Politics*, 8 (1956) pp. 238–63.

[5] See Edgar Furniss, Jr.: "A Re-examination of Regional Arrangements," *Journal of International Affairs*, 9, (1955) pp. 78–89.

[6] E.g., Leonard Binder: "The Middle East as a Subordinate International System," *World Politics* (April, 1958), pp. 408–29; Robert W. MacDonald: *The League of Arab States* (Princeton: Princeton University Press, 1965); Michael Brecher: "International Relations and Area Studies, The Subordinate State System of Southern Asia," *World Politics*, XV, 2 (January, 1963), pp. 213–35; Bernard Gordon: *The Dimensions of Conflict is Southeast Asia* (Englewood Cliffs: Prentice-Hall, 1966); I. William Zartman: *International Relations in the New Africa* (Englewood Cliffs: Prentice-Hall, 1966).

the number of career level diplomatic personnel sent from each of 104 nations of the world to every other nation in 1963–1964.[7] This enables us to construct a large table, or matrix of the exchanges. Each cell contains the total number of diplomats exchanged between the pair of states—the number accredited from A to B plus those from B to A, in each case as reported by the host country.[8] This exercise provides both a mapping of world diplomatic contacts, and an opportunity to test the relative strength of two competing but not entirely exclusive hypotheses:

a. Nations will be diplomatically salient to each other—that is, they will maintain high levels of personnel exchange—to the degree they share other measurable bonds of common interest. Diplomatic contacts would thus be heaviest within regional subsystems. To test this hypothesis we shall compare the result from this mapping with those obtained for group-ings defined by cultural similarity, commercial transactions, etc., in *International Regions*.

b. Nations will be diplomatically salient to each other to the degree they interact in international *politics* generally, regardless of other bonds of similarity or transaction. By this hypothesis we would expect a nation to maintain a large diplomatic staff in major neutrals or potential enemy states as well as in allied or friendly states, since it is sufficiently affected by the former's actions to require substantial information-gathering facilities in their capitals. Thus though the U.S. has far fewer cultural similarities to the USSR than to many other states, and conducts little trade with the USSR, we would nonetheless expect a high level of diplo-matic exchange between them.[9] But for minor powers, when looking with a global perspective one could hardly differentiate the data sup-porting this hypothesis from that which would be consistent with the previous one. Small states would be likely to concentrate their attention

---

[7] Steven J. Brams, "Transaction Flows in the International System," *American Political Science Review*, 60, 4 (1966), pp. 880–99, and *Flow and Form in the International System* (Ph.D. Dissertation, Northwestern University, 1965).

[8] Brams was forced to delete several countries from his analysis because of nonresponse to his request for information by several receiving countries. In two cases it was possible for us here to incorporate countries (Argentina and mainland China) on the assumption that the number of diplomats sent *by* each of those countries was the same as the number sent *to* them by every other state. Since Argentina and mainland China do not maintain diplomatic relations, leaving that cell blank with no diplomats was appropriate. We could not, however, add any other countries with missing data on this basis because to do so would have meant adding misleading zeroes. The assumption that the number sent equals the number received was checked with several states where full data were available, and found not to be seriously misleading.

[9] See Edward Gulick: "A balance-of-power system depends for operability on the watch-fulness of foreign offices over the various important states. This fact has been recognized from the very beginning of equilibrist strategy in the Renaissance. The major importance which has attached to the Ambassador as a diplomatic watchdog is evidence of it." *Europe's Classical Balance of Power* (New York: Norton, 1967) p. 16.

on one or two major powers within or adjacent to their region, and otherwise on other minor powers within the regional subsystem, powers with whom they would also have ties of transaction and relative similarity. A minor power is not likely to interact much with those other minor powers, or even most major ones, who are outside of this subsystem.

Since the fifteenth century, formal diplomatic theory has maintained that a combination of these two hypotheses should characterize diplomatic practice. Earlier, medieval diplomacy, operating under at least the assumption of a European Christian commonwealth, did not require the constant presence of diplomats at any given point within that community. "It [diplomatic representation] was a form of formal, privileged communication among the members of a hierarchically ordered society, and its exercise could be admitted or denied according to the relations of the parties concerned and the nature of the business at hand."[10] The medieval practice of placing the burden of a visiting legation's expenses on the receiving country underlined the belief that diplomats were expected to be of positive value to all the parties to a dispute. Similarly, the lack at that time of diplomatic immunities is explained by the belief that representatives should act according to the higher canon and civil law shared by all.

But if the medieval conception was summed up by Bernard du Rossier's admonition "The business of an Ambassador is peace," the modern view was stated as early as the late fifteenth century by Ermolao Barbaro: "The first duty of an Ambassador is exactly the same as that of any other servant of government, that is, to do, say, advise, and think whatever may best serve the preservation and aggrandizement of his own state."[11] With this new mandate the provision of complete and incisive information on foreign events became the main task of the diplomat. This new attitude toward the duties of the diplomat has pervaded normative writing on this topic down to the present day.[12] The pattern of diplomatic representation, it is held, should not merely reflect the state of a nation's favors, for diplomacy is a professional task that requires reconnoitering the enemies of the fatherland and committing the uncommitted as well as the flattering of faithful allies.

On closer examination, this textbook diplomacy breaks down. The most obvious instance is when the level of hostilities is felt to demand the breaking off of diplomatic relations entirely; the contemporary case of Israel and its Arab neighbors is an example. The Cold War has encouraged a new politicization of diplomacy also; the defeat, by no means certain at the time, of those who advocated full U.S. diplomatic representation in the new Communist China is an example. Finally, there are many new states whose explorations of

---

[10] Garrett Mattingly: *Renaissance Diplomacy* (Boston: Houghton Mifflin, 1955) p. 23.

[11] Ibid., pp. 42, 95.

[12] For a contemporary statement see Robert Rossow: "The Professionalization of the New Diplomacy," *World Politics*, 14, 4 (July, 1962) pp. 561–75.

national sovereignty are yet brief and tentative. In the third world, all international relations often take the form of "privileged communication" among a few members of an elite and "ambassadorial relations are frequently regarded as a sign of prestige and friendship than as an institution serving [any other] positive function."[13] Clearly an *inductive* analysis of patterns of diplomatic exchange is called for as a first step in understanding the role diplomatic representation plays in present-day international politics. To anticipate, we shall find evidence to support *both* hypotheses.

ASSUMPTIONS AND PROCEDURES

Three assumptions behind the mapping procedures employed in *International Regions and the International System* must be started again; the implications of those assumptions here are the same as in that book. The procedures adopted to meet them are discussed briefly here in the text, and at more length, with alternatives, in the methodological Appendix.

1. A means of *data reduction* is necessary. We can begin with a complete matrix of numbers of diplomats exchanged, but such a matrix is, in its raw form, exceedingly difficult to comprehend. Here it involves interactions among 106 political units, or more than 11,000 cells. Any attempt to find the major patterns directly from such a large matrix would inevitably be imprecise; the importance of some linkages would be exaggerated, others ignored. Thus some procedure, preferably one taking advantage of the data processing capacity of modern computers, must be employed.

   The basic technique chosen for data reduction was the principal components method of factor analysis, specifically *direct* factor analysis, a variant that operates directly on the data matrix rather than on a matrix of correlations of the original variables. The result is that the factors identify groups of countries that engage in a high level of diplomatic interaction among themselves. (This would not necessarily be true of the more common factor-analysis procedures where the variables, or countries, are first *correlated* with each other and the correlation matrix is factored.) The procedure is discussed in detail in *International Regions*, and will be presented only in outline here.[14]

2. The *relative impact* of diplomatic exchange is at the heart of our interests. We are concerned with the level of these bonds between two nations as compared with those between any other two nations. It is assumed

---

[13] Zartman: *International Relations in the New Africa*, p. 70.
[14] See Russett: *International Regions*, pp. 14–16, and 99–102 for details on the methodological considerations.

(except for the nonrecognition problem) that for a given nation (A) the size of the diplomatic staff accredited to and from each other nation is positively related to the impact each other state's actions have on the foreign policy making apparatus of A. Diplomatic staff is a measure of political attention, and thus correlated with domestic impact. This assumption allows for indirect as well as direct effects. We may assume, for instance, that Laos's *direct* impact on the U.S. is far less than its *indirect* effect through its actions toward the U.S. ally of South Vietnam. But this indirection requires the U.S. to maintain a large mission in the Laotian capital.

The matrix analyzed is one of diplomatic "proximity" coefficients, the mutal choice of partners for diplomatic exchange, with the entry in each cell varying with the number of persons sent and received.

3. The political effects of diplomatic exchange are subject to *decreasing marginal returns*. That is, the difference in effect between adding one more diplomat to an existing two-man delegation is far greater than from adding a single man to an existing 50-man delegation. Thus the measure of interdependence chosen must be more sensitive to increments at a very low level of exchange than to the same absolute increments at a high level. This is similar to a central assumption in much of economic theory, of the diminishing marginal utility of goods. It also corresponds to an assumption underlying one of the major alternative measures of interdependence, the Savage-Deutsch index of relative acceptance.[15]

To make the marginal impact of a change from a low level greater than that of the same absolute change from a high one, all the entries were subjected to a square root transformation. Then all input values were standardized to a range from 0 to 1.0, with 1.0 set equivalent to the square root of the highest level of exchange in the matrix. Values for the diagonal (a nation's attention to itself) were also arbitrarily set to 1.0. The result is a distribution which, except for the excessive number of zeroes (no exchange) at the low end, is roughly normal.

DIPLOMATIC EXCHANGE GROUPINGS IN 1963–1964

Table 4-1 shows all the major groupings, as identified by countries' loadings on the nine factors. All loadings of .30 or higher are given, and nations with two or more such loadings are identified by asterisks. Ten groups finally are identified, there being no reason for the number of groups to correspond exactly to the number of factors. Occasionally, as is here the case with factor eight, there will be one cluster of variables loading positively and another quite

---

[15] The role of this assumption is pointed out by Brams: "Transaction Flows," p. 884.

Table 4-1

Diplomatic Exchange Groupings, with Tentative Descriptive Labels

Factor 1†		Factor 2		Factor 3	
Eastern Europe	Loadings	Latin America	Loadings	Southeast Asia	Loadings
*USSR	.76	Peru	.58	Thailand	.72
Romania	.69	Mexico	.57	South Vietnam	66
Czechoslovakia	.68	Chile	.56	Philippines	.61
Bulgaria	.65	Panama	.55	South Korea	.54
Poland	.65	Colombia	.54	Taiwan	.54
Hungary	.63	El Salvador	.54	*Australia	.50
East Germany	.61	Ecuador	.50	*Japan	.50
Yugoslavia	.58	*Brazil	.48	*Burma	.46
*China	.55	*Spain	.48	*Indonesia	.42
*Cuba	.50	Uruguay	.48	Laos	.42
Austria	.39	Guatemala	.47	Malaysia	.36
*Egypt	.39	Nicaragua	.47	*U.S.	.35
*France	.37	*U.S.	.47	Cambodia	.34
*Greece	.37	*Argentina	.46		
*Turkey	.37	Venezuela	.43		
Albania	.36	Costa Rica	.42		
*Israel	.36	Paraguay	.39		
*Indonesia	.35	Honduras	.38		
*Algeria	.34	*Italy	.38		
*Finland	.34				
*Italy	.34				

Factor 4		Factor 5		Factor 6	
Middle East	Loadings	Large powers	Loadings	West Africa	Loadings
Iran	.61	*U.S.	1.45	Liberia	.54
Iraq	.60	*U.K.	1.02	Senegal	.51
Saudi Arabia	.56	*France	.82	Nigeria	.49
Jordan	.55	*West Germany	.72	*Ghana	.46
*Turkey	.54	*USSR	.48	Mali	.43
Syria	.50	*Italy	.47	Guinea	.42
*Morocco	.47	*Egypt	.42	Congo (Kinshasa)	.38
Lebanon	.46	*Japan	.40	Cameroun	.36
*Pakistan	.43	*Belgium	.35	Sierra Leone	.36
*Algeria	.38	*India	.30	Ethiopia	.30
*India	.37				
Libya	.36				
*West Germany	.36				
Afghanistan	.34				
Kuwait	.33				
*Sudan	.31				
*Spain	.30				

Factor 7		Factor 8		Factor 9	
Commonwealth and Outer Seven	Loadings	Positive and negative clusters	Loadings	Asia	Loadings
Canada	.67	China and friends		*India	.53
South Africa	.55	*China	.64	*Burma	.41
Netherlands	.48	*Algeria	.45	*China	.39
*Belgium	.46	*Cuba	.39	*USSR	.39
Portugal	.46	*Morocco	.36	Ceylon	.38
Sweden	.43			*Pakistan	.37
*U.K.	.43	Eastern Mediterranean		*Sudan	.36
Denmark	.40	*Greece	−.44	*Egypt	.34
Norway	.40	*Turkey	−.40	*U.K.	.34
*Australia	.36	Cyprus	−.38	*Australia	.33
Switzerland	.34	*Israel	−.37	*Ghana	.33
*Brazil	.33				
*Argentina	.32				
*Spain	.32				
*Finland	.31				
Ireland	.30				
New Zealand	.30				

Not in any group	Omitted from analysis (No data)
Central African Republic	Bolivia
Chad	Burundi
Congo (Brazaville)	Dahomey
Gabon	Dominican Republic
Haiti	Ivory Coast
Iceland	North Korea
Jamaica	Mongolia
Kenya	Niger
Luxembourg	Rwanda
Malagasy	Tunisia
Malta	Upper Volta
Mauritania	North Vietnam
Nepal	Yemen
Tanzania	
Togo	
Trinidad	
Uganda	

†Only nations with loadings of .30 or more are shown.   *Nations with loadings on two or more factors.

negatively on the factor, and they must be treated separately.[16] Each grouping is identified by a tentative descriptive label. Those countries at the top of each grouping are centrally associated with it, the others more peripherally.

Of the 10 groupings, all but two are clearly identifiable with familiar geopolitical clusters, loosely corresponding to regions. The first we have labelled "Eastern Europe" to fit the top eight countries on the list. It might well have been identified as "Communist states" since China and Cuba take up the ninth and tenth positions, but the European term is appropriate because of the relatively low standing of China and Cuba. With Albania somewhat further down the list, this factor includes all the Communist states for which we had data. Several other European and Afro-Asian nations that maintain good relations with Eastern Europe are also found here. Israel's presence is something of a surprise considering the more recent deterioration of Israeli relations with the Communist world.

A second major group is clearly identifiable with Latin America, and incorporates all the Latin American republics for which we had data, except Cuba and Haiti. As has been discovered in other analyses, Haiti's behavior is often quite distinct from that of her Spanish- and Portuguese-speaking neighbors; most of Cuba's neighbors have broken diplomatic relations with the Castro government. The presence of Italy, Spain, and the U.S. is also worth remarking upon, as is the absence of Canada and the former British colonies of the Western Hemisphere, Jamaica and Trinidad. We see here a strong geographic component, tempered both in inclusions and exclusions by cultural ties.

There are several distinct factors associated with Asian states. Factor three, the largest, includes all the Southeast Asian nations allied with the U.S., plus neighboring Australia and, toward the lower end of the list, several other Southeast Asian countries. Factor nine as well is made up largely of Asian nations, but without the pro-Western cast associated with the first group. It includes India, China, the USSR, and even Egypt. This division, corresponding in part to global political orientations, is significant. There is also a predominantly Asian factor four, labelled "Middle East," which incorporates all the Arab, several non-Arab but Moslem nations (Iran, Turkey, Pakistan, Afghanistan), plus a few non-Moslem countries which maintain special ties with the area. West Germany's moderate involvement is notable.

Three other regionally based groupings are evident. One includes many,

---

[16] A few of the loadings exceed unity, instead of varying merely between 0 and 1.0 as is most common. In direct factor analysis one is often working with a matrix that is not strictly gramian (i.e., the sum of positive eigenvalues may exceed the number of variables instead of being equal to it), in which case there may be loadings above unity. Except perhaps for its unfamiliarity this need not disturb the reader. Purists may object that such a matrix does not meet all the necessary requirements for factor analysis, but direct factor analysis can properly by applied to any matrix. The analyst who does so, however, must be careful to point out that he is not dimensionalizing the data matrix in any definitive way, but merely using the method as a crude data reduction technique. This fits our purposes, particularly as we are not saying that the world can be divided into exactly nine groupings (or any other number) as identified on any particular number of factors.

though not all, of the West African states. Some of the former French territories in that area do not show substantial diplomatic ties with their neighbors,
nor is the level of exchange with and among the former British East African
colonies sufficient for them either to fall in with the West Africans or to form
their own group. A group of economically developed middle level powers,
based firmly on the European-settled states of the British Commonwealth and
on Northern Europe, emerges on factor seven. This is more a culturally and
politically based group than a geographically based one, though the Northern
European element is strong. Many of these European countries, however,
have long had special trade ties with Britain, through the present "Outer
Seven," the former Sterling Area, or special preferential agreements. These
special economic relationships apply even to Portugal and Argentina, which
may otherwise seem a bit incongruous. Brazil and Spain are less easily explained, but their association with the group is quite marginal. Finally there is
a small group, on the negative pole of factor eight, called "Eastern Mediterranean," made up of the non-Arab states in that part of the globe.

Two other groups, however, cannot be associated in any way with geographical proximity. One is factor five, "Large powers." All the major actors of
international politics are there including, though out of order, those six states
(China excepted) with the largest economic power bases (GNP). Allowing
for the well-known diplomatic isolation of Communist China, the concentration of the great powers here is striking. This finding is a strong argument
against the hypothesis that levels of diplomatic exchange would be associated
solely with other measurable bonds of common interest such as cultural
similarity, economic transactions, or international organization comembership, as *no* such large power grouping was found by the other criteria (see
below). It supports the political relevance hypothesis, that the major nations
would maintain large diplomatic staffs in other *big* states almost *regardless
of political alignment;* that much diplomatic effort would go into watching
enemies and big neutrals as well as in maintaining the basis of cooperative
relations with friends. The intelligence-gathering function of diplomatic
missions is obviously of great relevance here. India's association with this
group is not surprising, considering that nation's size and in part self-
appointed role as leader of the neutralist states. More unexpected, however, is
that of Belgium and Egypt. Egypt probably owes this position to its status as
the largest of the Arab countries and its pretension to ideological leadership
of the third world, but Belgium's inclusion is less easily explained. The most
likely special influence may be the presence in Brussels of many of the European international organizations, so that a number of the major powers'
diplomats are accredited to that capital, less to conduct relations with Belgium
per se than to keep abreast of wider Western European developments.

In examining this factor we see the ambitions of potential powers for recognition as important international actors. Egypt, Japan, and India—all three
pretenders to great influence in their regional systems and quick to respond,
at least verbally, to global political issues—have expressed these desires in

an area particularly open to their control, deployment of the diplomatic corps. This diplomatic globalism serves to reinforce somewhat these middle powers' claims to be interpreters of world politics for their regional "constituents" and representatives of those constituents in the councils of the great.

The other politically based group is hard to label or explain, "China and friends." While the members of this group do maintain diplomatic relations with China, as many states do not, this hardly exhausts the list of states with embassies in Peking.[17]

Several observations can be made on the relevance of these results to the study mentioned above of regions of developing nations as subsystems in international politics. First, the West African grouping significantly contains ex-French and ex-British colonies as well as the two African states never subject to colonial rule, but includes none of the ex-colonial powers. This stands in great contrast to the analysis of patterns of trade exchange, for example, in which the ex-colonies fell into factors headed by former metropoles. We sense a striving, of little avail against international trade realities, towards regional integrity in the area of diplomatic exchange which permits a greater freedom of action. In the Asian groupings, however, the shadow of the great powers can be discerned behind even the diplomatic patterns. Many of the Asian countries in factor three have been anti-Communist stalwarts of the U.S. (itself a member of the cluster). Factor nine contains most of the professedly neutral states of the area, although it too includes great powers, the USSR and the U.K.

A virtue of this application of direct factor analysis is the way in which, for the countries most strongly associated with each factor, the *squared* factor loadings are related more or less linearly to the numbers in the original data matrix. This relationship is not perfect, but coupled with inspection of the data matrix it provides an approximate way of gauging the strength of the bonds (number of diplomats exchanged) among the core members of each group. For example, the U.S. and the U.K., with loadings above 1.0, exchanged a total of 155 diplomats, which represents the highest figure in the entire matrix. Typically also, they exchanged 70 to 80 percent of the maximum with France and West Germany. Rather lower exchange levels are typical of those sets of countries which, on other factors, lead their lists with loadings above .60. In those instances the exchange level is usually at least 30 percent of the U.S.-U.K. maximum, and in a few cases, as with the USSR's relationships with its East European allies represented by a loading of .76 on the first factor, the figure may go to 50 or 60 percent of the maximum. Loadings in the .50 to .60 range, as for example at the top of the Latin American and West African factors, usually indicate exchanges on the level of 20 to 30 percent of

---

[17] Neither of these politically based clusters emerged, it should be noted, in Brams's analysis. The reason is traceable to the size effect, which we have deliberately retained in this analysis, and which he removed by using the relative acceptance model. The finding of such high mutual salience for the great powers is thus newly documented from this data. Otherwise there is a high, though hardly perfect, degree of correspondence between his study and ours.

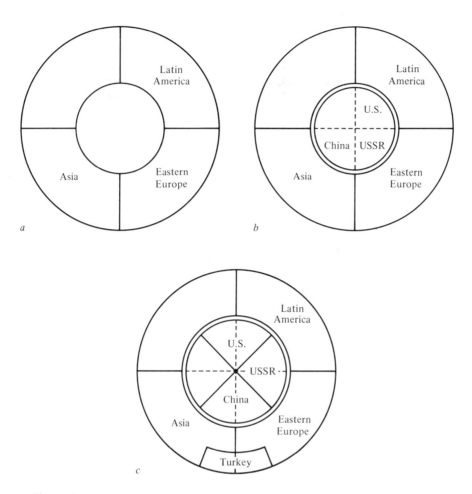

Figure 4-1
Several hypothetical international systems. *a*, Regional systems; *b*, International system with major powers and regional subsystems (spheres of influence); *c*, Major power penetration across subsystems.

the maximum. Thus, by far the highest levels of diplomatic representation occur *among the great powers* (hypothesis *b*), and within that group between great powers who are essentially *allied* with each other rather than hostile (hypothesis *a*). On substantive grounds, the high interchange among the East Europeans, especially with the USSR, is noteworthy.

The combination of regional subsystems plus heavy contacts among major powers in the larger international system deserves careful examination in juxtaposition to several other kinds of international systems that have or might have appeared in the past. Several such hypothetical systems are suggested graphically in the separate sections of Figure 4-1.

Figure 4-1, *a* illustrates one of the least complex possibilities imaginable, that of several regional systems, in turn composed of nation states who interact diplomatically with other states in their regions but not across systems. (The participant states, major and minor powers, are not portrayed in this simple diagram.) In effect there is no global system because of the absence of interaction across regions—perhaps something approximating this diagram might have applied to the world before the sixteenth century.

Figure 4-1, *b* portrays a true global system, with major powers, interacting with each other, in the center. In the outer ring are the smaller powers, who, lacking the capabilities or needs of the big states, concentrate their diplomatic exchanges within their regional subsystems. The term subsystem is now appropriate, because the major powers serve to knit the entire system together by their contacts. A major power does not, however, make heavy contact with *minor* states outside of its own region; except for keeping watch on its big allies and rivals, it confines its intense attention within the boundaries of its own "sphere of influence."

Figure 4-1, *c* represents a more complicated and probably more unstable world. Again it is characterized by major global powers and by regional subsystems, but there are no exclusive spheres of influence. Each major state has penetrated the subsystem of another great power, with the implication of rivalry and conflict, and most minor powers pay substantial diplomatic attention to at least two big states. In addition, some small powers also may carry on substantial exchanges with small states in other regions, so there is some overlap at low levels as well as at high ones. Turkey illustrates this in the hypothetical construct.

Figure 4-2 represents, in a schematized and necessarily incomplete way, the global pattern of exchange that was previously shown in Table 4-1. The regional subsystems previously identified are there, as are the major powers with supraregional interests. The ten members of the grouping we identified as "major powers" are within the double lined circle in the center, with the various regional groupings, and some of the smaller powers, represented in portions of the outer ring. States with ties to more than one region are represented as overlapping. Otherwise the size and location of the area marked for each state is of no significance, nor is the relative placing of the regions next to each other. They merely were juxtaposed in the best way to show the overlappings within the confines of a two-dimensional presentation. States outside of any regional grouping are not represented.

Most notably, there is *no* regional grouping that constitutes an exclusive sphere of influence. There are three not subject to any special penetration by any particular great powers,[18] but most show the activities of from two to four major states. Hence the figure illustrates some of the rivalry and conflict inherent in the current international system. From the small powers' vantage

---

[18] The Eastern Mediterranean group is probably penetrated by too many great powers to indicate the *special* presence of any *few*.

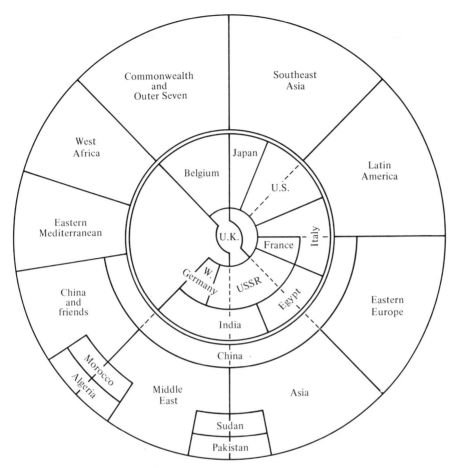

Figure 4-2
The international diplomatic system of 1963–1964.

point, perhaps it also suggests a certain degree of flexibility available to them; the necessity for members of a region to pay close diplomatic attention to more than one large state may in some instances present an opportunity for playing one off against the other. There are also a fair number of smaller nations (17 in all, though only a few could be represented in the figure) which have ties to more than one region. Such ties to more than one group would, according to some political and social theory, provide cross-pressure which would help to mitigate conflict and prevent the division of the world into rigidly distinct camps hostile toward each other.[19] On the other hand, a small power's strong diplomatic ties to two or more major powers may indicate, or invite, dangerous competition with more potential for conflict than would

---

[19] See Russett: *International Regions*, Chapter 14.

carefully delineated and agreed mutually exclusive spheres of influence. In any case, we lack any obvious base line to evaluate whether 17 small states with cross-national ties is "high" or "low" relative to some reasonable normative construct.

One other feature pointed out by the graphic representation is the wide-ranging political interest of mainland China, which has ties to four different groupings. Such global concerns are generally typical only of the major powers, yet China, because of her lack of diplomatic relations with several of the great powers, did not load on the major power factor. Although in part shut out of the normal processes of interaction among the mighty, China is nevertheless effectively sustaining her ambitions among a variety of lesser states. This concentration of attention on smaller nations, unmitigated by the usual amount of direct interaction with the major powers, is likely to have important consequences in Chinese behavior.

DIPLOMATIC EXCHANGE AND BONDS OF INTERACTION AND SIMILARITY

One original hypothesis was that the groups of countries joined together by high levels of diplomatic exchange would correspond in some measure to clusters of countries identified by other criteria, especially of similarity and interdependence. Some general likeness to "regional" groupings is already apparent in the majority of groups found above. This is true whether one uses the term "region" in a purely geographical sense, or whether the label is broadened to include social and political characteristics as well. But the evidence so far is vague and impressionistic, and a more rigorous comparison is required. The opportunity for such a comparison is presented by the data analyzed and reported previously, giving the groupings as defined by five objective criteria.[20] Two of those criteria concerned patterns of interaction (economic interdependence and common membership in international organizations), two concerned similarity (on a variety of social and cultural attributes, and in political behavior in the United Nations), and the other was simply geographic proximity. The data in each case are from the late 1950s (sociocultural groupings) or early 1960s (1962 or 1963 for all the others). Whatever slight difference in dates does occur makes little difference to the analysis, since it has been established that these groupings shift at a virtually glacial pace.

We may compare two factor analyses rigorously so as to measure precisely the degree to which the factor pattern in one resembles that in the other. In essence, the one factor matrix is rotated into the space defined by the other

---

[20] Ibid, Chapters 2, 4, 6, 8, and 10. The factor comparison technique used below is explained in Chapter 3.

factor matrix. The result is a product-moment correlation coefficient measuring the overall degree of agreement between the two patterns. Separate measures matching each factor in one study with each factor in the other are also provided. Thus one has not only a general picture of the correspondence, but an index also of where major differences lie, and of just which groupings match well and which poorly. Listed below are the squared correlation coefficients (r^2) for the *overall* comparisons between the diplomatic exchange analysis and each of the others.

Groupings by geographical proximity	.40
United Nations voting groups	.41
Sociocultural groupings	.42
International organization groups	.56
Trading groups	.56

The poorest fit is with the set of groupings defined by geography. This is of course not surprising, since we had already noted that on inspection two factors (five and eight) appeared to be politically rather than geographically based. Furthermore, geographical proximity is not subject to *inter*action with other influences; except as its effects may be mitigated by technological developments, it is not changed by diplomatic or other political acts. Thus whereas some feedback or other recursive mechanism may be plausibly hypothesized for the interaction of diplomatic exchange with any of the other influences (e.g., heavy commercial interactions promote a need for consular and ambassadorial personnel in the other country, and their presence then in turn facilitates even more trade), the causal relationship of diplomacy with geography must, if present at all, be merely from the latter. This finding then is theoretically plausible; it also corresponds empirically with a similar finding from the larger study, where the correlations between geography and the other four studies were appreciably lower than those *among* the other four.[21]

Two other r^2 in the above listing are not much higher, and those are the ones showing the correspondence between diplomatic exchange groupings and similarity as defined by sociocultural characteristics and by UN voting patterns. Slightly more than two-fifths of the variance is explained in both cases, as contrasted with the inter*active* sets of relationships at the bottom. Nations do *tend* to exchange numbers of diplomats with states that are politically or culturally similar to them, but this tendency is not particularly strong. It is considerably exceeded by the tendency to exchange diplomats with nations with which one is actively involved in some way, with nations that are salient because of active relationships. A state has relatively little choice as to what other states it may resemble culturally and even its voting behavior in global institutions may be determined as much by its domestic

---

[21] Ibid., p. 213.

preferences and policy choices as by interactions with allies or fellow caucusing group members. Trade and international organization memberships, however, are more clearly influenced by *international* pressures. Joining an international organization is certainly a political decision, and the relatively high correlation of those patterns with diplomatic exchange patterns, also politically based, is not surprising. The correspondence to trade groupings is less expected, particularly since the Communist countries, where foreign trade is conducted by state enterprises and hence subject to direct political control, are still a small minority of the world's nations. Yet international commerce even in free enterprise and mixed economies is subject to very substantial influence by national governments, not only in its total but in its direction, by preferential import duties and quotas, export subsidies, and a variety of special credit arrangements. The feedback relation between trade and the need for diplomatic representatives must also be remembered.

One other aspect of the above figures must be mentioned. These r^2 are sufficiently high to indicate some real "explanatory" power, but fall well short of the typical level achieved *among* the five sets of variables examined in *International Regions*. When the latter patterns were successively compared with each other, the average r^2 was .61. Here the average for each of the five with the diplomatic exchange factor pattern is but .46. This returns us to the original hypotheses of this chapter—diplomatic exchange patterns are in large measure explicable in terms of bonds of similarity and economic or institutional interdependence, but other factors, such as the relevance of states for each other in world politics, operate independently of those bonds.

Finally we shall look at the correspondences in detail. Table 4-2 goes below the overall level, and gives an index of agreement between each of the "regionally" based *factors* in the diplomatic exchange study with those, identified with descriptive labels, in the other analyses.[22] (The geographic factors are omitted as of less significance than the others.) An index is given for the degree of agreement between the diplomatic factor and that factor in each of the other analyses with which it has the closest fit. If there is no case of agreement as high as .30 this is indicated by a dash, since indices below that level are of little interest. The two nonregional or politically based factors in the diplomatic study are omitted, since in fact they did not correspond at all closely to any factors in any of the other analyses.

The East European or Communist countries find the greatest degree of correspondence across the board, with quite similar groups in each of the

---

[22] The index of agreement is derived from the measure employed in Russett, *International Regions*, but differs from it. On the principle that a factor from one study was rotated into the factor space of the other, the original index was the cosine of the angle between the factor (vector) in one study and a factor (or vector) in the other. A 90° angle would correspond to two orthogonal (uncorrelated) factors, and have a cosine of 0.0; perfect identity of the factors would be reflected in a 0° angle and a cosine of 1.0. This measure has an intuitive limitation, however, in that the relationship between degree of similarity and increases in the cosine is not linear; that is, the true midpoint is not .50 but .71 (the cosine for a 45° angle). Instead, we take as a linear measure I of similarity the angle θ between factors and norm it linearly: $I = 1 - \theta/90°$.

Table 4-2
Indices of Agreement between Diplomatic Exchange Factors and Factors from Other Analyses

Diplomatic exchange grouping from Table 4-1	Groupings from Russett's International Regions and the International System			
	Trade	Membership in international organizations	Sociocultural measures	UN voting patterns
Eastern Europe	Eastern Europe, .78	Eastern Europe, .87	Eastern Europe, .84	Communist countries, .70
Latin America	North and Central America, .78	Latin America, .87	Latin America, .82	Brazzaville Africans, .42
Southeast Asia	Asia, .84	Asia, .67	Afro-Asians, .34	—
Middle East	Arabs, .48	Arabs, .71	Afro-Asians, .42	Conservative Arabs, .41
West Africa	French Community, .66	Former French Africa, .60	—	Brazzaville Africans, .34
Commonwealth and Outer Seven	Western Europe, .49	Western Europe, .43	Western Community, .42	Western Community, .32
Asia	Asia, .45	Asia, .58	—	Afro-Asians, .47

other studies. (In the UN analysis this group was labelled Communists rather than East Europeans, but it is not notably different.) This finding reinforces previous evidence that the Communist nations form the closest equivalent to a subsystem, in the strict sense of the same boundaries being identified by a variety of empirical tests, as can be found in the current international system. But even there the correspondence from one criterion to another is far from perfect. Cuba, East Germany, Yugoslavia, China, and Albania are all borderline cases, sometimes clearly within the boundaries and sometimes not. With the diplomatic data they all were within the group, though Albania was distinctly marginal.

Also apparent is a substantial degree of correspondence for a Latin American group, at a somewhat lower level than is true of the Communist states. In two cases the fit is with a group that was labelled Latin America, and the other two, with poorer fits, are with a smaller and a larger group. In the trading analysis, Latin America was found to be divided into two separate groups, one centered on the South American continent and one on North and Central America. The diplomatic cluster most closely matches the North and Central American one, although it also produces an agreement index of .49 with the South American group (not shown in the table). The name "Brazzaville Africans" may seem strange for the best approximation in the UN study, but that is because in the 1963 session there was no clearly defined Latin American factor. Most of the Latin states did form a distinct group approximately midway between the Western Community of European states and a group of pro-Western African and Asian nations imperfectly labelled "Brazzaville Africans" to denote the caucusing group that formed the largest component of the voting cluster. Because of this peculiarity, there was no strictly Latin American *factor* available for a match, and it is reasonable to find the Latin diplomatic factor between the Brazzaville and Western Community factor (it has an agreement index of .20 with the latter, also not shown in the table).

The other diplomat groupings evidence appreciably less agreement generally. We found two distinct Asian subgroupings in the diplomatic data, and each fits fairly well with the larger single Asian or sometimes Afro-Asian group usually found in the other studies. The Middle Eastern and African states generally find moderate agreement with related groups in other analyses, but the boundaries vary quite a bit. The West African group is much more closely associated with the French African cluster of other studies, rather than with the separate British group that occasionally appears. The Commonwealth and Outer Seven cluster fits but poorly with groupings centered around Western Europe. On the relevant diplomatic factor many Western European states were prominent; but a number of the Europeans with a Latin culture were low or absent, and of course the old Commonwealth states were present, as they were not in the trade and international organization patterns.

One major finding that emerged from the overall comparisons is further documented in this more detailed examination. The correspondence between the diplomatic exchange patterns and those defined by interactive relationships (trade and international organization) is much stronger than between diplomatic and mere similarity groupings. Diplomats go where the action is.

APPENDIX ON METHODS

1. A great variety of other clustering procedures have been investigated, but none has emerged as clearly superior to direct factor analysis. This method has regularly been applied by sociometrists on problems analogous to the one here. We must also acknowledge that none of the available procedures is perfect; each mathematical paradigm is itself a theory about interrelationships, and the major computational alternatives all differ somewhat in the assumptions they make and the functional relationships they specify. Each will therefore produce somewhat different numbers of clusters or groupings. Inclusions and exclusions, especially at the margins, will vary from one procedure to another. In data reduction of the kind envisaged here, some information is always deliberately discarded in the search for general patterns. Efforts which do not make use of computers are faced with even greater problems in this regard and can rarely attain the levels of replicability and comparability made possible by the new technology.

Since we are using data that have been analyzed differently by Brams previously, it is appropriate to note the specific virtues of the two procedures and why we consider direct factor analysis superior. Brams's decomposition procedures have the important advantage of bringing out, more clearly than factor analysis can, hierarchical relationships among units. By this method the entire set is first broken into two large groups, each large group is then further subdivided, the smaller groups again subdivided, etc. Such hierarchies are not so easily discerned in the factor matrix. On the other hand, Brams's procedure requires that all originally ordinal or interval measures of interaction be arbitrarily transformed to dichotomous nominal measures where the interaction between each pair of states is found either above or below a threshold, and they are described either as linked or not linked. Within any single decomposition, the subtleties of different intensities of linkage are lost. Brams compensates for this limitation in part by an imaginative variation of the threshold from one analysis to another, but this is awkward and not fully satisfactory. At the least, the different advantages of the two procedures are sufficiently important to warrant a partial replication with our method. Furthermore, the factor-analytic technique has the virtue of lending itself well to precise comparisons of one study with another, as we illustrate in the text. There is a valuable method for, in effect, overlaying one factor matrix (e.g., diplomatic exchange) on another (e.g., trade patterns) to see in detail for what states and groupings they correspond and where they differ.

2. The concern for impact stands in contrast to other studies which ask whether the level of interaction is higher or lower than might be "expected" from the relative size of the countries involved. Such studies, while useful, are addressed to different theoretical concerns. This concern represents the second major difference between our procedures and those of Brams. His use of a null model, originally developed by Savage and Deutsch, is intended to control for the size effect. That is, if one *assumes* that two major powers, each with large foreign services, will maintain large embassies in each other's capital, it may be useful to know whether the actual exchange is in fact smaller or larger than one would "expect" from the nations' overall world activities. His index measures deviations from the expected value, and countries are considered linked to the degree those deviations exceed the expected value by a significant amount. While that is a useful and important inquiry, ours is intended to test hypotheses underlying that assumption. An even better measure of impact on the nations' decision-making processes might have been obtained by a ratio of the diplomats exchanged to the total number of foreign service personnel, or of all civil servants, employed by a government. This would have been analogous to previous efforts to relate the volume of foreign trade between two states to the total national income of each. In this case, however, the necessary data simply were not available.

3. We must acknowledge that the choice of this particular (square root) transformation is arbitrary. A case could also be made for a milder transformation, or for a more severe one (such as a logarithmic transformation). There is no evidence that the impact of diplomatic exchange on nations' decision-making processes is fully captured by *this* function (that the effect of a change from 1 to 4 is the same as that from 81 to 100, etc.). But in fact the practical implications of the choice of this transformation rather than some other (equally plausible theoretically) seem to be minimal. As a check we applied the much more drastic $\log_{10}$ transformation to the data and carried out the same analysis described for the square root data (including several rotations each employing a different number of factors). When the number of factors rotated was the same for both data sets, the patterns deriving from the two transformations were correlated with an average r^2 of .91. Even such a high correlation as this does not remove the desirability of applying some metric-free clustering technique to the data, but it makes us confident that, at least for this type of data, the scale problem need not concern us seriously. At the time of writing, nonmetric routines capable of handling matrices as large as ours simply were not available.

One other methodological point: Table 4-2 presents the results of the factor analysis as produced by varimax rotation of the original factor matrix. Rotation is a commonly employed procedure used to simplify the structure of the results, producing so far as possible a set of very high and very low loadings and relatively few moderate loadings. It has been employed in all the results reported previously in this project. Sometimes it is difficult, however, and was so here, to make a decision on the number of factors to rotate, and as is well known different decision rules will produce some variation in the final results. It is particularly difficult with direct factor analysis, where the most common rule, "rotate all factors with eigenvalues exceeding 1.0" is not strictly applicable. Use of that criterion here would have had us rotate more than 30 factors, producing very many small clusters of countries. Lacking clear-cut guidance, we decided to rotate only those factors with absolute eigenvalues exceeding 2.0, which in this case meant nine factors which together accounted for 35 percent of the variance in the matrix. This rule produced a set of factors that more or less corresponded in number to the maximum produced by the earlier analysis in this project, where the decision was easier to make. (In the study of UN voting groups in 1963 we examined loadings on six factors; for international organization and trade clusterings in the 1960s we examined seven and nine respectively.) About the same level of decomposition seemed important for comparability. The need for such a decision, however, emphasizes why one particular pitfall must be avoided. In the exposition, we do not in any way imply that the world is or should be, for all analytical purposes, divided into precisely nine or ten regional or other groupings. For different purposes finer or more gross divisions should be required. The minimum hierarchical insight that systems usually contain subsystems should be kept firmly in mind when examining the groupings shown in Table 4-2.

Importantly, however, even this problem is less severe than might have been thought. As a check on the amount of distortion that might have been produced by our rotation decision, we applied the method, otherwise identical, to a rotation of 16 factors, a figure deliberately chosen so as to exceed substantially the level of decomposition previously employed. We compared the 9 and 16 factor rotations for both the square root and the $\log_{10}$ transformations as discussed above; here the agreement was still quite high, with an average r^2 of .75. There were of course differences, especially with the more marginal members of some clusters, but basically the same large groups that emerged in the 9-factor rotations were also to be found, perhaps slightly attenuated, in the 16-factor rotations.

5

"Regional" Trading Patterns, 1938–1963

A TAXONOMY OF TRADING GROUPS

In my book *International Regions and the International System*[1] I examined the relationships over the post-World War II period among a number of variables generally considered relevant to delineating regional groupings of nations. The book-length examination was limited, however, to information on bonds among nations during the 1950s and early 1960s. Most of the basic data sources (aggregate data on national characteristics, international organization memberships) were not generally available or (UN voting patterns)[2] were inapplicable to the interwar period or earlier. There is, however, perfectly adequate information on the nation-to-nation linkages of international trade before World War II, data that could be matched with that for later years to map fairly long-term trends in the international system. In this chapter we shall examine those trends with a view toward quantitative description of a critical set of interactions that both affect, and are affected by, the events of international politics. Quite obviously patterns of international trade are influenced by national political decisions on trade quotas, colonial or other tariff preferences, and a government's financial or political support for foreign

---

Reprinted from *International Studies Quarterly*, 12, 4 (December 1968).
[1] Chicago: Rand McNally, 1967.
[2] Decisions in the League of Nations were usually governed by the rule of unanimity, hence there are no adequate voting data on patterns of disagreement.

investment either by its own nationals abroad or by foreign firms on its own soil. In turn, most theories of political integration regard international commerce as playing a central role in the development, or, less often, in the erosion, of bonds of community. Hence such a description, especially one that spans both the most destructive war in world history and the rise of a new bipolar international system, should be of some interest.

It should be noted, nevertheless, that we shall not here be testing *general* propositions about the relation between international trade and international politics. The effort is one of obtaining a more precise mapping or taxonomy of the global system. Furthermore, future empirical work will surely modify whatever groupings are offered in the primitive state of our current science. Doubtless there will be further important methodological refinements in the next few years as access to large computers spreads geographically and to a new generation of scientists. Yet we have at the moment so few data-based classifications, particularly on the international relations of earlier periods, that the following initial exercise seems warranted. *International Regions and the International System* examines trading patterns in 1954 and 1963. Here we shall look at trading patterns in the last year of peace before World War II, 1938, and compare them with what emerged in the later years.

As in the preceding chapter, three assumptions must be made and appropriate procedures adopted.

1. A means of *data reduction* is necessary, and as before we shall employ direct factor analysis to find patterns in the larger matrix of interactions.

2. We are concerned with the *relative impact* of trade. Here we assume that the political effects are some positive function of trade as a proportion of the entire economy. The matrix analyzed is one of "choice" of trading partners among all possible countries or partners. As a measure of impact, I decided on the volume of trade (T equals exports plus imports) between two nations as a proportion of the total national income (Y) of each in turn. That is, country j's economic impact on country i is equal to T_{ij}/Y_i and i's impact on j is T_{ij}/Y_j. We therefore produce a matrix of trade-to-income ratios that is square (each country is represented both by a row and by a column) but is asymmetric, since T_{ij}/Y_i is not equal to T_{ij}/Y_j. The same volume of trade between the United States and Guatemala has a much greater impact on the economy (and presumably the polity) of Guatemala than it does on the United States.

   This distinction is similar to that between choosers and chosen in the sociometric literature. If we are to find interdependent groups, we must have nations who both *choose* and *are chosen* by each other. (The man who names Tom, Dick, and Harry as friends, but who is not selected by Tom, Dick, and Harry as their friend, is in a real sense not *inter*dependent with them. He is *dependent* upon them, but the dependence is not reciprocated.) One factor analysis of such a matrix will pick out groups

of nations which depend on, or tend to "choose," similar trading partners—they will share the characteristic of having a higher than average
fraction of their economies devoted to trade with the same nations. But
if the matrix is turned on its side (transposed) and factored *again*, the
analysis picks out those states *into* whose economies they enter heavily,
and identifies countries which in common are "chosen" by, or depended on by, the same countries. These two analyses, labelled in
Tables 5-1 and 5-2 Chooser and Chosen, are equally legitimate and important. For a truly interdependent group we will require that a country
appear relatively high on *both* lists; hence the high-ranking countries
on each are listed in parallel columns. Note that this choice of the ratio
of trade to income is theoretically based, and is taken despite explicit
consideration of such alternatives as simply the total volume of trade,
or some deviation of actual trade from an "expected" value.[3]

3. As with diplomatic exchange, we assume that the political effects of trade
   are subject to *decreasing marginal returns*, and so must choose a measure
   more sensitive to additional increases in very small volumes of |trade
   than to absolute totals of high volumes of trade. Here I subjected all
   entries to a logarithmic transformation. The T_{ij}/Y values were first
   multiplied by 10,000 to remove the decimal and then logged to the base
   10. The input values were then standardized to a range from 1.0 to 0.
   As with the square root transformation of the diplomatic exchange data,
   the result here is a distribution which, except for the excessive number of
   zeroes for no trade (I substituted zeroes instead of the logarithm of zero),
   is roughly normal. Again, the particular transformation is arbitrary, and
   one could make a theoretical case for a milder or more severe one. But,
   as discussed in the appendix to the previous chapter, the practical implications of the choice seem to be slight.

---

[3] Russett, op. cit., pp. 122–7. The trade data are derived originally from United Nations, Statistical Papers, Series T, VI, 10, *Direction of International Trade* (New York: United Nations,
1956). They were compiled and punched under the direction of Karl W. Deutsch for one of his
projects, and graciously made available to me. I estimated some missing items as described in
Russett, op. cit., p. 128. This information on international trade is, relative to much of the data
employed in cross-national research, of good reliability. The income data, however, are less
satisfactory. They are obtained from W. S. Woytinsky and E. S. Woytinsky, *World Population
and Production* (New York: Twentieth Century Fund, 1953), pp. 389–90 and are subject to
substantial error, in some cases above 30 percent. A few entries are merely general estimates.
The effect on this analysis of poor income data, however, is trivial. The range of actual ratios of
trade to income runs from .01 percent to nearly 100 percent. Coupled with the logarithmic
transformation of the trade to income ratios (see below), an error of 30 percent in a single
income figure produces an error in the trade to income ratio that is only about 3 percent of the
entire range of empirically observed ratios. Furthermore, the error is constant for all entries for
that country. Such effects can properly be ignored in evaluating the results. For a generalized
discussion of the matter, see my "Techniques for Controlling Error," in *Statistical and Quantitative Methods*, Michael Haas, editor (forthcoming). The data, both the original matrix of
T/Y coefficients and the factor matrices discussed below, are available from the Inter-university
Consortium for Political Research, P. O. Box 1248, Ann Arbor, Michigan 48106.

Table 5-1
Trade Groupings in 1938

Choosers	Factor loading	Chosen	Factor loading
North and Central America			
Guatemala	1.52	United States	3.21
Honduras	1.47	Sweden	1.02
El Salvador	1.44	Canada	.80
Panama	1.11	El Salvador	.71
Peru	.88	Peru	.68
United States	.66	Norway	.57
Norway	.65	Honduras	.53
Sweden	.61	Guatemala	.48
Denmark	.57	Denmark	.46
Canada	.50	Panama	.43
South America			
Peru	1.67	Argentina	1.87
Argentina	1.58	United States	1.74
Uruguay	1.55	Germany	1.62
Chile	1.48	United Kingdom	1.55
Bolivia	1.35	Brazil	1.45
Brazil	1.31	Belgium-Luxembourg	1.38
Belgium-Luxembourg	1.13	Chile	1.38
Ecuador	.97	Peru	1.29
Cuba	.88	France	1.20
Sweden	.88	Japan	1.17
Switzerland	.86	Uruguay	1.14
Germany	.84	Italy	1.05
Netherlands	.79	Switzerland	1.05
Norway	.76	Sweden	1.03
Denmark	.75	Netherlands	1.01
United Kingdom	.74	Canada	.87
Italy	.73	Czechoslovakia	.76
Finland	.72	Bolivia	.75
Japan	.72	Denmark	.72
United States	.71	Norway	.59
France	.67	Ecuador	.58
Czechoslovakia	.60	Cuba	.56
Canada	.59	Finland	.48

(Continued)

Table 5-1

Trade Groupings in 1938 (Continued)

Choosers	Factor loading	Chosen	Factor loading
		British Empire	
Trinidad	1.92	United Kingdom	2.53
Jamaica	1.52	Canada	2.23
Canada	1.47	United States	2.14
Sierra Leone	1.20	Netherlands	1.33
United Kingdom	1.19	Belgium-Luxembourg	1.16
British Guiana	1.11	Australia	1.11
New Zealand	1.04	Trinidad	1.08
Ireland	1.01	Argentina	.92
Venezuela	.93	New Zealand	.87
Australia	.89	Jamaica	.83
Colombia	.80	Ireland	.67
Netherlands	.77	Czechoslovakia	.63
United States	.75	Venezuela	.59
Argentina	.71	Sierra Leone	.53
Belgium-Luxembourg	.70	Sweden	.53
French West Africa	.65	Brazil	.52
South Africa	.65	Colombia	.50
Brazil	.63	French West Africa	.50
Norway	.59	Switzerland	.49
Sweden	.57	British Guiana	.40
Czechoslovakia	.55	Norway	.40
Switzerland	.53	South Africa	.40
		Africa	
Tanganyika	1.56	Belgium-Luxembourg	1.52
Kenya-Uganda	1.43	India	1.15
Belgian Congo	1.20	Kenya-Uganda	1.12
South Africa	.92	South Africa	1.08
Belgium-Luxembourg	.81	Belgian Congo	1.07
Iran	.73	Tanganyika	.94
India	.61	Iran	.47
		French Union	
Algeria	1.79	France	2.40
Tunisia	1.64	Algeria	1.45
France	1.46	Belgium-Luxembourg	1.27
Morocco	1.45	Indochina	1.17
French West Africa	1.32	Netherlands	1.15
Indochina	1.18	Morocco	1.11
Belgium-Luxembourg	.98	Tunisia	.97

Choosers	Factor loading	Chosen	Factor loading
Madagascar	.90	Italy	.91
Netherlands	.83	French West Africa	.87
Switzerland	.67	Indonesia	.87
Portugal	.62	Switzerland	.66
Romania	.57	Spain	.61
Spain	.54	Madagascar	.46
Indonesia	.53	Portugal	.42
Italy	.52	Romania	.40

Northern Europe

Iceland	1.52	Norway	1.87
Norway	1.51	United Kingdom	1.78
Denmark	1.19	Germany	1.65
Belgium-Luxembourg	1.11	Sweden	1.60
Sweden	1.11	Denmark	1.44
Finland	1.05	Netherlands	1.35
Netherlands	1.04	Belgium-Luxembourg	1.21
United Kingdom	1.04	Spain	1.12
Portugal	.95	Portugal	1.06
Iran	.89	Argentina	1.01
Germany	.74	Poland	.99
Spain	.70	USSR	.97
Switzerland	.66	Brazil	.93
Brazil	.62	France	.91
France	.61	Finland	.85
Argentina	.58	Iceland	.81
South Africa	.58	Switzerland	.74
USSR	.58	South Africa	.72
Poland	.54	Iran	.56
Indonesia	.52	Indonesia	.49

Central Europe

Czechoslovakia	2.16	Germany	2.82
Greece	2.09	Czechoslovakia	2.28
Germany	1.87	United Kingdom	2.28
Romania	1.87	Italy	2.22
Switzerland	1.83	France	1.95
Belgium-Luxembourg	1.82	Poland	1.81
Hungary	1.78	Romania	1.80
Italy	1.74	Belgium-Luxembourg	1.78
Palestine	1.72	Hungary	1.77
Netherlands	1.69	Netherlands	1.74
Egypt	1.68	Sweden	1.71

(*Continued*)

Table 5-1
Trade Groupings in 1938 (Continued)

Choosers	Factor loading	Chosen	Factor loading
		Central Europe (Continued)	
Finland	1.66	Switzerland	1.71
Turkey	1.61	Greece	1.54
Poland	1.59	Yugoslavia	1.51
Denmark	1.58	Egypt	1.36
Sweden	1.58	Turkey	1.32
Bulgaria	1.53	Argentina	1.28
Malaya-Singapore	1.45	Denmark	1.25
Norway	1.45	Finland	1.22
United Kingdom	1.42	Bulgaria	1.20
Yugoslavia	1.38	Norway	1.06
Argentina	1.30	Brazil	.99
France	1.21	Canada	.92
Uruguay	1.20	Australia	.89
Syria-Lebanon	1.19	Palestine	.77
Brazil	1.07	South Africa	.74
French Morocco	1.05	Mexico	.67
Portugal	.95	Spain	.61
Iran	.91	Indonesia	.56
South Africa	.91	Uruguay	.53
Australia	.80	Iran	.49
Indonesia	.80	Portugal	.49
Canada	.73	Malaya-Singapore	.48
United States	.67	French Morocco	.45
Spain	.67	Syria-Lebanon	.40
		Middle East	
Syria-Lebanon	1.72	Egypt	1.63
Iraq	1.49	Saudi Arabia	1.61
Palestine	1.35	Syria-Lebanon	1.37
Cyprus	1.29	Iraq	1.19
Egypt	1.15	Palestine	1.16
Iran	.79	Romania	1.04
Saudi Arabia	.79	Iran	.98
Romania	.70	Cyprus	.83
Sudan	.63	Turkey	.68
Turkey	.59	Sudan	.44
Kenya-Uganda	.55	Kenya-Uganda	.40

Choosers	Factor loading		Chosen	Factor loading
		Asia		
Malaya-Singapore	3.14		United Kingdom	2.64
Ceylon	2.22		India	2.46
Indonesia	2.08		United States	2.45
Burma	1.92		Japan	2.28
Thailand	1.89		Malaya-Singapore	2.19
Japan	1.79		Indonesia	2.13
Iran	1.74		Australia	2.03
United Kingdom	1.64		Germany	1.85
Belgium-Luxembourg	1.57		Netherlands	1.69
Australia	1.56		France	1.60
Netherlands	1.54		Ceylon	1.58
Egypt	1.49		China	1.54
India	1.37		Belgium-Luxembourg	1.52
Philippines	1.34		Canada	1.52
South Africa	1.34		South Africa	1.50
New Zealand	1.33		Burma	1.40
Iraq	1.33		Thailand	1.32
Canada	1.23		Italy	1.30
Kenya-Uganda	1.22		Egypt	1.25
Norway	1.22		Sweden	1.22
Indochina	1.21		Iran	1.13
Sweden	1.14		Switzerland	1.08
Switzerland	1.13		New Zealand	1.05
Czechoslovakia	1.10		Czechoslovakia	1.00
France	1.10		Indochina	.95
United States	1.09		Philippines	.93
Denmark	1.07		Norway	.85
Saudi Arabia	1.06		Denmark	.80
China	1.05		Argentina	.77
Germany	1.01		Poland	.77
Finland	.99		Mexico	.57
Italy	.89		Finland	.52
Argentina	.80		Mauritius	.52
Mauritius	.76		Chile	.45
Chile	.71		Iraq	.44
Mexico	.65		Saudi Arabia	.44
Poland	.64		Kenya-Uganda	.40

	Not listed in any group			
Albania	Ethopia		Gold Coast	Nigeria
Costa Rica	French Cameroons		Haiti	Paraguay
Dominican Republic	French Equatorial Africa		Nicaragua	Taiwan

TRADE GROUPINGS IN 1938

With these methodological points cleared away we are now ready to examine the clusters of trading nations as they are discovered for 1938. In Table 5-1 we list Chooser and Chosen factors in parallel columns. Only countries that show loadings exceeding the mean factor loading (averaged over each of the two entire matrices) on *both* factors are listed. The Choosers are given first, since they more nearly resemble geopolitical regions in their orderings. The list of Chosen countries is often led by one or more of the major industrial and trading powers of the world, especially the United States or the United Kingdom. The countries at the top of the list are most closely associated with the cluster, and we approach the more marginal members as we move down. A country which is toward the bottom of both lists is obviously rather peripheral to the grouping; so, in the sense of a somewhat weak *inter*dependence, is a state that appears near the very end even of one. Relatively pure cases of interdependence are toward the top of both. The numbers following the name of the country in each column represent the country's loading on that particular factor.[4]

Nine groups of economically interdependent states emerge, corresponding to nine factors in the factor analysis. The Western Hemisphere was, in 1938, divided into two commercial groupings. The smaller of the two is identified roughly with most of the continental states of North and Central America, especially the latter. Even in 1938 the Central American states conducted a fair amount of trade with each other, as well as with the United States and, to a lesser degree, with Canada. Only Peru from the South American continent was much involved with them. The group did not include all the independent states of the Caribbean area, however. Costa Rica and Nicaragua were omitted, as were Mexico, Haiti, the Dominican Republic, and Cuba. The last one tended to be tied in more with the South American nations, and all six were linked less to Central America than directly to the United States and, to a lesser degree, to Europe. When the Central American Common Market was formed in the 1950s, it may be noted, Costa Rica joined 18 months after the others had initiated it. Note too the association, in a peripheral way, of several Scandinavian states with this group. Unlike most Western European countries in 1938 the Scandinavians had no tropical colonies for preferential trading arrangements, and so seem to have turned to the independent countries of Central America.

A second Western Hemisphere group incorporates most of South America except for the northernmost states of Colombia and Venezuela. It is a large cluster, however, that also includes substantial though lesser trading ties to

---

[4] The procedure was the principal components method of factor analysis, with orthogonal rotation. Ten factors (all those accounting for one percent or more of the total sum of squares in the original matrix) were rotated. The tenth was small with very few substantial loadings, and is omitted here as being of no substantive interest. The nine factors shown together account for 81 percent of the sum of squares in the original matrix.

Western Europe. The United States involvement in this group is much less intense than in the more northern grouping first examined. Many of these South American nations have long maintained important markets and supply sources in Europe.

A third group, affected importantly by geographical factors but even more by political considerations, included much of the British Empire. The first eight states on the Choosers list were part of the Empire in 1938, as were Australia and South Africa somewhat further down the list. The British colonies of the Caribbean (Trinidad, Jamaica, and British Guiana) that did not show up in the first grouping are here instead, with few relations to the Latin states. So too are several Western European countries. The latter include several of the states (Norway, Sweden, Switzerland) that two decades later joined Britain in the "Outer Seven" of the European Free Trade Association. This cooperative effort had its roots in long-term association with the British Commonwealth. In 1938 the Scandinavian states were 'part of the Sterling Area and its arrangements for pooling foreign exchange reserves and pegging exchange rates to the pound. The Anglocentric trading system was also held together by the scheme of Imperial Preferences. While no continental European nations were tied to that, several Latin American countries did have preferential agreements with Britain. Most notable of those was the Roca-Runciman agreement signed between Britain and Argentina in 1934. Such agreements doubtless account in part for the presence of several South American nations on this list; bonds among some of the Caribbean colonies and independent states (including Colombia and Venezuela) also play a role.

Another grouping that includes several other members of the British Empire has been labelled "Africa." It is much smaller than the whole African continent, with only a few British and Belgian sub-Saharan colonies, and the Union of South Africa. In addition there is a modest Asian component plus Belgium, largely because of the latter's ties with its own colony. Most, though not quite all, of the French African and Asian colonies go, with the metropolitan country, into a grouping identified as "French Union." The first six units on the Choosers list are French, as is Madagascar. The West European (except for Germany) elements of this group also should not be overlooked, nor should Romania's presence, alone of the East European states. The Romanians of course speak a Romance language and before World War II had security ties to France.

Two larger groups, however, are more clearly and centrally identified with Europe. The first, called "Northern Europe," is composed primarily of Scandinavia, the Benelux states, and the United Kingdom. Other European polities, and a few non-European ones as well, are more peripheral. It is the most dramatic of several groups notable for their composition by essentially similar and competing economies which nevertheless find much to sell to each other. Cultural, political, and geographical factors obviously matter much.

The second, and still larger, group is labelled "Central Europe." It incorporates virtually all the European nations between Iberia and the Soviet Union, and this economic integrity of Europe is of some interest. Note also the presence, though not in a central way, of a number of Middle Eastern states. But the USSR is *not* included here, but rather in the preceding Northern Europe list. Its strong *present* economic ties to Eastern Europe are thus traceable to the political changes that have taken place there since World War II rather than to economic or geographical constants.

The Middle Eastern countries and colonies form a unit among themselves. This is mostly an Arab grouping, modified by the addition of Cyprus, Iran, Romania, Turkey, and Kenya-Uganda. It is about as geographically compact a cluster as any in the table. The Arab colonies of the North African Maghreb are not part of it, however, being instead closely tied to France and some of France's other colonies. These colonies, though Arab, are of course physically somewhat removed from the predominantly eastern Mediterranean center of this group. Finally there is a large Asian cluster, centering around Southeast Asia but covering most of the continent and its periphery, as well as the major colonial powers.

One general point can now be made not only about interdependence *within* trade groupings, but about the bonds *between* groups. If the most central members of a group are found at the top of a list, we can conceive of other members as falling within increasingly distant concentric circles as we move down the list. Furthermore, the circles, especially the outer ones, surrounding one core often intersect with circles around other cores. Countries listed with one group are frequently found with one or more other clusters as well, and most groupings overlap with other groups. Thus the world is not divided into several watertight, isolated regional compartments, but into groups with quite indistinct boundaries. A number of nations, especially but not exclusively the industrial developed states, have broad and even worldwide trading interests and serve to link the otherwise fairly autonomous groups. Particularly wide ranging are small, developed countries *without* large colonial empires; e.g., Belgium, Netherlands, Sweden, and Switzerland. In systems language the global economic system is indeed built on several partly, but not completely, decomposable subsystems.[5]

THE EFFECTS OF WAR AND COLD WAR

Three substantive hypotheses about the effect of international political events on trading patterns can be investigated with the data (for 1938, 1954, and 1963) that are now available.

1. The patterns of interdependence in 1938 will be less like those for 1954 than 1954 is like 1963. There are four possible reasons.

---

[5] Herbert A. Simon, "The Architecture of Complexity," *Proceedings of the American Philosophical Society*, 106, 6 (December 1962), pp. 467–82.

    a. The time elapsed is greater, and changes in commercial habits are to some degree a function of time.

    b. Political changes on the Eurasian continent, specifically the communization of Eastern Europe and China, have cut old trading bonds and created different ones.

    c. Decolonization has weakened the bonds among the former British and French colonial empires.

    d. The physical damage and economic disruption of World War II left much of the world, especially Europe, with a severe "dollar shortage" in the first postwar decade. As a consequence Europeans' links to former markets and sources of supply outside their political spheres of influence were gravely weakened. This was particularly severe in the case of the Latin American countries which competed with the primary producing economies of the African and Asian colonies and former colonies.

2. The patterns of interdependence in 1938 will be less like those for 1963 than 1963 is like 1954 because of factors *a–c* above. Item *d*, the dollar shortage and its consequent monetary restrictions, had been relieved by 1963.

3. The patterns of interdependence in 1938 will be more like those in 1963 than like 1954 because of the absence of condition *d* in 1963 and the modification of condition *b*. These changes may be somewhat counteracted by condition *a* and the further progress of *c*.

As before, we can compare any two factor analyses both overall and by individual factors so as to see just which groupings have changed over time.[6] Table 5-2 lists the squared correlation coefficient, r^2, for the overall comparisons, and Table 5-3 shows the most important similarities among particular factors.

The relationships are essentially the same whether one looks at the Choosers or at the Chosen comparisons. There is *substantial*—perhaps surprising—*continuity* over time despite the intervention of political upheaval. Nevertheless there are shifts, and hypotheses 1 and 2 (similarity 1938–1954 less than similarity 1954–1963; similarity 1938–1963 less than similarity 1954–1963) are clearly confirmed in general terms, though the detailed influences suggested have yet to be examined. But hypothesis 3 (similarity 1938–1963 more than

---

[6] The variables (countries) have to be the same in both analyses in order to make this comparison. Some of the polities included in the postwar analyses thus had to be dropped. In the case of some units which became divided after World War II, more or less arbitrary equivalencies were established between the older unit and the largest of the new ones. Kenya-Uganda is matched with Kenya, Malaya-Singapore with Malaya (in 1954; with Malaysia in 1963), Syria-Lebanon with Syria, Indochina with South Vietnam, and Germany with West Germany. French West Africa and French Equatorial Africa are simply dropped from the 1963 comparison for lack of sufficient correspondence with any of the several smaller units formed from those areas.

Table 5-2

Overall Similarity Indices (r^2) among Factor Analyses of Trading Patterns in 1938, 1954, and 1963

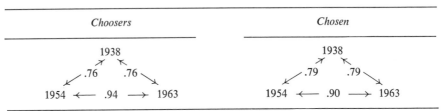

Choosers	Chosen

1938
.76   .76
1954 ← .94 → 1963

1938
.79   .79
1954 ← .90 → 1963

similarity 1938–1954) must be rejected, since in neither case is 1938 more nor less like 1963 than like 1954. Table 5-3 below helps us to understand the particulars. For parsimony the comparisons are presented only for Choosers, not for Chosen. Although the details are not quite the same in comparisons among Choosers groups as among the Chosen, most of them are close (within about .08). More important, the Chosen groupings, because of their tendency often to rank highly the major industrial states with worldwide commercial interests, give a less useful picture of the linkages among the smaller states and of the geographical, cultural, and political influences on trade. Indices lower than .40 are largely omitted as of little interest.

On the specific components of hypotheses 1 and 2, we see each moving in the expected direction. The Central European group's composition changed somewhat, and the group became transformed into one focusing on the Communist countries of Eastern Europe. There is evidence of the effects of decolonization in both the French and British empires.

We can focus most effectively on the *components* of hypothesis 3, which was disconfirmed with a finding of no *net overall* difference between the 1938–1954 and 1938–1963 fits. Political change on the Eurasian continent did have trade-diverting effects, though not enormous ones. The basic continuity despite the communization of Eastern Europe is evident in the very high indices of agreement (.76 and .87) between the original Central Europe and that labelled Eastern Europe in the later years. But it is also true that the 1938–1954 fit is the weaker of the two, and the end of Stalinist autarchy by the 1960s is reflected in the movement back nearer the 1938 pattern. Several non-Communist countries, states that had conducted quite a bit of trade with Central and Eastern Europe in 1938 (notably Egypt) had by 1963 restored many of their earlier bonds with the area.

Secondly, the effects of decolonization are also evident. The French Union (Community) shows very high continuity over the entire period; nevertheless there is real slippage between 1954 and 1963 as ties, formerly politically imposed rather than based on firm economic interest, were allowed to atrophy by newly sovereign states. The British Empire (Commonwealth) shows less impressive continuity in any case, but the fractionation of the 1950s and early 1960s is still apparent. In the 1954 analysis there was only one grouping clearly

Table 5-3

Indices of Agreement between "Choosers" as Measured with 1938 Trade Factors and Factors Defining "Choosers" for 1954 and 1963

1954	←→	1938	←→	1963
North and Central America	.71	North and Central America	.66	North and Central America
South America	.40	South America	.63	South America
Commonwealth	.66	British Empire	.59	British Caribbean
(Middle East	.38)	Africa	.70	Commonwealth
French Community	.82	French Union	.73	French Community
North Atlantic	.58	Northern Europe	.67	Western Europe
Eastern Europe	.76	Central Europe	.87	Eastern Europe
Middle East	.67	Middle East	.58	Arabs
Asia	.76	Asia	.69	Asia

identifiable with the British Commonwealth; in 1963 there were two. But as we have noted there were also two in 1938, since the small Africa grouping had a heavy component of British colonies. It is likely that the immediate postwar international monetary situation helped temporarily to knit the Commonwealth together as an economic unit.

The effects of wartime and postwar economic disruption on the trade of the Western European states also show up here. In the 1954 analysis there was no limited group identifiable with Northern or Western Europe, only a larger "North Atlantic" cluster in which the United States and Canada played major roles. Europe's postwar dollar shortage problem stemmed, after all, from a need for too many imports from the United States; North America was virtually the only supplier of many manufactured goods that were essential to European recovery. Trade across the North Atlantic was substantial though European exports to the Dollar Area were not sufficient to pay for as many imports as the Europeans wanted. The consequence of this difficulty, however, was a set of tight restrictions on "unessential" trade imports that had to be paid for in dollars. Trade with the *rest* of the Western Hemisphere therefore was reduced well below its prewar levels, and where possible European nations developed new sources of tropical products in their colonies (e.g., tobacco and coffee in British Africa). We can see this both in the existence of the 1954 North Atlantic grouping and in the changes that took place in the South America factor. In 1938 the South America group was very large, in fact including quite a number of European nations. By 1954 it became a small group of only seven states—six geographic South Americans and the Philippines (also in the Dollar Area). But in 1963 the South American group had enlarged to include a few Europeans, and much more nearly resembled the prewar cluster (and the Philippines had dropped out). Yet it still did not include as many West Europeans as before, suggesting a permanent loss of access as a result of the temporary dollar shortage. In addition, intra-European trade grew greatly between 1954 and 1963 (by a factor of four within the EEC) and Western Europe again became an interdependent trading area fairly distinct from North and South America.

For the other groups, continuity is the primary feature. Over the 25-year period the Asia factor changed relatively little; the Middle Eastern group also was quite constant except for an increasing tendency, over time, for it to narrow down to a set of ties among *Arab* states, leaving out non-Arabs like Iran and Turkey on the periphery, not to mention Romania and Kenya. The other very notable change in the Middle East is of course the shift in Palestine's linkages. In 1938 the Palestine mandate was at the core of Middle Eastern trade; by 1963 Israel was isolated from the Arab Middle East and joined instead to Western Europe. Israel's isolation from the Arabs is obvious, but Palestine's previous integration with the area is less widely appreciated, and may in large part explain the Arabs' sense of injury and loss.

Substantial continuity is also apparent in North and Central America. The major observable difference there is a widening of the group to include by 1963 all six of the Central American states (probably as a result of the Central American Common Market) and, on the periphery, Venezuela and Colombia. The division of the Western Hemisphere into rather separate Northern and Southern components, formalized recently in the creation of both CACM and LAFTA, can actually be traced back many decades.

In conclusion, let us return to the finding of surprising continuity over the entire 25-year period. There are essentially the *same* trading groups, and the same *number* of groups (nine in both 1938 and 1963, eight in 1954). There is no discernible long-run trend toward a merging of trading groups or the fissioning of existing ones. The globe has become neither more splintered nor more concentrated into fewer tightly interacting groups. In *International Regions and the International System*, my study of changes over the 1954–1963 decade, I remarked about the glacial pace at which patterns of international interaction changed. This longer look, even though it spans a period of immense political system change, confirms and strengthens the earlier finding. Trading relationships are rooted in long-term habits, preferences, and expectations. And this inertia reinforces the imperfections of the international market. Over a wide range of products, the degree to which one nation's products will willingly be substituted for another's is seriously limited. Some of the causes of these imperfections are doubtless political. And as economic bonds in turn condition political choice, the long-term continuity of trading groups suggests important underlying forces for the continuity of international political ties.

6

The Asia Rimland as a "Region" for Containing China

THE COMMON DEFENSE OF NON-COMMUNIST ASIA

By any of the traditional criteria of national power China is the strongest nation on the Asian mainland, superior in military potential to any of its neighbors. To try to prevent the piecemeal subjugation of a number of smaller nations United States policy makers have implicitly or explicitly guaranteed the security of most non-Communist Asian states, whether by limited military aid and tacit assurances (India), bilateral treaties (Japan, Taiwan), multilateral pacts (SEATO), or the active commitment of large numbers of American ground troops (South Korea and South Vietnam). Most of these acts, however, are regarded not as permanent measures but only as more or less temporary expedients, to be superseded in time by the efforts and local resources of the Asian nations themselves. Sometimes, as at present, that goal seems to fade into the distant future, but Americans nevertheless look forward with much hope and some confidence to the day when, at the minimum, Vietnamese type involvements can be avoided without leaving the way clear to the further spread of Chinese influence.

In principle, local resources are not unimpressive. A rimland arc of non-Communist nations runs from Afghanistan through India, Southeast Asia, and the East Indies, and up to Taiwan, Korea, and Japan. Combined, these states possess military forces and total population half again as large as China's

Reprinted from *Public Policy XVI*, John Montgomery and Albert Hirschman, editors (Cambridge: Harvard University Press, 1967).

and a gross national product more than twice that of China.[1] If they could act together, with a coordinated foreign policy on the most crucial matters, they doubtless could, by their own efforts and without the active assistance of European or Western Hemisphere powers, achieve the containment if not the outright defeat of Communist China.[2] The rub, of course, is precisely in the requirement for common action and coordination, since even together the margin is not impressive and singly no nation is quite a match for the Peking regime. With the advantages of topography and a defensive stance India or Japan might possibly hold off a Chinese attack on itself, but would not alone be able to give sufficiently effective aid to a smaller state. For the latter, a coalition or perhaps even a formal alliance is required, and the coalition must include at the very least two of these three: India, Japan, and virtually all the major states of Southeast Asia. Actually just two of these components alone would be able to produce only a very marginal and precarious superiority; long-term prospects of reasonable success probably demand the inclusion of all three elements. The individual units by themselves are too weak, and only a fairly large number of nations acting together can make this experiment in collective security work. (See Table 6-1.)

Table 6-1
Some Indices of Relative National Strength in Asia, 1966

	Population (in millions)	Total GNP (in billions of dollars)	Military personnel (in thousands)
India	495	28	879
Japan	98	64	246
Taiwan	13	3	544
South Korea	29	3	572
Pakistan	113	10	278
Indonesia	105	10	352
Other non-Communist Asia	159	24	840
Total non-Communist Asia	1,012	144	3,711
Mainland China	700	55	3,486
North Korea and North Vietnam	30	4	624

This is not to imply that the Chinese challenge to the rest of Asia is exclusively military, or that the threat of war should be or has been the sole or ulti-

---

[1] The data, given in more detail in Table 6-1, are from Institute for Strategic Studies, *The Military Balance, 1966–67* (London: Institute for Strategic Studies, 1966); and also from Bruce M. Russett et al., *World Handbook of Political and Social Indicators* (New Haven: Yale University Press, 1964); and United Nations, *Statistical Yearbook, 1965* (New York: United Nations, 1966). Some figures are but general estimates.

[2] For an imaginative if not wholly convincing treatment of the relative strength of various combinations of forces in Asia, see David S. Neft," Macrogeography and the Realms of Influence in Asia," *Journal of Conflict Resolution*, V, 3 (1961), pp. 254–73.

mate concern of regional activity. Economic and political cooperation among the non-Communist Asian nations might well strengthen even relatively small groups of states, like those in the Mekong basin, against various kinds of external pressures. But resistance to such pressures is especially difficult in the shadow of long-term military danger, even in the absence of a direct threat of violence. In this chapter we shall discuss some of the conditions for success in long-term coordination of foreign policy among independent nations, and will explore—with some rather depressing conclusions—the degree to which these conditions are, and are likely to be, fulfilled along the Asian rimlands.

REGIONS AND ALLIANCES

In the 1950s United States foreign policy was diagnosed as suffering from a severe case of "pactomania." That disease may now be largely cured, but it has been succeeded by a related affliction, "regionitis." Policy makers originally tried to constitute a number of military alliances, each focused on a particular geographic area but including one or more of the major Western powers. As instruments for militarily containing the Soviet Union, these alliances were fairly adequate, but much less so in a broader political sense or as directed against China. More recent attempts have gone to functional groupings still regionally focused but ostensibly directed to nonmilitary problems, primarily economic development and integration. Quite explicitly the architects of these organizations hope, by avoiding overt military commitments, to include neutralist states that would not otherwise join. But for Americans, at least, it is clear that these groupings have a double purpose, and this is especially true of the activities in Southeast Asia. They hope that these functional efforts will in time develop into areas of regional solidarity capable of providing, at least implicitly, a basis for collective defense and containment. The goal has not changed as much as has the public appearance of the instrument. And the existence of common interests in these areas still is often assumed as much as it is examined; simple geographical proximity is thought to provide the basis.

The literature on regional description and delineation is immense; I have attempted to review some of it elsewhere.[3] It has intellectual roots and counterparts in material applied to regions within a country (e.g., the American "South") as well as to regions of the world. The term is used with a wide variety of not always rigorous meanings, but most commonly it applies either to *nodal* or to *homogeneous* regions.[4]

A homogeneous region is simply one where the various subunits (or nations in this instance) are similar in the characteristics considered relevant. Such

[3] Bruce M. Russett, *International Regions and the International System* (Chicago: Rand McNally, 1967), especially Chapter 1.

[4] Cf. Brian J. L. Berry and Thomas D. Hankins, *A Bibliographic Guide to the Economic Regions of the United States* (Chicago: University of Chicago, Department of Geography, 1963).

characteristics are invariably the result of arbitrary choice, but commonly include social structure, political system, culture, race, and perhaps average income level, language, and religion. *How similar* is a tricky problem seldom tackled with precision, but it is generally agreed that the subunits should be more like each other than like units left outside of the grouping. Whether they have to be very similar to *every* unit in the group, or merely to some mean or average, varies with the user.

A nodal region, on the other hand, is a spatial system defined by patterns of communication or transaction; in the strict sense it is merely an area all the subunits of which are joined at least to a central point or node—the hub of a rail network, or of a metropolitan newspaper which is diffused to the provinces. More generally, but also more demandingly, it may mean a group of subunits which all are interconnected with each other fairly directly and not only through some central switchboard. As the first usage connotes an axle with spokes, the second is the full wheel including the rim, or even better, a spider web.

A further variation in using the term region may merely signify a geographical area with some physical distinctiveness, or a unit—a continent perhaps—but for scientific or policy purposes it is likely to be less useful than one which employs, instead or in addition, some of the above social phenomena. In any case, for reasons which are not hard to theorize about, there is often substantial correspondence between nodal or homogeneous regions and areas of geographical propinquity. Furthermore, in international relations nodal and homogeneous regions frequently encompass much the same territory. Some of this will be clear from the illustration below. The major exception is the *empire*, which may be geographically dispersed and very heterogeneous, but with components joined by institutional and economic bonds. What remains of both the British Commonwealth and the French Union tends to fit this pattern, except that the transactional links look much like the axle and spokes for the Commonwealth, and more like the spider web for the former French territories.[5]

Political acts do not occur in an environmental vacuum. Whether one feels more at home intellectually with the "limits of foreign policy" viewpoint of C. B. Marshall, the Sprouts' "environmental possibilism," or the interdisciplinary "unified science" approach of the general systems theorists,[6] most observers agree that effective political choice depends heavily upon social and economic conditions, as well as on technological ones. Such conditions may not *determine* the political outcome, but they set the limits within which political choice can be made. Sometimes they may make it virtually impossible

---

[5] For this distinction and an illustration of a shift from the former to the latter pattern in Colonial America, see Richard L. Merritt, *The Growth of American Community* (New Haven: Yale University Press, 1966).

[6] Cf., respectively, C. B. Marshall, *The Limits of Foreign Policy* (New York: Henry Holt, 1954); Harold and Margaret Sprout, *The Ecological Perspective on Human Affairs* (Princeton: Princeton University Press, 1965); and many of the articles in *General Systems: Yearbook of the Society for General Systems Research*, Vols. I–XI (1955–1966).

for a national policy maker to reverse his associations or alliances (even if President deGaulle wished to do it, could he actually take France out of the Common Market?), or more often, to create an association when the environmental conditions are absent (it takes more than President Nasser's fond desire to bring about an Arab union).

INFORMATION AND ALLIANCES

The regional approach is a useful one precisely because it identifies some of the conditions that seem to be essential to the long-run coordination of national policies implied by either a formal or tacit alliance. At base it comes down to the requirement for information as the essential—though not sufficient—condition for cooperative policy. Without information about conditions or consequences, action involves risk: without information about another's preferences and perceptions, one can hardly coordinate action with the other. The independent actions of two parties will be the same, or compatible, only if their independent preferences and perceptions happen to be identical or compatible. Good but ignorant intentions are unlikely to suffice. Tacit communication requires different kinds of channels than does the explicit variety, yet channels for observing the other's behavior must still exist. Information is not always dependent upon current communication, since it may be stored from previous experience. But stored information is of little use in dealing with changes in the environment.

> A large continuous flow of information makes it possible to mobilize the requisite experience and data quickly ... it may also bring the anticipated crisis to the attention of the decision makers sooner than would otherwise occur. Large flows of information ... make it possible to reduce the chances of blundering into international conflicts.[7]

This is not to say, of course, that information alone is enough. Information increases interdependence; it is a necessary ingredient for antagonism as well as for cooperation.

Creators of alliances usually recognize these points. Having established that their nations share certain interests in common—perhaps they perceive another power as a threat to both of them—they seek to construct conditions that will magnify the flow of information between them, and perhaps also to create additional common interests on other issues. The architects of NATO, for example, did not rest content with a mere declaration to defend each other

---

[7] Richard L. Meier, "Information, Resources, and Economic Growth," in *National Resources and Economic Growth*, J. J. Spengler, editor (Washington, D. C.: Resources for the Future, Inc., 1961). Quincy Wright in his *The Study of International Relations* (New York: Appleton-Century Crofts, 1955) has declared flatly, "Considering all its aspects, communication can be studied as central in all the social sciences. . . . The study of communication is more fundamental than the study of power or of trade because it is the condition for both." Cf. also the excellent theoretical statement by Steven J. Brams, "Flow and Form in the International System" (unpublished Ph.D. dissertation, Northwestern University, 1966).

from external attack. They built numerous institutions for military coordination and the exchange of information; exchanges among service personnel and the creation of institutions like the NATO War College helped produce common values and perceptions. President Kennedy's "Grand Design" for an Atlantic Community had as its keystone the promotion of commercial exchange among the member states; his Trade Expansion Act was intended to have profound political as well as economic effects. Other institutions for the coordination of policy have grown up in a variety of domains: sometimes they are explicitly political like the Benelux caucusing group in the United Nations General Assembly, or, more remotely, they promote public health or commercial advantage, linked only secondarily to the common defense as well. It is arguable that the failure to build more and stronger institutions for the entire NATO area in the 1950s was responsible for the divergent interests that surfaced at the beginning of the 1960s.[8]

Below we must set out just a bit more of the theory behind these statements. The basic outlook is not so very different from elements common to the position of such writers on the theory of international integration as Deutsch, Etzioni, Haas, and Jacob, notable parts of whose thought derived from Wright and from a broad spectrum of social scientists, both current and classical.[9] Physical proximity, for example, is certainly associated with the exchange of information and, *ceteris paribus*, promotes it. It is widely acknowledged that communication tends to be greatest between units that are near each other.[10] But other things—physical and social barriers and channels for communication—are not usually equal, and one must look, in addition, at other factors.

MEASURES OF HOMOGENEITY AND INTERDEPENDENCE

In a longer study cited previously[11] I sought to identify clusters of countries throughout the world by four major sociopolitical criteria, two of which led

---

[8] A much better job was done in building primarily European institutions, especially continental ones. I have developed some of these arguments at greater length in Chapter 12 of this book and in my *Community and Contention: Britain and America in the Twentieth Century* (Cambridge: M.I.T. Press, 1963).

[9] E.g., Karl W. Deutsch et al., *Political Community and the North Atlantic Area* (Princeton: Princeton University Press, 1957); Amitai Etzioni, "The Epigenesis of Political Communities at the International Level," *American Journal of Sociology*, XXVIII, 3 (1963), pp. 407–21, and *Political Unification* (New York: Holt, Rinehart and Winston, 1965); Ernst Haas, *The Uniting of Europe* (Stanford: Stanford University Press, 1957), and "The Challenge of Regionalism," *International Organization*, XII, 3 (1958), pp. 440–8; Philip E. Jacob and Henry Teune, "The Integrative Process: Guidelines for the Analysis of the Bases of Political Community," in *The Integration of Political Communities*, Philip E. Jacob and James Toscano, editors (Philadelphia: Lippincott, 1964); and Quincy Wright, *A Study of War* (2 vols.; Chicago: University of Chicago Press, 1942). See also Chapter 18 of this volume.

[10] E.g., Bernard Berelson and Gary A. Steiner, *Human Behavior: An Inventory of Scientific Findings* (New York: Harcourt, Brace and World, 1964), p. 349; and James G. March and Herbert A. Simon, *Organizations* (New York: Wiley, 1958), pp. 128–9.

[11] Russett, *International Regions and the International System*.

essentially to nodal groupings, and the other two of which were more useful for finding homogeneous groups.

One of the criteria was simply groups of nations that were heavily interdependent economically, nations which accounted through foreign trade for a higher portion of each other's national income than did states outside the grouping. The measure was trade between the pair (exports plus imports) expressed as a percentage of the gross domestic product (GDP) of each.

A second criterion required a search for groups of nations that were politically interdependent, in the sense that each nation belonged to a large number of international organizations along with the governments of the others. The organizations themselves covered the complete range of intergovernmental institutions, from military alliances to customs unions to commodity marketing organizations, and to institutions devoted to fostering health, disease control, communications, and cultural exchange.

The third set comprised nations which exhibited similar political behavior on a wide variety of issues in international politics. The measure employed was simply the frequency with which nations voted together in the UN General Assembly across the entire spectrum of issues before that organization—not just the Cold War, but problems of colonial liquidation in Africa, the desired role of the United Nations itself, and a number of less frequent concerns. Strictly speaking, it was a measure only of the behavior of governments, not national attitudes on the issues in question; but such a study over a decade and a half has revealed remarkable stability in nations' positions on these issues, despite changes of governmental personality, party, and, within limits, even of regime.

The remaining grouping criterion was of nations which were similar across four major sociocultural dimensions, taken together. Two of these dimensions were essentially cultural (one concerned with the basic domestic political system, and the other addressed to religious or theological orientations); the other two were more nearly directed to broad aspects of the structure of social systems (economic development and land use patterns).

In this study it was argued that foreign trade serves as a channel of communication which brings to those who engage in it a variety of ideas and information to which they would otherwise not be exposed. Several other studies have demonstrated that commercial contacts result in changed attitudes, frequently in the direction of greater understanding and sympathy for the needs, broadly defined, of people in the other nation.[12] Furthermore, it gives the trader a material stake in conditions in the other nation. Sometimes this may merely mean exploitation (or perceived exploitation) if the stake is conceived in narrow immediate terms, but it is unlikely if the relationship is at all symmetrical; that is, if mutual trade does not represent an extraordinarily

---

[12] Daniel Lerner, "French Business Leaders Look at EDC," *Public Opinion Quarterly*, XX, 1 (1956), pp. 212–21; Russett, *Community and Contention*, Chapter 9; Raymond A. Bauer, Ithiel de Sola Pool, and Lewis Anthony Dexter, *American Business and Public Policy* (New York: Atherton Press, 1964) suggest a rather more complicated interaction.

greater share of the income of one nation in the pair than of the other, problems of felt exploitation are seldom major. They are most likely to arise between a metropolitan state and a small or poor colony, and are much less serious between economic and political equals.

There are cases of diverse economic size in Asia (as great as between Japan or India and Laos), but all the states now have a common political status; and the economic differences, though great, are much less than between, for example, the United States and the republics of Central America. Mutual trade as a proportion of the total income or product of each state thus gives us an indirect approximate measure of the size of interest groups which can serve as information channels, and which, from another viewpoint, can be mobilized to buttress mutually beneficial decisions. Like the point about favorable attitudes and understanding, there are some important *ceteris paribus* qualifications that need to be entered, but our restricted focus here, on independent Asian nations, avoids some problems that otherwise might be more pressing.

Like foreign trade, common membership in international organizations is no panacea ensuring that nations will be able successfully to coordinate their behavior and pursue mutually rewarding goals. One can certainly point to cases where the institutions have been ineffectual and essentially irrelevant or, in some instances, where the joint membership has produced or deepened conflicts that would not otherwise have arisen. Common institutions, notably the common federal government, made salient to the American North and South two major disputes—over slavery and the tariff—that would have been much less relevant to the relations between separate nations. In a less severe way intergovernmental organizations can have the same kind of effect. But again, as with trade, the theoretical argument is not that common institutions suffice to promote policy cooperation, nor that they may even do the opposite sometimes. Instead the argument is that for nations that are already interdependent and whose governments *want* to cooperate, institutions become an element of the necessary conditions. An institution can be described as essentially a set of channels for processing information, solving problems, and transmitting communications. And along with their more manifest functions, they may serve in latent ways to further cooperation by promoting new perspectives, common loyalties, and personal friendships among the participants.[13]

As to similarity of political behavior (especially to the degree it manifests similar and not just compatible goals and values) and similar social and cultural patterns, the evidence is more clear-cut and better accepted. The grounds for scepticism are obvious enough—both parties may value something

---

[13] Cf. Leon Lindberg, *The Political Dynamics of European Economic Integration* (Stanford: Stanford University Press, 1963), p. 9; and Chadwick F. Alger, "Non-Resolution Consequences of the United Nations and Their Effect on International Conflict," *Journal of Conflict Resolution*, V, 2 (1961), pp. 128–45, and "Personal Contact in Intergovernmental Organizations," in *International Behavior: A Social Psychological Analysis*, Herbert C. Kelman, editor (New York: Holt, Rinehart and Winston, 1965). This theme is strong in the sociology literature. Cf. Robert Merton, *Social Theory and Social Structure* (Glencoe: The Free Press, 1957), pp. 60–64.

only one of them can have—but so are the grounds for the more positive arguments. Despite Shaw's witticism about the common language and the dangers of taking ease of communication for granted, surely information is transferred more readily between individuals who share similar experiences, outlooks, and cultural patterns than between those who do not.

Sometimes the causal chain can become quite complex. George Homans, for instance, in dealing with small groups, explains that interaction is likely to lead to similarity both in sentiments and in activities.[14] Furthermore, the causal chain need not always proceed from interaction, to similar sentiments, to common activities; the last may also promote the others, and a feedback cycle, in which it may be virtually impossible to identify the initial spark which set off the process, is not at all uncommon. Homans in fact built his entire theory on just this principle of reciprocal causation.[15]

This mutually reinforcing relation between similarity and interaction helps explain, therefore, the substantial congruence that is found empirically between international groupings identified by homogeneity, and nodal groupings characterized by substantial interdependence. We can push the conclusion yet further: For sustained long-term cooperation among states, *both* conditions must be present in significant degree. To some extent perhaps commercial intercourse can substitute for formal institutions, or both for cultural similarities, but we would expect the substitutability to have its limits. Each of these different channels contributes somewhat different information to different points in the political system. Unfortunately there is so little solid reliable evidence on the subject that we simply cannot say with any confidence what kinds and amounts of substitution are possible. We can, however, assert the converse proposition with rather more assurance: The long-term prospects for cooperation among states that share substantial trade, institutional bonds, common political orientations, and basic social and cultural similarities should be better than for states sharing only three or fewer of these bonds.

CURRENT ASIAN GROUPINGS

A further question—*how much* of each of these four criteria is "enough"—remains and will vex us again in the discussion below. For the moment we shall turn to a limited mapping exercise, the results of a quest for a group of

---

[14] George C. Homans, *The Human Group* (New York: Harcourt, Brace, 1950), passim., especially p. 120.

[15] Similar points of view are shared by authors in many disciplines. For example, sociologist Amos Hawley, in *Human Ecology: A Theory of Community Structure* (New York: Ronald Press, 1950), pp. 3 ff. describes his approach to "the world of life as a system of dynamic interdependence"; psychologist Kurt Lewin develops a field theory of interdependence in *Field Theory in Social Science* (New York: Harper, 1951); and geographer Brian J. L. Berry shares this conception as applied to problems of regional differentiation and is currently analyzing data on India to provide a rigorous test with a mathematical model. See his *Essays on Commodity Flows and the Spatial Structure of the Indian Economy* (Chicago: University of Chicago, Department of Geography, Research Paper No. 111, 1966).

Asian states where the within-group bonds are numerous compared with those between members and nonmembers.[16] The procedures were entirely inductive, and not constrained by any requirements for producing a group of nations that was, in the language of legislative districting, compact and contiguous. (Hence they are what geographers call "regional types" rather than regions.) I merely put together separate sets of data, one for each of the four criteria, on roughly one hundred sovereign nations and major colonies in the world. Each of these sets of data was analyzed by a computer directed to identify those clusters with relatively dense within-group bonds; generally a cluster was found for Western Europe (or a wider Western Community), one for Eastern Europe, one or more for Latin America, and often one for the Middle East and one or more each for Africa and Asia. Overall the boundaries for excluding and including countries varied rather substantially, and more so for Asia than for most other geographical areas.

The complete analyses were extensive and are presented in the longer study; here we shall merely look at those groupings that can be identified post hoc as containing a large number of Asian states. By looking at each set successively we then can see what aggregate of Asian states hangs together on all four criteria.[17] To a degree this overview, drawn as it is from a worldwide focus and oblivious to some of the finer details, will seem rather presumptuous and possibly naive to a regional specialist, but in fact I think the two perspectives complement rather than compete with each other.

The data are for the late 1950s and early 1960s. Table 6-2 shows the grouping by each of the four criteria. The countries are listed in descending order of the clarity with which they can be identified with the group; those at the bottom are most marginal. All of the sixteen states are listed for reference, but those italicized at the bottom did *not* make the grouping.

Strikingly, and in no way predetermined by the procedures, it is clear that on three of the four criteria there is a single grouping that accounts for the majority of Asian nations. This is most obvious for trade and international organization membership, where in each case there was only one group which included many Asian states, and that group numbers thirteen of the sixteen. Afghanistan and Nepal are absent from both. Both states are landlocked and physically isolated; neither carries on much intercourse with Asia or with the wider world in general. Cambodia, while belonging to some of the Asian regional organizations, directs most of its trade elsewhere. Most importantly, it still maintains substantial commerce with France and with several other

---

[16] This is not to say, for instance, that trade interdependence between a given Asian nation and one or two states outside the group may not be as high or higher than that between it and the group—only that no nonmember is highly interdependent with several of the members.

[17] A few non-Asian nations found their way into each of the groupings to be presented; however, no state, other than the sixteen non-Communist nations in the arc from Afghanistan to Japan, appeared in a grouping defined by more than two of the four criteria. Hence, for clarity, we shall eliminate from present consideration all countries other than the sixteen, even though they were examined in the initial stages of the analysis.

Table 6-2

A Core Group of South and East Asian Nations Emerges on All Criteria

Economic transactions	International organizations	Social cultural homogeneity	National political behavior (UN)	
Malaysia	Thailand	India	Afghanistan	Thailand
Thailand	India	Malaysia	Indonesia	Malaysia
South Vietnam	Pakistan	Thailand	India	Pakistan
Taiwan	Philippines	South Korea	Burma	Philippines
Philippines	Burma	Burma	Cambodia	
Japan	Ceylon	Taiwan	Ceylon	
Indonesia	Malaysia	Ceylon	Nepal*	
Burma	South Vietnam	Indonesia	Laos*	
Laos	Indonesia	Pakistan		*South Korea‡*
South Korea	Japan	[Afghanistan]†		*South Vietnam‡*
Ceylon	Cambodia	[South Vietnam]†		*Japan*
Pakistan	South Korea	[Laos]†		*Taiwan*
India	Laos	[Cambodia]†		
Afghanistan	*Afghanistan*	[Nepal]†		
Nepal	*Nepal*	*Philippines*		
Cambodia	*Taiwan*	*Japan*		

†No firm data, but would probably be included if appropriate information were available.
*Very marginal membership in group.
‡Not UN members; hence no data. Probably would vote like Taiwan (not a member of an Asian grouping) but might behave more like SEATO members.

former French colonies. Taiwan (Nationalist China) carries on a brisk trade in South and East Asia, but is politically something of a pariah. Unlike the Peking government it at least was represented in the major universal institutions like the UN, but most of those organizations set up to deal with Asian cultural, economic, or security matters have excluded both Chinas.

There also is a single grouping as defined by the set of social and cultural criteria, though one or two caveats must be entered. The first is fairly trivial: There simply were insufficient data available on five countries for them to be included in the formal analysis. On the basis of what is known about these societies and the others, however, it seems unlikely that they are much more different from the first nine states than the nine differ among themselves. Tentatively, then, I included them, but have enclosed the names in brackets to indicate the more subjective nature of the decision.

The second caveat is more critical, and involves some limitatons in the original choice of dimensions which do not necessarily allow results most relevant for a study of Asian groupings. These dimensions are more appropriate for worldwide analysis, and the most serious problems arise with regard to the religious factor. Essentially, this dimension distinguished between predominantly Christian and non-Christian states, and it accounts for the absence of the Philippines from this group. The Christian–non-Christian distinction is in fact an extremely important and pervasive one, going as it does beyond religion to basic Western–non-Western cultural differences. I would contend that the gulf between values and behavior in the Philippines and elsewhere in Asia is indeed both deep and broad; it involves not only religion but the predominance, exclusively in the Philippines, of Western languages and the relative success (rare though not limited exclusively to those islands) of representative democracy. I think these distinctions are more important than those between the Moslem and Buddhist or Hindu states of Asia. At the same time the latter are surely very great also, and one must bear fully in mind how heterogeneous this remaining "homogeneous" grouping really is. It is a point to which we shall return shortly.

In the United Nations, however, two distinct groupings, each containing Asian members, were apparent. The larger identifies states associated with the broader Afro-Asian neutralist group. As other analyses have shown, these nations are anticolonial and vote often with the Communist countries on strictly Cold War issues (while they retain very different perspectives from the Communists as to the role the organization should play in international politics). The smaller group comprises states that are not much less anti-colonial than the chief Afro-Asian cluster but generally agree with the NATO powers on Cold War issues. They tend to vote with a larger grouping that incorporates most of the Latin American countries (not listed here). Japan and Taiwan are even more dependable, for the West, on Cold War issues, and in addition tend to support the "northern powers" on those colonial questions that do not isolate the Europeans too drastically. In a sense these two states could be considered marginal members of the West-oriented Asian group, and this ambiguous status is indicated by their listing in that column even though their names are italicized. The divided states of Korea and Vietnam are of course not UN members, but if they were it is likely that they would be sufficiently sympathetic to, and dependent upon, the United States to behave much like Nationalist China.

A NON-COMMUNIST ASIAN "CORE"

Across the four criteria, eight states appear on all, though their UN position split the eight into two groups with different political orientations. India, Indonesia, Burma, Ceylon, and, marginally, Laos, the "neutralist" Afro-Asians, appear on each of the first three lists, as do Thailand, Malaysia, and Pakistan, the "pro-Western" Asians. In addition, Cambodia, the Philippines, South Korea, and South Vietnam make three of the four lists. Cambodia is politically associated with the neutralists; and the Philippines, South Korea, and South Vietnam are likely to be rather sympathetic with the pro-Western Asians, though perhaps the divided states would be even more closely tied to the NATO powers. Afghanistan, Nepal, Taiwan, and Japan are each absent from two criteria. Afghanistan and Nepal are relatively small and unimportant; together they account for less than three percent of the population, industry, or military forces of the rimland states. They have some strategic significance for the defense of India against conventional land attack, but little more.

Taiwan's isolation produces a rather more serious gap. Though small in population (about twelve million), with South Korea it supports one of the largest and best trained and equipped military establishments in the area. While its anti-Communist orientation is hardly to be doubted for the reasonable future, its lack of ties with other states could substantially reduce the possibilities for utilizing effectively its resources for joint action. Despite the Western desire to utilize more Asian troops in the South Vietnam war, for instance; despite the presence there of large numbers of Korean soldiers; and despite the availability of several divisions of Nationalist Chinese troops, no use of these forces was contemplated. The reasons, of course, are well known and substantial, but they do illustrate barriers to employing this potential resource. Perhaps Taiwan's isolation from many joint efforts will have to continue as long as the fiction that Taipeh governs China continues. A two-Chinas policy, aimed at recognizing facts and integrating "little China" into non-Communist Southeast Asia, would have a great deal to recommend it.

The absence of Taiwan from collective efforts may be regrettable, but it will seldom be critical. Japan's isolation is much more likely to deserve the latter description. Allowing for some margin of error in the data, its total GNP is at least as large, and probably greater than, mainland China's; and as a major industrial power and the world's fourth largest steel producer, it could make an enormous contribution to common Asian enterprises. But it is precisely its wealth and industrialization that accounts for much of the social distance between Japan and its neighbors. Its income level and, hence, patterns of production, consumption, and living, are much nearer the average of Western Europe than of Asia. This is the reason Japan did not fall within even the very mixed area of social and cultural "homogeneity" occupied by most other Asian states. It has joined many of the international organizations formed by the developed states, and is the only nation outside the North Atlantic area to join the Organization for Economic Cooperation and Development (OECD). The underdeveloped countries increasingly share the perception of Japan as not one of them and frequently exclude her from their deliberations, as at the June 1964 UN Conference on Trade and Development.[18] Japanese policy makers are not very happy with this situation, and would prefer to retain a foot in either camp. Their activity in helping to create a new regional organization, the Asia and Pacific Council (ASPAC), reflects this concern. Some of their isolation too is a consequence of World War II and its aftermath, which cut Japan off from its neighbors. In the past few years they have recovered

---

[18] Cf. Saburo Okita, "Japan and the Developing Nations," *Contemporary Japan*, XXIII, 2 (1965), pp. 1–14.

their membership in most local international organizations and greatly expanded their economic activities in Southeast Asia, but the task is not yet complete.

A question to be asked about the majority of Asian states, those that appeared on all or all but one of the lists, is how seriously the *political* division, manifested in the United Nations by the split between neutral and Western-allied Asians, should be taken. Some flexibility and shifting does go on. India and especially Indonesia have, as a result of international and domestic events respectively, notably moderated their anti-American policies. Many Indians now regard themselves as America's allies, in a limited and tacit way to be sure, against China. Pakistan, starting from the pro-Western side, has moved appreciably toward a neutralist position, particularly with respect to China. It is also true, however, that the split has often hindered cooperation in the past, and is unlikely to disappear. Despite the shifting, no state has yet actually moved from one side to the other, only toward middle positions. Perhaps over the long run a gradual convergence of the now distinct groups can be anticipated.

If one is willing to discount the long-term gravity of the present political division, there is a group of Asian nations, joined by a variety of bonds, that is rather interdependent and has built up a number of channels for transmitting information among them. Japan and Taiwan, however, are distinctly marginal to this group, and their absence would very severely jeopardize the power position of any attempted tacit or formal Asian non-Communist alliance. Equally serious is the qualification pertaining to the absolute strength of those bonds, one that goes beyond the question of whether the relative strength is greater within Asia than between Asians and non-Asians, or between Communist and non-Communist Asians.

DISTINCT, BUT HOW COHESIVE?

The problem of cohesiveness first appeared with the identification of a socially and culturally "homogeneous" grouping of Asian states. Even on a worldwide basis the groupings obtained from the larger study were homogeneous only in a relative sense. Clusters of similar size in the main study, for example, brought together most of Latin America in one, and Western Europe in another. It is apparent that the heterogeneity of the Asian cluster is much greater. In Western Europe the same alphabet and related languages are employed; religious differences among Protestants, Catholics, and even agnostics educated in the Judeo-Christian tradition are less deep than the divisions in Asia; and political institutions and cultures are, except for Spain and Portugal, not so terribly different across the non-Communist part of the continent. Compared with this, Asia's uniformity is slight indeed.

The level of unity implied by trade ties and international organizations is also deceptive; the links are much less numerous in Asia than in several other

Table 6-3

Institutional and Economic Bonds Are Relatively Sparse among Asian Nations

Intragroup trade as percent of GDP (1963)		Number of common memberships in international organizations (1962)	
Western Europe	20	Western Europe	75
Middle East	9	Latin America	42
Eastern Europe	7	Middle East	35
Non-Communist Asia	7	Non-Communist Asia	30
Africa	3	Eastern Europe	28
Latin America	2	Africa	20

regions, again notably in Western Europe. Table 6-3 summarizes the intragroup bonds for six such clusterings, showing the average level of intragroup trade as a percentage of GNP for each, and the number of international organizations to which the most deeply involved states belong in common with each of the others. (The figures apply to such centrally involved states as those of the European Six rather than to the more peripheral ones.)

The Asian grouping falls well down the rank orders in both columns, far below the example set by Western Europe. The networks of trading and of organizational memberships are far more dense in Western Europe than in non-Communist Asia, by an order of two to three times in each case. Even Eastern Europe, which used to be thought of as held together primarily by the threat of Soviet military force, does almost as well. And while commercial exchange among the Latin American countries is slight, the number of institutional bonds uniting them is fairly impressive. Most Asian nations may have more bonds with each other than with outsiders, but the achievement is not substantial compared with what has been accomplished in other parts of the world.[19]

Nor do the *consequences* of those bonds look very impressive. Among proximate nations which already have common interests and potential sources of conflict, one would suppose that bonds such as we have discussed would facilitate, if not inexorably produce, capabilities for preventing or controlling the outbreak of international violence. There have, in fact, been no deadly quarrels, however small, among the nations of continental Western Europe since the end of World War II, except for the conflict between the distinctly peripheral states of Greece and Turkey over Cyprus. The performances of

---

[19] For a similar conclusion see Michael Brecher, "International Relations and Asian Studies: The Subordinate State System of Southern Asia," *World Politics*, XV, 2 (1963), pp. 229–33. For a comparative assessment of the integrative output of certain institutions, see Robert W. Gregg, "The UN Regional Economic Commissions and Integration in Underdeveloped Regions," *International Organization*, XX, 2 (1966), pp. 208–32, who rates ECAFE lower than ECLA (Latin America) and not much above the far younger ECA (Africa).

Latin America and of Communist Eastern Europe are not quite so impressive, but even there only two clashes (a small one between Cuba and the Dominican Republic in 1959, and the bloody Hungarian uprising crushed by the Russians) have resulted in as many as one hundred fatalities.[20] Non-Communist Asia, however, has been jolted by three major clashes between India and Pakistan; a far from trivial guerrilla war waged by Indonesia against Malaysia; and numerous skirmishes, below the hundred deaths level, between others such as Pakistan and Afghanistan, and among the three states of Indochina. Likewise, on the positive side of cooperation and joint action, Asia looks weak by comparison with the other areas listed in Table 6-3. For example, it is the only area where there is no military alliance binding the parties against outside attack (though admittedly the Arab League looks better in word than in deed).

The absolute level of information-carrying capabilities among Asian nations is not high. Furthermore, in international relations these bonds grow slowly (as also they decay slowly, except in wartime or perhaps high crisis). For years in the early 1950s the same kind of analysis as produced Table 6-2 was performed for trade and institutional bonds and for UN voting patterns. The results were not notably dissimilar, showing essentially the same countries in the same positions. The only appreciable difference—perhaps a significant and important one—was the rise of Japan to a middle position in the 1963 trade and international organization groupings from a marginal spot in 1954. This return of Japan to what is probably its prewar level of peaceful involvement in the area should not be overlooked, even though on the other criteria the Japanese still lag behind.

COHESION PRODUCED BY EXTERNAL THREAT?

In other areas of the world an assiduous searcher can discover a fair number of cases where the individual countries may go their separate and even conflicting ways in "normal" times, yet with or without an overt alliance manage to submerge their differences in the face of a common interest in defense against an external threat. Well-documented examples go back at least to the Greek city-states and ancient Persia. But so too do instances of treachery and "Medizing" by Greeks with the "common" enemy. Certainly there is little evidence that mainland China is yet seen by the rimland states as a sufficiently threatening common enemy to produce unified resistance. To the contrary, the only military alliance in the area, SEATO, is weak, restricted in membership and scope, and utterly dependent upon the assistance of non-Asian powers. Some comments in the literature of social science suggest that if the threat were to grow the cohesion of an opposing coalition could be expected to counter it. Quincy Wright, for instance, concluded part of his massive empirical

---

[20] Russett, *International Regions and the International System*, Chapter 12.

and theoretical study with the words, "Human communities larger than the primary group have usually been organized by conquest, enlarged by more conquest, and integrated internally through the fear of foreign invasion."[21]

Surely the apparent passing of a threat can lead to the dissolution of an otherwise shaky coalition. Raymond Aron and Daniel Lerner decided that one of the most important reasons for the failure of the French Parliament to pass EDC was the seeming diminution in the external threat posed by the Soviet Union, and thus a reduction in the need for a tight European coalition. If not supported by underlying bonds, an alliance is a fragile thing.[22] Examples, from the American-British-Russian alliance during World War II to the recent experience of NATO, could be multiplied far beyond their utility in the absence of rigorous comparative study.

It would appear that an external threat often serves as a discriminating variable. Where the integration of a community of nations is already high, to the point that an external threat is seen by members of the group as a mutual danger and not a potential ally for one side in internal quarrels, it becomes a force that promotes further integration. A common cultural experience frequently promotes mutual identification, a sense of oneness against external pressures. But if the area is poorly integrated at the time the threat appears, the possibilities of securing such an external ally, or disagreements over priorities and the degree of necessity to cope with the threat, are likely to produce further disintegration. Karl Deutsch et al. concluded essentially this from their comparative study of historical cases, and Georg Simmel has declared, in a form that states the problem though it hardly points to prediction, "A state of conflict, however, pulls the members so tightly together and subjects them to such uniform impulse that they either must get completely along with, or completely repel, one another."[23] An important review of the theoretical and empirical literature on this point is that of Robert Hamblin. He produces limited but persuasive experimental evidence that even with the other necessary conditions a crisis or external threat increases a group's integration only if a cooperative solution to the crisis can be perceived; otherwise the group moves toward disintegration. Though the cooperative containment of China is a possibility, it is so tenuous a hope that other Asians may indeed not perceive it.[24]

It can be concluded from past experience that the prospects that most or all of the Asian nations bordering on China could unite to repel an attack on one

---

[21] Wright, *A Study of War*, p. 1038.

[22] Raymond Aron and Daniel Lerner, *France Defeats EDC* (New York: Praeger, 1957). Among many others, George Liska, *Nations in Alliance* (Baltimore: The Johns Hopkins University Press, 1962) has some useful comments on this matter.

[23] Deutsch et al., *Political Community;* and Georg Simmel, *Conflict and the Web of Group Affiliation*, K. H. Wolff and Reinhard Bendix, translators (Glencoe: The Free Press, 1955), p. 57.

[24] Robert Hamblin, "Group Integration During a Crisis," *Human Relations*, IX, 1 (1958), pp. 67–76.

of them look very slim indeed. A few, like the government of Prince Sihanouk in Cambodia, decided that the chances were slight and made the best arrangements they could with Peking. More have simply reached the conclusion that they are too poor to be able to afford a major conflict on the behalf of others, and they will rely on time, China's good intentions, or aid from the United States to repel any attack that should occur. Even should a coalition be put together, chances are that it would be temporary and easily broken, lasting only while the danger was most pressing and immediate, and subject to rapid melting during the first real or imagined thaw. Despite the fact that the potential power for the containment of China exists on the mainland and its offshore environs, the power would have to be put together by a diverse coalition made up of many disparate elements. Except in a world of superproliferation where many Asian states had nuclear weapons, the atomic and hydrogen bombs do not change this conclusion. The bonds and information-carrying capabilities among these nations seem now to be too weak to sustain the heavy and continuing weight that can be brought to bear on them.[25] American hopes for the future in Asia will have to built of less chimeral stuff than a regional all-Asian non-Communist coalition. Efforts can be begun in that direction— ASPAC is surely a first step—but it will be decades before they can be fulfilled in the dramatic and far-reaching manner desired.

If one believes that the threat of Chinese expansionism stems primarily from the revolutionary nature of the current Peking regime, one can, of course, hope for a mellowing and a decline in xenophobic zeal. If, on the other hand, one holds that the war proneness or instability of an international system depends more upon the number and relative size of the major actors within it, rather than upon domestic political conditions, the outlook is considerably less sanguine. So it is too if one clings to the domestic origins theory but feels that the Chinese are unlikely to become less expansionist until they have in fact secured their borderlands and purified the continent of Western influence. By this theory we are caught in an endless cycle of American containment and Chinese hate.

Overall, the outlook is not encouraging. Very possibly the long-run chance to contain China by Asian powers alone vanished with Mao's victory and subsequent unification of China in 1949. Should that be the case, American policy makers may be faced with their current dilemma for decades to come. Either the United States must indefinitely maintain a humanly and materially expensive presence in the Asia rimlands, or it must reconcile itself to living in

---

[25] For similar scepticism based on more traditional analysis of the foreign policies of nations in the area see, for example, three articles by Bernard K. Gordon: "Regionalism and Stability in Southeast Asia," *Orbis*, X, 2 (1966), pp. 438–57; "Problems of Regional Cooperation in Southeast Asia," *World Politics*, XVI, 1 (1964), pp. 222–53; and "Economic Impediments to Regionalism in Southeast Asia," *Asian Survey*, III, 2 (1963), pp. 235–44; and John D. Montgomery, "Regionalism in U.S. Foreign Policy: The Case of Southeast Asia," in *Prospects for Southeast Asia*, Kenneth Young and Gilbert White, editors (New York: Praeger, 1967).

a world, a tightly interknit system, where the Middle Kingdom has restored its control over much of Southeast Asia, and India and Japan live in awe of it. Such Chinese influence, by what might for centuries remain a poor and backward nation, may be a tolerable price—but it may nevertheless define the true limit of American choice.

7

Is There a Long-Run Trend toward Concentration in the International System?

NATIONAL SIZE IN HISTORICAL SYSTEMS

Many theories of international politics draw major propositions from the structure of the international system; that is, from the number and relative size of the nations that go to make up the system, the degree to which population or other power bases are concentrated in a few states. We have theories that a bipolar system is or is not more "stable" than a balance of power system, or, extending the argument, that a world with very small nations would or would not be less prone to severe wars than would a multipolar world with only a few major powers.[1] These theories are not at the moment entirely satisfactory for making reliable statements about the contemporary world. Either they rest upon unrealistic assumptions, or they require many qualifications. Yet, some preliminary efforts to test alternative hypotheses do suggest that over the past century and a half the structure of the system has been a moderately good predictor to the amount and nature of violent conflict

Reprinted from *Comparative Political Studies*, 1, 1 (April 1968).

[1] See, e.g., M. A. Kaplan, *System and Process in International Politics* (New York: Wiley, 1957), Part I; K. W. Deutsch and J. D. Singer, "Multipolar Power Systems and International Stability," *World Politics*, 16, 3 (April 1964); K. Waltz, "The Stability of a Bipolar World," *Daedalus*, (summer 1964), pp. 881–909; and R. N. Rosecrance, "Bipolarity, Multipolarity, and the Future," *Journal of Conflict Resolution*, 10 (September 1966), pp. 314–27.

in the system.[2] These theories have a long and for the most part honored place in the history of international relations theory and contain at least the seeds of important explanations. By analogy, similar theories have substantial explanatory power in economics for the behavior of firms—in a number of significant ways one can specify "the difference it makes" whether a market is basically duopolistic (only two firms, or at least two firms very much bigger than any others), oligopolistic (several large firms), or approximating perfect competition (many small firms, none of them large enough in isolation to affect the price or quantity of goods sold).

If it is conceded that there is something relevant, for policy as well as for theory, in the structure of the international system, it behooves us to devote some effort to description—to get some sense of the *current* distribution of nations by size—and to test some hypotheses about what that distribution *has been* in the past so as to be able to offer some further hypotheses, however speculative, about what that distribution may *be becoming*. In this chapter we shall look at the evidence available as to trends in the distribution of nations by population size. The data include information on the "birth" and "death" of nations of various sizes, population growth rates, and static data for the distribution of nations by size at particular points in time and from which we can test some inferences about random processes that might have generated those distributions. To anticipate, we find that the available data are ambiguous, but at least there is no good evidence that the distribution is changing or that there are forces at work which are notably increasing or weakening the degree of concentration.

While population alone is not a good index of power in current international politics, the data for population are very much better than for indices such as military capability or economic strength that might be theoretically more preferable. Furthermore, the number of people is a relevant measure of size for many purposes, and in the long run it may be a more important dimension of power than it seems at present. Its current disabilities stem from the power that Western organization and capital accumulation conveys in the industrialized countries, but over most of history the differentials across the globe were far less than they are at present. And they may become less again at some time in the future. Hence, we shall limit our empirical investigation to concentration of population, while acknowledging that a study of the distributions of power more generally would cover other variables also.

The first crude bit of evidence suggests that over the *very* long run the relative size of the largest nations has not changed greatly. For virtually all of recorded history the largest state in the world has been China. Currently, China's population of 700 million represents approximately 21 percent of the people

---

[2] J. D. Singer and M. Small, "Alliance Aggregation and the Onset of War," in *Quantitative International Politics: Insights and Evidence: International Yearbook of Political Behavior Research*, J. D. Singer, editor, Vol. VI (New York: The Free Press, 1968).

of the world; its estimated 1939 population of 452 million was also about 21 percent of the world's people then. On a much longer time scale, a census in the second century A.D. turned up 59.5 million Chinese; estimates for world population at that time are roughly 210–250 million. This would put China at about 25 percent—a remarkably constant proportion, all things considered.

The picture is not much different if we look at heterogeneous empires rather than units that more nearly approximate nation states. The United Kingdom and the non-self-governing parts of the British Empire in 1939 amounted to possibly 524 million people, or about 24 percent of the then current world population, and estimates of the extent of the Roman Empire contemporary with the census for ancient China put it at around 55 million, or perhaps just under 25 percent of the total. So however we choose to define the appropriate political unit for long-term comparison, it would seem that over at least a 2000-year period the largest has contained on the order of one-fifth to one-fourth of the entire world's population.[3]

GROWTH RATES AND ECONOMIES OF SCALE

Pure description of present and past distributions by itself offers little guidance in suggesting what may occur in the future. Fortunately, however, it is possible from the descriptive material on the size distribution of nations to make some inferences about how the distribution got that way. Essentially, the problem is: do large nations have any particular advantages of scale, so that big states are likely to grow faster than small ones (and, hence, become proportionately bigger), or, on the contrary, do big countries face diseconomies of scale so that they typically grow at slower rates than smaller ones? This brings to mind traditional economic explanations for the relative size of firms, explanations that depend upon assumptions about the structure of costs.

One such explanation is that the larger a firm is, the more efficient it will be, i.e., it will be able to produce at a lower cost per unit of output. Obvious examples stem from the contrast of production-line to handcrafted techniques of manufacture. If there are efficiencies that can be achieved only with a very great output relative to the size of the market, then small firms will have difficulty competing with large ones, and the likely result will be an oligopolistic industry. But another explanation contends that per unit costs do not decline indefinitely as the size of firm increases, that eventually there comes a point where unit costs begin to rise again and the larger firm becomes inefficient.

Clearly, very small firms do suffer real disadvantages, but it seems unlikely that *dis*economies of scale can be traced simply to production methods or that over a long enough time span to allow for plant and staff expansion there is, even for a particular industry, any "optimum" firm size. It is possible,

---

[3] W. S. Woytinsky and E. S. Woytinsky, *World Population and Production* (New York: Twentieth Century Fund, 1953), pp. 33–34.

however, that the size of firms may be limited by organizational difficulties and problems of management control of very large firms.[4] There are a variety of theories about loss of control in large institutions, especially those that are hierarchically organized.

There is evidence, however, that for many industries long-run costs are stable once some minimal firm size has been reached. Except for the costs of entry that keep very small firms out entirely, size would otherwise be irrelevant to a firm's prospect of success. The *proportionate* growth rate would thus be a random variable in the sense of being uncorrelated with the absolute size of a firm or with its relative performance in the previous time period. Size would then be determined by the statistical "law of proportionate effect," sometimes named "Gibrat's law" for its maker. The assumption that proportionate growth is independent of size means not that the distribution of firms by size will be normal, but that it will be highly *skewed*, with a clustering of most firms toward the left-hand (small size) side of the scale and a sharply decreasing number as one looks further to the right. If Gibrat's law holds, the resulting distribution will be a *lognormal* one. That is, if for the numbers representing the firms' size we were to substitute their logarithms, *then* the distribution of the logarithms would be normal (bell shaped).

A normal curve is generated when a large number of small, independent, random forces act on a variate in an additive manner: and a lognormal curve can be generated if they act multiplicatively. In the present context this means that the determinants of the growth of firms tend to change the size of firms by randomly distributed *proportions*. . . .

The first implication of this simple model is that large, medium, and small firms have the same *average* proportionate growth. The second implication is that the *dispersion* of growth rates around the common average is also the same for large, medium, and small firms. The third implication is that the *distribution* of proportionate growth rates is also lognormal. Thus if in any period firms on average stay the same size, so that average proportionate growth is unity, just as many firms double as halve their sizes. . . . Since this applies to all firms, it follows that if *x* percent of large firms *double* their size, *x* percent of small firms *halve* their size. Therefore a fourth implication of the simplest lognormal model is that the relative dispersion of the sizes of firms tends to increase over time. In this analysis the disparity of the sizes of firms increases over time, in spite of the fact that large firms have the same average proportionate growth as medium and small firms: this is so because 50 percent of large firms with above average growth include firms which were formerly among the smallest in the class of large firms but which enter the ranks of the very largest firms and overtake some of the former leaders.[5]

---

[4] J. Williamson, "Profit, Growth, and Sales Maximization," *Economica*, 33, 1 (February 1966), pp. 1–16; and O. E. Williamson, "Hierarchical Control and Optimum Firm Size," *Journal of Political Economy*, 75, 2 (April 1967), pp. 123–38.

[5] P. E. Hart, "The Size and Growth of Firms," *Economica*, 29, 113 (February 1962), p. 30. For the basic paper, see G. U. Yule, "A Mathematical Theory of Evolution Based on the Conclusions of Dr. J. C. Willis, F.R.S.," *Philosophical Transactions of the Royal Society of London*, 213 (1924), pp. 21–87.

Thus, a lognormal curve is circumstantial evidence that costs are constant and that large firms have no particular efficiency advantages. The fact that several investigations have turned up highly skewed and in some cases lognormal distributions has been cited as evidence against the existence of economies of scale.

It is essential to note that this entire subject—both on the empirical evidence and the theoretical explanations—is a matter of considerable dispute among economists. The wide range of empirical phenomena to which such distributions can be fitted, however, together with the accuracy of the causal explanations in many cases where they can be fully tested, indicates that the appearance of similar phenomena in international politics would deserve very careful study, despite the skepticism which "curve fitting" may initially provoke.[6] Short-run projections of concentration would, of course, be done more effectively through the aggregation of demographers' single country models of individual birth and death rates. The question to be investigated here is more general and more fundamental.

THE SIZE DISTRIBUTION OF NATIONS

This discussion is relevant to the international system not simply because of any crude analogy between the distribution of firms and the distribution of nations, but because some of the causal hypotheses advanced about the size of firms and of nation-states are so similar. There is, of course, the proposition that only rather large nations are "efficient" and can provide necessary or desirable services to their people at minimum cost. Rather powerful are the arguments that recall economists' points not about efficiencies, but about the market power of large firms—big states, because of their power, can coerce smaller ones so as to obtain a more favorable cost-to-revenue ratio. Or it is contended that very large nations are inefficient, that they must incorporate such diverse peoples, and incur so many bureaucratic costs from hierarchy, that they are ill suited to survive.

In fact, the distribution of nations by population size in three different years, for which we have reasonably good data, *is* highly skewed and provides

---

[6] I do not pretend to know this literature thoroughly, but in addition to the references cited previously and in the following pages, see, among many others, Stephen Hymer and Peter Pashigian, "Turnover of Firms as a Measure of Market Behavior," *Review of Economics and Statistics*, 44 (February 1962), pp. 82–87; E. Mansfield, "Entry, Gibrat's Law, Innovation, and the Growth of Firms," *American Economic Review*, 52 (December 1962), pp. 1023–51; R. E. Quandt, "On the Size Distribution of Firms," *American Economic Review*, 56 (June 1966), pp. 416–32; and T. R. Saving, "The Four-Parameter Lognormal, Diseconomies of Scale, and the Size Distribution of Manufacturing Establishments," *International Economic Review*, 6 (January 1965), pp. 105–14. Y. Iriji and H. A. Simon, "Business Firm Growth and Size," *American Economic Review*, 54 (March 1964), p. 79, have shown that the law of proportionate effect does not require that the percentage change in size of a unit from one period to another be independent of the unit's size, but only that the change in size of *the totality of firms in each size stratum be independent of stratum.*

a very good fit to the lognormal distribution. Figures 7-1, *a*, *b*, and *c* show graphs for the size distribution for nation-states in 1967, 1957, and 1938. The skewness has been removed by substituting logarithms for the original figures for population in thousands. The actual distribution is shown as the number of nations in each of a number of uniform (by logarithms) size classes, and the curve superimposed illustrates what the ideal normal distribution would be.[7]

Allowing for the effects of grouping, the fit is, indeed, very close, and for each of the three years. Employing a chi-square goodness of fit test to test the null hypothesis that the distribution is *not* normal, we obtain values of about 3.6, 7.0, and 6.6, respectively, for 1938, 1957, and 1967. For 1967 this is statistically significant only at the .88 level, meaning that almost nine-tenths of the time we would correctly *reject* the null hypothesis in favor of the alternative hypothesis of normality. For 1938 and 1957, when the range was narrower and the total number of nations was less, I used fewer size classes and, hence, there are fewer degrees of freedom. Their chi-square values are both significant at the .73 level, meaning that one properly would reject the hypothesis of non-normality only about three-quarters of the time. But all three of these figures together indicate a strikingly good and consistent fit.[8]

The three separate years are given to show the effect of adding so many ex-colonies to the international system during the past three decades. As is apparent, the effect has not been great. There has been an increase in the dispersion (as the lognormal model of efficiency uncorrelated with size would

---

[7] Data are from B. M. Russett et al., *World Handbook of Political and Social Indicators* (New Haven: Yale University Press, 1964), pp. 18–20; United Nations, *Demographic Yearbook, 1966* (New York: United Nations, 1967); United Nations, *Demographic Yearbook, 1962* (New York: United Nations, 1963); United Nations, *Demographic Yearbook, 1958* (New York: United Nations, 1959); and *World Almanac and Book of Facts, 1944* (New York: World Telegram and Sun, 1944). Some data are estimated. "Sovereign state" is defined in 1957 and 1967 to include all members of the UN, plus Switzerland and the nations excluded by Cold War politics, whose existence is acknowledged if not always recognized. Byelorussia and the Ukraine, however, are not counted, despite their formal UN membership. Ministates that are not members of the UN (e.g., Andorra, Monaco) are not counted because they are too small (below the minimum firm size) to carry on even the minimal activities of international politics that the small UN members do. The 1938 country list is compiled from B. M. Russett, J. D. Singer, and M. Small, "A Standardized List of Political Entities in the Twentieth Century," *American Political Science Review*, 62, 3 (September 1968), applying UN memberships retroactively, and including the Baltic states.

[8] If significance levels of .88 and .73 don't seem very impressive, bear in mind that we are reversing the normal procedure where one takes a theoretical distribution such as the normal one, and sets the *null* hypothesis that the distribution is normal. One typically hopes to find evidence that the null hypothesis can be rejected and the alternate hypothesis of nonnormality can be accepted, but to do so one must have rather high confidence that the departure from normality is not induced by chance alone. Since one would usually demand a significance level of .05 before rejecting the hypothesis of normality, levels of .88 and .73 look pretty good for the reverse procedure.

In calculating the chi square, I collapsed the last two size classes at each tail into a single category so as to raise the expected frequency in that class above 1. With expected frequencies below unity the chi-square test is not appropriate. Some statisticians would insist on frequencies of at least 5, but this seems too conservative. See W. G. Cochran, "Some Methods for Strengthening the Common x^2 Tests," *Biometrics*, 10 (December 1954), pp. 417–51.

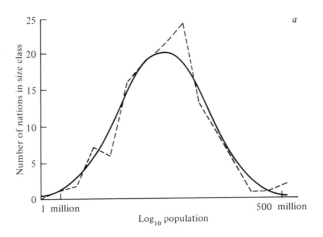

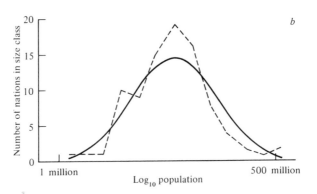

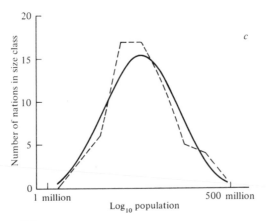

Figure 7-1
Log$_{10}$ population distribution of nations by size classes. a, For 1967 (128 nations); b, For 1957 (89 nations); c, For 1938 (65 nations). Dashed lines show actual distribution; solid lines show hypothetical normal curve.

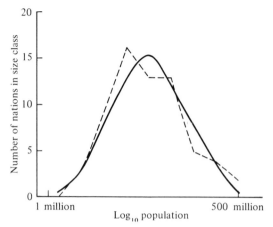

Figure 7-2
Log_{10} population distribution of the 65 nations of 1938 (as depicted in Figure 7-1, c) with the addition of the populations of colonies in appropriate cases, by size classes. Dashed line is actual distribution; solid line shows hypothetical normal curve.

predict), and despite world population growth, the mean size of nation has shifted slightly downward, from the logarithm for almost 7 million to just over 5½ million. But the overall fit has remained good throughout the period.

A problem arises, however, as to how we should treat colonial empires. Are we concerned with the growth or shrinkage of the national core, or of all of the peoples under centralized rule from that core? There are reasons for limiting attention to the nation-state itself—for instance, if we are concerned in some sense with power, colonial people are rarely as great an addition to the power of a nation as are those in the metropole—but doing so would omit some of the most interesting political (rather than biological) processes of growth and so lose important information. Accordingly, it seems necessary to present the data both ways, and so Figure 7-2 gives the data for the same nations of 1938, except that for the ten (Belgium, Denmark, France, Italy, Japan, Netherlands, Portugal, Spain, United Kingdom, United States) that had colonial empires I have added the colonies' population to that of the metropolitan territory. This change weakens the fit somewhat, raising the chi square to 4.2, significant at the .65 level. Apparently, the random growth model fits better for core nations than for the dynamics of empire, although we shall continue to check our findings on both sets.

While actual events may not fit the model's assumptions precisely, it serves as a useful approximation. As Iriji and Simon note, Galileo's law of the inclined plane, that the distance traveled by a ball rolling down the plane increases with the square of the time

does ignore variables that may be important under various circumstances: irregularities in the ball or the plane, rolling friction, air resistance, possible electrical or magnetic fields if the ball is metal, variations in the gravitational field—and so on, ad infinitum. The enormous progress that physics has made in three centuries may be partly attributed to its willingness to ignore for a time discrepancies from theories that are in some sense substantially correct.[9]

For the moment accepting the hypothesis of a lognormal distribution, we have the circumstantial evidence that big countries typically grow neither more nor less rapidly than smaller ones, and there is no overall tendency for either a decline or an increase in concentration in the international system. This corresponds fully with what poor evidence we cited earlier for millennia-long periods. Of course, if one thinks of nations as growing in population only by the biological processes of birth and death among their citizenry, then such a finding is not surprising. On that basis there would be few plausible hypotheses that big nations would have an advantage except by some rather involved mechanisms, such as a correlation between size and per capita income and, consequently, faster (or slower) natural rates of population increase in the larger and, thus, richer countries. But this hypothesis, at least, is poorly supported empirically,[10] and in any case natural life processes certainly do *not* provide the only way that nations grow or shrink. Nations accept immigrants and provide emigrants. Furthermore, they annex other areas, fission, or, in turn, are annexed. When these processes are recalled, various alternative hypotheses about the advantages (or handicaps) accruing to big countries in international competition are not so implausible. They just do not seem to meet with much support here.[11]

SOME ALTERNATIVE MODELS

Yet this rather neat fit to the lognormal distribution, with the consequent deductions we can make for speculating about how the distribution might have been generated is, unfortunately, complicated by some alternative models and hypotheses that cannot easily be rejected. Herbert Simon, for example, has suggested that if in addition to random growth rates one assumes a process of birth for new firms, the consequence is the Yule distribution, which looks like the lognormal one except that there are a few more very large firms:

Let us assume that there is a minimum size, S_m, of firm in an industry. Let us assume that for firms above this size, unit costs are constant. Individual firms in

---

[9] Iriji and Simon, op. cit., p. 78.

[10] See Russett et al., op. cit., p. 277, where the correlation is shown to be below .20.

[11] Data on nations' size by measures such as total GNP are, as indicated earlier, less reliable than population data, especially for changes over time. A test of the distribution of nations' GNP in 1957, nevertheless, powerfully supports the major hypothesis of this chapter; it fits a lognormal distribution with a chi square of 4.5 at a significance level of .92, even higher than any test of the population data. This needs to be examined further. Data from Russett et al., op. cit., pp. 152–4.

the industry will grow (or shrink) at varying rates, depending on such factors as (*a*) profit, (*b*) dividend policy, (*c*) new investment, and (*d*) mergers. These factors, in turn, may depend on the efficiency of the individual firm, exclusive access to particular factors of production, consumer brand preference, the growth or decline of the particular industry products in which it specializes, and numerous other conditions. The operation of all these forces will generate a probability distribution for the changes in size of firms of a given size. Our first basic assumption (the law of proportionate effect) is that this probability distribution is the same for all size classes of firms that are well above S_m. Our second basic assumption is that new firms are being "born" in the smallest size class at a relatively constant rate. . . . What distinguishes the Yule distribution from the lognormal is not the first assumption—the law of proportionate effect—but the second— the assumption of a constant "birth rate" for new firms. If we assume a random walk of the firms already in the system at the beginning of the time interval under consideration, with zero mean change in size, we obtain the lognormal. If we assume a random walk, but with a steady introduction of new firms from below, we obtain the Yule distribution.[12]

Simon has also developed an alternative model, allowing for the death of small firms at the same rate as the birth of some new small firms, that again produces a Yule distribution.[13] A distribution more like the Yule than the lognormal can also be produced when there are some efficiency advantages to be gained only by extremely large size.

One analyst has reconciled the basic proportionate effects model with what many economists have described *empirically* as a *progressing* degree of concentration in quite a number of industries. He does it by assuming that the average firm does grow some, and by distinguishing between average *growth* rates and *survival* rates. He attributes lower survival rates to the smaller firms. The analysis recalls a variety of phenomena in international politics—large nations' attempts to secure safety through control over foreign sources of vital supplies, the coercive market power of big countries in international politics, and the alleged greater caution and "responsibility" or conservatism which many observers attribute to great powers.

> The fact that mortality decreases with size, that firms—at least in free enterprise conditions—are subject to high infant mortality but that very large firms rarely succumb, is well established. . . . Now if big firms have a better chance of survival then firms of smaller size, this will readily explain why, in the course of time, they obtain more scope for themselves, as a group, than the others. . . .
>
> Simultaneously, the difference in the chance of survival can also offer an explanation of . . . what becomes of the advantage of big firms in large scale economies of operation—what do they do with it? They use it, not to earn more and to grow faster, but to survive better than the smaller firm.

---

[12] H. A. Simon and C. P. Bonini, "The Size Distribution of Business Firms," *American Economic Review*, 48 (September 1958), pp. 607–17. Note some of the analogies between reasons for the growth or shrinkage of firms and those for nations.

[13] H. A. Simon, *Models of Man* (New York: Wiley, 1957), Chapter 9.

It will be appreciated that a firm can use its advantages over its competitors in either of two ways: either to earn more, or to have more safety—that is, either to increase the mathematical expectation of the profit rate or to decrease the variance of it. . . . A firm may increase its chances of survival at the expense of the rate of profit by holding more reserves of various kinds, such as financial reserves in the form of liquid assets, government bonds, etc, but in many cases also as stocks of raw material. It may also acquire sources of raw materials, not very profitable, but essential for operation in certain contingencies. Or again, it may diversify its production program in a way which will entail a sacrifice in efficiency (higher cost) but will reduce the impact of a failure in any one line. . . .

Thus the greater profit and growth rate of "bigness" exists—at least to a large extent—only potentially, and is not realized owing to the preference of big firms for safety.[14]

These models mean that there are several different mechanisms by which an increasing degree of concentration could arise in a system such as the international system. They are relevant because, in fact, the Yule distribution does fit our empirical distributions of nations at least as well and perhaps a bit better than the lognormal one, and because of our interest in finding the *why* behind the *is*. From the graphs it is apparent that the number of very big countries at the upper tail is slightly greater than predicted by the normal model. This evidence must be taken with a good deal of skepticism, however, since it is based on the deviations of only one or two countries from their "expected" point in the distribution. As some of the analogous controversies in economics have indicated, it is often virtually impossible to decide just which of several hypothetical distributions actually provides the best fit to a set of data and, even after obtaining a fit, to decide which variant of the law of proportionate effect offers the proper causal description. We cannot differentiate among them with purely static data.

FOUR HYPOTHETICAL SOURCES OF CONCENTRATION

An international system is *concentrated* to the degree that a high proportion of the total population is contained in a small proportion of the countries. There are several ways in which increasing concentration could occur.

---

[14] J. Steindl, *Random Processes and the Growth of Firms* (New York: Hafner, 1965), pp. 218–21. W. J. Baumol suggests that the managers of firms may prefer to avoid even moderate risk so as not to antagonize their shareholders. Losses attributable to risk taking may provoke immediate shareholder disaffection, and even windfall gains from successful risk taking may provoke ultimate dissatisfaction if they lead to expectations of *continued* high gain that cannot be met. Cf. *Business Behavior, Value, and Growth* (New York: Macmillan, 1959), especially Chapters 6, 7, and 10. Governments similarly may wish to avoid risk taking for fear of reprisal from their constituents. Marshall Hall and Leonard Weiss, "Firm Size and Profitability," *Review of Economics and Statistics*, 49, 3 (August 1967), pp. 319–31, show that the rate of profit *is* higher for large firms than for smaller ones even controlling for the degree of concentration of the industry.

1. More rapid growth rates for the very largest nations than for smaller ones.

2. The "death" of small nations by annexation or merger at the same or greater rate as new ones were being born, while large nations retained high survivor rates.

3. A great increase in the number of very small nations (births in the lowest size class).

4. The birth of one or two very large nations, either by merger or by entry into the list of sovereign nations from a former state of colonial dependency.

The finding of a perfectly lognormal distribution would have been strong disconfirmation of the first hypothesis, but the suggestion that a Yule distribution fits equally well limits the confidence with which that hypothesis can be rejected. What is now required for further differentiating among these plausible alternatives, or for rejecting all in favor of a finding that concentration is not increasing, is to look at the actual data on observed *growth rates* as well as the size distribution. We must also have data on the *births* and *deaths* of nations. This can be done successfully only with data spread over quite a long time period, measured in several decades as an absolute minimum. Unfortunately, such information is not very accurate even for the Western developed nations, let alone for the underdeveloped world. Population censuses have not been sufficiently reliable for a long enough time to permit the fine measurement really demanded here.

We can, however, go a bit farther. First, we have nearly complete information, if of less than desirable accuracy, on national population growth rates over the period 1939–1965.[15] We can divide the distribution into several subsets and see if big countries have, in fact, grown faster than smaller ones. The first row of Table 7-1 (next page) shows the average growth rate for the countries in each quartile of the distribution. The second row allows for the decline of empires, giving the quartile means of the growth rates for the same units except that for the empires I have combined the population of the colonies with that of the metropolitan territory in the prewar year, and in 1965 for those that still had colonies.

1. The hypothesis that big nations have been growing faster than smaller ones is unambiguously rejected. This finding is not merely an artifact of the

---

[15] The data are for 1939–1965 population growth, but it seemed relevant to do the analysis for the political units that existed in January 1938, before the largely temporary elimination of a number of independent states from the international scene immediately before and during World War II. Data are from United Nations, *Demographic Yearbook, 1958* (New York: United Nations, 1959), Table 4, and United Nations, *Demographic Yearbook, 1965* (New York: United Nations, 1966), Table 4. The prewar population estimates for Afghanistan, Liberia, Saudi Arabia, and Yemen were too crude to use here.

Table 7-1

Mean Growth Rates (in Percent) of Nations' Population, 1939–1965, by Quartile

	Top quartile	Second quartile	Third quartile	Bottom quartile	Overall mean
Nation-states	142	143	149	183	154
Nations and empires	104	151	149	183	147

grouping by quartiles, nor does it hide higher growth rates for the few nations at the very high end. Of the eight largest states, only China, and that barely (155 percent), had a growth rate higher than the rate achieved by the average nation overall (154 percent). Size does make some differences in growth, but opposite from the way expected. Growth rates for the *smallest* quartile of nations have been well above the average for nations as a whole. This is even more true if empires rather than nation-states are included in the computations, and there, reflecting the breakup of colonial holdings after World War II, the *largest* quartile shows by far the *least* growth.

Incidentally, there are other reasons for questioning whether the law of proportionate effect is the source of the size distribution of nations. According to the second and third implications of the law as drawn by Hart, the *standard deviation* of growth rates should be the same for small nations as for large ones, and the distribution of growth *rates* should itself be lognormal.

Investigation turns up little evidence of these properties. Table 7-2 shows the standard deviations of nations' 1939–1965 growth rates for each quartile of the distribution. For the three lowest quartiles the dispersion is virtually the same, but for the top quartile, whether one looks at nations only or at nations and colonial empires, the measure of dispersion is much *higher* than for the other quartiles. Thus, it not only appears that the proportionate effects model does not strictly apply for the largest states, but that big countries are prone to more risky behavior than are smaller ones. Apparently, a nation or empire has to *take chances in order to grow big* and to stay big, and is likely as a result to expand or shrink by a greater proportional amount than most countries.[16] Note, however, that this seemingly more risk-prone behavior was not re-flected in lower *survival* rates for big countries. Shrinkage rates are not so sharp, or the "cushion" available to a big country is large enough, that over the time

---

[16] This finding in a way complements that of Stephen Hymer and Peter Pashigian, "Firm Size and Rate of Growth," *Journal of Political Economy*, 70 (December 1962), pp. 566–9, who looked at the standard deviations of growth rates of firms in different size classes. Because of the possibilities large firms have for diversification to spread their risks, they predict a *sharply inverse* relation between size and the variation in growth rates. Although they do find a some-what inverse relationship, the fact that the standard deviation for large firms' growth rates is greater than predicted (though less than for smaller firms) brings them to conclude that large firms are also prone to greater risk-taking behavior. While all the *assumptions* of their model are not appropriate for transferring an expectation of an inverse relationship from firms to nations, the *finding* is nevertheless relevant.

Table 7-2

Standard Deviation of Growth Rates of Nations' Population, 1939–1965, by Quartile

	Top quartile	Second quartile	Third quartile	Fourth quartile
Nation-states	48.7	33.6	35.1	35.1
Nations and empires	59.8	33.9	35.1	35.1

period studied no states above the smallest size class actually dropped out of the international system of sovereign entities (see point 2).

As for the implication that the distribution of proportionate growth rates should be lognormal, it too is not borne out in the crude data available. Figure 7-3 shows the actual distribution superimposed on the hypothetical normal curve. The curve is vaguely normal with bunchings toward the middle, but more nearly bimodal. The chi square for goodness of fit is 9.8, significant at the .13 level. We probably would *reject* the hypothesis of normality, though with a .13 probability of error and, hence, without much confidence. (The curve for empires is an even poorer fit [slightly skewed] and not shown.) It is true that the data for time changes are rather gross for a procedure requiring fine measures, and also that they are incomplete in a way that may be relevant. There are four nations with missing data (Afghanistan, Liberia, Saudi Arabia, and Yemen), and from what crude information that is available it is clear they would fall somewhere in the middle of the distribution. Should most or all of them belong in the middle category, they would moderately improve the worst aspect of the fit. The significance level and the problem of data error do leave open the possibility that some implications of the proportionate effects model may not be so inapplicable as they appear here.

2. Another of the four possible sources of concentration listed previously was that large nations would have substantially lower death rates (Steindl) or, ideally, that all "deaths" of nations would be in the smallest size class (Simon). On the whole, the differential death rate models simply do not apply—only four permanent deaths by annexation or merger have occurred since 1938. The Baltic states of Estonia, Latvia, and Lithuania were absorbed into Soviet Russia in 1940, and Zanzibar joined Tanganyika in 1964, shortly after achieving independence. It is true that these few deaths all involved nations with populations under three million, so they are not inconsistent with the hypothesis; but they were so few compared with the number of births (67) as to be essentially irrelevant to the characteristics of the distribution.

3. We said that a great increase in the number of very small states could produce a Yule distribution. That is a substantial oversimplification of what has actually happened. True, a much larger proportion of new than of old states *do* fall in the very small size class. The smallest four—Maldive Islands, Iceland, Barbados, and Gambia—are all post-1938 nations, and of the 15

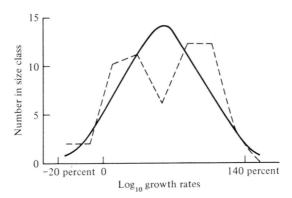

Figure 7-3
Log$_{10}$ distribution of nations' population growth rates, 1939–1965.

under one million only Luxembourg was in existence at the beginning of the period. But above that level there is no relation between size and post-1938 independence. And the new sovereign states of the past twenty years include India, Pakistan, and Indonesia, each now with over 100 million people. Thus, attributing part of the departure from lognormality to the introduction of new small states is plausible, but incomplete. In addition to the large new nations that do not fit the model, the process of introduction has not been "at a relatively constant rate." Forty percent of the countries that became independent over the entire 30-year period did so between 1960 and 1962.

4. A single very big country—India—was born during the time period in question. Its birth would, with the other birth and death patterns noted previously, in large part account for the departure from lognormality in the upper tail observed earlier, and its position in the number two ranking has tended to increase the degree of concentration. But it is difficult to generalize from the single case to any longer-term trends in the system. India is the first state to join the community of nations near the top of the size distribution since Germany did so a century ago.

STABLE CONCENTRATION, 1938–1967

Having checked out the various mechanisms by which concentration might have increased in the post-1938 era, we can now return to the actual data on what did happen. Figure 7-4 shows the Lorenz curves for the distribution of nation-states by population in 1938 and 1967. A Lorenz curve is drawn by ranking nations from smallest to largest and computing the percentage of the total *population* held by various percentages of the *total number* of nations, starting at the lower end. The further the curve is from the line of equality

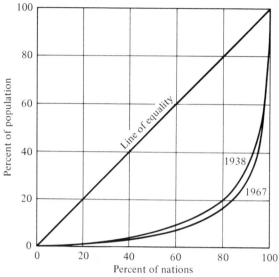

Figure 7-4
Lorenz curves of population concentration by nations, 1938 and 1967.

bisecting the square from lower left to upper right, the greater the degree of concentration.[17]

The two curves are similar, but not identical, with some indication of an increase in concentration over the period. The Gini index of concentration (which measures the area between the Lorenz curve and the line of equality) increased from .746 to .776. Virtually all that difference occurred between 1957 and 1967, since the 1957 curve (not drawn) is almost identical with the 1938 one and has a Gini index of .748. If we look at the extent of colonial empires as well as of nations, however, we find that the curve has been effectively unchanged. For 1938, empires and nations together the Gini index is .785, or very *slightly more* concentrated than the distribution in 1967. By this interpretation the post-World War II end of empire has not really varied the distribution of a major power base, population, from what it was three decades ago. The results of those events do not offer any support for a prediction of greater concentration in the future.

SUMMARY

We examined the size distribution of nations at several points in time and explored several possible mechanisms by which that distribution might change. Some questions were resolved; others remain open.

---

[17] H. R. Alker and B. M. Russett, "Indices for Comparing Inequality," in *Comparing Nations*, R. L. Merritt and S. Rokkan, editors (New Haven: Yale University Press, 1966).

1. There is no evidence that the largest states are proportionately either larger or smaller than 2000 years ago.

2. The *size distribution* for recent years is nearly lognormal and hence consistent with a random growth model implying no correlation between size and proportionate growth.

3. The *size distribution* also, however, departs slightly from lognormality in a way that leaves open the possibility that the very largest states may be growing faster.

4. The *size distribution* also departs slightly from lognormality in a way that is consistent with a Yule distribution that could be generated by various models employing random growth and certain birth and death rates.

5. Over recent decades large nations have *not grown faster* than smaller ones, contrary to the possibility suggested by item 3.

6. The *distribution* of observed *growth rates* does not fit the requirements of the random growth model (item 2) well, but the data are not highly reliable for the fine measurements required.

7. A combination of the *death* and especially the *birth* patterns for nations in recent decades could have produced a departure from lognormality roughly in the direction suggested by item 4.

8. The actual change in the degree of *concentration* in the system over the past three decades has been very small.

8
The Ecology of Future
International Politics

THE RANGE AND PROBABILITY OF
FUTURE OUTCOMES

The prediction of future world events is frequently an exercise in political sociology. Or perhaps more accurately, it is a problem in political ecology, one concerned with the relationship between the political system and its social and physical environment.

A statement that nothing will change over the next few decades would hardly be credible, and anyway it would be boring. On the other hand, to quote one of my favorite books on prediction, "If a man predicts large but not very large changes, the public will regard him as a man of imagination; but if he predicts extremely large changes, his audience will replace imagination by phantasy."[1] I would like, in this chapter, to avoid both extremes. In any case, my recent menus have offered neither sheep livers nor chicken entrails, so I am unable to engage in prophecy. I will not attempt to foretell a specific event on a specific occasion, nor to paint a detailed picture of a particular political future. But I am a restrained believer in the outlook aptly labelled by Charles Burton Marshall as "the limits of foreign policy."[2] Without getting into the determinist-free-will debate—which in the still youthful state

Reprinted from *International Studies Quarterly*, XI, 1 (March 1967).
[1] H. Thiel, *Economic Forecasts and Policy* (Amsterdam: North Holland, 2nd edition, 1961), p. 156.
[2] Charles Burton Marshall, *The Limits of Foreign Policy* (New York: Henry Holt, 1954).

of our sciences is largely irrelevant anyway—we can, I think, agree generally with the idea that political prediction is best concerned with the future state of the *milieu* within which decisions have to be made. In this context we are interested in *negative* prediction—we aspire to narrow the range of possibilities, to eliminate some events as unlikely, and to produce a range of outcomes within which future developments will lie.[3]

In effect, we want to do what we do as scientists when generalizing from our samples to larger populations; we want to make a prediction that states both a *range* of possibilities—the confidence interval—and the probability, or *significance level*, that we attach to the likelihood that the true value will fall within that range. If we give as a "best guess" some point within that interval, we recognize that it is really only shorthand for a much more complicated statement. I think this is true whether we are making explicitly quantitative statements, such as the number of people who would be killed in a nuclear war, or whether we are talking about apparently discrete events, such as whether or not "war" will occur. We may simplify our analytical models to talk about war versus peace, but we know that there are many shades and varieties of each, and that in *many* respects the "war" we refer to is less a step jump from the level of previous states than the mode of a distributional curve. We have learned this well from our recent experiences with civil unrest and insurgency. All of us know too about the problem of subjective probabilities and the inappropriateness of assigning a probability to a unique event; when we make a prediction that is not based on a sample from a known universe we are beyond the limits within which the assignment of precise probability levels is permissible. Yet without some such effort, however crude and subjective, the analysis is incomplete and misleading.

Suppose that we have a prediction that a particular kind of war promises to bring death to between 5 and 25 million Americans. The President of the United States must decide in a crisis whether that is a price the country should pay in order to defend Western Europe. However he chooses to phrase his question, he must ask further, "What are the *probabilities* that the casualty level will actually fall within this range?" Presumably his decision would be quite different if his advisor could say he was *very* confident (say, a 99 percent probability) that casualties would not exceed the upper limit of this range, than if he thought there was as much as one chance in three that the upper limit might be exceeded. Without both elements, the apparent precision of a

---

[3] See Harold and Margaret Sprout, *The Ecological Perspective on Human Affairs* (Princeton: Princeton University Press, 1965), pp. 180, 199. See also Thiel, op. cit., Chapter 1; and Nicholas Rescher, "Discrete State Systems, Markov Chains, and Problems in the Theory of Scientific Explanation and Prediction," *Philosophy of Science*, 30 (1963), pp. 325–45; and, for a similar if less rigorous and overly cautious statement, Saul Friedlander, "Forecasting in International Relations," in *Futuribles: Studies in Conjecture*, II, Bertrand de Jouvenel, editor (Geneva: Droz, 1965), p. 99. On the difficulties of predicting particular events, relevant comments include those by Wilbert E. Moore, *Social Change* (Englewood Cliffs: Prentice-Hall, 1963), pp. 3–4; and Kenneth E. Boulding, "Expecting the Unexpected: The Uncertain Future of Knowledge," in *Conference on Designing Education for the Future*, Denver, Colo., July 1966, Edgar Morphet and Charles Ryan, editors (New York: Citation Press, 1967).

quantitative confidence interval smacks of scientism, and the consumer would be better off with a vague but honest, "I am rather confident" or "only moderately confident" that the actual casualty level will be within the range, than he would be with a statement that gives no inkling whatever of the probability the forecaster may have had in mind.[4]

But this is not meant to be a treatise on the statistics of deadly quarrels, nor on scientific method either. I now want to consider another kind of prediction—how one can examine smooth changes in order to identify more or less discrete ones, in effect to anticipate system change. I will, however, stay within the framework outlined at the beginning—we will not be trying to predict particular events, but changes in the social and technological environment that will produce political and further social changes of one sort or another, changes that will lead to quite different social and political systems and present to future decision makers the opportunity, and usually the necessity, for choice.

RIGOR, INFORMATION, AND IMAGINATION

Imagination is often useful, and sometimes essential, for accurate prediction. Yet there have *always* been some men who had imagination, and only in recent decades has prediction been dramatically improved in many areas. We now predict economic conditions, elections, demographic trends, with imperfect but notably better success than we used to. This success is dependent less upon flights of imagination than upon a mixture of information and rigor.

Formal rigor means eliminating contradictions, preventing obscurity, and avoiding leaps in logic. Perhaps even more important, the rigorous formulation of a problem very often identifies a trend that wouldn't be apparent from mere intuition or imaginative speculation. Deductive reasoning has been the great strength of traditional sociology, and, sometimes without the sociologists' rigor, of traditional political science too. Now, rigor is frequently supplied by mathematics or symbolic logic. Despite the occasional abuse of mathematics and symbols, these tools have a remarkable ability to show up relationships that would otherwise escape notice. A primary reason for the greater success of economists and demographers in predicting future developments has undoubtedly been their increased use of rigorous—that is, mathematical—theories.[5]

---

[4] I am thinking, of course, of Herman Kahn, *On Thermonuclear War* (Princeton: Princeton University Press, 1960), though he is by no means the only offender, and his use of ranges was a notable improvement over all previous efforts in this area.

[5] Obviously there are plenty of examples where economists and demographers have fallen on their faces in prediction, though not so grossly in recent years as in the earlier stages of their sciences' development. In general, it is fairer to compare present social science's predictive power with that of its predecessors than to disparage it by comparing it with its natural science contemporaries. See Bernard Barber, *Science and the Social Order* (Glencoe: The Free Press, 1952) p. 243.

One of the most striking and popular applications has long been the projection of exponential growth rates from the past into the future. An exponential growth rate is of course simply like compound interest, where a quantity regularly increases by some *proportion* of itself, rather than by a standard absolute *amount*. Hence, when graphed, the pattern is of a rising and ever steeper curve, rather than an upwardly sloping straight line. It is in fact one of the simplest of all models, known in the trade as a first order system.[6] Yet for limited periods of time, and under stable conditions, it is an extraordinarily useful model. Probably the most familiar example is that for the population explosion, where the world's current annual rate of population increase, about two percent or a doubling every 35 years, is projected forward and the density of the land areas of the globe is projected to a level exceeding present-day Hong Kong's by the year 2200. Similar growth rates have been publicized by Derek Price for the expansion of science. The household phrase about "almost 90 percent of all scientists who ever lived are alive today" comes directly from his work.[7] As we go on I shall identify some other social phenomena that have grown at exponential, and often remarkably steady, rates for years or decades.

The fact that so many processes have exhibited exponential growth rates is no accident, nor is the rate itself merely a coincidence or a statistical construct forced on the unwilling data. Science feeds upon itself, with some scientific progress making possible the cumulation of further progress. The growth of *science* has made possible many *technological* changes, as of course the demand for these improvements has provided the material basis for science to grow. While all the rates have not been precisely the same, and as we shall see the recent doubling periods vary between about every 35 years (for population) and every four years (scientific expenditures, and the destructive radius of weapons), a neat identity would be too much to expect. The rapid growth in each of them is nevertheless closely interrelated and interdependent. As such they comprise a system in dynamic but stable equilibrium; change is interrelated in a highly dependable manner, and if we can for a moment forget the *rapidity* of change about us, looking backward over recent decades the highly "predictable" nature of that change is impressive. It has been like a rocket taking off from its launching pad—slowly gathering momentum until very great speeds are attained, but the acceleration has been quite steady and not at all fortuitous.

Yet *rigor* is only a part of the modern success story in prediction. The other major element is simply *information*, scads of it, precisely, in fact, one of the exponentially growing phenomena being measured. Price's statements about scientists are primarily inferences from the volume of scientific information; the most familiar set of data in his presentation refer to the number of scientific and technical journals, which has now reached over 100,000. Without

---

[6] Boulding, op. cit.

[7] Derek J. de Sola Price, *Science since Babylon* (New Haven: Yale University Press, 1961), Chapter 5. See also his *Little Science, Big Science* (New York: Columbia University Press, 1963).

this information explosion we would not know in a precise and detailed way, even to the degree necessary for fitting very rough exponential growth curves, about all the other changes. It has made possible the *inductive* generalization that marks so much current work in both sociology and political science. (Though many historians and political scientists have always held to a notion that "the facts speak for themselves.")[8] But large bodies of quantitative information are expensive and time consuming to produce, and could never have been gathered by scholars working under nineteenth century conditions.

And curve fitting is a tricky business. Formally speaking, many possible curves can be fitted to a single set of points.[9] The "best" curve is highly ambiguous, and if one has only a few observations, gathered perhaps for only a short period of time and subject to substantial error in measurement, the hazards are multiplied. With little data a straight line, an exponential growth rate, or even a cyclical pattern of hills and valleys superimposed on a rising trend may all be equally "correct" mathematically, and we may have little basis for preferring one or another. Even the fact of a rising trend may be misleading, especially as it may be related to a longer-term cycle. So the information-gathering side of things is crucial, and we need all the public and private data-gathering services in existence—at the same time that we need to devise means to prevent being snowed under in a blizzard of trivia.

Even rigor and information, the twin pillars of modern social wisdom, suffice only for limited tasks. The uncritical projection of exponential growth rates provides some of the worst examples of simpleminded curve fitting. Quite obviously the world's rate of population increase will *not* continue unabated until the earth's density exceeds Hong Kong's; some kind of control, deliberate or natural, felicitous or disastrous, will prevent it.[10] Still, the ease and attractions of simple projection have subverted many a would-be prophet. G. K. Chesterton, in his slightly pompous Victorian way, amply satirized the outlook:

> When we see a pig in a litter larger than the other pigs, we know that by an unalterable law of the Inscrutable it will some day be larger than an elephant—just as we know, when we see weeds and dandelions growing more and more thickly

---

[8] This strain is exemplified by Henry Adams's writings on American history, especially his *History of the United States of America* (London: Putnam, 1891–1892, 9 vols.).

[9] Arthur C. Clarke, *Profiles of the Future* (New York, Harper and Row, 1962), Chapter 1 is a popular but sophisticated statement of this problem. He notes (p. 7) "Mathematics is only a tool, though an immensely powerful one. No equations, however impressive and complex, can arrive at the truth if the initial assumptions are incorrect."

[10] Such a density would imply a total world population above 400 billion. Actually the upper limit to a population living "moderately well" is probably around 50 billion. One of the more buoyant pro-natalists (Colin Clark, "Agricultural Productivity in Relation to Population," in *Man and His Future*, Gordon Wolstenholme, editor [Boston: Little, Brown, 1963], pp. 23–35), and one of the most creative minds working on the problem of how that population might be sustained (Richard L. Meier, *Science and Economic Development: New Patterns of Living* [Cambridge: M.I.T. Press, 1966, 2nd edition], p. 147), seem to have arrived at this figure independently. Both describe the prospective living conditions in some detail; they might be characterized as appreciably better than those now prevailing in Latin America but probably inferior to—and certainly different from—those now typical of Europe.

in a garden, that they must, in spite of all our efforts, grow taller than the chimney pots and swallow the house from sight, so we know and reverently acknowledge, that when any power in human politics has shown for any period of time any considerable activity, it will go on until it reaches the sky.[11]

Some political and social predictions based on the extrapolation of apparent growth rates are only a little less absurd, yet even a sensible-appearing use may go very far wrong.[12] Upward trends do *not* go on forever, but at some point, for some reason, level off, oscillate, or go into a downturn. A child doubles in height between the ages of 2 and 18—but he won't (I trust) double his height again before he is 35. But political history is full of examples of failures to anticipate the system break, the turning point, when what used to be appropriate is no longer so. Generals' alleged preparedness to fight the last war is just such an instance. A national population policy which stressed producing large numbers was appropriate for an era when the number of soldiers a state could field was a major basis of its power; some countries, like Italy, carried that policy over into an age when per capita wealth was equally important as a power base. Political goals, as well as political methods, must be adapted to changes in the social and technological environment. Perhaps we have reached a period when the simple goal of maximizing the "national interest"—whatever that is—has become inappropriate in a world where heavy symbiosis and cooperation are unavoidable. We also must have sufficient discrimination to know which growth rates are important to us. By 1870 there was, within the British government, a clear awareness that Germany's growing steel production would intersect with Britain's before the end of the nineteenth century. For another decade, however, they thought that the country they had to worry about, for political reasons, was France, not Germany. Here then, are still a variety of crucial roles for imagination.

This is the kind of thing to which I want to devote the rest of this chapter: to examining some of the features of the environment of the international political that have undergone very rapid change in recent years, suggesting what the prospects are for their continued growth, and what their political consequences may be. There are at least four possible ways in which a smooth, continuous rate of growth in something may eventually have a discontinuous effect on other aspects of the system, producing what may be called step level change or system transformation.[13]

---

[11] G. K. Chesterton, *The Napoleon of Notting Hill* (London: John Lane, 1904), p. 19.

[12] One of the most forceful statements about the utility of prediction via extrapolating exponential growth curves is Hornell Hart, "Predicting Future Trends," (New York: Appleton-Century Crofts, 1957), pp. 455–73, and a good argument for caution, trying instead to anticipate jumps and quantum leaps, is Gardner Murphy, "Where is the Human Race Going?" in *Science and Human Affairs*, Richard E. Farson, editor (Palo Alto, Calif.: Science and Behavior Books, 1965), pp. 7–17. A more general treatment of how exponential growth rates change is Daniel Bell, "Twelve Modes of Prediction: A Preliminary Sorting of Approaches in the Social Sciences," *Daedalus*, 93, 3 (1964), pp. 845–80.

[13] An early use of this approach in political science is, of course, Morton Kaplan's *System and Process in International Politics* (New York: Wiley, 1957).

CROSSING A THRESHOLD

One is an increase which crosses a threshold, a rate of growth that continues until, on reacting with some other aspect of the social or political system, it produces a discrete change. A given equilibrium may be unstable. In forest ecology, forms of life, adapted to their environment, grow and develop in an area, but in so doing they modify their environment until it has changed so that they are no longer adapted to it. Hardwood trees, for instance, first become established in sunny, relatively open areas. But as they grow up and mature over many decades, they shade the ground beneath them, and in the shade young conifer trees thrive better than new hardwoods. In time, as the large hardwoods die out they are replaced by conifers, which in turn create even deeper shade that prevents the growth of any more hardwoods. The resulting "climax" forest is then in a static equilibrium, and will maintain itself indefinitely except for exogenous change introduced by the activities of man, fire, or other natural disaster. An obvious political example is the slow growth of a voting bloc that, on passing the 50 percent mark, is able then to effect a sharp change in policy.[14] Even here the change may not be all that discontinuous—some political change is likely to occur in response to the pressure of any large bloc, and some further change will arise in anticipation of its majority status as it approaches the halfway mark. But the principle, even though not entirely unambiguous in most empirical examples, is clear enough.

If in the future we have a world government, with effective authority over its member states or over individuals, this example might be of more importance for international politics than it now seems to be. Already the poor states (those with a per capita income of less than $300 a year) form more than a majority in the United Nations, and actually they have the two-thirds majority which is required for issues defined as "important." If they were able to enforce their collective will they doubtless would expand United Nations assessments many times over, spreading the new revenues around for economic development. But though for years they have had the votes necessay to pass this assessment—and have been able to band together to defeat the rich powers on other occasions—they have not done so with the tax rate. It is one thing to assess taxes, quite another, in the current state of international organization, to collect them. So for the present they avoid a show of parliamentary strength that would merely expose their executive weakness.

Another example of this phenomenon which might have more immediate effect is provided by relative power relationships in the Middle East. Despite Israel's numerical inferiority to her neighbors (on the order of one to twenty) her wealth, organization, and external assistance, plus the divisions among the Arabs, allow her to remain militarily equal to her antagonists. But a sustained growth in income and organizational efficiency in Egypt could over

---

[14] Bertrand de Jouvenel, "Political Science and Prevision," *American Political Science Review*, 59, 1 (1965), p. 34.

the long run tip that balance in the Arabs' favor. The notion of a sharp system change or step-level jump is an oversimplification, but at least subjectively, if not objectively, Egypt could reach a point where its leader could decide that from then on he had the power to crush Israel. Whether he really was able to do it, whether he miscalculated and was beaten again, or whether Israel changed the whole threat system by going nuclear, the effect would nevertheless be of a slow and smooth change in one parameter that had, at some pretty clearly identifiable point, produced a discrete change in the system.

More generally, something of this sort has happened in the international system as a whole. Kenneth Boulding has adapted from economics what he calls the "loss of strength gradient," or the rate at which a nation's power declines with distance from its borders.[15] For the major industrial powers this gradient has been steadily pushed outward since the Napoleonic Wars, as fewer and fewer states have remained "unconditionally viable." (He calls a nation unconditionally viable if it can prevent foreign imposition of drastic change of political or social organization inside its own borders.) The ability of one nation to coerce another even at a great distance was strengthened first by social changes (such as the *levée en masse*, the aggregation of large nation-states, and revolutionary ideology), and then technological innovation (the steamship, tanks, aircraft, and finally the atomic bomb). For many years this meant that only six or so great powers were viable against any opponent, and that these great powers could conquer even far away small states.

The cumulative effect of these trends, however, produced a dramatic system change at the end of World War II, when only the two superpowers could dependably resist the domination of any other state. The erosion of all other nations' unconditional viability is in effect what we mean by the transformation of the international system in the early postwar years.

And the bipolar system as we knew it only a decade ago has itself become transformed by the maintenance of the very same trends that first produced it. Continuing technological change, moving from atom bombs and manned bombers to thermonuclear weapons and intercontinental missiles, has removed the sanctuaries that the superpowers used to enjoy in their homelands. Thus there has been a limited revival in the independence of the middle powers, as the great powers can no longer provide such a credible deterrent umbrella. Yet though smaller states are not now so dependent on the big powers for protection—not dependent simply because they are not so confident in it—they still could never hope to *defeat* a superpower. Thus we are somewhere between a bipolar situation and a balance of power world with many foci of more or less equal strength.

Changes in transportation and destructive capacities produced fairly discontinuous changes in the political system, first by cutting the number of great powers to two, and then by restoring to those at the middle level *some*

---

[15] Kenneth E. Boulding, *Conflict and Defense* (New York: Harper and Row, 1960).

of the independence they had possessed before bipolarity. The elimination of *all* states from the "unconditionally viable" category makes the need for new political forms for the international system more pressing then ever. We hear less about this now than a few years ago when the balance of terror was thought to be unstable, but I think the passing of extreme bipolarity *increases* the long-run requirement for political change.

Possibly these trends will have further sharp effects on the international system. The most likely way would be if technology were for a while to favor strongly the defender, especially in the development of an antiballistic missile system for continental defense. Apparently such development has progressed a good bit farther than most of us would have expected a couple of years ago, and an effective anti-ICBM defense no longer seems utterly out of the question for the two big and rich powers.[16] If successful, and if not merely outflanked by chemical or bacteriological weapons, it would return its possessor to the unconditional viability of the good old days. But at the moment that still seems to be a long shot, and I suspect we must look in other directions for new ecological influences on the political system.

DEMAND AND SUPPLY AS LIMITS TO GROWTH

The previous example was of a smooth trend that, on reacting with some other characteristics, produced a marked change in the system. There are in addition several possibilities for trends to stop moving along at their previously established rates—the growth stops, or at least is drastically modified. Our *second* class, then, is of a development that reaches a so-called "logical" ending point, where it stops because of a change in the needs, perception, and behavior of men, because the *demand* which initiated it has essentially been fulfilled. One such is probably in the destructiveness of modern weapons that I alluded to a moment ago. During the century preceding World War II the destructive radius of the biggest weapons then available grew at a doubling rate faster than every 10 years, with the perfection of explosive chemicals and the development first of large cannons and finally of blockbuster bombs. The explosion of the first atomic bomb marked a certain discontinuous jump here, and in the two decades following it the doubling period shortened, to about every four years, culminating in the 100 megaton weapon that can collapse an ordinary frame house within 30 miles of its explosion point. But there is an obvious limit to the destructiveness of modern weapons—the size of anything worth destroying. At the doubling rate of four years, another twenty would be quite sufficient for a weapon capable of obliterating an entire continent; less than a decade more would produce a doomsday machine with a destructive radius exceeding that of the globe. More than that would appear to be a

---

[16] See Jeremy J. Stone, *Containing the Arms Race* (Cambridge: M.I.T. Press, 1966), pp. 224–32, and Chapter 11 of this volume.

waste of scarce resources. Weapons development and improvement might well continue, but along other dimensions like reliability, discrimination (as between men and structures in the neutron bomb), and "cleanliness."[17]

Many of the characteristics of what has been termed the "mobiletic" revolution are likely also to fall into this category, and also rather soon. Mobiletics is a slightly inelegant but useful term coined to cover the whole range of movement—of things, of energy, and of information.[18] One of its components is the transportation of men and other high value per unit volume goods. In the nineteenth century the speed at which men could travel over transcontinental or intercontinental distances doubled more or less every 25 years. It began at the speed of the sailing ship or horse and carriage (depending on the medium), which was hardly more than five miles an hour over sustained distances in the early 1800s. This progressed through the perfection of clippers, the steamship and the railroad. After the Wright brothers this rate speeded up, with a doubling about every ten years, reaching around 600 miles an hour in the late 1940s and the 2000-miles-an-hour bomber in the early 1960s. The built in limits to the trend are fuzzy but fairly obvious, at least on this small earth. Something like a man-carrying intercontinental rocket is the top; 5000 mile missiles make the entire trip from point to point in under 30 minutes or roughly 10,000 miles per hour. Extrapolation of the 10-year doubling rate since the turn of the century would bring us to this limit sometime in the 1980s. Since the 2000-miles-per-hour airliner is not expected to be operational until after 1970 this projection for the rocket seems rather overoptimistic, and the social demand for human travel at 10,000 miles per hour instead of 2000 miles per hour is not likely to be so great as to require that the "schedule" imposed by extrapolating past changes be kept. In the longer run faster speeds for manned travel to the planets and beyond are to be expected, but even here the extrapolation to 30,000 miles per hour in the year 2000 is, give or take a few years and tens of thousands of miles, about as long as current rates of growth can go unabated. According to most scientific authorities, by then there would appear to be more payoffs in suspended animation, or instellar travel by colonies that would reproduce themselves en route. The real upper limit to man's travel capabilities may be only at the speed of light, but it is unlikely to be approached at the current high rates of increase. This, then, is another rate of change that will, within the lifetimes of some of us, slow down drastically.

With the advent of the telegraph, communication became virtually instantaneous, at the speed of light plus processing time, over short distances. The changes are not so orderly that any simple exponential growth curve can be fitted to this one, but modern improvements have concentrated on eliminating the need for fixed channels of communication such as wires, on lengthening

[17] The data in this and the following paragraph are from Bruce M. Russett, *Trends in World Politics* (New York: Macmillan, 1965), Chapter 1.
[18] Bertram E. Gross, *Space-Time and Post-Industrial Society* (Syracuse, N.Y.: Syracuse University, Maxwell School of Citizenship and Public Affairs, 1966, mimeo.), p. 4.

the distance that could be covered, and on providing facilities for transmitting a wider variety of messages, from electrical impulses that had to be translated from Morse code into letters, to impulses that could be made into faithful reproductions of sound and sight. When these developments culminate, as they will shortly, in the installation of a worldwide system of relays to carry television impulses around the earth within two seconds, the most important dimension of the communication revolution will be completed.[19] Further work will be left to clean up the quality and variety of transmission possibilities and to proliferate transmitters and receivers. These mobiletic changes, therefore, are now approaching their natural completion. Probably they will pick up again on some now hardly imaginable dimensions,[20] but it is unlikely that in the next fifty years or so they will again produce such a sudden change in the environment of international politics as they have just put us through.

These are growth rates that will slow down essentially as the *demand* is satisfied. Making an effective decision to speed up or slow down their growth is not always within the capabilities of our social and political systems, but at least the growth is not so autonomous that we need anticipate any particular difficulties when the "natural" slowdown points approach. This is by no means universally the case with rapidly growing social phenomena, so we are led to a *third* category—growth rates that come to a halt because the *supply* of some basic commodites is exhausted.

Behind all the changes just listed has been the explosion of science and technology. Since the eighteenth century the number of scientists in the world has doubled approximately every 15 years; in the United States alone the doubling rate has been faster, roughly every 10 years. This clearly can't go on. The number of scientists and engineers has now reached almost one percent of the total population,[21] and if one eliminates the temperamentally and intellectually unfit (eliminates them only for analytical purposes), they amount to possibly one fifth of those who have the capacities to become productive scientists. Even if we forget about leaving high IQ individuals for commerce, administration, and the arts, it is clear that this exponential growth curve has a built in ceiling. We will see the end of it well before the century is out; it will affect our professional lives and especially those of our graduate students. Some mitigation may be in sight; for instance, utilizing the brain drain of high IQ people from underdeveloped countries, a reservoir that may not dry up for another fifty years or so; or extremely sophisticated computer usage; or hiring more secretaries; or improving information retrieval; or various ways of relieving scientists of the substantial drudgery that still remains in

---

[19] See John R. Platt, "The Step to Man," *Science*, 149 (August 6, 1965), p. 608.

[20] Sometimes this mutation and revival is called "escalation." See Gerald Holton, "Scientific Research and Scholarship: Notes Towards the Design of Proper Scales," *Daedalus*, 91, 2 (1962), pp. 369–99.

[21] This is from a projection and adaptation of figures for 1962–1964 in U.S. Bureau of the Census, *Statistical Abstract of the United States, 1966* (Washington, D.C.: U.S. Government Printing Office, 1966), p. 547–8. I am assuming that the potential talent pool includes all those of working age with an IQ of at least 120.

their work. Yet this kind of relief only postpones the day when surgery will be necessary. Federal obligations for research and development in the United States doubled roughly every four years between 1950 and 1964.[22] But from 1964 to 1967 they levelled off at about three percent of national income. This is nearly a third of what we spent on defense then, and even allowing for growth in real national income (perhaps a doubling every 20 years at an annual rate of about four percent) it is hard to see how science spending can grow very much more. Depending upon how it is handled, the levelling off of this trend could lead to a period of regrouping and digestion in science, as better means are perfected for making us aware of other people's research and avoiding some of the duplication that is currently so prevalent. In the world at large, it is conceivable that a levelling off of the growth in science could slow down some of the more wasteful and dangerous aspects of international technological competition. In any case, the levelling has already begun.

THE SOCIAL CONTROL OF GROWTH

This leads us to a distinction which ushers in our *fourth* class of growth patterns—between growth rates that are brought to a halt *only* by resource limitations, and rates that are controlled, short of the physical limits, by deliberate social policy.[23] John Platt's fascinating essay on "The Step to Man" also mentions some of the growth curves I have detailed, and forecasts their orderly levelling off.[24] But orderly transition may be the exception. A growth rate may reach its ceiling and, in the absence of social control or an escalation that picks up again on some other dimension, bump along the ceiling. In effect this is oscillation around the equilibrium level, and I will illustrate it with the outcome foreseen for the population explosion according to one model.

Imagine an island with no foreign trade and where there is neither emigration nor immigration—a closed system. The area of agricultural land is fixed, and for some time it has supported a population, growing at a constant rate, that has not yet required all of the available land. As land utilization reaches

---

[22] Ibid., p. 544, and *Statistical Abstract of the United States, 1959*, p. 539. The figures are not fully comparable, but the general pattern is unmistakable.

[23] I distinguish between this *planned diminution* and the simple relatively autonomous slackening of demand discussed as the second category. Note too that the first and third categories apply to environmental limitations that act regardless of human cognition, whereas the second and fourth operate only as a consequence of perceptions. This useful distinction between different environmental effects is made by Sprout and Sprout, op. cit.

[24] Platt, op. cit. An initially exponential curve that bends over smoothly in an S-shape is the logistic curve. An early example in demographic prediction is Lowell J. Reed, "Population Growth and Forecasts," *Annals of the American Academy of Political and Social Science*, 188 (November, 1936), pp. 159–66. The logistic curve may have looked applicable to U.S. population in the 1930s but it does not fit later developments. The article is nevertheless useful as an explicit answer to the projection of exponential rates to infinity.

100 percent and the level of technology remains constant, the population will approach the maximum that the island can support. But if technology is evolving, as it has been in the Western world over the past several centuries, the ceiling may continually be pushed upward and the population may continue to grow at its exponential rate. Let us assume, however, that at some point the local farmers' ingenuity gives out and they exhaust all methods for substantially increasing the yield of their land. When this point is reached the population of the island will have reached its ceiling. Growth may not stop absolutely short in its tracks, for there may be some belt tightening possible. But it must stop soon, and not necessarily as a simple levelling off to a smooth plateau. On the contrary, after the first steps of belt tightening the next consequence is likely to be a disease epidemic in a population made vulnerable by malnutrition, or there may occur a natural disaster which drastically cuts food production in a situation where there is no margin to spare. Instead of simply levelling off, the population will drop sharply in response to the sudden rise in death rates. But after this immediate disaster is past, there will again, at the advanced technological level achieved, be a surplus of land relative to population. So, for a short period, unless reproductive habits have been changed, the population will again shoot upward, at the previous rate, until the gap is filled once more. And again, the population will become vulnerable to disease or nature, will fall once again, and so on. Here is the classic Malthusian trap in which population is forced into equilibrium with limited productive resources. The pattern, however, is one of violent oscillations to and from a ceiling imposed by "nature."[25]

Such a perpetual unhappy fate is nevertheless not the only possible denouement to the exponential growth curve. If, instead of allowing resource limitations to determine the situation, it is subjected to human volition and social control, a better solution is feasible. If the birth rate is brought down fairly quickly and made equal to the death rate before the ceiling is reached, the curve can be made to taper off smoothly and culminate in an even plateau without wild oscillation. Presumably there will be some fluctuation for a while, as the social controls are perfected and the right mix is found to depress the birth rate just to, and not beyond, the equilibrium level. But in principle the proper procedures could be worked out.

Going from the abstract model of the isolated island to the current world demographic situation brings, I would guess, substantial cause for optimism. Many sociologists and economists are more expert on demographic matters than I, and I will not try to encroach on their territory. It appears to me,

---

[25] A good example of thinking that hitting the ceiling is the only probable outcome to such demographic pressures is Sir Charles Darwin, "Forecasting the Future," in *Frontiers in Science*, Edward Hutchings, Jr., editor (New York: Basic Books, 1958), pp. 100–16. Richard L. Meier, *Modern Science and the Human Fertility Problem* (New York: Wiley, 1959), pp. 53–63, forecasts something much like this happening in certain areas of the world, notably the island of Mauritius. For a similar result with a different mechanism (the stress syndrome) see Hudson Hoagland, "Mechanisms of Population Control," *Daedalus*, VI, 3 (1964), pp. 812–29.

however, that this represents a growth rate that is on the verge of being brought under control, at least sometime before the end of the century. I doubt very much that the world will look like our mythical island, or even like Hong Kong. For what is, by comparison with the funds expended for military research and development, a very modest investment, we have come up with a variety of extremely promising methods for population control, and have still more in the works. Even a cosmic pessimist would have to admit that the technical side of this problem is being licked before our eyes. The social side—how to bring about widespread acceptance and use—is not so easy, but with the new attitudes in developed and underdeveloped countries alike, it does not seem so formidable as it did only a few years ago. I should perhaps say these things in a still small voice, since I am assuming a high degree of public awareness and determination to defeat the threat, a degree that has not yet been reached and must be maintained for decades if my prediction is to come true. It could, if it makes us complacent, become a self-defeating prophecy. And I am aware that the details of solving this problem could yet be very difficult, and that the quality of life on earth may well depend less on *whether* the demographic revolution is brought to its thermidor, than on how quickly. A delay of a generation will mean almost twice as many people to accommodate, and give us some very serious economic and political crises throughout Asia—crises that may be partly avoided by more rapid action. Thus I am very much in sympathy with those who are in a hurry. But this is nevertheless a promising area. With some luck, determination, and dedication, it may become an example of how a social pattern, an exponential growth rate of enormous import, was brought under control before it reached its built in ceiling and burdened mankind with its oscillations.

Here then is a prediction, imbued with I think only a small component of overoptimism, for the turn of the coming century. The population explosion will be, at least for macro purposes, ended. We may not have reached the state of equal birth and death rates and hence a stable population, but the rate of growth should be much reduced. The world food crisis will have been met and surmounted. (Notice, however, that I did *not* say avoided. I do not think we will get off that easily. Before population control takes full effect we will have to deal with mass famine in Asia.) The problem of economic development will still be with us, and perhaps in even more pressing form. But it will be in *different* form, for rapid population growth will no longer be a major brake on the developmental process, demanding heavy inputs of capital investment just to stay in place. The major problems instead will be in the areas of organization, determination, and the difficulties of controlling the social and political unrest that is associated with the middle stages of economic development. How to cope with rising expectations, with wants that increase even faster than growing satisfactions, will not be an easy question. The last stages of the mobiletic revolution, in bringing to even the poorest members of world society images of how foreign and domestic rich live, will enormously exacerbate problems we can already see.

THE END OF STABLE CHANGE

For the past century men in the Western world, and more recently over the rest of the globe, have lived in a period when change was the usual state of affairs. Though the change has been exciting, disruptive, and demanding for the individuals undergoing it, all of us have become accustomed to it; our parents with some head shaking, our children in a way that takes space travel and other wonders in stride as normal and utterly expectable events. Prediction of the ecology of international politics has been difficult primarily because for most of the time we have been so ignorant about the precise magnitudes of change and its predictable regularities. Had we before us accurate information about past experience, and courage enough to extrapolate, much of the present situation could have been predicted merely by expecting more of the same that had prevailed—not the same levels, but the same change rates. Relatively speaking, *political* prediction would have been easy (given today's data sources and theoretical achievements). Persistence forecasting, or the extrapolation of mildly sloping trends, would have been accurate. But until recently much of the necessary quantitative information simply had not been assembled, and since one can hardly extrapolate a trend without knowing what the trend is, we have a clear example of a case where neither imagination nor rigor were, by themselves, sufficient for adequate forecasting. Where precise data are still lacking, the normal difficulties of forecasting have been compounded recently by the rapid changes implied in the high levels now reached on many of the exponential growth curves, where a doubling in eight years instead of twelve can make a very great difference in the absolute changes with which society must cope.

Some of these problems will remain in future years, but as more and better data become available, and as social science develops greater rigor and a better understanding of our environment, they are being eased. For a brief period prediction may have great success in a world of rapid but dependable change. It will soon be shaken, however, by the system breaks that can be discerned in the not so distant future. The new qualities of imagination will be required, both to *predict* and to *determine* what the world will be like. Much of the future will depend upon which growth rates change first, and whether by orderly deliberate control that brings them to a plateau with a minimum of oscillation, or whether they bump up and down against a ceiling imposed by the environment. Doubtless we all would prefer a world where population growth was brought to a regulated halt, rather than one where Malthus reigned supreme and the population rose and fell with epidemics and bad harvests. And because many of these growth rates *are* interrelated, an uncontrolled change in one is likely to have far-ranging effects.

For several generations we have been living in an era of transition between great system changes. That era is now coming to a close, and a period of instability is ahead. We have a limited amount of time to break loose from habit, inertia, and administrative routine, to decide which trends we most need to control, and to devise ways of doing it. Without adopting a naive eighteenth-century faith in the omnipotence of science, it is nonetheless true that when a social need is strongly felt *some* solution is often found, even though no one could have predicted in advance precisely what that solution would be.[26] On the whole, I am hopeful that the necessary social and technological innovations can be found under pressure, although the time is short and the margin for error not at all wide. The population control experience is a good omen here. Only ten years ago one could not have said which, if any, of the possibilities then being explored might pay off; now we find unanticipated degrees of freedom. Maybe something of the sort will arise for international politics and world order. Right now no one can produce a scheme for the year 2000 that really looks workable, but as the pressure comes on, ingenious men may be able to develop something.

While trying to improve our predictive powers we must, at the same time, avoid *depending* on a high level of predictive success. We must maintain a pluralist approach as as to be able to adapt to the unexpected; we must have several possible alternatives and "keep our options open." It is worth recalling a statement by Alfred North Whitehead that is even more appropriate now than when he wrote it almost fifty years ago:

> We must expect that the future will be dangerous. It is the business of the future to be dangerous, and it is among the merits of science that it equips the future for its duties. . . . The middle class pessimism over the future of the world comes from a confusion between civilization and security. In the immediate future there will be less security than in the immediate past, less stability. . . . There is a degree of instability which is inconsistent with civilization. But, on the whole, the great ages have been unstable ages.[27]

---

[26] See Bell, op. cit., and John R. Platt, *The Excitement of Science* (Boston: Houghton Mifflin, 1962), Chapter 4, for good discussion of how this may be true, and also L. B. Slobodkin, "On the Present Incompleteness of Mathematical Ecology," *American Scientist*, 53, 3 (1965), pp. 347–59. It is important, however, to distinguish between what an *observer* might diagnose as social needs, and effective social *demands*.

[27] Alfred North Whitehead, *Science and the Modern World* (New York: Macmillan, 1925), p. 291.

9
The Rich Fifth and the Poor Half: Some Speculations about International Politics in 2000 A.D.

AFFLUENCE AND POVERTY

Many modern utopians foresee a coming perfection of social man, stemming from great changes in his physical environment. They see the problem of evil as basically intractable in a world of pain, ignorance, and deprivation, but soluble where the ancient bonds of man's mortality have been loosened. They still consider that raising incomes in poor countries, or improving the physical lot of poor citizens within rich countries, will solve the problem of political instability. In posing the question, "Who can be interested in democracy when he has an empty belly?," they derive social and political optimism from the prospects for future economic growth.

Such optimism may have a hollow ring in light of some unanticipated and threatening events of recent years. Political instability in many industrialized nations—most notably the United States—throws doubt both on the above political theory and on the prospects for an industrialized society sufficiently stable to maintain its economic growth. Furthermore, even should productivity continue to increase, pollution threatens either actually to diminish the quality of life or to force cleanup efforts so expensive as to absorb most of the production gains merely to stay in place in terms of environmental quality. Pollution

Reprinted, with substantial revisions and additions, from an essay appearing in *Virginia Quarterly Review*, 44, 2 (spring 1968). Presented to the Conference on Comparative Analysis of Highly Industrialized Societies in Bellagio, Italy, August 1971.

endangers industrial and developing nations alike. Over the past two decades energy consumption in the advanced states has grown at a rate of more than 4 percent a year, almost all of it from fossil fuels. A continuation of this trend would produce a fourfold increase in worldwide energy requirements between now and the end of the century. Energy consumption is both a source of pollution and, paradoxically, a necessary component of any effort to diminish pollution. Recent, and perhaps temporary, cuts in government support for science and technology also make one uneasy.

Nevertheless the threats of pollution and of political instability still contain large unknown elements as to their nature, magnitude, and timing. Even such work as that by Donella and Dennis Meadows and Jay Forrester for the Club of Rome puts the environmental crisis sometime into the twenty-first century. For now let us assume that those problems can, for at least the next 27 years, be managed without greatly reducing the otherwise projected growth, and consider whether even then the optimists' image of a stable, growing, and affluent world is plausible. I believe, rather, that clearly discernible trends in the international social system will first produce a crisis of international government.

By many tests the world of the not so distant future will be, for many of its inhabitants, far better than the present one. We have confident and compelling predictions of vast automation, greatly diminishing the amount of physical drudgery required in production and freeing members of the labor force either for leisure or for intellectually stimulating and satisfying work. Time and facilities for the leisured pursuit of science and the arts seem within reach for many. We have the prospect of major breakthroughs in medical science, with artificial organs and the control of killer diseases. We are promised (or threatened with) supersonic transports to circle the earth at three times the speed of sound, and instantaneous electronic communication with data banks and libraries anywhere. A computerized financial system for pay, credit, and tax collection is virtually in preparation. Despite funding cuts, NASA scientists still talk of the likelihood of a manned landing on Mars and of a permanent base on the moon by 2000 A.D. There is held out to us the image of a new Eden, a stable period wherein many of the most unsettling aspects of modern life may be brought under control and we can more fully reap its great benefits.

But how many of the six billion or so people on this globe will be able to afford to circumnavigate it? How soon will the Indian peasant install his automated farm and devote himself to experimentation in his laboratory? Have *you* paid a bill for private hospital treatment lately? It is crucial to recognize that the gains from these developments will not apply at all equally to all men. The most dramatic benefits will accrue to those who can afford substantial sums of money to pay for them. A world view that sees material prosperity as providing the opportunity for the resolution of discord may be attractive (if simplistic as political or social theory), but it will not be very relevant to a society where only a minority possess the necessary wealth. And that is precisely what will happen. The absolute gap in living standards between rich and poor nations is widening much more rapidly than would be implied by a simple juxtaposition of growth rates, and the rich are becoming a self-perpetuating elite.

1965 AND 2000 A.D.

Table 9-1 shows some basic information and forecasts about the world, listing items roughly in the order in which we shall refer to them in the course of this chapter. It treats the world as divided into three groups of nations: a rich quarter where the mean per capita gross national product (GNP) in 1965 was at least $900 and averaged over $1,900 for the entire group; a poor half where no nation had a mean GNP per capita as high as $200 and where the average was hardly more than $100; and a middle quarter between the two extremes. (Because of its slow projected population growth the rich *fourth* becomes a mere *fifth* of the world's population by 2000 A.D.) The rich group is composed of northern Europe (east and west including the USSR but excluding the Iberian and Balkan peninsulas), Canada, the United States, Puerto Rico, Australia, New Zealand, Israel, Kuwait, and Japan. The poor group includes most of Africa excluding South Africa, and most of Asia except for Japan. The remaining parts of Europe go with most of Latin America into the middle group. Since the purpose of this chapter is to contrast living conditions and political potential at the two extremes, the table ignores the middle income group and we shall do likewise in the text.[1]

Columns 1 and 3 in the table show the situation as of 1965, and columns 2 and 4 give my "best guess" estimates for the situation of the year 2000. Some of the predicted figures are derived simply from projections of recent rates of growth. Others reflect natural "ceilings," or otherwise modified growth rates.[2] Still others reflect what I consider to be likely shifts in preferences (e.g.,

---

[1] Except for the data on nuclear weapons and life expectancy, all information in the table is from Charles L. Taylor and Michael C. Hudson, *World Handbook of Political and Social Indicators*, second edition (New Haven: Yale University Press, 1972). Life expectancy data are from *UN Demographic Yearbook, 1969* (New York: United Nations, 1970). Nuclear weapons data are for *1971* and are estimated from Stockholm International Peace Research Institute, *Yearbook of World Armaments and Disarmament, 1968/69* (Stockholm: SIPRI, 1970). On the basis of its economic performance since 1965 Japan is included in the rich group despite an average per capita GNP of only $861 in 1965. All averages in the table are *weighted* averages; that is each nation is weighted by its population so that the United States, USSR, China, and India weigh very heavily in their respective groups. This was done because we are interested here in the situation of the average *individual* in each group, not in the average *country*.

[2] Comparing *rates* of growth in rich and poor countries can be deceptive since for many variables (literacy, infant mortality, or calories, for example) the rich countries are already at or near a natural "ceiling"; hence their growth rates will now be low. Theodore Caplow, "Are the Poor Countries Getting Poorer?," *Foreign Policy*, 3 (summer 1971), pp. 90–107, has nevertheless shown that the current rates of increase of growth in poor countries are lower than those achieved by the present rich countries at comparable stages in their development. Hence in terms of what could be "expected" at a stage of early growth the poor countries are in fact falling behind.

toward more health and education expenditures in developed countries and a virtual halt in net migration to central cities in developed countries.) Some of the reasoning behind the predictions is spelled out in the text or in notes to the table. While the 1965 data are quite reliable, the predictions are of course subject to considerable challenge. I nevertheless believe that, as statements about order of magnitude, they are defensible within the basic assumptions of the chapter—no nuclear war between superpowers, no breakdown of the international economic or monetary system, and no political breakdown in a superpower.

There is, it is true, a widening gap even as the per capita GNP growth rates are measured. Some of the poor countries, such as South Korea and until recently Pakistan, have done well, but they are more than balanced by big states like India and Indonesia, which have hardly done more than keep pace with rising population. On the other hand, no figures are available for China, where there almost surely has been real growth. Adjusting the figure in the table for Chinese performance *might* raise GNP per capita growth rate in poor countries to as much as 3 percent—perhaps not too great a difference from that of the rich, though it implies a doubling rate of income in not less than 24 years as compared with 17 for the rich.

The catch in any such argument, however, is in its frame of reference—*percentage rates* of growth. While it is hardly fair to expect a poor country to add the same *total* amount to its income each year as does a rich one, the failure to do so nevertheless causes a widening of the *absolute* gap. When the differences between rich and poor are as great as they are in the world today, the cumulative results are very striking. Let us suppose that the poor nations with annual per capita incomes in 1965 of $105 grew at a yearly rate of 3 percent until the end of the century. The outcome would be average incomes of about $300 in the year 2000 A.D. Frankly it is hard to imagine how this performance could be much improved upon, given the shortages of skills, capital, and social incentives for growth in these areas. Except for a few special cases, the problem is more than simply one of bottlenecks where the injection of some key components, like money, might quickly trigger self-sustaining growth. Even on the most optimistic assumption of a 4 percent per annum growth rate the per capita GNP in the underdeveloped world would still be less than $400 in the year 2000.

If, however, we assume even the modest annual growth rate of 3 percent in the developed countries, the beneficence of compound interest will bring a most impressive absolute level of wealth. The average annual GNP per head of under $2,000 would go to about $5,400, a figure at least 18 times that in the poor half of the globe, and which means an *absolute gap of at least $5,000 instead of $1,800*. On more optimistic assumptions, for the industrialized countries the income level would go to about $7,500 at 4 percent interest, or an absolute gap of over $7,000 and a differential of 20 to 25 times. With the post-Keynesian understanding of fiscal and monetary policies, generally well applied in modern nations, this is an entirely plausible projection in the absence of world war. Both the present and the prospective relative difference of rich and poor *between nations* is extremely great by comparison with the income

Table 9-1

Contrasts between Rich and Poor in 1965 and "Best Guess Estimates" for 2000

Bases for contrast	Rich fifth		Poor half	
	1965	2000	1965	2000
1. Total population (thousands)	908,148	1,300,000	1,858,548	3,500,000
2. Average per capita GNP (U.S. dollars)	1,912	>5,000	105	<300
3. Average GNP per capita growth rate (percent)	4.3	3	1.4*	<3
4. Average energy consumption per capita (kilotons of coal equivalents)	4,746	14,000†	260	1,000†
5. Public health expenditure per capita (U.S. dollars)	51	300	1	3
6. Public health expenditure as percentage of GNP	3	6	1.1	1.1
7. Physicians per million population	1,506	2,000	165	300
8. Infant mortality rate per thousand	25	20–25	82	60
9. Life expectancy (females at age 0)	74	90?	43	60
10. Annual population growth rate (percent)	1.3	<1.0	2.1	<2.0
11. Enrollment in higher education per million population	14,944	20,000	1,976	3,000
12. Total scientific journals	28,045	50,000	1,945	5,000
13. Public education expenditure per capita (U.S. dollars)	103	350	3	12
14. Public education expenditure as percentage of GNP	5.5	7.0	2.9	4.0
15. Percentage of adults literate	99	99	39	55
16. Primary and secondary public school enrollment as percentage of age group	88	90	41	60
17. Calories per capita per day	2,947	3,000	2,088	2,500
18. Protein units per capita	88	100	55	70
19. Total GNP (millions of U.S. dollars)	1,732,311	6,500,000	195,566	1,000,000
20. Total energy consumption (million metric tons of coal equivalents)	4,310	18,200	493	3,500
21. Total military expenditures (millions of U.S. dollars)	109,194	380,000‡	11,658	60,000‡
22. Military expenditure per capita	121	300‡	6	19‡
23. Military expenditure as a percentage of GNP	5.9	5.9?‡	5.9	5.9?‡
24. Nuclear warheads (1971)	>100,000	>100,000	<100	>5,000
25. Foreign trade as percentage of GNP	19.8	25	14.3	15–20
26. Deaths from domestic political violence (1960–1970)	736	?	>800,000	?
27. Gini index of *sectoral* income inequality	14.0	?	24.2	?
28. Population per square kilometer	16.1	23.0	44.7	83.6
29. Percentage of population in cities over 100,000	38	40	9	25
30. Radios per thousand of population	440	1,000	14	>100

†4 and 20 assume approximate 4 percent growth in 2000 A.D. poor countries with development, but that antipollution efforts keep growth to 3 percent in the rich countries.
*No data for China.
‡21–23: no change assumed for military share of projected GNP from present, though one can hope for a decline, and *possibly* a shift in rich countries from military spending toward foreign aid.

160

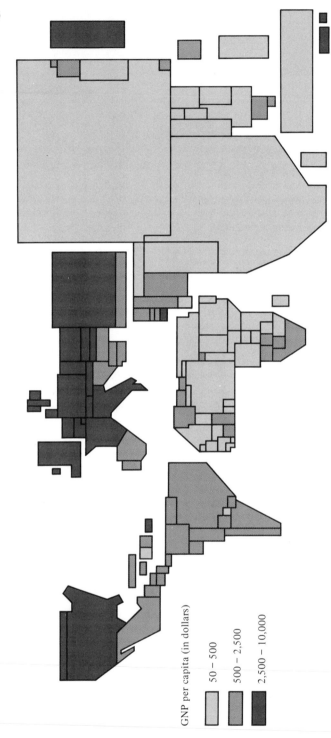

Figure 9-1
Distribution of population according to GNP per capita projected for 2000 A.D. Country areas are drawn to reflect projected population sizes.

GNP per capita (in dollars)

50 – 500

500 – 2,500

2,500 – 10,000

inequalities typical *within* nations. The difference in average per capita GNP over the entire range of the richest and poorest states (United States versus the poorest Africans) is now on the order of 70 to one; within the United States the difference between Connecticut and Mississippi, at the extremes, is hardly more than two to one.

Now, as every economist warns, cross-country comparisons of per capita incomes in dollars are treacherous. A dollar will buy much more, fully two or three times as much, of the necessities of life in a poor agricultural nation as in a rich urban one. But however measured, the gap between rich and poor remains, and will remain, enormous. Many of the other items for comparison in the table convey some sense of the current gap, and we shall explore their implications further in sections below. Moreover, it is precisely the kinds of things that are expensive in anyone's currency that are some of the most exciting products of modern science and technology. They promise to be produced largely in industrialized societies and by industrialized societies—and because of their cost, *for* industrialized societies as well.

THE HEALTH GAP

What will you be able to buy with money if you have lots of it in the world of a generation hence? For one thing, there is life itself. Organ transplants and organ banks will probably be common. We are on the verge of mass use of artificial organs in the United States. Hospitals all over the country now operate artificial kidneys; artificial livers, lungs, and most importantly, hearts are clearly near development. Millions of middle aged and elderly Americans and Europeans will doubtless shortly wear pacemakers—instruments to provide a regular electrical stimulus to the heart, preventing what is by far the most common cause of cardiac arrest. The complete pump for an artificial heart is at present cumbersome, but it will not remain in its now primitive form. Such replacements of natural functions as radar to substitute for the eyes of a blind man are fully contemplated. With all these organs replaceable, it is not hard to visualize the next step—it would be entirely possible to keep a severed head, or perhaps just a brain, alive almost indefinitely if attached to a device for circulating blood (or other fluid) containing nutrients and removing waste products. While it may hardly seem to us a desirable form of nearly eternal life, tastes may change. It represents only one of the most dramatic ways in which the degenerations of aging may be postponed or evaded.

Short of this still rather fantastic outcome are the more modest current and prospective achievements of modern medicine. In addition to the artificial organs there is the prospect of modest control over aging and an eventual cure for several major diseases, including many forms of carcinoma. For more than 20 years life expectancy in the United States and Europe inched forward;

within the past decade there has been almost no change at all. But some of these prospects suggest that another major breakthrough is imminent.

Few of these achievements, however, are likely to be cheap, either in the costs of their research and development or in their application to particular patients. Major surgery or a series of drug and radiation treatments for cancer are far from inexpensive; medical care is the fastest rising item in the cost of living index. The annual cost per user of an artificial kidney machine exceeds the total income of most of its potential recipients even in the United States; where it is nevertheless made available some form of subsidy is required. Within rich and integrated societies some form of insurance or burden sharing doubtless may bring them within reach of virtually everyone. But it is extremely difficult to imagine how they can be brought within range of the price that any but a tiny fraction of the people in Asia, Africa, or even Latin America will be able to pay, and their societies will not be able to afford subsidies on anything approaching a mass basis.

In 1960 the expectation of life for a newborn infant in India was 41 years, less than two-thirds that of a North American or West European baby born at the same time. By contrast, Ceylon, with a per capita income only about 70 percent higher than India's, had in 1962 an average life expectancy of 61 years, much nearer to that typical of Western Europe and North America (about 74 years) than to India's. Ceylon had been the subject of major public health projects which in a few short years dramatically cut its death rate by more than half. As is implied by the low per capita income of Ceylon, the means for doing this were cheap. Probably the most significant was the use of insecticides,[3] at a cost of only a few cents per person, to kill mosquitoes and eradicate malaria. Some of these measures have now also been introduced in India and the others will be, though there the problems are greater and incomes so low that even cheap public health is not always within their means. But basically the Ceylonese experience is an archetype of the population problem in the underdeveloped world, a consequence of the drastic reduction in death rates, and hence life expectancy, which has been achieved rapidly at very low cost.

This near convergence of life expectancies in the rich countries and in some poor ones may not last long. It takes a great increase in the wealth of a nation to add those additional 13 years (between Ceylon and Europe) that will equate its life expectancy figures with those currently found in an industrialized country, and only the very rich will be able to afford the technological innovations of the next three decades. Very possibly the year 2000 will see a continued differential of three to two between the number of years a poor child can expect to live and the number to which a newborn citizen of the privileged West may reasonably aspire—a difference between perhaps 60 years in the former case, and something approaching a century in the latter.

---

[3] Specifically, with DDT. Substitutes will be at least temporarily more expensive.

EDUCATION AND LEISURE

Education is a prime example of the desirable aspects of future life that will be available only to those who live in very affluent societies. The United States is notorious in its lavish proliferation of colleges and universities, with almost half the eligible age groups so enrolled. At no foreseeable time will under-developed countries be able to afford this, unless possibly as the crudest and most transparent effort to keep young people out of a swollen labor force for a little longer, and in any case only to send them back with higher aspirations but little more in the way of relevant skills.

Furthermore, there is more than one measure of education. As practiced in the better Western institutions, higher learning is a very capital-intensive process. Fifteen of the top private universities in the United States, for example, have an average endowment exceeding $25,000 per student—and even so tuition and fees approximate $3,000 apiece for undergraduates at these institutions. Typically the faculty-to-student ratio is about one to six, not so very remote from Mark Hopkins's ideal. The end product is a graduate who has had a good deal of seminar experience, substantial criticism of his writing, and even in a time of research rewards to faculty, a fair amount of interaction with at least some of his teachers if he desired it. At the same time he has been at a place where exciting, relevant research has been conducted on a large scale, and where what he has been taught was not too far removed from the frontiers of knowledge. Such an experience cannot even remotely be approached in an underdeveloped country. (Berkeley students might enroll in Calcutta to discover what anomie is *really* like.) This is not to deny that underdeveloped countries may be able to provide a minimal education for most of their citizens. Whereas the typical rate of literacy in low income countries is now just under 40 percent, by the end of the century most people will probably have the most basic skills for reading and writing—for the past decade or so the literate proportion of the population has grown even in the most hard-pressed areas. But the quality of that education, in terms of financial, social, and intangible personal rewards, is very different from that accruing to the graduate of Cornell, or for that matter, of Manchester or Heidelberg.

Even leisure varies enormously in quality between these two parts of the world. In the developed West, and especially for middle and upper class citizens, leisure is a commodity of great productive value. It is of such value that people may not feel they have much of it, but in terms of time spent away from the office, even the busiest actually have a good bit. Executives are forced to take vacation time whether or not they want it. And though they may have little enough time for strict rest and relaxation, many hours are spent on community or personal activities only tenuously related to earning a livelihood. Education is rapidly becoming a respectable use of leisure hours, if not for some a near necessity. Extensive automation, profoundly affecting every trade and profession by 2000 A.D., can but strengthen these tendencies.

The difference between leisure in a rich society and in a poor one involves images which hardly need drawing, though their consequences may require emphasis. For its constructive use, leisure demands expensive education or facilities, or both, of the sort utterly unavailable to the masses of Africa and Asia. In the latter area the phenomenon of underemployment is already rampant, with millions of agricultural workers occupied only a fraction of the year. On the farm such a situation may be deplorable because of the human potential it wastes, but unemployment in the cities is far more dangerous for social and political stability. Often amounting to more than a quarter of the labor force, urban unemployment means the existence of a mass of men without income and often without prospects, but located in a part of the country where they can readily be used by demagogues for violent demands on the government.

This pessimistic picture should not be viewed as implying that *none* of the wonders of the future will be of any benefit to the underdeveloped areas. Many of them surely will be, including the economical desalinization of sea water; cheap, effective, and widespread fertility control; and the commercial synthesis of protein for food. Another is the profitable "mining" of sea water, probably coupled to the same plants that desalinate for drinking and irrigation. This will make available to states with coastlines the minerals that do not lie in exploitable quantity within the land parts of their domains. Some poor nations, however, are likely to emerge as net losers when this new source provides a cheaper alternative to existing mines. The commercially useful production of tin from sea water, for instance, would demolish the already precarious economy of Bolivia. The cheap manufacture of palatable synthetic food also is likely to be something of a mixed blessing for predominantly agricultural societies.

But the trouble with these prospective developments, even ignoring the substitution effects of mineral extraction from the sea or synthetic protein manufacture, is that they cannot upgrade the basic quality of life much above subsistence in the poor areas. They may raise food production to a calorie level near that in the rich world and so avoid starvation; they may avoid the most utter and abject misery and may even prevent the further expansion of populations in already densely packed lands while at the same time they improve basic sanitation and cut infant mortality and other deaths from the traditional scourges of famine and epidemic. None of these improvements, however, will make available to the poor man the kind of benefits a rich man will be able to buy for himself.

THE DISTRIBUTION OF POWER

This is not to suggest that the consequence of relative deprivation in vast areas of the world, even of an increase in the relative differences that seems so probable, will be successful violent revolution against the worldwide order or the decline of the West in terms of sheer power. On the contrary, technological innovations are likely to favor the industrialized nations here too. Among the more exotic probabilities are procedures for manipulating the weather; the perfection of nonlethal chemical agents to destroy the will to resist without causing permanent damage to the organism; and perishable arms for counter-insurgency forces, which would deteriorate rapidly if lost or captured. Surely many of these developments can already be discerned. The United States may not have done very well in its unhappy adventure in Vietnam. But the reason it was able to hold on even as long as it did was its wealth. Simple calculations show a cost of $250,000 a head for every Viet Cong (or bystander) who showed up in the body count. (At its peak the war cost over two billion dollars a month, and Viet Cong casualties ran at about 8,000 a month according to American official—and probably exaggerated—figures.) The enormous weight of wealth and technology which Americans can bring to bear against a small country, even at that distance, makes outright failure in antiguerilla warfare unnecessary for the politically determined. The military uses of outer space, if they prove to be significant, will be exploitable only by nations rich enough to pour many billions of dollars into the effort. (Note that Table 9-1 shows the military expenditure of rich nations to be ten times that of the poor nations, and their advantage in total resources or GNP to be about the same.)

Not even the proliferation of nuclear weapons will change this situation. A few atomic or even hydrogen bombs, plus a crude delivery system, make no equalizer for the small state against a superpower. At best a small nation, even if able to deliver its weapons, could not prevent a crushing retaliation capable of utterly destroying it as a functioning social system. The threat to use nuclear weapons against the United States or Russia could be credible only in the most dire corner. More important is that, even ignoring the promise of retaliation, delivery is hard and will not necessarily become easier. Recently the American government was in the midst of a most painful debate—whether or not to build an antimissile system. An antimissile would be of some, but marginal, utility for diminishing the damage inflicted by a hypothetical Soviet attack using missiles with the sophisticated penetration aids the Russians undoubtedly can produce. But it would be of much greater use, perhaps to the point of nearly perfect success, against the kind of primitive attack that even China will be able to launch for the next decade or two. Getting through a good ballistic missile defense system will require much knowledge of the effects of nuclear weapons and some very clever engineering, plus some extremely fancy and expensive electronics. Underdeveloped countries simply do not and will not have the resources to acquire that detailed and extensive know-how, nor the money to build the equipment if they knew how to do so.

Thus superpower antimissile systems would not in any notable way change the relative power of the United States and the Soviet Union vis-à-vis each other. Such systems would cost both powers a lot of money that could be spent elsewhere, and perhaps threaten the stability of their mutual strategic

balance. But they would have the consequence of pricing small or poor nations out of the market for nuclear deterrents with regard to the superpowers.
They might blow each other up to the hearts' content of their leaders, but they
could not effectively confront the two great military states that so dominated
international politics during the 1950s. An antimissile system would therefore restore the bipolarity and United States-Soviet nuclear preeminence
that so recently seemed to be slipping, and dash any hopes the small powers
may retain of being able to coerce the great states militarily.

HARASSMENT

Thus in the world of 2000 A.D., perhaps even more so than now, the poor
half of the world will not be able to challenge the rich fifth for control—but
it will have the ability to harass the rich and bring the entire system into chaos.

The world of the foreseeable future will be one of great interdependencies of
many sorts; the complex exploitation of material resources that will be necessary to sustain the living conditions of the rich will require extremely dense
and complicated communications and transportation systems. The whole
system, relying as much of it will on very close man-machine interactions (as
with artificial limbs and organs), will leave many people extremely dependent,
for their very lives, on constant inputs from an extremely artificial man-made
physical environment. (What happens, for instance, to the man with radar
eyes if he cannot get replacement parts? Or to a system geared to electronic
data banks when the power goes off?) Even if an antimissile system could
prevent an underdeveloped nation from wreaking major direct physical havoc
on the developed world, the hazards of interruption, destruction, and temporary or local chaos might still be very severe. All the more so if the promise of
guerilla sized nuclear weapons for the future should become reality.

Primitive man rarely lived to old age; like the animals he preyed upon,
every man, when no longer in his prime, became vulnerable to the abundant
natural enemies which before might not have been able to challenge him successfully. Even during the peak of life sudden death from animals, other men,
or weather, was common enough. Civilization, however, has cut the odds of
sudden destruction to a fraction of what they once were. We still are conscious
of the hazards of our man-made environment, especially the automobile,
but only because other causes of death for the young and middle aged become
almost insignificant by comparison with their former toll. But the world of the
future might well restore the dangers from new sources, and raise the risks
of sudden death. Man-made interruptions to the delicate interdependent system would be the new threat, and those largely from the underdeveloped
world. (As a crude and very partial measure of the developed world's greater
susceptibility to interruption, note in the table its higher foreign trade ratio—a
ratio which also has been growing much faster for the industrial countries in
recent years.)

Domestic difficulties have sometimes led to foreign adventures by the heads of underdeveloped states: Sukarno's behavior in West Irian and Malaysia was one example.[4] Wars among poor and frustrated nations may become more common. If nuclear weapons were used in those wars a few would certainly affect the interests of rich nations. Or more seriously, the poor states would acquire harassment capabilities to deliver (possibly by individuals rather than by governments which might readily be held responsible) nuclear bombs. There are literally hundreds of ways in which a determined, embittered, and perhaps nonofficial minority of people in the have-not areas could prevent the rich from full enjoyment of their prosperity.

Incentives to violence will be there in ample measure. Marx thought revolutions were born from the growing absolute impoverishment of the masses. If so there would be little for powers of the status quo to fear, since there is small reason to think many of the poor countries will actually slip downhill. But the evidence of the past century indicates clearly that Marx was wrong in this respect. De Tocqueville had a contrasting theory derived from eighteenth-century France—that revolutions arise not from increasing poverty, but from an improvement in the fortunes of the poor after ages of hopeless degradation. New expectations, aroused but by no means satisfied by a modest upturn, provide the impetus to revolution.

More recent theory combines something of both Marx's and de Tocqueville's. It suggests that the most likely point of revolution is when, after a rather sustained period of betterment for the poor, a fairly sudden stagnation or sharp downturn is experienced. New hopes and demands may be satisfied just enough to control things while the growth continues, but they will not tolerate much of a reversal.[5] None of these theories has yet been throughly tested, but there is some interesting evidence for the latter. If it does indeed indicate a general principle of revolutionary activity, it would seem vital, in their own interests, for the rich nations to help the poor at the least to maintain their growth at existing rates.

A better evaluation of the political and social potential of economic conditions in the poor half of the world at the end of this century, however, can be gained by remembering some particular aspects of the basically impoverished conditions of life to be expected there. Although not educated to high levels, the bulk of the population will be literate. They will be heavily if not predominantly urban, with perhaps a quarter living in cities of 100,000 or more. They will have access to the mass media of communication—their urbanization, literacy, and the cheap transistor radio will see to that. Furthermore,

---

[4] An example does not, of course, prove the general point. It remains a complex and unanswered question as to the relative frequency of and conditions for domestic instability to lead to the initiation of foreign conflict by underdeveloped countries. For a recent effort and review see Jonathan Wilkenfeld, "Models for the Analysis of Foreign Conflict Behavior of States," in *Peace, War, and Numbers*, Bruce M. Russett, editor (Beverly Hills: Sage, 1972).

[5] See James Chowning Davies, editor, *When Men Revolt and Why* (New York: The Free Press, 1971), and Ted Robert Gurr, *Why Men Rebel* (Princeton: Princeton University Press, 1970).

they will have immediate acquaintance with, if not experience of, life in the rich fourth of the world. Communication satellites, television sets in central city and village locations, and all the worldwide paraphernalia of instant communication will assure the breakdown of their previous insulation. Though poor and uneducated, they will not be ignorant of what they are missing. Whereas once they could compare their status only with that of the village landowner, now they will have the example of the whole rich West to instruct them in their relative deprivation.[6] And they will realize that the structure of the world political and social system makes it impossible for them, *as individuals*, to improve their lot. Barriers to immigration will keep them in their physical places.

In short, Asia and Africa are likely to comprise a huge slum in the social as well as material sense, with close parallels to present-day Harlem. The difference will be in the degree to which the fate of the privileged will even more closely be linked to that of the slum dwellers, who will be a virtual majority, not a relatively small segment of the population that might be effectively isolated in a ghetto and forgotten. The privileged class will be a distinct minority, and the "middle class" buffer will not be much larger. Ideologies which blame poverty on exploitation by the rich will exacerbate international tensions.

FINDING A TOLERABLE WORLD ORDER

Several courses of action, some of which must be concurrent rather than substitutes for each other, are open to the rich world for the next few decades. One is obvious and attractive to our humanitarian traditions—assistance to the underdeveloped nations to keep the level of income growing at a steady if unspectacular rate. But recent trends have been in the direction of diminishing aid. Felt inequalities within the rich countries, especially the United States, militate against external assistance. And the prospect of extremely expensive medical treatment, extending life expectancies in the rich countries of 2000 A.D., means that heavy external assistance might come at the cost of life itself, not just life style, for citizens of rich countries. If so, the resistances will be great.

Moreover, the prescription of economic assistance is hardly more than a tiresome cliche at this point in our experience and disillusionment with foreign aid as an instrument of development. It is much easier to specify ingredients— money, technical assistance, leadership training, flexibility and long-term dependability, etc.—than to make them work. Part of the problem is that the

---

[6] My assumption that people in the poor countries will use those of the rich countries as reference groups, and hence the basis for a sense of relative deprivation, is of course challengeable. They might look back on their own (or their parents') past and not feel deprived. There is some evidence that the latter is a relatively early phenomenon in a group's consciousness, but that the former regularly occurs if there is little social mobility into the elite.

doctors have expected too much. The rate of growth that can realistically be achieved will not eradicate unrest, violence, or the threat of violence. The hope must be only to reduce their incidence. Aid must be complemented by scientific research seeking to lower drastically the cost of at least some elements of the "good life." Certain aspects of education, coupled with teaching machines and communications satellites, may be especially appropriate for cheap mechanization. Others should appear if an intensive effort is made.

At the same time, this is only part of the prescription for a tolerable world order. Another element requires strengthening and multiplying the existing institutional bonds among nations—in effect a move in the direction of world government for the sake of political control over the poor states. Of course such a government, in most of the probable and all of the ideologically pleasing forms, would entail control *by* as well as *of* the poor world. Any pluralistic variety of political organization for the globe would involve concessions by the rich and some kind of substantial taxation. But this need not conjure up images of utter leveling and loss of privilege—the rich usually manage to retain a power and influence over decisions that is very disproportionate to their numbers. Their skills will give them great advantages in manipulation and an essential ingredient for world growth that can be bartered for a substantial price. Nor need we think of such institutions as highly centralized with great authority over wide issues. Modes of loose confederation can also be models for ultimate world organization.

Efforts to implement the strategies of aid and global institution building are vital because the alternative is not so ideologically attractive. The threat of violence does not operate merely in an economic and social environment; it is not simply the product of expectations, frustrations, and growth rates. Behavior also is subject to political controls; the resort to violence can be contained by repression. A world government *could* be a powerful one initiated and firmly controlled by the rich. Or the governments of the developed states could ally themselves with authoritarian or totalitarian oligarchies in the poor world, with regimes that are able, with extant and yet-to-be devised instruments of surveillance and control, to keep the lid on their domestic politics. The payment would be privileges for the governing elite in these countries, a sharing in the benefits of 2000 A.D. material culture that could never be paid to the masses. (Note the sharp degree of income inequality already typical of the poor countries. And recall how often a foreign statesman from the underdeveloped world, when paying an official visit to the United States, spends a day at Walter Reed Hospital for a thorough physical examination. Access to such facilities may be worth years to him in terms of his life expectancy.) These oligarchies might continue to mouth the ideology of development and ultimate prosperity for their citizens, and even provide, with outside assistance, the basis for a modest improvement in their peoples' physical condition. Yet they would retain the ability to control change and suppress dissent, acting in part as agents of the rich world.

This is a repugnant prospect, and I do not advocate it. To do so, especially now before we have made a proper effort with the first two elements, would be a despairing counsel. Until much greater resources have been devoted both to research and practice in development and international organization, a further alliance with the oligarchies would be intolerable. There are more than enough elements of it in the foreign policies of present Western governments. At some point, however, after energetically trying the other ways at substantial sacrifice, the compromise may seem more beguiling. It may come for the simple reason that the world and its civilizations will not, we hope, come to an end in the year 2000 A.D. It might be justified by motives other than selfish parochial interest. Men must build for ages to come, and construction cannot take place in chaos.

PART II

International Violence:
Deterrence and Restraint

10
Cause, Surprise, and No Escape

A CONCEPTUAL SCHEME

What causes a war? For as long as there have been wars and historians to write about them, controversy has raged over what the precise factors were which resulted in a particular war. Explanations have ranged from simplistic "war guilt" accusations to the despairing answer that wars have myriad causes and we can never hope to untangle the web of causation. Many of the difficulties, however, stem from the lack of a systematic framework of analysis to apply to the problem. The usefulness of such conceptual frameworks is being demonstrated to an increasing extent in other areas of political science, particularly comparative government.[1]

In this chapter we shall attempt once again to assess the causes of World War I, using the classic study by Sydney Bradshaw Fay as a starting point.[2]

Reprinted from *The Journal of Politics*, 24, 1 (February 1962).

[1] For instance, see Gabriel A. Almond, "Comparative Political Systems," *Journal of Politics*, XVIII, 3 (August 1956), pp. 391 ff.; Gabriel Almond and James Coleman, *Politics of the Developing Areas* (Princeton: Princeton University Press, 1960); Roy C. Macridis, *The Study of Comparative Government* (Garden City: Doubleday, 1954); and Edward Shils, *Political Development in the New States* (The Hague: Mouton, 1960).

[2] *The Origins of the World War*, 2 volumes (New York: Macmillan, 1928). While some of Fay's interpretations have since been challenged and new material made available, we shall not attempt to reevaluate his conclusions in the light of this new evidence. The question of his accuracy is not directly relevant to the purpose of this chapter, which is to offer a possible system of analysis.

In an effort to clarify the problem we shall employ an accounting scheme originally designed to identify the causes of an automobile accident.[3] It is hoped that this analysis will be useful in suggesting similar ways to study other periods of international tension, and to build a body of comparative data. In the final section of the chapter we shall use the conceptual scheme and analysis as springboards to consider some possible ways in which the conflict might have been avoided, and to discuss the relevance of the analysis to contemporary problems. Particularly, we shall attempt to identify opportunities for improved strategic intelligence, and areas where such intelligence might contribute to current inquiries into problems of credibility and predictability in an age of nuclear war. The examination is, of course, in no sense intended as definitive, but rather as a discussion to promote further thought and research.

The use of an "accident" accounting scheme obviously implies certain assumptions about the origins of the war. Specifically, it assumes that the outbreak of war, at least on a scale involving several major powers, was an accident rather than the result of a deliberate aggressor's plot. "War guilt" is rejected. This was Fay's major contribution, for by identifying the numerous interwoven causes of the World War and showing that the Central Powers neither wanted a European war nor, for quite a while at least, realized how close they were to having one, he eliminated war guilt as a satisfying explanation. Instead we assume that, as in an automobile accident, no power wanted a general conflict—a driver does not usually deliberately run his car into a tree. Rather, the war or accident arises because of numerous acts of commission and of neglect, acts whose probable consequences were not foreseen at the time. Thus there are numerous causes, a point of sudden surprise when the seriousness of the consequences becomes known, and a point when those consequences can no longer be avoided. We do not deny that there have been instances when a war was deliberately planned for the achievement of specific aims. But this does not appear to be such a case; if it were, a quite different system of analysis would be required.

The accounting scheme we shall employ is as follows:

Cause

This will refer only to those events or factors about which we can say, "If it had not existed, there is an overwhelming probability that the war would not have occurred." There is naturally an element of imprecision in the term "overwhelming probability." We shall use it, however, because of the impossibility of absolute certainty that its absence would have prevented

---

[3] Adapted from J. Stannard Baker, "A Framework for the Assessment of Causes of Automobile Accidents," reprinted in *The Language of Social Research*, Paul F. Lazarsfeld and Morris Rosenberg, editors (Glencoe: The Free Press, 1955), pp. 438–48.

the outbreak. At the same time, we wish it to be clear that the factor in question seems almost certain to have been essential, thus eliminating mere "contributing factors" from the analysis. When possible we shall use Fay's interpretation as to whether a particular factor was necessary to produce the final catastrophe. Where he is ambiguous we must be somewhat arbitrary. Some arbitrariness, while regrettable, cannot be avoided in such a brief analysis, and does not hinder its usefulness for illustration. Finally, a cause, while seemingly necessary, need not be a sufficient factor.

Remote Cause

We shall use this term to describe any condition which made possible the chain of events leading directly to the outbreak of hostilities. Thus we mean conditions of neglect or factors such as those binding one country to the support of another. In short, it means any condition which either made the occurrence of an "incident" very likely, or which made it very difficult to correct short of war any such incident once it had occurred.

Mediate Cause

Three types may be distinguished:

1. Conditions which exist in the period immediately preceding the outbreak of hostilities and which affect the actors involved.
2. The acts or neglect which lead quickly up to surprise.
3. The acts after surprise which make the situation worse, or the failure to mitigate the seriousness of the accident.

Direct Cause

The behavior of an actor which leads directly to the *key event*. It thus refers to a single act only. Furthermore, it need be in no way autonomous, as it may be wholly determined by factors up to and including the point of *no escape*.

Key Event

The actual declaration of war or the commencement of hostilities on a large scale, whichever should occur first. One qualification, not applicable to this situation, might be made regarding the declaration of war. In some cases, as the period of "phoney war" in 1939–1940, large-scale hostilities do not follow the declaration of war for some time. In the "phoney war," for example, a number of political leaders seem to have hoped for several months that an agreement might be reached, and each side avoided provoking the other.[4] Under such circumstances the *key event* occurred only with the German invasion of the Low Countries, and the point of *no escape* may have followed rather than preceded the declarations of war in September 1939. This situation, however, is not applicable to 1914. With the possible exception of England, each of the major powers was engaged in large-scale conflict almost immediately after the declaration of war. Germany, for instance, hastened the declaration lest German troops enter France before this formality had been met.

Point of Suprise

The moment when those controlling the foreign policy of a state realize that something is going wrong and is likely to involve their state in war. While the awareness may exist to some degree for a very long period before the *key event*, there is usually a point which can be identified as signalling a sharp increase in the awareness of danger. It is not the moment when the danger actually develops, as it may develop before the actors are aware of it.

Point of No Escape

That point in time after which the war cannot be prevented. Nothing the actors can do will save them from hostilities. It may also be argued that there is a second point of *no escape* when the military situation gets out of hand. Thus both sides in the Korean War undoubtedly expected a far more limited war then they eventually were forced to conduct. (The North Koreans certainly did not expect a massive injection of United States ground forces, and the Americans in turn ignored Chinese threats to intervene.) In World War I it is safe to assume that none of the participants expected to conduct a four-year war of attrition. While this would be an extremely important matter to investigate, it lies beyond Fay's work and the analysis of this study. We shall limit the discussion to the events leading to the opening of hostilities.

An examination of the pattern of events suggests that the analysis can best be carried on by dividing those events into four stages. The first concerns the war between Serbia and Austria, which did not spread to include the other powers until four days after the Austrian declaration. In this case the chain of events producing the conflict is necessarily the same for both parties. Thus a

---

[4] Winston S. Churchill, *The Second World War*, I, *The Gathering Storm* (Boston: Houghton Mifflin), pp. 484–5, 582–3.

war is different from an automobile accident, which requires only one participant even though it may, of course, include more. A second stage concerns
the events which culminated in the German declaration of war on Russia.
This resulted in the addition of two more belligerents, again with the same
causal chain. We shall also analyze separately the events leading France, and
finally England, into the war. Fay makes no mention of the declarations of
war between Austria and the Entente powers, but given the situation and the
Austro-German alliance, Austria's wider participation necessarily followed
Germany's.

We thus shall deal separately with the events resulting in the broadening
of hostilities at each stage. Naturally those events which caused the original
(Austria-Serbia) conflict are also causes of the war engulfing other states;
they must be understood as such even though we shall not repeat them for
each actor. While logically there is no reason why a cause may not be unique
to a single stage, in fact the involvement of each power in World War I was
contingent on the inclusion of all those who entered earlier. England, for
example, would not have gone to war if the Austria-Serbia conflict had not
spread to Russia, Germany, and France. The image of a row of falling dom-
inoes is particularly appropriate.

We may note also that the point of *surprise* may be different for every actor;
it need not, for instance, have been the same for Austria as for Serbia. Although it was identical for a local war between the two, the point of *surprise*
for a European war occurred appreciably sooner for Serbia than for Austria.
Where there are more than two antagonists the point of *no escape* also need
not be the same for every one of the ultimate participants. In cases of ambiguity we shall note the actors to whom a particular event applies, as
Surprise[AE] indicates the point when *Austria* became aware of the acute danger
of a *European* war involving at least one other great power.

Table 10-1
The Scheme Applied: World War I

AUSTRIA-HUNGARY-SERBIA

Remote causes

    Frictions and irritations among all powers, due in turn to the arms races, alliances, national-
ism, economic imperialism, and irresponsible newspaper activities. No one of these, however, seems essential to this friction.

    Failure to comprehend the severity of the consequences of a general European war.

    Progressive decay of the Ottoman Empire, particularly in the Balkans.

    Serb nationalism.

    Pan-Slavism, and Russian encouragement to Serb nationalism.

    Presence of many Serbs in parts of Austria, thus making Serb nationalism a threat to Austria's
national integrity.

    Hungarian oppression of Serbs in Austria.

    Lack of plan or leader in Austria to accommodate Slavs in country.

(Continued)

Table 10-1

The Scheme Applied: World War I (Continued)

AUSTRIA-HUNGARY-SERBIA (*Continued*)

Decline of Austria's power and prestige.

Serb government's long standing toleration of agitation against Austria.

Serb certainty of Russian support in any conflict with Austria.

Conspicuous failure of London Conference on Albania in 1913 and equally conspicuous success of Austria's unilateral ultimatum to Serbia.

Thus, conviction in Austria that Serbia could be dealt with only unilaterally.

German need for Austria as her one dependable ally (see RUSSIA-GERMANY for causes of this).

Mediate causes

Serb government's failure either to take action to prevent the attack on Archduke Franz Ferdinand or to warn Austria adequately of the plot.

Surprise^{AS}
Surprise^{SA} } Assassination of Franz Ferdinand.
Surprise^{SE}

Mediate causes

Serb government's failure to deprive Austria of excuse by itself taking prompt action to apprehend all involved in assassination plot.

Russian military weakness, but growing strength; therefore,

Austrian conviction that an immediate war with Serbia could be localized whereas a later one could not.

Austrian conviction that strong action could restore prestige as a great power.

Germany fails to restrain Austria; instead assures support for whatever action Austrians deem necessary to deal with Serbs.

Austria decides to use assassination as excuse to crush Serbia.

Austria issues Serbia an ultimatum which is designed to be unacceptable, war to follow if all points not accepted.

France and Russia refuse to participate in mediation.

Serbian government fails to comply with ultimatum.

No escape^{AS}

Germany rejects Grey's conference proposal.

Direct cause^{AS}

Austria rejects all conference proposals.

Key event^{AS}

Austria declares war on Serbia (or possibly, Austrian bombardment of Belgrade).†

Surprise^{AE}

News of Russia military preparations (before mobilization) reaches Austria.

No escape^{E}
Direct cause^{E} } See equivalent events at these entries under RUSSIA-GERMANY.
Key events^{E}

---

†It might even be contended that we should not regard the key event as occurring until the Austrian invasion of Serbia was begun; that is, after the other powers had been brought into the war. In this instance it is not an important distinction, however, as once the Austrian government was firmly resolved to invade, and the other powers for one reason or another had refused mediation or conference, it is most difficult to see how that invasion might have been forestalled.

RUSSIA-GERMANY

Remote causes

Frictions and irritations among all powers.

Failure to comprehend the severity of the consequences of a general European war.

Pan-Slavism and Russian encouragement to Serb nationalism.

Failure to maintain Re-Insurance Treaty between Russia and Germany.

Russian-Austrian antagonism in the Balkans.

Alliance with France and entente with England.

French conviction alliance is essential to her interests (see FRANCE); English conviction that entente must be maintained (see ENGLAND); thus,

Russian confidence of support from France and England.

Previous Russian humiliations and defeats, giving "need" to restore prestige.

Growing Russian military capabilities and confidence, as evidenced by contemplation of "preventive war" on Turkey in early 1914.

Military advantages of being first nation to mobilize in war and serious handicap of being attacked before own mobilization is complete.

Technical military reasons why mobilization, once begun, could not be halted short of war.

Russian military's failure to plan for partial mobilization, which could be directed at Austria only, without weakening German front.

Major role of military in Russian government.

Tsar's personal weakness; follows advice of the last adviser who speaks with him.

Enmity of France toward Germany (see FRANCE).

German failure to accept proffered alliance with England.

German-English friction, due to combination (no one essential) of English opposition to Baghdad Railway, naval rivalry, formation of Entente, Boer War, and competition for colonies.

Fear of encirclement and need for Austria as Germany's one dependable ally.

Mediate causes

Absence of moderate and conciliatory men like Kokovtsev from Russian cabinet.

Surprise[R]

Austrian ultimatum to Serbia.

Overwork, worry, and fatigue of leaders.

Because of Pan-Slavism and earlier encouragement to Serbs, feeling that Russia could not abandon Serbia if she were attacked.

French failure to restrain Russia, and promise of support.

English failure either to restrain Russia or to warn Germany she would not be neutral in a European war (see ENGLAND).

Russian distrust of German motives; conviction that Germany was egging Austria on rather than restraining her.

Military leaders declare partial mobilization against Austria only leaves Russia at the mercy of Germany in the event of a general war.

Surprise[G] (only one day before Austrian declaration of war on Serbia).

Austria declares war on Serbia.

Austria fails to accept "pledge plan" to halt at Belgrade and not crush Serbia.

Russian military leaders decide war is inevitable.

Tsar approves order for general mobilization.

Russian general mobilization begun.

(*Continued*)

Table 10-1
The Scheme Applied: World War I (Continued)

RUSSIA-GERMANY (*Continued*)

No escape
German government decides delay would be fatal, must declare war immediately if Russia does not halt mobilization.

Direct cause
Russia refuses to rescind mobilization order.

Key event
Germany declares war on Russia.

FRANCE

Remote causes
Frictions and irritations among all powers.
Failure to comprehend the severity of the consequences of a general European war.
Franco-Prussian War, and German annexation of Alsace-Lorraine.
Recurrent irritations and bad feelings toward Germany.
Passionate French desire for *revanche*.
French fear of having to face Germany alone in another war.
Alliance with Russia, and conviction that it must be maintained.
French entente with England (see ENGLAND).
Anglo-French military and naval conversations, and subsequent impression of English "moral commitment" in case France had to fight a nonaggressive war.
Firm French expectation of English support in case of such a war.
German geographical position and inferiority to combination of Russia and France in number of troops, giving
Military decision, if general war seemed certain, to crush France quickly, then turn on Russia.

Mediate causes
All events leading to Russian general mobilization.
Overwork, worry, and fatigue of leaders.

Surprise[F]
Probably the Austrian ultimatum to Serbia.

No escape
German government decides delay would be fatal, must declare war immediately if Russia does not halt mobilization.
Germany asks French if they will stay neutral in case of a German-Russian war.
France declares she will "respect her obligations."
Russia refuses to rescind mobilization order.

Direct cause
Germany declares war on Russia.

Key event
Germany declares war on France.

ENGLAND

Remote causes
Frictions and irritations among all powers.
Failure to comprehend the severity of the consequences of a general European war.

German rejection of proffered alliance with England.

German-English antagonism (naval rivalry, colonies, etc.); English distrust of Germany and German militarists.

English fear that a German victory over France would upset the continental balance of power.

Desire to maintain solidarity of entente (which would prevent England from putting firm pressure on either France or Russia in case of danger).

Anglo-French military and naval conversations, and subsequent "moral commitment" to aid France.

English form of government, which made it impossible for leaders with any certainty to warn another power that a particular action would lead to war.

Mediate causes

All events leading to German declaration of war on France. Note specifically England's failure to warn either Germany or Russia against precipitate action.

Overwork, worry, and fatigue of leaders.

Surprise[E]

Austrian ultimatum to Serbia.

Grey decides England is morally bound to fight with France if war develops.

Germany decides it must declare war on France and Russia.

No escape

Unionist Party assures Grey of its support if he decides for war with Germany.

Direct cause

Germany declares war on France. (*Note*: We do not consider the German violation of Belgian neutrality as either the *direct cause* or the point of *no escape.**)

Key event

England declares war on Germany.

---

*It is somewhat inaccurate to label a decision, such as that of the Unionist Party to support Grey, as the point of *no escape*. As long as the decision has not been implemented by military or diplomatic moves it can, in principle, still be reversed. The Tsar's first order for general mobilization was, in fact, rescinded in time, even if only to be repeated a day later. Yet in the English case it seems that Grey's mind was made up, and once he was assured of parliamentary support it is very unlikely that anything could have changed his decision. For this reason we do not call the invasion of Belgium either the point of *no escape* or the *direct cause*. Grey had already decided to fight, according to Fay. The German invasion made it easier for Grey to justify his decision to the public, but did not cause it. Also because of Grey's decision to fight we do not treat the actual commitment of English forces on the continent as a relevant *key event*.

AVOIDING ACCIDENTS

At this point we shall evaluate some of these events to discover possible ways of avoiding the outbreak of war. We shall move from the analytical scheme to areas where prewar strategic intelligence can be improved.

Perhaps the matter which deserves most attention is the period between *surprise* and *no escape*. Note that in the above analysis, *surprise* for a war precedes its point of *no escape* for every actor. In each case, therefore, it was possible for the leaders of the nation to pull back after they had discerned the immediate danger. Yet *surprise* did not occur at the same moment for each power, indicating that the point of *surprise* is to a great extent determined by the development and perceptiveness of one's intelligence services, and by the perceptiveness of top policy makers.[5] For Serbia, Russia, France, and England, news of the Austrian ultimatum to Serbia seems to have introduced *surprise* for a general European war; until then the danger of a major war did not appear great. For Germany, however, *surprise* probably did not occur until just before the Austrian declaration of war on Serbia—three days after *surprise* for the other powers. This delay made it much harder to reverse the trend toward war. The Austrian point of *surprise* for a general European war, however, only occurred after the declaration of war on Serbia and the arrival of news about Russian military preparations. Thus the point of *no escape* from a war with Serbia had already passed, and while that for a general war had not yet occurred, time was very short and many serious irreversible moves had been made.

Even for those states in the most favorable circumstances, the period between *surprise* and *no escape* was only six days, or between the arrival of news of the Austrian ultimatum and Germany's decision that it could not tolerate Russian mobilization (for France and Russia). Although England had three more days before she was irrevocably committed to war herself, a continental war was inescapable after the German decision. It was, in fact, extremely difficult to avoid after Russian mobilization had begun. The period within which action could be taken was therefore very short for all powers concerned. And insofar as we have listed overwork, fatigue, and worry as a cause of the war for all participants (except perhaps for Austria), the short time becomes even more important. A final factor that can be very important when there is such a short span of time is overload of the decision-making system. England's attention was seriously diverted by the smoldering Irish situation, and while this was not listed above because it did not seem *necessary* to produce English belligerency, the diversion of attention at this vital time was certainly a major contributing factor in preventing a peaceful solution.

One of the primary causes of the war was the growth of nationalism, particularly in the Balkans. We now have measures which enable us to identify areas where nationalist tensions are strong and the rate at which they are increasing.[6] Such measures need not be listed in detail here, but their use might have been extremely beneficial to the Austrians. With them they might have more accurately identified the dangers in the Balkans, both within and without the Dual Monarchy, and might then have taken proper steps to alleviate tension.

Another important cause was the failure of the powers to recognize the nature of the ties among the major states. Had the Central Powers been certain that England would not stay neutral it is improbable that they would have acted so precipitately. Nor would Austria likely have decided to crush

---

[5] Note the conclusion of Benno Wasserman ("The Failure of Intelligence Prediction," *Political Studies*, VIII, 2 [June 1960], p. 165) that in very many cases "the *failure of intelligence prediction is due to faulty evaluation and not to lack of available information*" (author's italics).

[6] See K. W. Deutsch, *Nationalism and Social Communication* (Cambridge: M.I.T. Press, 1953), especially Chapter 5.

Serbia in 1914 had she known the degree to which the Russians felt committed to Serbia's support. And Germany would not have been so quick to reject the proffered English alliance much earlier, had she known of the likelihood of an understanding between England and France and Russia.[7]

Fay refers to one possible means of identifying such close ties when he marks the great influx of Englishmen to the Paris World's Fair as the beginning of the Anglo-French entente. Other now familiar methods of analyzing communications flows, such as trade, mail, travel, and migration,[8] would have been of great use, particularly in warning Germany despite the lack of an explicit warning of England's intentions. In addition to identifying current directions and long-term trends, it seems possible that discontinuities or sudden shifts in the direction of a nation's policy could be predicted by looking for sudden shifts in its attention pattern. For example, five of six countries experiencing "neutralist" shifts in foreign policy between 1955 and 1959 showed a marked increase in trade with the Soviet Bloc either in the year of the shift or up to three years before.[9] In each case exports to the Bloc increased by 85 percent or more from one year to the next, exports to the Communist area totalled at least 6 percent of the nation's total exports, and this percentage was higher than that of 1952, showing that the increase was not merely a recovery from a bad year. Even though in some cases the shift in trade did not occur until the year of the political shift, the Communist nations usually deal through trade agreements, which must be concluded up to a year before the goods begin to flow. Thus on-the-spot observers in these countries, watching the flow of goods and the progress of trade negotiations, could have predicted the change in foreign policy before it occurred.

Similarly, an analysis of newspapers, both elite and mass, in terms of some sort of ratio of favorable to unfavorable editorial comment toward particular states would have helped discern a nation's probable moves even before its

---

[7] It is doubtful whether threatening policy statements alone could correct misapprehensions of this sort. The recent decline in American willingness to depend solely on a strategy of massive retaliation illustrates some of the difficulties involved in making a threat credible. "Overadvertisement" of one's readiness to go to war can, if not believed, create as much dangerous uncertainty as the "underadvertisement" of 1914.

[8] See especially K. W. Deutsch et al., *Political Community and the North Atlantic Area* (Princeton: Princeton University Press, 1957), pp. 144–6; and Deutsch, "Toward an Inventory of Basic Trends and Patterns in Comparative and International Politics," *American Political Science Review*, LIV, 1 (March 1960), pp. 34–57.

[9] The shifts that could have been "predicted" by this test were: Yugoslavia (rapproachement with Soviets—1955), Egypt (arms purchase—1955, the first clear indication of a change in Egyptian policy), Syria (arms purchase—1956), Iceland (Communist election gains and near expulsion of U.S. from its NATO base—1956), and Lebanon (revolution—1958). No such trade increase was associated with the Iraq revolution of 1958, in part because approximately 90 percent of the country's exports are controlled by the Western owned oil companies. The proposed test would also give a few false positives, but as in a hypothetical cancer test it is far more important that the test locate most actual cases than that it identify *only* true cases of cancer.

Data from United Nations, Statistical Papers, Series T, Vol. X, No. 8, *Direction of International Trade*, New York, 1958.

leaders had made a decision. Possibly also the relative frequency of references to "peace or neutrality" (or both) versus "solidarity with allies" (admittedly a very crude measure; better ones could be suggested by clues in the content of the papers) would be a useful predictive tool. Insofar as certain editorials in elite papers can be identified as government inspired their importance increases, as possibly the dependence on quantitative analytical techniques decreases.

Another very useful measure applicable to newspaper editorials might be something on the order of a "frustration ratio." Three of the participants in World War I had felt frustrated in the achievement of several major aims of foreign policy. Thus the crisis after Sarajevo offered an opportunity to wipe away previous frustrations through a military or diplomatic victory which would raise their self-esteem and their prestige in the eyes of others. While none of them deliberately created a major war, their feelings of frustration made them more willing to incur the risk. A "frustration ratio" might measure column inches in newspaper editorials referring to the achievement of goals of national foreign policy as the denominator, and inches referring to the frustration of perceived goals, either by foreign powers or by domestic ineptitude, as the numerator. A particularly high frustration ratio might warn of a sudden desperate move (as is sometimes alleged to have been the case with the Anglo-French attack on Suez). A particularly low ratio, on the other hand, might warn of an appetite that grows with the eating. As with all these measures, it is important to watch trends in the ratio, not just the absolute level at any time.

Yet another possible use of newspaper scrutiny would be a warning when *surprise* has occurred for other actors. In most cases, when a government decides war may be imminent it takes action to prepare the attitudes of its public. It may begin violent denunciation of the prospective enemy, or place special stress on its own virtue and readiness to defend itself. Awareness of such a sharp shift in others' expectations should induce *surprise* in the mind of the analyst.[10]

Finally, improved military intelligence might have warned Austria that Russia was not as weak militarily as the Central Powers believed, and at the same time warned Russia that her relative military power was not yet sufficient to allow her to defeat Austria. In this way a mutual inspection system, by providing a more realistic assessment of the other side's capabilities, might have prevented hasty moves. Several other possible consequences of arms inspection must be considered, however:

1. By providing one side with information about the other's perhaps temporary weakness, it may stimulate an immediate "preventive war" attack.

---

[10] Ithiel de Sola Pool ("Public Opinion and the Control of Armaments," *Daedalus* [fall 1960], p. 996) has pointed out that the frequent reiteration of one's peaceful intentions to a domestic audience may make one's own troops undependable in any attempt to launch a first strike. Yet a sudden shift to warlike propaganda may surrender the advantages of surprise.

2. It may, on the contrary, give the weaker side an incentive to catch up before its weakness becomes serious.
3. It may reduce those tensions which stem from a fear that the opponent may have some secret weapon giving him a great qualitative advantage.

A properly operating inspection scheme would make the presence or absence of any such weapon known. In general, it is unlikely that inspection would cause an arms race or exacerbate an existing one. An arms race proceeds best where there is some information on the opponent's capabilities but where that information is inadequate. The Anglo-German naval rivalry before World War I is an excellent example. Had both sides possessed more complete information the rivalry probably would have been less serious rather than more so.[11]

Though the discussion so far has been largely in terms of the world of 1914, the problem is very much a current one. Military technology has changed immeasurably since World War I, but war by mistake remains a distinct possibility. In 1914 each of the continental powers had a mobilization scheme that called for the immediate dispatch of great numbers of troops to the frontiers and into the other country, using split-second railroad scheduling. To allow the enemy to mobilize without doing so oneself meant leaving one's frontiers undefended. Yet once mobilization had actually begun, it was impossible to stop it without creating utter chaos with fragmented units scattered across the country's railways. Thus once either side was convinced that the other had begun to mobilize, conflict was inevitable. The point of *no escape* was passed.

The present situation is analogous. With the advent of nuclear weapon-carrying missiles a premium attaches to identifying an enemy attack immediately, and launching retaliation without delay, for delay could under certain circumstances result in the loss of the ability to retaliate. If an attack seems to be in progress, the defender's soft missiles must be in the air before the enemy's strike. But once launched they cannot be called back.[12] The points of *surprise* and *no escape* thus become practically simultaneous. If the attack is real, *no escape* actually precedes *surprise* for the attacked party. But if there really is no attack, *no escape* can follow almost immediately on the heels of *surprise*. The "attacked" party has little time to evaluate the ambiguous evidence, and if it decides to "retaliate" war is on. The system may be very vulnerable to false alarms, which could launch "retaliation" merely because certain signals (meteors on the radar scope) were misinterpreted.

---

[11] See Samuel P. Huntington, "Arms Races: Prerequisites and Results," in *Public Policy*, Carl J. Friedrich and Seymour E. Harris, editors (Cambridge: Harvard University Press, 1958), pp. 41–86, for a further examination of these problems. See also Malcolm W. Hoag, "On Stability in Deterrent Races," *World Politics*, XIII, 4 (July 1961), pp. 505–27, and Anatol Rapoport, *Fights, Games, and Debates* (Ann Arbor: University of Michigan Press, 1960).

[12] Theoretically they might be destroyed in the air, but since any power which believed itself under attack would expend a great many missiles in the first shot, it might find itself practically defenseless if it then destroyed them.

The danger of such an event rises during periods of international tension, such as that over Quemoy. Each major power may fear that events are likely to get out of hand and that the other may launch a deliberate or a preemptive attack. Because of this fear, each may instruct its radar operators to be less cautious in their interpretations of possibly hostile moves. On seeing ambiguous blips they would be less likely to interpret them as normal benign occurrences than they would be in a period of lesser tension. Therefore the "threshold," or the amount of provocation necessary to trigger a "retaliatory" attack is dependent not only on weapons development and the adequacy of the warning system, but also on the general tension level; that is, the degree to which either side holds it probable that the other will attack unexpectedly.

Measures to prevent this sort of occurrence can be classified either as attempts to hasten the advent of *surprise* or to postpone the point of *no escape*. There have been a number of suggestions for improving intelligence so as to hasten surprise. Kissinger and Schelling have suggested means for exchanging information about capabilities or for making it possible to determine the extent of each other's preparations for launching a surprise attack.[13] The now very much outdated open skies proposal fell into this category, as in some respects do unilateral measures like the use of reconnaissance satellites.[14] Proposals for crash arms control, whereby in a great crisis both sides might temporarily find it worthwhile to accept far-reaching inspection, are highly stimulating. One can easily imagine circumstances under which a power would be desperately anxious not only to assure himself that the enemy was not planning to strike, but to offer his enemy tangible proof of his own intentions and so prevent mistaken preemption.[15] Schelling also offers provocative comments on procedure in the so-called "coordination game," where both powers try to devise means to communicate to the other the stakes they consider important and worth fighting for, thus preventing the other from unknowingly stepping over the line to unavoidable war.[16]

Alternatively, we might concentrate on postponing the point of *no escape*. In terms of the 1914 situation, limited progress has been made in this area, with improved machinery for consultation and mediation, as well as changes in military procedures and the requirements of mobilization. Had any of the

---

[13] Henry A. Kissinger, "Arms Control, Inspection, and Surprise Attack," *Foreign Affairs*, XXXVIII, 4 (July 1960), and T. C. Schelling, "Reciprocal Measures for Arms Stabilization," *Daedalus* (fall 1960), pp. 892–914.

[14] See Albert Wohlstetter, "The Delicate Balance of Terror," *Foreign Affairs*, XXXVII, 2 (January 1959) for demolition of the notion that aerial inspection could detect an imminent surprise attack with current weapons.

[15] T. C. Schelling, "Arms Control: Proposal for a Special Surveillance Force," *World Politics*, XIII, 1 (October 1960), pp. 1–18.

[16] *The Strategy of Conflict* (Cambridge: Harvard University Press), 1960. Just this kind of communication failure seems to have occurred in Korea during the fall of 1950, especially in the American failure to take seriously Chinese warnings about advancing into North Korea. By the time the Americans became seriously alarmed, China had committed herself to enter the war. (*No escape* preceded *surprise*.) See Allen S. Whiting, *China Crosses the Yalu* (New York: Macmillan, 1960).

proposals for conference or mediation been accepted, for example, World War I might have been prevented. Note that German rejection of Grey's conference proposal was given as the point of *no escape* for an Austro-Serbian conflict. Even though the participants had decided for war, hostilities might have been prevented by the action of a third party.

In a thermonuclear world, an additional set of measures is required. To some extent they may be undertaken unilaterally rather than only by negotiation or explicit understanding. *No escape* may be postponed or avoided by hardening missile bases or making them mobile. If one can be sure that a substantial number can survive a first strike by an enemy, one may wait, after *surprise*, for indisputable evidence that one has been attacked. A complementary result can be obtained by the large-scale construction of fallout shelters, or the evacuation of one's metropolitan population in time of great crisis.[17] These measures provide some protection not only against imagining an attack when there is in fact none, but against the possibility of "catalytic" war.[18] The last is where a small, adventurous power attacks a larger one with the intention of creating a conflict among the major powers. If the attacked nation can take time to ascertain the source of a few missiles which have just hit it, the chance of a mistaken retaliation is reduced.[19]

It should be noted that several suggestions for stabilizing the military environment need not necessarily have the desired effects. A huge shelter program in one country, ostensibly for stabilizing purposes, might actually tempt the other power to make a preemptive attack before the program was complete, for afterward the sheltered power might be in a position to risk nuclear war without losing too great a proportion of its civilian population. Similarly, suppose that a program of mass evacuation from its cities was worked out by the Soviet Union, and one day the Russians announced that they were testing the system. Once the evacuation was complete, they would then be in an extremely advantageous position to blackmail the United States. The position might be so dangerous to America, in fact, that it might consider preempting before the evacuation was complete. The Soviets might

---

[17] Getting one's missiles off the ground is of course no way to protect one's population from a first blow if the enemy is already attacking, but it can prevent their death in a second strike, or at least make the difference between winning and losing a war. On the principle that "winning" and "losing" are not necessarily wholly inappropriate to nuclear warfare see Herman Kahn, *On Thermonuclear War* (Princeton: Princeton University Press, 1960).

[18] Arthur L. Burns, *The Rationale of Catalytic War*, Research Monograph No. 3, Center for International Studies, Princeton, 1959.

[19] Aaron Wildavsky has suggested in "Nuclear Clubs or Nuclear Wars," *Yale Review*, 51, 3 (spring 1962), pp. 345–62, that chances of international military stability may actually be *increased* by the spread of nuclear weapons to additional powers. While the possibility of a deliberate or accidental explosion is increased by such a spread, it may induce restraint in retaliation. Under present conditions if a major power saw a nuclear explosion on its territory it would "know" where it came from, but if many nations had nuclear capabilities it would be more alert to the possibility of hoax or accident. For other arguments about the possible stabilizing effects of nuclear dispersal see the debate on a NATO capability and Morton Kaplan's discussion of the "unit veto" system (*System and Process in International Politics* [New York: Wiley], 1957, pp. 50–52).

actually be testing their system in complete good faith, but one could well imagine situations where the United States would not dare to trust them. Finally, despite all the attention to problems of arms control and inspection, there has been little careful discussion of what is to be done if a violation of the arms control agreement should be detected.[20] If the violation was well advanced and seriously disequilibrating, it is possible that the violator might elect to attack immediately on his exposure. Or if he had the capabilities to do so, the discoverer might under certain circumstances prefer to preempt rather than publicly expose the violation. The purpose of these points is not to disparage fallout shelters, civil defense, or arms control agreements, but to urge more thorough examination of the consequences.

We have dwelt largely on situations where no major power wants war, even though under some conditions it would initiate one in order to avoid being attacked. When considering a war launched with a large measure of deliberate planning and calculation the problems of inducing surprise at an earlier moment become quite different, and in many ways easier to solve. Almost all of the above measures could be adapted to this purpose, and many others added.[21]

We do not, therefore, contend that all wars are of the "accidental" variety, and so amenable to the kind of cooling off treatment which can take place between the points of *surprise* and *no escape*. Hitler in 1939 consciously ran at least the high risk of war for the achievement of certain aims, and the resulting conflict was not "accidental." It may further be contended that there is at least one other type of war-producing situation—one where a crisis drags on for some time and where, despite the early advent of *surprise*, either the situation is not amenable to diplomatic procedures or the possible

---

[20] Fred Iklé, "After Detection—What?," *Foreign Affairs*, XXXIX, 2 (January 1961), pp. 208–20, is the most thorough discussion of these matters at present, but it leaves many questions. See also Robert Bowie, "Basic Requirements for Arms Control," and Lewis B. Sohn, "Adjudication and Enforcement in Arms Control," *Daedalus* (fall 1960), pp. 708–22 and 879–91.

[21] Seymour Melman, editor, *Inspection for Disarmament* (New York: Columbia University Press, 1958), remains the most complete published examination of detection methods. See also Bernard T. Feld, "Inspection Techniques of Arms Control," *Daedalus* (fall 1960), pp. 860–78, and the references there.

Evidence of the usefulness of the kinds of quantitative techniques suggested earlier for predictive purposes is still somewhat scanty, but there have been a number of studies which indicate that they can substantially increase the reliability of forecasts. Alexander George (*Propaganda Analysis* [Evanston: Row Peterson, 1959]) used content analysis quite successfully to predict Axis moves during World War II, and Ithiel de Sola Pool, *Symbols of Internationalism* [Stanford: Stanford University Press, 1951]) showed a high correlation between the degree of favorableness of elite newspaper editorials and more intuitive *post hoc* judgments about relations between a number of pairs of countries at various periods. Richard L. Merritt (*Symbols of American Community, 1735–1775* [New Haven: Yale University Press, 1966]) shows the relationship between newspaper content and the emergence of feelings of separateness and commonality in colonial America. Results similar to Pool's, using data like that cited in footnote 8, will be presented by Karl W. Deutsch and I. Richard Savage (*Regionalism, Trade, and Politital Community*, forthcoming). For the relation of about 30 indices of communication and transaction to trends in Anglo-American relations see my *Community and Contention: Britain and America in the Twentieth Century* (Cambridge: M.I.T. Press, 1963).

steps are not taken. Perhaps the long-term crisis over Berlin, which first really alarmed a number of responsible officials in the State Department in the spring of 1959, was such a case. For years thereafter little of consequence was done to relieve the situation, and one might even argue that no permanent solution is possible short of near capitulation by one side. The conceptual scheme might well be modified to cover such a case, possibly by distinguishing two separate points of *surprise*. The first would be when responsible officials become acutely aware of the danger, and the second when certain identifiable steps to avert it are begun. In any case, it is not argued that lengthening the period between *surprise* and *no escape* necessarily prevents war. It merely provides an opportunity to explore possible preventive measures. Yet this does suggest ways in which the framework can be adapted to apply to more than one type of war-producing instance. Further inquiry will determine the degree to which such adaptation is possible and the kinds of modification needed.

Much of this discussion has dealt with means of making certain actions of one power more readily predictable to other powers, and particularly to prospective opponents. This is in sharp contrast to much of traditional diplomacy, with its frequent emphasis on keeping the opponent off balance by being unpredictable. But by apprising each side of the other's desire to avoid general war, and furnishing tangible evidence of intentions, part of the edge can be removed from the present hair trigger. By reducing the danger of "accidental" war, all powers can gain.

11

The Complexities of Ballistic Missile Defense

Ever since the limited nuclear test ban, two growing clouds have come to dominate the horizon of national security policy: the spread of nuclear weapons, and the prospects for an antiballistic missile system, or ballistic missile defense. Other arms control issues, such as the continuing hope for some detente in Europe or for formal restrictions on the great powers in space, have received attention, but the first two become ever more pressing. There is now a consensus both in government and in the wider national security community that major decisions on both will have to be taken before the end of the 1960s.

One finds a high level of agreement as to what basically ought to be done about the spread of nuclear weapons (stop it!) even though there is much less common understanding of how to do it, or how to live with the situation if proliferation cannot be halted or drastically limited. The problem of ballistic missile defense, however, finds no agreement even at such an elementary level. Unfortunately the issue has emotional proponents on both sides, each arguing in black and white terms without a common frame of reference. Often the debate is conducted on a very complicated set of considerations perhaps amenable in the end only to detailed and technical information of a sort available neither to the general public nor to those who aspire to a slightly more than trivial role in the formation of national policy. But an effort to understand at least what the basic considerations are is essential to useful

Reprinted from *The Yale Review*, 56, 3 (spring 1968).

debate. Furthermore, they are not irrelevant to the other major issue, nuclear proliferation. The political ramifications of building an American antimissile system will be widespread and extremely serious. This is a classic situation where cost and narrow military effectiveness, so well analyzed by current techniques, must not be the sole criteria. There are sound *political* reasons for urging restraint, so the arguments should not be based on *technical* misapprehensions.

In the following discussion we shall address questions only about the desirability of a ballistic missile defense system to protect cities. A defensive system designed merely to secure strategic retaliatory forces against attack is widely considered desirable, *if* feasible at an appropriate price. Invulnerable retaliatory forces are an essential component of contemporary nuclear deterrence. The defense of population centers against attack, and against retaliation, is much more controversial. On the one hand it seems humane; on the other it poses serious questions for the stability of the balance of terror.

Some years ago the late Premier Khrushchev boasted that his country had built an antimissile missile that could "hit a fly in the sky." This may sound like an impressive feat, but it is really both insufficient and unnecessary for an effective program of ballistic missile defense. What is involved is a complex tradeoff between offensive and defensive capabilities in which each tries to degrade the other, with an ability on the part of the defense to score a direct hit quite irrelevant. The details are doubtless available in a good deal of classified material in the government, and with substantial digging in the trade and technical press to the scientifically trained and assiduous. Some distortion and simplification is unavoidable in a general discussion, but in essence the situation can be illustrated in one type, not necessarily always the most critical, of consideration.

The hope of ballistic missile defense depends upon the specific vulnerabilities of the incoming thermonuclear warhead it must intercept. In its simplest form a nuclear, or atomic, bomb is composed of two or more pieces of fissionable material, enriched uranium (U^{235}) or plutonium. The original masses of radioactive metal are subcritical; that is, the masses are small enough so that a large proportion of the neutrons emitted will escape beyond the area of the material; if the mass were sufficiently larger the neutrons would combine to produce a chain reaction or nuclear explosion. An implosion bomb, of the type used at Nagasaki and later, is composed of several subcritical masses loosely packed and surrounded by a chemical explosive. When this chemical explosive is properly detonated it applies great inward force to the loosely packed uranium, bringing it together at a high density so fast that the uranium very quickly reaches its critical mass and explodes, or *fissions*.

A thermonuclear weapon, or fission-fusion bomb, is constructed essentially by surrounding a fission device (usually one of enriched uranium) with heavy hydrogen (deuterium and tritium) that explodes, or undergoes *fusion*, when subjected to the very intense heat generated by fission. The outer rim of this combination would be composed of some dense and tough material capable of withstanding the blast of the fission just long enough to hold the device together while the heat builds up to set off the heavy hydrogen. Initially an inert metal was used for this jacket, but clever engineering made it possible to substitute natural uranium (U^{238}) in the jacket. The latter improvement meant that further fission, in addition to that occurring in the core, could be created so as to increase the total explosive yield of the weapon without changing its weight. This natural uranium does not produce as much yield as would enriched uranium or heavy hydrogen, but it is a good bit better than inert metal.

An antiballistic missile defense system could be effective by sheer force, as by splitting apart or knocking off course an incoming thermonuclear warhead. This would, in effect, be hitting the fly in the sky. But the mechanics of the device itself provide a number of points at which it can be rendered harmless or exploded prematurely and inefficiently, without depending on the physical blast to produce gross damage to the warhead in the crude sense. There are several such possibilities, but examination of one in some detail will make the point.

When a nuclear or thermonuclear weapon explodes it creates heat, blast, and radiation. One element of the radiation is the emission of a vast number of neutrons just like those normally emitted, at a much slower rate, from ordinary radioactive material—like those given off by the subcritical masses of enriched uranium. If enough neutrons should reach any subcritical mass *from outside* the effect would resemble that of bringing together enough fissionable material to create a critical mass—a chain reaction would be set off. It would not necessarily be an efficient explosion utilizing all the potential of the mass, since the engineering problems are extremely complex and a proper explosion cannot easily be achieved in such a crude way. Many nuclear physicists have testified, for instance, that there is no "secret" to the atomic bomb. But the fission will nevertheless occur, setting the bomb off prematurely and ineffectively in such a way that it would cause little or no damage to its intended target. The amount of *fusion* produced would be extremely minimal if the core of a thermonuclear weapon was set off this way. The range at which an exploding antiballistic missile (ABM) could produce such an effect would depend upon a complex pattern of variables (including protective measures that might be undertaken on behalf of the intruder), but ranges on the order of half a mile or even a mile seem not unreasonable—surely no need to hit a fly in the sky.

To prevent premature explosion the designers of the attacking warhead can, for instance, shield it with a heavier jacket designed to reduce the number of neutrons that penetrate to the enriched uranium core. Virtually all such countermeasures require, however, sacrificing some of the weapon's explosive yield. Even if the protection meant only increasing the amount of natural uranium in the jacket, for a given weight of warhead this would have to be achieved by reducing the amount of heavy hydrogen (which despite its name is much lighter than uranium). Since the hydrogen fusion releases more energy than does the uranium, the critical ratio of yield to weight has been affected, adversely from the point of view of the attacker, beneficially for the ingenious deployer of the ABMs. Because existing delivery vehicles cannot simply take on heavier and heavier warheads (to keep the yield constant), the defender has in fact scored a gain even if his ABMs fail to intercept and destroy a single attacking missile in wartime—he has reduced the total explosive megatonnage that his opponent is able to deliver onto his soil. (Because of the greater lift power of the bigger Soviet missiles the relative gain would be higher for a Russian ABM system against American penetration than vice versa, an important asymmetry that should not go unnoticed by advocates of such a defense for the United States.) Other possibilities for the defense include utilizing the effect of electromagnetic radiation which might shock the chemical explosive, or heat to melting some of the delicate circuitry required to make a thermonuclear warhead detonate. Depending upon the designs of both the attacking and defending weapons this might occur at closer or greater distances than the neutrons would have their effect. But there are several possibilities, and all of them increase the uncertainty for the attacker and may require him to build into his warheads a variety of protective devices, in each case at the expense of explosive power that might be carried in the absence of any active defense.

A warhead launched by a rocket over great distance comes in, as its name implies, on a ballistic trajectory; that is, it is carried very high above the atmosphere by its booster and falls onto its target at an angle not too far removed from the vertical. On the descent, decoys are especially effective in confusing the defense. An example of a decoy is simply the release of inflatable balloons early in the descent. If of a proper size and material composition they would, in the near vacuum of the outer atmosphere, appear on the defender's radar with much the same behavior as the thermonuclear warhead. (Falling bodies all descend at the same rate, regardless of their mass, in a vacuum.) But as the descent continues, and especially as they reach denser atmosphere, the lightweight balloons will gain velocity less rapidly than the heavy warhead, and the defender's radar can then discriminate between warhead and balloon decoy by their aerodynamic characteristics, and concentrate its interception system on the former.

For every response by the defender there is of course some more or less feasible counterploy by the attacker. In this case it is to use, instead of balloons, dummy warheads with essentially the same weight and aerodynamic qualities as the real warhead, making effective discrimination impossible. Yet if one is going to incur the cost of a dummy in payload-free weight, one might as well make more "productive" use of it. Hence the idea of *multiple* warheads, each containing a thermonuclear device but launched by the same missile. And there are other penetration aids, such as devices for actively confusing the interceptor's radar, which can complicate the defender's task. The better these devices, and the better the dummies that can be devised without incurring all the weight costs of additional warheads, the longer the defense must study the patterns of descent before being able to pick out the crucial incoming targets.

Thus the Nike-X system is composed of two missiles, one for long range, high altitude interception, and the Sprint for low altitude interception. The latter is capable of very rapid climb to moderate heights, and permits the defender, if the high altitude missile has failed to take out all the incoming objects, to delay his final effort until a better discrimination among the remaining ones is possible. All the devices, however, especially dummies or multiple warheads, impose a cost on the attacker—they have decreased the yield-to-weight ratio, and diminished the effective destruction any single missile can deliver. Even if all the multiple warheads are delivered, they will tend to be scattered around the intended target. So again the defense can score a gain even if not a single warhead is actually intercepted in the actual duel, and the attacker must compensate for it by building more or larger missiles. Also, in adding to the attacker's uncertainty about the effectiveness of the *defense*, the ABM system may contribute to *deterring* attack.

On the other hand, even complete "success" for the defender is not without its weaknesses. The attacker could try to foil the defense by building "dirty" warheads and detonating them himself, above their optimum altitude but before they are fouled by the ABM, or by aiming them at points farther removed both from the defense and his preferred targets. In either case he would hope to achieve by fallout many of the antipopulation effects lost by lesser heat and blast damage. So the earlier interception can be made, the better off the defender is.

Because like any falling body a missile gains in velocity the longer it falls, the rocket is most vulnerable at its zenith, and becomes progressively harder to hit as it descends. Furthermore, while dummy warheads might be released during the rocket's upward swing before it reaches the peak, it is likely to be harder to make them look like the real thing at that point. So for a variety of reasons the defender will prefer to improve as much as possible his high altitude or "exoatmospheric" interception capabilities. But doing so is not easy, given the speed with which information must be processed and the anti-missile missile launched. There is, nevertheless, in the information which has seeped through to the public, an intimation that major strides have been made toward effective exoatmospheric interception. Despite a few hints it seems very unlikely that such a system will ever be good enough to eliminate the necessity for a Sprint-like vehicle and fallout shelters, but it could ease the pressure somewhat. It also would raise the prospect of an effective defense of wide areas of the nation, a prospect that would have some political appeal beyond the confines of the cities that could be ringed with point defense.

As we have seen, the precise costs and benefits of various defensive systems and their countereﬀorts are impossible to calculate in the abstract with any confidence, and one should be highly suspicious of such calculations even for carefully detailed systems, given the error margins which must inevitably apply. But the basic idea of ballistic missile defense, for damage reduction for cities, is not absurd even though the idea of actually hitting a fly in the sky may be. It need not be fully effective to have some use, nor should the simple argument that defense is likely to be more costly than countermeasures (including more and more powerful intercontinental ballistic missiles) be accepted uncritically. Even should it be correct, the United States is about twice as rich as the Soviet Union. While the notion of our spending the Russians into bankruptcy is not very plausible, in an arms race propelled to a much higher level than at present we doubtless either could outspend them on this one, or force them to keep up with us only by sacrificing other programs which, if we were in a strictly competitive bipolar state of world politics, would rebound to America's advantage.

This kind of discussion assumes that the United States might goad the Soviets, by our example, into another spiral of defense spending, on antimissile missiles. The reality, of course, is that we risk being goaded *by* the Soviets into acquiring an ABM system. The numerous intelligence reports about a widespread system apparently being constructed by the USSR have produced political pressure on the present American Administration to match it. And that pressure comes at a time when the Administration, widely unpopular because of Vietnam and its failures in our cities, is in a difficult position for determined resistance.

Some of the disadvantages of a large-scale ABM program are fairly obvious, others less so. The unmistakable element is economic cost. Different sets of figures are quoted for systems with various levels and mixes of capabilities, but some rough orders of magnitude can be discerned. A light Nike-X system, capable of a high degree of success against any anticipated Chinese attack, might cost a total of 10 billion dollars or more spread over about five years. A larger system, intended for partial protection from a Russian attack, would be much more expensive. Figures on the order of 20 to 50 billion dollars, again spread over a number of years, seem fairly appropriate. This system would have to include not just the Nike-X or its successors, but major fallout shelter facilities and an improved air defense system directed against penetration by manned bombers. At the moment bombers are an inefficient means of attack, but an effective ABM system would make them relatively if not absolutely attractive. Such a system might have the ability to reduce by one-third to one-half the number of casualties anticipated from a Soviet attack that was directed from its early stages toward American urban centers. Even so the country would be vulnerable to myriad end-runs such as biological and chemical warfare. Furthermore, building a fallout shelter system would involve the American public much more than would ABMs alone, thus greatly complicating any efforts to retain some political psychology of detente.

By the standards of United States involvement in Vietman, currently at least 20 billion dollars a year, a missile defense capability is not enormous. But on top of the Vietnam embroglio, in an inflated economy, the cost is not trivial. Even the small China-oriented system would cost more than the rate of spending on the domestic poverty program (less than 2 billion dollars) and the larger one, for the Russians, would exceed American expenditures on the entire world poverty program, domestic and foreign economic aid, which currently amount to little more than 4 billion dollars. Machiavelli thought it better for a prince to be feared than loved, but he probably would have qualified his statement with the principle that any good policy can be carried to excess. Considering our current programs of expenditure for the instruments of fear we should perhaps demand that further increments in that direction be especially well justified.

A common argument against all measures for protecting the civilian population from nuclear attack, whether by active defense (ABMs) or by purely passive defense (shelters), has been that such programs risk communicating the wrong intentions to the other side, that they suggest an intention to protect our populace so well that under certain circumstances we might actually strike first. By this argument our civilians are hostages for our good intentions. A large segment of the American strategic analysis community has advocated just such a balance of terror to restrain both sides, and has not been displeased to see the Soviet Union take better steps to protect its retaliatory vehicles, so that it could have confidence they would survive to make a second strike. Fallout shelters alone would not change this situation, since those protected just against radioactivity would still be exposed to the blast and heat effects of an opponent determined to kill them in retaliation for attack. Shelters merely make plausible the idea of a "counterforce" war, which would involve attacks on each other's strategic delivery vehicles avoiding deliberate or at least early strikes against cities. Without protection many people would die from radioactivity even if not attacked directly; with fallout shelters most might survive a rather fearsome counterforce exchange.

A highly effective antimissile system for one or both sides might remove important restraints on a first strike under provocative circumstances. To the degree that American acquisition of such a system communicated (erroneously or otherwise) such an intention to the Russians the results would on balance be unfortunate, even if the Russians did not reciprocate. But again, these are not the present circumstances. The Soviets, more than we, have initiated this round, and we are left in the far more difficult position of trying to use our restraint to keep them from pushing on to a bigger and more sophisticated system, and this after our past restraint in this area was not enough to keep them from starting.

It may be contended that a ballistic missile defense system will not really be that effective, and so the harm done will not be all that great. The Americans and the Russians will have wasted money, but just money, and the consequence will merely be better penetration and continued vulnerability in the long run. But in deterrence as in other aspects of life, no man steps twice into the same river. The flow of events will create a new set of forces which inevitably will not, in their effects, precisely mirror current ones. The present river is rather smooth and satisfactory; stable deterrence based on vulnerable populations is a goal toward which many of our policy makers have been striving for years. A shift away from those conditions would imply grave risks unless new incentives to the opponents' good behavior were devised.

The peculiar irony of the present situation is that United States construction of a ballistic missile defense would be triggered by *Russian* action, but suitable in size for the *Chinese*, and perhaps later against other new nuclear powers as well. It is freely admitted that a system only marginally effective against a Soviet attack using large numbers of delivery vehicles with sophisticated penetration aids would probably be very effective indeed against the kind of small and primitive threat the Chinese will be able to mount for the next decade or so. If the Administration does succumb to the pressures on it, it may do so, or at least rationalize its behavior, on the grounds of the system's utility against China. Thus the very fact that the world is not simply bipolar may prove the most effective argument for an ABM.

Many of the system's proponents urge it as an answer to the proliferation problem. If we cannot prevent other nations from acquiring nuclear weapons—and one encounters increasing pessimism on this score—or from blowing up *each other*, we can at least protect ourselves. An ABM system would have the consequence of pricing small powers out of the deterrence market vis-à-vis the superpowers; the United States and Russia could retain their invulnerability against smaller powers that had bombs and delivery vehicles but could not afford great quantities or complex penetration aids. We would thus restore the bipolar world which has so recently begun to loosen.

The temptations to do so are strong. A need to be sure we can contain China hardly requires emphasis. United States and Soviet systems effective against small powers would take a good bit of the wind out of French sails. The individual countries of Western Europe would on the one hand find their own extant or prospective deterrent forces degraded by the Soviet ABM system, and on the other could be offered American ABMs for partial protection from attack. Their dependence on the United States would be very great, since the rate of obsolescence in ABMs promises to be rapid and the cost beyond any but the greatest states. Making it possible for—indeed virtually forcing—Europe to return to the American nuclear umbrella for protection must have very great attractions for harassed American statesmen. Even that outcome, however, would not be guaranteed. If separateness is weakness and dependence should be repugnant, the option of a purely *European* deterrent and ABM might look feasible and desirable to our present allies.

In retrospect the bipolar years from 1945 to the early 1960s were perhaps not so bad after all; not only can we see with hindsight that we did not have a major war, but we can see with more accurate information than then existed publicly that the Russians were at all times in a position of marked military inferiority to the United States. If we attribute to them only a reasonable caution it seems hardly likely that they could ever have been very near a readiness to take a serious risk of all-out war.

Yet we must not let analysis turn to nostalgia. The very loosening of bipolarity at present, bringing our troubles with Europe and, more importantly, the Russians' with China, has made possible the present however tenuous degree of detente that we find so comfortable. Now we hardly want to advocate the spread of nuclear weapons, which has so many frightening features. And we can hardly be so attached to the notion of loosening bipolarity as to forego otherwise virtually cost-free opportunities to strengthen ourselves vis-à-vis third powers. But an ABM system, even against China, is not cost free, nor nearly so.

On the matter of intentions, there is a subtle but in the long run especially corrosive kind of communication that would be read from American purchase of an ABM system effective against China. During most of the initial two decades following the Second World War the Soviet Union had at first no ability at all to deliver nuclear weapons on the continental United States, and even rather late in those years its capacity was weak and vulnerable to surprise attack. The Soviets doubtless saw this situation as far less than optimal, but still tolerable for one reason—they could always occupy or devastate Europe, regardless of American actions, even if they could not greatly damage the United States itself. They thus saw our allies and neutrals, the ancient states of Western Europe, as hostages to our good behavior. There is no way to know whether the presence of such hostages was ever necessary to restrain American belligerence; though I personally doubt it the situation nevertheless existed, and the Soviets say it reassured them.

The case for ABMs against China is that we must retain, and more importantly be seen to retain, our ability to use nuclear weapons against China without ourselves sustaining much damage, if Peking's belligerence should ever make it essential. But implicit in such a position is the idea that we would be much more restrained by what the Chinese could do to us than by what they could do to our allies and friends along the Asia rimlands. Under threat men always draw a distinction between their immediate selves (including their families) and their more peripheral associates and acquaintances. It is inevitable that we will not run the same risks for non-Communist Asia that we would run for Americans. But do we want to dramatize the distance—social as well as physical—that separates us from Asia, and that makes Asia so much more distant than Europe? A China-oriented missile defense would have to be supplemented with concrete military capabilities designed to protect non-Communist Asia from devastation before our retaliation against China could take full effect. This is a subtle point, but our friends in India, Japan, and elsewhere are neither so naive nor so confident in us as to ignore it for long, especially if we choose to make it with a "Fortress America" that builds its citadel facing the Pacific.

Let us return finally to the problems of bipolar confrontation. The Russians are probably building a system for defense against ballistic missiles. Though we cannot ignore the possibility, neither should we assume they do it from malevolent intentions toward the United States. In the first place, they too have their China problem, one which is magnified by their proximity to China's conventional as well as nuclear capabilities. While their present ABM system is not China-oriented—Peking is not yet a missile threat anyway—this is a long-term problem for Russia. Second, there is a long and powerful strain in Soviet political and military thought that emphasizes the virtues of a strong defense. Stalin's apparent wish for a reverse *cordon sanitaire* in Eastern Europe; the principle of socialism in one country; earlier emphasis on air defense; and various rejections of the "best defense is a good offense" principle—all suggest a policy of insuring the retention of hard won gains by a cautious Bolshevik defense of the homeland. While they *could* be preparing the conditions for an attack on us or on our allies, that is not the only or the likeliest explanation.

In any case, the appropriate response to such a Soviet system is not simply to imitate or surpass it. Our military positions are far from symmetrical, and we never in the past have tried to match them gun for gun. As a great continental land power the Soviet Union has always put more resources into ground forces than were appropriate for the United States. Similarly we have not attempted to match ship for ship their enormous submarine fleet, but rather have concentrated on the appropriate counter, antisubmarine warfare, supplemented by our traditional strength in surface vessels. The *emotional* response to an anti-missile missile may well be another anti-missile missile; the *military* response is to improve our intercontinental ballistic missile capabilities. Hence our Polaris submarines will be refitted with larger Poseidon missiles capable of carrying bigger warheads and more penetration aids. The cost of this, approximately 60 percent of the original price of the submarines, will not be insignificant.

It has been powerfully demonstrated that the United States decision to build the H-bomb stemmed far less from a confidence that it had a clear military utility than simply from a fear of what might happen if the Russians built one first. It may well be that under the circumstances that was the wisest decision. But it would be a pity to repeat history without trying a little harder to break the pattern of simple reaction.

12
The Calculus of Deterrence

A COMPARATIVE STUDY OF DETERRENCE

A persistent problem for American political and military planners has been the question of how to defend "third areas." How can a major power make credible an intent to defend a smaller ally from attack by another major power? Simply making an explicit promise to defend an ally, whether that promise is embodied in a formal treaty or merely in a unilateral declaration, is not sufficient. There have been too many instances when "solemn oaths" were forgotten in the moment of crisis. On the other hand, more than once a major power has taken up arms to defend a nation with whom it had ties appreciably less binding than a formal commitment.

Some analysts, such as Herman Kahn, maintain that the determining factor is the nature of the overall strategic balance. To make credible a promise to defend third areas the defender must have overall strategic superiority; that is, he must be able to strike the homeland of the attacker without sustaining unacceptable damage to himself in return.[1] This analysis implies, of course, a strategy which threatens to retaliate, even for a local attack, directly on the home territory of the major power antagonist. Advocates of a strategy of limited warfare retort that, in the absence of clear strategic superiority, the capacity to wage local war effectively may deter attack.

Reprinted from *Journal of Conflict Resolution*, 7, 2 (June 1963).
[1] Herman Kahn, *On Thermonuclear War* (Princeton, N. J.: Princeton Univ. Press, 1960).

Other writers, notably Thomas C. Schelling, have suggested that the credibility of one's threat can be considerably enhanced by unilateral actions which would increase the defender's loss if he failed to keep his promise.[2] One of the best examples is Chiang Kai-shek's decision in 1958 to station nearly half his troops on Quemoy and Matsu. While the islands were of questionable intrinsic importance, the presence of so much of his army there made it virtually impossible for Chiang, or his American ally, to abandon the islands under fire.

All of these explanations tend to stress principally the military elements in what is a highly complex political situation. There are, however, numerous non-military ways in which one can strengthen one's commitment to a particular area. A government can make it a matter of prestige with its electorate. A nation might even deliberately increase its economic dependence upon supplies from a certain area, the better to enhance the credibility of a promise to defend it. W. W. Kaufmann's classic piece identified the elements of credibility as a power's capabilities, the costs it could inflict in using those capabilities, and its intentions as perceived by the enemy. In evaluating the defender's intentions a prospective attacker will look at his past actions, his current pronouncements, and the state of his public opinion.[3]

Kaufmann's formulation is better than simpler ones that stress military factors exclusively, but it needs to be expanded and made more detailed. One must particularly examine the potential costs to the defending power if he does not honor his commitments. In addition, propositions about factors which determine the credibility of a given threat need to be tested systematically on a comparative basis. On a number of occasions, for example, an aggressor has ignored the threats of a major power "defender" to go to war to protect a small nation "pawn" even though the defender held both strategic superiority and the ability to fight a local war successfully. Hitler's annexation of Austria in 1938 is just this kind of case, and one where the aggressor was correct, moreover.

In this chapter we shall examine all the cases, during three decades, in which a major power "attacker" overtly threatened a "pawn" with military force, and where the defender either had given, prior to the crisis, some indication of an intent to protect the pawn or made a commitment in time to prevent the threatened attack.[4] A threat may be believed or disbelieved; it may be a bluff, or it may be sincere. Often the defender himself may not be sure of his reaction until the crisis actually occurs. We shall explore the question of what makes a threat credible by asking which threats in the past have been

---

[2] Thomas C. Schelling, *The Strategy of Conflict* (Cambridge, Mass.: Harvard Univ. Press, 1960).

[3] W. W. Kaufmann, editor, *Military Policy and National Security* (Princeton, N. J.: Princeton Univ. Press, 1956).

[4] These definitions are employed purely in an analytical sense with no intention of conveying moral content. The British-French "attack" in 1956, for instance, was certainly provoked to a large extent by the Egyptians themselves.

respected and which disregarded. Successful deterrence is defined as an instance when an attack on the pawn is prevented or repulsed without conflict between the attacking forces and regular combat units of the major power "defender." ("Regular combat units" are defined so as not to include the strictly limited participation of a few military advisers.) With this formulation we must ignore what are perhaps the most successful instances of all—where the attacker is dissuaded from making any overt threat whatever against the pawn. But these cases must be left aside both because they are too numerous to be treated in detail and because it would be too difficult to distinguish the elements in most cases. Who, for example, really was the "attacker"? Was he dissuaded because of any action by the defender, or simply by indifference? Such questions would lead to too much speculation at the expense of the careful analysis of each case in detail.

Deterrence fails when the attacker decides that the defender's threat is not likely to be fulfilled. In this sense it is equally a failure whether the defender really does intend to fight but is unable to communicate that intention to the attacker, or whether he is merely bluffing. Later we shall ask, from the viewpoint of the attacker, which threats ought to be taken seriously. At this stage we shall simply examine past cases of attempted deterrence to discover what elements are usually associated with a threat that is believed (or at least not disbelieved with enough confidence for the attacker to act on his disbelief) and therefore what steps a defender might take to make his threats more credible to his opponent. Table 12-1 lists the cases for consideration.[5]

These cases are not, of course, comparable in every respect. Particularly in the instances of successful deterrence the causes are complex and not easily ascertainable. Nevertheless, a systematic comparison, undertaken cautiously, can provide certain insights that would escape an emphasis on the historical uniqueness of each case.

DETERRENCE IN RECENT DECADES

First, we may dismiss as erroneous some frequent contentions about deterrence. It is often said that a major power will fight only to protect an "important" position, and not to defend some area of relatively insignificant size or

---

[5] Note that we have excluded instances of protracted guerrilla warfare. While preventing and defeating guerrilla war is a major problem, the differences from the matters considered here require that it be treated separately. The Berlin crisis was not included because, at the time of writing, it was still unresolved. Also excluded are those cases of aggression in the 1930s and 1940s where no particular power had given a previous indication of a readiness to defend the pawn. By "previous indication" we mean either at least an ambiguous official statement suggesting the use of military force, or the provision of military assistance in the form of arms or advisers. The League of Nations Covenant is not considered such an indication because, barring further commitments by a particular nation, it is impossible to identify any one defender or group of defenders.

Table 12-1

Seventeen Cases of Threatened Military Action, 1935–1961

Pawn	Year	Attacker(s)	Defender(s)
		Success	
Iran	1946	Soviet Union	United States Great Britain—Secondary
Turkey	1947	Soviet Union	United States
Berlin	1948	Soviet Union	United States Great Britain } Secondary France
Egypt	1956	Great Britain France	Soviet Union†
Quemoy-Matsu	1954–1955 1958	Communist China	United States
Cuba	1961	United States (support of rebels)	Soviet Union
		Failure: pawn lost	
Ethiopia	1935	Italy	Great Britain France
Austria	1938	Germany	Great Britain France Italy
Czechoslovakia	1938	Germany	Great Britain France
Albania	1939	Italy	Great Britain
Czechoslovakia	1939	Germany	Great Britain France
Romania	1940	Soviet Union	Great Britain
Guatemala	1954	United States (support of rebels)	Soviet Union
Hungary	1956	Soviet Union	United States
		Failure: war not avoided	
Poland*	1939	Germany	Great Britain France
South Korea	1950	North Korea (supported by China and Soviet Union)	United States
North Korea	1950	United States	Communist China

†Despite its efforts to restrain the attackers, the United States was not a "defender" in the Suez affair. It neither supplied arms to the Egyptians before the crisis nor gave any indication that it would employ military force against Britain and France. In fact, the United States government explicitly ruled out the use of military coercion. See *New York Times*, November 7, 1956.

*Possibly the Polish case is not really a failure at all, for Hitler may have expected Britain and France to fight but was nevertheless prepared to take the consequences. A. J. P. Taylor presents an extreme version of the argument that Hitler expected Poland and/or Britain and France to give in. See A. J. P. Taylor, *The Origins of the Second World War* (New York: Atheneum, 1962).

population. As we shall see below, this is in a nearly tautological sense true—if, by "important," we include the enmeshment of the defender's prestige with the fate of the pawn, the symbolic importance the pawn may take on in the eyes of the other allies, and particular strategic or political values attached to the pawn. But if one means important in terms of any objectively measurable factor like relative population or gross national product, it is not true.

As Table 12-2 shows, in all of our cases of successful deterrence—Iran, Turkey, Berlin, Egypt, Quemoy-Matsu, and Cuba—the pawn's population was well under 15 percent, and his GNP less than 5 percent of that of the principal defender.[6] (Britain was not Iran's chief protector.) Yet in five of the eleven cases where the attacker was not dissuaded the territory in question represented over 20 percent of the defender's population (Ethiopia, Czechoslovakia in the Sudeten crisis and again in 1939, Poland, and Romania). Poland in 1939 constituted the largest prize of all, yet Hitler may not have been convinced that Britain and France would go to war to save it. Nor can one discover any special strategic or industrial importance of the pawn only in cases of success. Austria and both Czechoslovakian cases met these criteria but were nevertheless overrun, and the United States did not expect Communist China to fight for North Korea, despite its obvious strategic significance.

Table 12-3, page 206, shows the apparent effect of various alleged influences in all the cases. Clearly, it is not enough simply for the defender to make a formal promise to protect the pawn. Only in one case of success was there what could be described as a clear and unambiguous commitment prior to the actual crisis (Berlin). In the others the commitment was either ambiguous (Iran, Cuba, Quemoy-Matsu) or not made until the crisis was well under way (Turkey, Egypt). The United States' principal precrisis commitment to Iran was the Big Three communique from Teheran in 1943 (written chiefly by the American delegation) guaranteeing Iranian "independence, sovereignty, and territorial integrity."[7] Britain was allied with Iran, but the Russians recognized that any effective resistance to their plans would have to come from the United States rather than from an exhausted Britain. In July 1960 Khrushchev warned that the Soviet Union would retaliate with missiles if the United States attacked Cuba, but this was later qualified as being "merely symbolic" and the precise content of Soviet retaliation was left undefined. Neither Congress nor the President has ever stated the exact circumstances under which our formal guarantees of Taiwan would apply to the offshore islands.

---

[6] On the other hand one might argue that they were not of sufficient potential value to the attacker for him to run even a relatively slight risk that the defender might actually fight. A complete formulation involving these factors would have to include both the value of the pawn to the attacker and his estimate of the probability that the defender would fight. See the next section of this chapter.

[7] See George Kirk, *The Middle East in the War: Royal Institute of International Affairs, 1939–46* (New York: Oxford Univ. Press, 1952), p. 473, on the Iranian case.

Yet in at least six cases an attacker has chosen to ignore an explicit and publicly acknowledged commitment binding the defender to protect the pawn. Britain, France, and Italy were committed by treaty to Austria, France by treaty to Czechoslovakia in 1938, France by treaty and Britain by executive

Table 12-2

Size (Population and Gross National Product) of Pawn in Relation to Defender(s)

Pawn	Defender(s)	Pawn's population as percent of defender's population	Pawn's GNP as percent of defender's GNP
	Success		
Iran	United States	12	†
	Great Britain	37	4
Turkey	United States	13	1.7
Berlin	United States	1.5	†
	Great Britain	4	3
	France	5	3
Egypt	Soviet Union	12	2
Quemoy-Matsu	United States	†	†
Cuba	Soviet Union	3	1.5
	Failure: pawn lost		
Ethopia	Great Britain	28	1.8
	France	31	2
Austria	Great Britain	14	7
	France	16	8
	Italy	16	17
Czechoslovakia (1938)	Great Britain	30	14
	France	34	16
Albania	Great Britain	2	†
Czechoslovakia (1939)	Great Britain	23	11
	France	26	12
Romania	United Kingdom	33	11
Guatemala	Soviet Union	1.6	†
Hungary	United States	6	1.0
	Failure: war not avoided		
Poland	Great Britain	73	25
	France	82	29
South Korea	United States	14	†
North Korea	Communist China	2	3

Sources: Population data are from United Nations, *Demographic Yearbook, 1948* (New York: United Nations, 1949) pp. 98–105; United Nations, *Demographic Yearbook, 1961* (New York: United Nations, 1962), pp. 126–37. GNP data are from Norton Ginsburg, *Atlas of Economic Development* (Chicago: University of Chicago Press, 1962), p. 16. GNP data are approximate and sometimes estimated.

†Less than 1 percent.

Table 12-3

Presence or Absence of Various Factors Alleged to Make Deterrent Threats Credible

Factors alleged to make deterrent threats credible	Attacker holds back						Attacker presses on — Defender does not fight								Attacker presses on — Defender fights		
	Iran	Turkey	Berlin	Egypt	Quemoy-Matsu	Cuba	Ethiopia	Austria	Czechoslovakia (1938)	Albania	Czechoslovakia (1939)	Romania	Guatemala	Hungary	Poland	South Korea	North Korea
Pawn 20 percent + of defender's population	*						X		X		X	X			X		
Pawn 5 percent + of defender's GNP	?	X	X		?	?	?	X	X	?	X	X		?	X		
Formal commitment prior to crisis		X	X		?	?	?	X	X	?	X	X		?	X		X
Defender has strategic superiority	X				X		X	X	X	?	?			?		X	?
Defender has local superiority							X	X	?	X				?		?	?
Defender is dictatorship				X	X	X		*					X				X
Pawn-defender military cooperation	X	X	X	X	X	X			X		X	X	X		X		X
Pawn-defender political interdependence	X	X	X		X							X	X			X	X
Pawn-defender economic interdependence	*	X	X	X	X	X		*								X	X

×Factor present.　　?Ambiguous or doubtful.　　*Factor present for one defender.

agreement to Czechoslovakia in 1939, Britain by executive agreement to Romania, Britain and France by treaty with Poland, and China by public declaration to North Korea. In three others there was at least an ambiguous commitment on the "defender's" part that might have been more rigorously interpreted. By a treaty of 1906 Britain, France, and Italy pledged themselves to "cooperate in maintaining the integrity of Ethiopa," Britain and Italy agreed in 1938 to "preserve the status quo in the Mediterranean" (including Albania), and in the 1950s American officials made references to "liberating" the satellites that were tragically overrated in Hungary. Of the failures, in fact, only Guatemala and possibly South Korea lacked any verbal indication of the willingness of their "protectors" to fight. (In these instances, the defenders showed their concern principally by sending arms to the pawns before the attack.) The analyst who limited his examination to the present cases would be forced to conclude that a small nation was as safe without an explicit guarantee as with one. At least such guarantees existed in fewer instances of success (one in six) than in cases of failure (six of eleven).

We must also examine the proposition that deterrence cannot succeed unless the defender possesses overall strategic superiority; unless he can inflict far more damage on an aggressor than he would suffer in return. It is true that the successful deterrence of attack is frequently associated with strategic superiority, but the Soviet Union had, at best, strategic equality with the United States at the time of the Bay of Pigs affair. While Russia was clearly superior to Britain and France when it threatened to attack them with rockets in 1956, it just as clearly did not have a credible first strike force for use against their American ally.[8]

Furthermore, in at least five cases where the attacker was not dissuaded, it nevertheless appears that the defender definitely had the ability to win any major conflict that might have developed (in the cases of Ethiopia, Austria, Czechoslovakia in 1938, Albania, and South Korea) and in two others (Czechoslovakia in 1939 and Hungary) the defender had at least a marginal advantage. (*Post hoc* analysis of the relevant documents indicates this superiority was more often perceived by the attacker, who went ahead and took the chance it would not be used, than by the defender. Hitler consistently recognized his opponents' strength and discounted their will to use it.)

Even less is it necessary for the defender to be able to win a limited local war. Of all the cases of success, only in Egypt could the defender plausibly claim even the ability to fight to a draw on the local level. In the other instances the defender could not hope to achieve equality without a long, sustained effort, and local superiority appeared out of reach. Yet in at least two failures the defenders, perhaps individually and certainly in coalition, had local superiority (Ethiopia and Austria) and in four others (Czechoslovakia in

---

[8] In both of these instances we must recognize that the "attacker's" failure to persevere to defeat of the pawn was probably due less to Soviet threats than to pressures from the "attacker's" own allies and world opinion.

1938, Albania, and the Korean cases) the defenders seemed to have been more or less on a par with their prospective antagonists.[9]

Yet if these two kinds of capabilities—local and strategic—are analyzed together, it would seem that a defender may not be clearly inferior in both and yet hope to restrain an attacker. Although the Soviet Union could not dream of meeting the United States in a limited war in the Caribbean, at least in 1961 its strategic nuclear capabilities seemed roughly on a par with America's.[10] And although Russia was inferior to Britain-France-United States on the strategic level, Soviet chances of at least matching their efforts in a local war over Egypt seemed a little brighter. Success requires at least apparent equality on one level or the other—this is hardly surprising—but when we remember that even superiority on both levels has often been associated with failure we have something more significant. *Superiority*, on either level, is not a condition of success. *Equality* on at least one level is a *necessary*, but by no means *sufficient*, condition. The traditionally conceived purely military factors do not alone make threats effective.

Nor, as has sometimes been suggested, does the kind of political system in question seem very important, though it does make some difference. Often, it is said, a dictatorial power can threaten much more convincingly than a democracy because the dictatorship can control its own mass media and present an apparently united front. Democracies, on the other hand, cannot easily suppress dissenting voices declaring that the pawn is "not worth the bones of a single grenadier." This argument must not be overstated— four of our successful cases of deterrence involved a democracy defending against a dictatorship. Yet in all of these cases the democracy possessed strategic superiority, whereas the other two successes, by a dictatorship, were at best under conditions of strategic equality for the defender. And in all but two (North Korea and Guatemala) of the eleven failures the defender was a democracy. Thus a totalitarian power's control over its citizens' expression of opinion may give it some advantage, if not a decisive one—particularly under conditions when the defender's strategic position is relatively weak.

INTERDEPENDENCE AND EFFECTIVENESS

With some of these hypotheses discarded we may now examine another line of argument: the effectiveness of deterrence depends upon the economic, political, and military interdependence of pawn and defender. Where visible ties of commerce, past or present political integration, or military cooperation

---

[9] See Winston Churchill, *The Second World War*, I, *The Gathering Storm* (Boston: Houghton Mifflin, 1948), pp. 177, 270–1, 287, 336–7 on the military situation prevailing in various crises before World War II.

[10] American intelligence reports were, however, far from unanimous. By the end of 1961 it was clear to those with good information that the Soviets' strategic forces were distinctly inferior to America's.

exist, an attacker will be much more likely to bow before the defender's threats—or if he does not bow, he will very probably find himself at war with the defender.

Military Cooperation

In every instance of success the defender supported the pawn with military assistance in the form of arms and advisers. In one of these cases, of course (Berlin) the defenders actually had troops stationed on the pawn's territory. The military link with Iran was somewhat tenuous, for Teheran received no shipments of American military equipment until after the 1946 crisis was past. Yet an American military mission was stationed in the country at the time, and 30,000 American troops had been on Iranian soil until the end of 1945.[11] America had given a tangible, though modest, indication of her interest in Iran. But in only five of the eleven failures were there significant shipments of arms to the pawn. France extended large military credits to Poland, and the British gave a small credit ($20 million) to Romania. The Americans and the Chinese sent both arms and advisers to their Korean protégés. The Soviets sent small arms to Guatemala but no advisers, and they did not give any explicit indication of an intent to intervene in any American move against the Guatemalan government. A French military mission was stationed in Prague before and during the two Czechoslovakian crises, but no substantial amount of French equipment was sent (in part because of the high quality of the Czechoslovakian armament industry). In none of the other failures was there any tangible military interdependence. Some degree of military cooperation may not always be sufficient for successful deterrence, but it is virtually essential.

Political Interdependence

This is a helpful if not essential condition. Four of the instances of successful deterrence include some kind of current or recent political tie in addition to any current alliance. Western troops were stationed in Berlin and the three Western powers participated in the government of the city by international agreement. America and Nationalist China had been allies in a recent war. Turkey became allied with the Big Three toward the end of World War II. Iran had been occupied by British troops until early 1946 and American troops until the end of 1945. In the case of failures only four of eleven pawns had any significant former tie with a defender. Britain and Romania were allies in World War I, as were the USSR and Guatemala in World War II. Obviously, neither of these ties was at all close. The other two, however,

---

[11] Kirk, op. cit., p. 150.

were marked by rather close ties. United States forces occupied South Korea after World War II, and the government of the Republic of Korea was an American protégé. The Communist Chinese had close party and ideological ties with the North Korean regime, and not too many decades previously Korea had been under Chinese sovereignty.

Economic Interdependence

We shall work with a crude but simple and objective measure of economic interdependence. In 1954 all countries of the world, other than the United States, imported a total of $65 billion of goods, of which 16 percent came from the United States. South Korea, however, took 35 percent of its total imports from the United States, a figure well above the world average. This will be our measure: does the pawn take a larger than average proportion of its imports from the defender or, vice versa, does the defender take a larger than average proportion of its imports from the pawn? To repeat, this is a crude measure. It does not tell, for example, whether the defender is dependent upon the pawn for a supply of a crucial raw material. But there are few areas of vital economic significance in this sense—almost every commodity can be obtained from more than one country, though not always at the same price— and attention to overall commercial ties gives a broad measure of a country's general economic stake in another.[12] In none of the cases where this test does not show general economic interdependence is there evidence that the defender relied heavily on the pawn for a particular product.

In five of the six cases of successful deterrence either the pawn took an abnormally high proportion of its imports from the defender or vice versa. In the remaining case, the Iranian economy was closely tied to Britain if not to the United States, but in only three of the eleven failures was there inter- dependence between pawn and defender. A higher than average proportion of Austria's trade was with Italy, though not with France and Britain, the other two parties bound by treaty to preserve her integrity. Both Korean regimes also traded heavily with their defenders. Economic interdependence may be virtually essential to successful deterrence.

DIVINING INTENTIONS

Briefly we may also examine the question from the viewpoint of the attacker. If the defender's threat is not challenged, one may never know whether it

---

[12] In the cases of Berlin and Quemoy-Matsu we must rely on trade figures for a larger unit (West Germany and Taiwan). West Germany conducted an above-average proportion of her trade with the United States and France in this period, but her trade with Britain was below average. Yet as Allied resolve in the Berlin crisis clearly depended upon American initiative it seems correct to include Berlin in the class of economically interdependent pawns.

truly expresses an intention to fight or whether it is merely a bluff. Perhaps the defender himself would not know until the circumstances actually arose. But we can examine the eleven cases where deterrence was not sufficiently credible to prevent attack. Previously we asked what differentiated the instances when the attacker pressed on from those in which he restrained his ambitions. Now, what distinguishes the cases where the defender actually went to war from those where he did not?[13]

"Size," as defined earlier, again is not crucial. Poland, for which Britain and France went to war, was a very large prize but neither North nor South Korea represented a significant proportion of its defender's population or GNP. Of the eight instances where the defender's bluff was successfully called, four of the pawns (Ethiopia, Czechoslovakia on both occasions, and Romania) represented over 20 percent of the defender's population and four (Austria, Czechoslovakia both times, and Romania) over 5 percent of its GNP. Proportionately "large" pawns were more often the subject of "bluffs" than of serious intentions. Nor is there necessarily a formal, explicit commitment in cases which result in war. There were such commitments over Poland and North Korea, but South Korea is an obvious exception. And there was such a commitment in the case of half the "bluffs" (Austria, Czechoslovakia twice, and Romania), and a vague, ambiguous one in three other cases (Ethiopia, Albania, Hungary).

The state of the military balance does not seem to have much effect either. In at least four "bluffs" (Ethiopia, Austria, Czechoslovakia in 1938, and Albania) the defenders were clearly superior *overall* and in two other cases (Czechoslovakia in 1939 and Hungary) they were at least marginally so. Yet despite their bad military position Britain and France fought for Poland in 1939. And although the Chinese made some bold "paper tiger" talk they really could have had few illusions about their position should the United States counter their move into North Korea with its full conventional and nuclear might. In no instance where a defender fought did he have the ability to win a quick and relatively costless *local* victory. But in the two cases where the defender probably did have this ability (Ethiopia and Austria) he did not employ it. Neither does the defender's political system appear to matter much. The Chinese fought to defend North Korea, but dictatorships did nothing to protect Austria and Guatemala.

Yet bonds of interdependence—economic, political, and military—do turn out to be highly relevant. In every case where the defender went to war he

---

[13] Remember that we have been dealing only with those cases in which deterrence was visibly in danger of failing, and not with instances where it was fully successful, i.e., where the attacker was dissuaded from ever making a serious explicit threat. As noted earlier the latter cases are extremely difficult to identify; nevertheless it seems likely that analysis would show similar results to those above. American protection of Western Europe is an excellent example. The political, economic, and military interdependence of Europe and the United States is great enough to make America's threat highly credible (though perhaps not as credible as we might sometimes wish).

had previously sent military advisers and arms to the pawn. Only four of the eight "bluffs" were marked by either of these activities, and none by a significant level of both. The two Koreas both had important prior political ties to their eventual defenders, but only two of the instances of "bluff" (Romania and Guatemala) were marked by even very weak ties of previous alliance. The two Korean states also were closely tied economically to their defenders, but of all the seven instances of bluff, only Italy-Austria show a bond of similar strength. Again it is the nature of the defender-pawn relationship, rather than the attributes of either party separately, that seem most telling in the event.

We must be perfectly clear about the nature of these ties. Certainly no one but the most inveterate Marxist would assert that the United States entered the Korean War to protect its investments and economic interests. The United States went to war to protect a state with which it had become closely identified. It was rather heavily involved economically in Korea, and its prestige as a government was deeply involved. It had occupied the territory and restored order after the Japanese collapse; it had installed and supported an at least quasi-democratic government; and it had trained, organized, and equipped the army. Not to defend this country in the face of overt attack would have been highly detrimental to American prestige and to the confidence governments elsewhere had in American support. Even though it had made no promises to defend Korea (and even had said it would not defend it in a general East-West war) the American government could not disengage itself from the fate of the Korean peninsula. Despite the lack of American promises, the American "presence" virtually guaranteed American protection.

MAKING DETERRENCE CREDIBLE

It is now apparent why deterrence does not depend in any simple way merely upon the public declaration of a "solemn oath," nor merely on the physical means to fight a war, either limited or general. A defender's decision whether to pursue a "firm" policy that risks war will depend upon his calculation of the value and probability of various outcomes. If he is to be firm the prospective gains from a successful policy of firmness must be greater, when weighted by the probability of success and discounted by the cost and probability of war, than the losses from retreat.[14] The attacker in turn will determine whether

---

[14] See Daniel Ellsberg, *The Crude Analysis of Strategic Choice*, RAND Monograph P-2183 (Santa Monica, Calif.: RAND Corporation, 1960). Formally, the defender will pursue a firm policy only if, in his calculation:

$$F \cdot s + W(1 - s) > R$$

where F = the value of successful firmness (deterrence without war), W = the value (usually negative) of the failure of firmness (war), R = the value (usually negative) of retreat, and s = the probability that firmness will be successful.

to press his attack in large part on his estimate of the defender's calculation. If he thinks the chances that the defender will fight are substantial he will attack only if the prospective gains from doing so are great.[15]

The physical means of combat available to both sides are far from irrelevant, for upon them depend the positions of each side should war occur. A defender's commitment is unlikely to be believed if his military situation is markedly inferior to his enemy's. Yet even clear superiority provides no guarantee that his antagonist will be dissuaded if the defender appears to have relatively little to lose from "appeasement." At the time of the Austrian crisis Neville Chamberlain could tell himself not only that appeasement was likely to succeed, but that prospective losses even from its possible failure were not overwhelming. In particular, he failed to consider the effects appeasement would have on Britain's other promises to defend small nations. By autumn 1939, however, it was clear that further appeasement would only encourage Hitler to continue to disregard British threats to fight, as British inaction over Austria in fact had done.

Under these circumstances the effectiveness of the defender's threat is heavily dependent on the tangible and intangible bonds between him and the pawn. If other factors are equal, a potential attacker is more likely to hold back, the greater the number of military, political, and economic ties between pawn and defender. No aggressor is likely to measure these bonds, as commercial ties, in just the way we have sketched them here, but he is most unlikely to be insensitive to their existence.

Strengthening these bonds is, in effect, a strategy of raising the credibility of deterrence by increasing the loss one would suffer by not fulfilling a pledge. It illustrates in part why the American promise to defend Western Europe, with nuclear weapons if necessary, is so credible even in the absence of overwhelming American strategic superiority. Western Europe is certainly extremely important because of its large, skilled population and industrial capacity. Yet it is particularly important to the United States because of the high degree of political and military integration that has taken place in the North Atlantic Area. The United States, in losing Western Europe to the Communists, would lose population and industry, and the credibility of its pledges elsewhere. To put the case another way, America has vowed to defend both Japan and France from external attack, and there is much that is convincing about both promises. But the latter promise is somewhat more credible than the former, even were one to assume that in terms of industrial capacity, resources, strategic significance, etc., both countries were of equal

---

[15] Precisely, he will press the attack only if:

$$A \cdot s + W(1 - s) > P$$

where A = the value of a successful attack (no war), W = the value (usually negative) of an attack which is countered (war), P = the value of doing nothing in this instance (peace), and s = the probability of a successful attack.

importance. The real, if not wholly tangible, ties of the United States with France make it so.[16]

Interdependence, of course, provides no guarantee that the defender's threat will be believed. There have been a few cases where an attacker chose to ignore a threat even when relatively close interdependence existed. But if one really does want to protect an area it is very hard to make that intention credible *without* bonds between defender and pawn. If the United States wishes to shield a country it will be wise to "show," and even to increase, its stake in that country's independence. Because the strength of international ties is to some degree controllable, certain policy choices, not immediately relevant to this problem, in fact take on special urgency. Implementation of the Trade Expansion Act, allowing the American government to eliminate tariffs on much of United States trade with Western Europe, will have more than an economic significance. By increasing America's apparent, and actual, economic dependence on Europe it will make more credible America's promise to defend it from attack.

The particular indices of economic, military and political integration employed here are less important in themselves than as indicators of a broader kind of political and cultural integration, of what K. W. Deutsch refers to as mutual sympathy and loyalties, "we feeling," trust, and mutual considera-tion.[17] These bonds of mutual identification both encourage and are encour-aged by bonds of communication and attention. Mutual attention in the mass media, exchanges of persons (migrants, tourists, students, etc.), and com-mercial activities all make a contribution. Mutual contact in some of these areas, such as exchange of persons, tends to promote contacts of other sorts, and often produces mutual sympathies and concern for each other's welfare.[18] This process does not work unerringly, but it does work frequently neverthe-less. And these mutual sympathies often are essential for the growth of a high level of commercial exchange, especially between economically developed nations rather than nations in an essentially colonial relationship with each other.[19]

---

[16] This point is further illustrated by the 1962 Cuban crisis. The American government took great pains to indicate that it was reacting to the threat of Soviet missiles on the island, and only demanded their removal, not the overthrow of the Castro regime. To have directly threat-ened the existence of a Communist government in which the Soviets had such a heavy military and economic investment would have carried a much greater risk of Soviet military retaliation.

[17] Karl W. Deutsch, *Political Community at the International Level* (Garden City, N.Y.: Doubleday, 1954), pp. 33–64.

[18] The theoretical and empirical literature on this point is voluminous and cannot be dis-cussed in more detail here. I have presented elsewhere a general theoretical examination of these problems and their application to Anglo-American relations. See Bruce M. Russett, *Community and Contention: Britain and America in the Twentieth Century* (Cambridge, Mass.: M.I.T. Press, 1963).

[19] Few markets are perfectly analogous to the model of perfect competition, as the products of two sellers are seldom identical, at least in the mind of the buyer. Customs, habits, traditions, and "myths" about the goods or the seller differentiate two seemingly identical products. A seller who speaks the language and understands the mores of his customers has a great ad-vantage over one who does not. Past habits can affect current prices through credit terms. Goods coming across a previously established trade route can be shipped more cheaply than those across one which has not yet developed much traffic.

In addition to the loss of prestige and of tangible assets, there is yet another way in which a defender may lose if he fails to honor his pledge. New Yorkers would sacrifice their own self-esteem if they failed to defend Californians from external attack; some of the same feeling applies, in lesser degree, to New Yorkers' attitudes toward Britishers. Though broad and intangible, this kind of relationship is nonetheless very real, and knowledge of it sometimes restrains an attacker.

Communication and attention both produce and are produced by, in a mutually reinforcing process, political and cultural integration. Table 12-3 demonstrates the degree to which economic, military, and political interdependence are correlated. All this raises the "chicken and egg" kind of question as to which comes first. In such a "feedback" situation there is no simple answer; sometimes trade follows the flag, sometimes the flag follows trade.[20] Yet these are also to some extent independent, and the correlation is hardly perfect. From the data available one cannot identify any single factor as essential to deterrence. But as more are present the stronger mutual interdependence becomes, and the greater is the attacker's risk in pressing onward.

---

[20] Ibid., Chapter 4.

13

Pearl Harbor: Deterrence Theory and Decision Theory

AN "INEXPLICABLE" DECISION

When General Hideki Tojo was Japanese Minister of War in September 1941 he advised Premier Konoye that at some point during a man's lifetime he might find it necessary to jump, with eyes closed, from the temple of Kiyomizu-dera on the heights of Kyoto into the ravine below.[1] Other Japanese officials used less colorful words invoking the necessity to take great risks, or to plunge with faith into the sea of the unknown. Partly because of these remarks, but more because objectively Japan was so obviously overmatched in resources for undertaking a war with the United States, many observers have attributed the Japanese decision to an act of irrationality, a choice that cannot be explained by any calculation of utilities and probabilities that would be arrived at by decision makers of another nation.[2] Such an interpretation easily leads

Reprinted from *Journal of Peace Research*, 2, 2, 1967.

[1] From the memoirs of Prince Konoye, cited by Robert J. C. Butow, *Tojo and the Coming of the War* (Princeton: Princeton University Press, 1961), p. 267.

[2] For example, see Sir Winston Churchill: "A declaration of war by Japan could not be reconciled with reason . . . But governments and peoples do not always take rational decisions. Sometimes they take mad decisions, or one set of people get control who compel all others to obey and aid them in their folly . . . However sincerely we try to put ourselves in another person's position, we cannot allow for processes of the human mind and imagination for which reason offers no key." (*The Grand Alliance*, Boston: Houghton Mifflin, 1950, p. 603). Masao Maruyama, a Japanese scholar, describes the country's leaders as acting "with their hands over their eyes." See his *Thought and Behaviour in Modern Japan* (London: Oxford University Press, 1963), p. 88.

to an emphasis on those peculiarities of Japanese national character that could bring them so grossly to distort reality in their calculations, or to a reiteration of the risks involved in a strategy of deterrence under high tension. According to the latter argument, it is precisely those times—great crises— when deterrent threats are most immediate that men are least able to weigh calmly the cost of their acts and the likelihood of counteraction.

Probing the personalities of decision makers is often an essential task in explaining political events. Provided that one brings a sophisticated approach to the analysis of national character, looking for *modal* behavior patterns (How is the average Japanese different from the average American, not how are all Japanese different from all Americans?), an explanation in terms of particular behavior or attitude patterns may be essential to understanding the motivations underlying a decision. But although such considerations have sometimes been invoked for the decision to attack Pearl Harbor and cannot be ignored as potential influences on any foreign policy decision, I contend that a satisfactory explanation can be offered with a model that is more general than those which depend heavily upon the personality characteristics either of national cultures or of more limited aggregates.

Most especially, an explanation does not require postulating that the Japanese leaders acted "irrationally." Rationality is a poorly defined and ambiguous concept in much of social science, but in this context its absence presumably could mean one of several things. The decision maker may, because of high stress, fail to perceive information or alternatives that would otherwise be apparent. Second, despite the receipt of information, he may distort it so seriously that his assessment of the probabilities of various events differs markedly from what another observer would conclude. Thus he might wildly exaggerate the probability of conducting a successful attack. Finally, he may have a grossly distorted set of value preferences that affect his motivations. For example, a retreat might be so painful to his personal self-esteem that he would unconsciously take action which imposed very severe risks on his nation.[3]

Most of these explanations depend either upon a situation of great stress, which would warp the actions of all or most of the participants in the decision process, or really apply only to circumstances where a single individual in fact makes the decision. Some of Hitler's most costly mistakes in World War II, for example, were highly individualistic decisions for which he alone was responsible. Typical of the pattern was his order to stand and fight at Stalingrad rather than allow his army to retreat and regroup. High stress plus the

---

[3] These correspond to the elements of an "ideal type" definition of means—ends rationality offered by Sidney Verba in his excellent "Assumptions of Rationality and Non-Rationality in Models of the International System," *World Politics*, 14 (October 1961), p. 108: accurate information, correct evaluation, and consciousness of calculation. By this definition peculiarities of value orientation, such as *conscious* extreme protection for one's self-esteem, would be "rational" but still require particularistic explanation. Some of the literature from experimental psychology, especially regarding the effects of time pressure, is cited by J. David Singer, "Inter-Nation Influence: A Formal Model," *American Political Science Review*, 57 (1963), pp. 420–30.

peculiarities of the Fuehrer's personality produced a command different from what other man would have given.

The Japanese decision to attack Pearl Harbor, however, was neither the decision of a single individual, where much of his behavior could be explained by his own personality structure, nor a decision arrived at under time pressures. It was reached incrementally and reinforced at several steps along the line. On July 2, 1941, it was decided to press ahead with expansion in Southeast Asia even though this meant a high risk of war with the United States. After deep consideration by high Japanese military and naval officials for months, a formal commitment was made at the Imperial Conference of September 6 that either negotiations must result in lifting the United States embargo on strategic raw materials, or Japan would have to fight the Americans. October 15 was set as the deadline for success in negotiation. But even though the *strategic* commitment (in the sense of a decision for the next move dependent upon the opponent's reaction to this one) had seemingly been made, it was the subject of a great deal of reexamination over the subsequent three months. Prince Konoye's government resigned following the expiration of the deadline, but the new cabinet formed under General Tojo took office not as a regime determined to take the nation into war, but rather as one still seeking a way out of the dilemma. Serious negotiations with the United States continued through November; a new secret deadline of November 25 was once set, "after which things are going to happen automatically," but it too was extended until November 30.[4] Whatever the nature of the decision to go to war, it was arrived at and reinforced over a long period of time, and was not the result of anyone's possibly "irrational" impulse.

In any case, the decision was in no important sense the act of a single man whose personality traits can thus be used to explain it. Premier Tojo never had a control over his government's actions that even remotely approached Hitler's. Though he was formally in the key position, the decision to go to war was pressed upon him by the Army High Command and was fully approved by the Navy and even by the relatively pacific Foreign Minister Shigenori Togo. The decision-making machinery was extremely loose, with an attempt to coordinate policies being made by such institutions as the Four Ministers' Conference, the Liaison Conference, or the Imperial Conference. The central problem was of reaching and carrying out decisions at all, not of having them imposed by the Premier. Tojo said after the war about these problems:

> When the Prime Minister, to whom is entrusted the destiny of a country, has not the authority to participate in supreme decisions, it is not likely that the country will win a war. Then again, the Supreme Command was divided between Army and the Navy—two entities that would not work in unison. I did not hear of the

---

[4] Butow, op. cit., p. 321.

Midway defeat till more than a month after it occurred. Even now I do not know the details.[5]

Tojo certainly knew the details of the proposed attack on Pearl Harbor, but he did not impose it—in fact he only found out about the plan after the Navy had already adopted it as its preferred strategy. Further examples of Army and Navy independence could be multiplied. The oubreak of the Sino-Japanese conflict in 1937 can be traced directly to unauthorized action by elements of the Army. And Army-Navy cooperation was so tenuous that in anticipation of landings in the Southwest Pacific it was decided that the area would be divided into two zones of occupation. Hong Kong, the Philippines, Malaya, British Borneo, Sumatra, and Java were to be in the Army's zone; the rest, including the other Dutch East Indies, were to be under Navy jurisdiction. So difficult was cooperation between the two branches that a Solomon solution had to be devised.[6]

In the light of what we know of the Japanese decision-making process, and the time it took to settle on the attack, any effort to explain the decision as an irrational "leap in the dark" would depend upon a notion of *collective irrationality over a period of many months*—no explanation at all. In fact, the rational-irrational distinction is for most purposes *not* a useful one, and we shall develop another way of examining individuals' preferences and evaluations in order to suggest how they make decisions.

A DECISION THEORY OF DETERRENCE

The Japanese attack on Pearl Harbor represents one of the most conspicuous and costly failures of deterrence in history; as such it deserves careful examination to see if any general propositions can be extracted. A full investigation of the personalities and attitudes of the major participants in Japan's decision is quite beyond the scope of this chapter, although enough memoirs and official documents are available to permit an effort in this direction by other scholars. The purpose of the chapter is quite different: to show that in this and probably many other instances a satisfactory explanation can be given largely without reference to idiosyncratic factors. The intent is to put the Japanese decision into the context of a more general theory of deterrence and a more explicit look at the foreign policy making process than is sometimes

---

[5] Quoted in the memoirs of Mamoru Shigemitsu, *Japan and Her Destiny: My Struggle for Peace* (London: Hutchinson and Company, 1958), p. 271.

[6] David J. Lu, *From the Marco Polo Bridge to Pearl Harbor: Japan's Entry into World War II* (Washington, D. C.: Public Affairs Press, 1961), p. 224. Maruyama, who is no apologist for the prewar governments, nevertheless vividly pictures the instabilities and insubordinations of the time, what he calls "the rule of the higher by the lower," and the differences between this situation and the decision-making system of Nazi Germany. See his *Thought and Behaviour*, op. cit., Chapter 3.

taken. Particularly, we want to examine some of the elements in common between this situation and other cases in the recent past. What is required is a theoretical framework that combines explanations on the level of the international system and the national decision-making system.

In the preceding chapter I offered a model, derived from decision theory, for analyzing the success or failure of nations' attempts to deter other nations from attacking smaller third parties. The decision theory model was cast in a utility-probability framework, in common with models suggested by several other writers.[7] It isolates certain variables in the mind of the formal decision maker of a nation as he decides whether or not to attack a small nation which is to some degree under the protection of another power. The situation under scrutiny is one of deterrence in third areas (what Herman Kahn long ago labelled Type III deterrence), and has since the end of World War II been a major consideration of American policy makers: how to prevent a Soviet (or Chinese) attack on allies or on exposed neutrals. Simplifying for the moment to a single set of calculations in the mind of a single decision maker, the prospective attacker must weigh the expected gains (utilities) to accrue from each of the following events:

1. W—an attack on the small nation, or pawn, which is countered by war on the part of the potential defender of that pawn; in other words, the utility—positive or negative—of having to fight a *war* with the major power;

2. A—an attack on the pawn which is not met by war with the defender; in other words, a successful act of "*aggression*";

3. P—a decision not to attack the small nation; this outcome is in effect an aggregate of many possible courses of action; for simplicity, if somewhat inaccurately, we shall refer to it as "*peace*" or choosing not to attack at all.

P—the decision not to attack at all—is a choice fully under the control of the prospective attacker, and will occur or not as he decides. The other two possible outcomes, however, are not fully under his control, and he can only estimate the likelihood that the defender will or will not go to war. Therefore he has to attach subjective probabilities to those two outcomes, and their utilities must be weighted by those probabilities. The utility of A must thus be discounted by whatever the attacker thinks is the probability, s, that he will actually get away with it, and the utility or disutility of W must similarly be weighted by its apparent likelihood $(1 - s$ in this simplified analysis). The final decision thus rests upon the relative values of two ex-

[7] Related utility-probability models are employed by Daniel Ellsberg, *The Crude Analysis of Strategic Choice*, RAND Monograph P-2183 (Santa Monica, California: RAND Corporation, 1960); Singer, op. cit.; and Glenn H. Snyder, *Deterrence and Defense* (Princeton: Princeton University Press, 1961).

pressions: P (do nothing) on the one hand; and the summed utilities, weighted by their subjective probabilities, of A and W on the other. According to this formulation, the potential attacker will actually press ahead with his attack only if A times s plus W times $(1 - s)$ is greater than P. Since these are variables, of course, the same decision might be reached on the basis of quite different values in the formula. If the potential gains even from a successful attack (A) on the pawn are relatively low compared with "peace" (P), and the disutilities of a major war (W) are very great, even a small subjective probability that the defender will fight is enough to deter attack. On the other hand, the relative gains from a successful attack on the pawn might be quite high, but if the subjective probability of an unresisted attack were low, the aggression would still not be carried out.

Now of course this model is grossly oversimplified, since a decision maker is virtually always faced with a great variety of potential courses of action, not simply an attack-or-don't-attack dichotomy, matched with a fight-or-don't-fight choice by the potential defender. Nevertheless, each of these possibilities can, for analytical purposes, be thought of as aggregates of many shades of action. Another objection might be that political decision makers certainly do not calculate utilities and probabilities in any precise way, though "strategic thinkers" and men versed in game theory may attempt to do so. But despite the fact that they may not try to put numerical values into an explicit model, decision makers surely do weigh the probable costs and gains of various alternatives. Finally, the model is hardly operational as a predictor of events in international politics because of the extreme difficulties associated with any attempt to measure utilities and especially subjective probabilities. The problems are formidable in the laboratory, and virtually insuperable with real world political leaders.[8] But despite the fact that we cannot actually measure even these implicit values with precision, the model will serve its purpose if it helps us identify relevant influences on a decision.

Empirical content was put into this model by a comparative study of 17 instances in the period 1935–1962 where a potential attacker threatened a smaller state that was to some degree under the protection of another power. I was able to suggest several factors associated with successful deterrence and, in addition, to identify several which, though hypothesized in the national security literature to be relevant, seemed not to make a great difference in the outcome. Among other things, this *post hoc* experiment indicated that while military equality between the attacker and the defender was required at either the local or strategic level, military *superiority* by the defender, on either or both levels, was *not* a *sufficient* condition for deterrence. In terms of the above decision model, even though the potential disutilities of an

---

[8] Some experiments, however, have measured utilities and probabilities under laboratory conditions. Cf. Ward Edwards, "Utility and Subjective Probability: Their Interaction and Variance Preferences," *Journal of Conflict Resolution*, 6, 1 (1962), pp. 42–51, and the references cited there. Also useful is Robert M. Thrall et al., editors, *Decision Processes* (New York: Wiley, 1954).

attack might be very high to the attacker, that alone was not sufficient to restrain him. The other variables, and especially the attacker's subjective probability that the defender would actually fight—were highly relevant.

Pursuing this line of reasoning further, I found that certain characteristics of the *relationship* between the small state and the potential defender were far more closely associated with successful deterrence. The major hypothesis to which this led was: If other factors are equal, an attacker will regard a military response by the defender as more probable the greater the number of military, political, and economic ties between pawn and defender.

There are of course two substantial inferential leaps implied in the above statement. One is from the *existence* of such bonds between defender and pawn to their *perception* by the decision makers of the potential attacker, and the second is from their *perception* to their *entry* in a significant way *into the calculations* of those who are deciding whether or not to press the attack. We are precisely in the middle of the old problem of confounding correlation with causation; the mere presence of the bonds does not prove that they influenced the outcome. The observed correlation has merely increased our interest in what was at the outset perhaps a plausible, if unsubstantiated, hypothesis. To go further we must move from the examination of many cases to the study in depth of one or more particular instances to discover whether these factors really were observed by the decision makers and what importance they took on. Even so we will not prove the hypothesis—scientific hypotheses can only be disproven, never proven with certainty—but we can add substantially to our confidence in it as a guide to policy and to theory. We return, then, to the Pearl Harbor case.

JAPAN PERCEIVES AMERICA'S COMMITMENT

As we shall see, crucial elements in Japan's decision to attack Pearl Harbor were its need for the resources of Malaya and especially the Dutch East Indies, the realization that these resources could be obtained in sufficient quantity only by force, and the conviction that the United States would declare war on Japan if those colonies were attacked, whether or not the Japanese themselves initiated hostilities with America. Japanese analysts reached the latter conclusion despite the absence of any American threat or promise.

At the Atlantic Conference, Roosevelt and Churchill discussed a "war warning" with regard to any further conquests by Japan in the Far East. No such warning was ever issued. The nearest equivalents were two statements by President Roosevelt to Ambassador Nomura in July and August of 1941. The first read:

> If Japan attempted to seize oil supplies by force in the Netherlands East Indies, the Dutch would, without the shadow of doubt, resist, the British would im-

mediately come to their assistance, and, in view of our policy of assisting Great
Britain, an exceedingly serious situation would immediately result.[9]

On the second occasion Roosevelt stated:

> If the Japanese Government takes any further steps in pursuance of a policy or
> program of military domination by force or threat of force of neighboring coun-
> tries the Government of the United States will be compelled to take immediately
> any and all steps which it may deem necessary toward safeguarding the legitimate
> rights and interests of the United States and American nationals and toward
> insuring the safety and security of the United States.[10]

Despite its firm language, this was not the unequivocal warning discussed
with Churchill at Argentia.[11] On presentation to Nomura it was, as Langer
and Gleason point out, not given the status of a "written statement" or even
of an "oral statement." It was merely private "reference material" for Nomura's use in communicating with his own government. No unequivocal
warning could be given, simply because Roosevelt could not be sure of
American's reaction in the actual event of crisis. He was fully aware of the
need to secure Congressional approval for war, of the strength of isolationist
sentiment in the United States, of the difficulties involved in demonstrating
that an attack on British or Dutch colonies was a direct threat to American
interests, and of the dangers inherent in going to war with the country divided.

By autumn 1941, however, opinion was crystalizing in the highest levels of
the American decision-making system. In November, Roosevelt informally
polled his cabinet on the question of whether the country would support war
against Japan in the event of attack on Malaya or the Indies. All members
responded in the affirmative. General Marshall and Admiral Stark, the Chiefs
of Staff, concluded that the United States should fight if Japan attacked
British or Dutch territory, or Siam west of 100 degrees East or south of 10
degrees North. On the morning of December 7 in Washington (before the
Pearl Harbor raid, which took place at dawn, Hawaii time), Secretaries Hull
(State), Knox (Navy), and Stimson (War) discussed the anticipated Japanese
attack on Siam or Malaya. They agreed the United States should go to war
if the British did. Roosevelt then expected to go before Congress the next day
to explain why a Japanese invasion of Siam threatened the security of the
United States.[12] Nevertheless the President had not, to the knowledge of any

---

[9] Quoted in William L. Langer and S. Everett Gleason, *The Undeclared War* (New York:
Harper, 1953) p. 650.

[10] Ibid., p. 695.

[11] A warning originally drafted by Churchill for Roosevelt's possible use read "Any further
encroachment by Japan in the South-West Pacific would produce a situation in which the
United States Government would be impelled to take countermeasures, even though they might
lead to War between the United States and Japan," (Churchill, op. cit., p. 440).

[12] Herbert Feis, *The Road to Pearl Harbor* (Princeton: Princeton University Press, 1950), p.
340.

of his advisers, definitely reached this decision. He clearly leaned in that direction and there was near consensus among his advisers, but no more.[13]

Thus the Japanese conviction that war could not be limited to the British and Dutch had to be based wholly on inference. Yet it was a solid conviction, as shown by the otherwise inexplicable risk they took at Pearl Harbor.

Rather close links had been forged between the United States and the colonies of Malaya and the East Indies, bonds that were known to the Japanese and considered to be of great importance. These ties, furthermore, closely resemble the kinds of links that we earlier indicated have been associated with the successful deterrence of attack on third parties. The Southwest Pacific area was of undeniable economic importance to the United States— at the time most of America's tin and rubber came from there, as did substantial quantities of other raw materials.[14] American political involvement in the area was also heavy. The United States was cooperating closely with the British and Dutch governments, and according to the Japanese evaluation, if the United States failed to defend the Indies it would lose its influence in China and endanger the Philippines.[15] Premier Tojo even referred in this context to the approval given Pan American World Airways to establish an air route between Singapore and Manila.[16]

Unilateral American actions to build up its military forces, both generally and in the Pacific in particular, were seen as evidence of aggressive intent.[17] But most convincing of all were the military ties apparently being established among the ABCD (American-British-Chinese-Dutch) powers. The United States was known to be supplying munitions and arms, including aircraft, not just to China but to British and Dutch forces in the Pacific. In cooperation with the British, Dutch, Australians, New Zealanders, and the Free French (at New Caledonia) the United States had begun construction of a string of airfields to the Philippines. Furthermore, the United States had participated in staff conversations with British and Dutch military personnel at Singapore.

---

[13] Charles A. Beard (*President Roosevelt and the Coming of the War*, 1941 [New Haven: Yale University Press, 1946], pp. 538–49) contended that the United States did assure the British that it would support them if they resisted Japanese incursions. The evidence he adduced was, however, far from conclusive, and it seems unlikely that any such assurance was actually given at the highest level. Even if it was given it was only just on the eve of the attack (Beard's best evidence is from a communique dated December 6, 1941) and not as early as November when the Japanese finally reaffirmed the decision to go to war with America. And in any case that assurance, if indeed it was given, was in the strictest secrecy and never known to the Japanese.

[14] The economic importance of the area to the United States was not left to Japanese imagination. On July 11, 1940 Ambassador Grew pointed out to Foreign Minister Arita that in 1937 15.8 percent of the foreign trade of the Netherlands East Indies had been with the United States, and only 11.6 percent with Japan. He further emphasized the interest of the United States in continuance of the open door there. See F. C. Jones, *Japan's New Order in East Asia; Its Rise and Fall, 1937–45* (London: Oxford University Press, 1954), p. 238, citing Cordell Hull, *The Memories of Cordell Hull* (New York: Macmillan, 1948), Vol. I, pp. 895–6.

[15] Cf. The Japanese Foreign Office memorandum of early November 1941, International Military Tribunal for the Far East (hereafter cited as IMTFE), *Document* No. 1559A. Similar conclusions were expressed in the Liaison Conference meetings of October 1941, according to Butow, op. cit., pp. 317–8.

[16] Butow, op. cit. p. 225.

[17] IMTFE, *Transcript of Proceedings*, p. 36246.

The Japanese came to associate these conversations with an "Anglo-American policy of encirclement against Japan in the Southern Pacific Ocean."[18] This notion of encirclement appears time and again in Japanese official documents and memoirs. The freezing of Japanese assets by the United States, British, and Netherlands East Indies governments occurred on the same day, July, 26, 1941. Although that act was in direct response to Japan's occupation of Southern Indochina, her leaders nevertheless saw it as the final link in their bondage.[19]

As early as spring 1941, in fact, the Japanese army and navy general staffs had agreed among themselves that military action in the Southwest Pacific meant war with the United States. As we have seen, no definite decision by the United States had been or would be reached, due largely to the state of American public opinion. But President Roosevelt and Secretary Hull were quite willing to have the Japanese believe that a joint American-British-Dutch plan for defense of the Indies existed.[20] The conviction only grew stronger with time, and was reinforced by the intelligence received from the Japanese embassy in Washington. On December 3, 1941, for example, the Washington embassy cabled Tokyo: "Judging from all indications, we feel that some joint military action between Great Britain and the United States, with or without a declaration of war, is a definite certainty in the event of an occupation of Thailand."[21] Here is explicit evidence that the decision makers of the prospective attacker did look at the ties between pawn and defender and did take them into account in their calculations of probabilities. We must now try to understand the utilities they attached to various outcomes.

HOBSON'S CHOICE

As we saw, Roosevelt and Hull pursued a strategy of deterrence by ambiguity. Because of domestic political constraints they were unable, even had they been willing, to make a firm or public commitment to the defense of British

---

[18] Cf. the Foreign Office memorandum so entitled, July 1941, IMTFE, *Defense Document No. 1982.* Foreign Minister Shigenori Togo in his memoirs (*The Cause of Japan* [New York: Simon and Schuster, 1956] pp. 84, 156, 163) repeatedly refers to the conversations this way.

[19] IMTFE, *Transcript*, p. 36273.

[20] Feis, op. cit., p. 190.

[21] Quoted in U.S. Congress, Joint Committee on the Investigation of the Pearl Harbor Attack, *Investigation of Pearl Harbor Attack: Report of the Joint Committee*, 79th Congress, 2nd Session, (Washington, D.C.: U.S. Government Printing Office, 1946), p. 172. Other analysts have tended, retrospectively, to treat the American-British-Dutch relationship as one of virtual alliance despite the absence of any firm public or private commitment. For example, Roberta Wohlstetter, *Pearl Harbor: Warning and Decision* (Stanford, Calif.: Stanford University Press, 1962), says, "Our own standard of logic pointed to the easier British and Dutch targets [as probable objectives] but the Japanese regarded the American-British-Dutch alliance as a real one." See also Wohlstetter, p. 381. If one uses the term "alliance" merely to indicate nations with bonds of common interest linking them in common action this is fairly accurate, though clarity might sometimes be served by a more restrictive definition. A tacit or secret "alliance" may well be binding—although special difficulties arise in a democracy—but it can have no *deterrent* effect unless the intention is somehow made manifest or inferred by the prospective attacker.

and Dutch Pacific colonies. But they were quite prepared to have the Japanese *think* that America was ready to go to war under those circumstances, and hoped that such a perception would deter the Imperial government. And in one sense it worked, since the Japanese policy makers did indeed think the United States would fight. Why then did *deterrence* fail; why did Japan not only attack the Indies anyway, but also directly attack the United States as well?

The model set forth in the preceding chapter was explicitly one with a number of elements. While from the empirical study of 17 cases it was established that certain kinds of pawn-defender links were *closely associated* with successful deterrence, those bonds were by no means a *sufficient* condition. There were several instances in which, despite them, the attacker was not deterred. Recall the formulation, which said that deterrence would succeed only if the utility of fighting a major war times its apparent probability was less than the utility of no attack, or "peace." We have established that, for the Japanese, the subjective probability that the United States would fight to defend the Indies was very high. Thus even though the utility of an attack on the British and Dutch territories would have been very high, if unresisted by the Americans, its probability was thought to be so slight that it amounted to little in their calculations.

On the other hand, the utilities attached by different members of the Japanese elite to not attacking was extremely low. In 1940 fuel oil and scrap iron were brought under the new National Defense Act of the United States as goods which could not be shipped out of the Western Hemisphere without an export license. Although commerce in these products with Japan was not cut off for another year, the threat of scarcity of raw materials was obvious to Japan. Following the freeze on Japanese assets in the United States of July 1941, and the consequent cessation of shipment of oil, scrap iron, and other goods from the United States, Japan's economy was in most severe straits and her power to wage war directly threatened. Her military leaders estimated that her reserves of oil, painfully accumulated in the late 1930s when the risk of just such a squeeze began to be apparent, would last at the most two years. She was also short of rice, tin, bauxite, nickel, rubber, and other raw materials normally imported from the Netherlands Indies and Malaya. Negotiations with the Dutch authorities to supply these goods, plus extraordinary amounts of oil from the wells in Sumatra, had failed, ostensibly on the grounds that the Dutch feared the material would be re-exported to the Axis in Europe. The United States, and the British and Dutch, made it quite clear that the embargo and freezing of assets would be relaxed only in exchange first for a return to the status quo in Indochina before July 1941 (in other words, Japanese withdrawal from air and naval bases there) and an agreement which would mean the end of the Japanese involvement in China and the abandonment of any right to station troops in that country. The purpose of the Western economic blockade was to force a favorable solution to the "China incident."

Under these conditions, the High Command of the Japanese navy demanded a "settlement" of one sort or other that would restore Japan's access to essential raw materials, most particularly oil. Without restored imports of fuel, the fleet could not remain an effective fighting force for more than a year and a half. While the Navy might have been willing to abandon the "China incident," it was utterly opposed to any long continuation of the status quo. Either raw materials supplies had to be restored by a peaceful settlement with the Western powers, or access to them, from Thailand, Malaya, and the Indies, would have to be secured by force while Japan still retained the capabilities to do so.

If the Navy demanded either settlement or war, most members of the Japanese elite were opposed to any settlement which would in effect have meant withdrawal from China. The long war in China, begun in earnest in 1937 but tracing back to the seizure of Manchuria in 1931, was making little progress. Japanese forces had occupied most of the coast and most of China's industrial capacity, but with a trickle of American aid the Nationalist armies hung on in the interior. Yet no serious consideration was given to the possibility of peace with Chiang's government. To do so would have meant the end of all hopes of empire and even, so it was thought, of influence on the continent of Asia. Herbert Feis describes the reaction of moderate Foreign Minister Togo to the most forceful statement of American demands, on November 27, 1941: "Japan was now asked not only to abandon all the gains of her years of sacrifice, but to surrender her international position as a power in the Far East. That surrender, as he saw it, would have amounted to national suicide."[22]

In any case, the Army High Command simply would not have tolerated any abandonment of its position in China. Its own prestige and influence had been built up step by step during the war there, and its position in China became its power base in Japanese domestic politics. And the pursuit of the war had allowed the Army to achieve a degree of internal unity quite surprising in view of its earlier factional strife. General Tojo, by no means the most violent of Army war hawks, feared that any concession on the China issue would risk an actual revolt by extremist elements in the Army.[23] In fact, on the resignation of Prince Konoye's government in October 1941 Tojo had urged the appointment of Prince Higashi-Kuni as Premier, on the principle that should a settlement with the United States be decided upon only a member of the royal family would have a chance to control the Army and make peace. In the context of Japanese politics of the 1930s, when there had been several plotted *coups* and when one after another of the political leaders thought to be too conciliatory toward foreign elements were assassinated by extreme nationalists, this was hardly a farfetched fear. Togo once characterized the

---

[22] Feis, op. cit., p. 327.
[23] Lu, op. cit., passim, describes vividly and convincingly the position of the Army on these questions.

Japanese internal political situation in these terms to Joseph Grew, American Ambassador to Tokyo: "If Japan were forced to give up suddenly all the fruits of the long war in China, collapse would follow."[24] And there was, after all, an attempted Army revolt in August 1945, when the Japanese government finally did accept the Allied terms of surrender.

Thus, to the various members of the Japanese decision-making system, and for somewhat different reasons, a peaceful settlement was utterly unacceptable. They could not accede to the American demands, and they could not even continue to drag out the negotiations because of the increasingly precarious nature of the war economy and especially the Navy's fuel supplies. On rejecting this unpalatable alternative they were again thrown back on the other; the necessary raw materials could be obtained only by seizing Thailand, where there was rice; Malaya, with its sources of tin, nickel, and rubber; and the Netherlands Indies, with their oil. But, according to the Japanese calculations, the United States was certain to fight if British or Dutch territory in the Far East were attacked. The American fleet in the Pacific, while inferior to the Japanese in many respects, was strong enough to endanger seriously a sustained offensive and quite possibly strong enough to postpone Japan's effective occupation of the Indies until her raw materials ran out. The oil fields might be put out of operation for many months, and in any case the shipment of these supplies to Japan under the threat of American air and naval attack would be too risky. Japan simply dared not undertake such operations while the American fleet remained intact.[25]

With these considerations in mind the Japanese leaders were faced with a true dilemma. An attack on the British and Dutch territories in the Pacific which was not resisted by the United States looked highly attractive, but highly unlikely. Much more probable was American resistance, and that promised substantial disutilities—a near-certain Japanese defeat. But the choice of a negotiated settlement with the United States was out of the question.

The only escape from the dilemma was by blunting one of its horns—to accept war with the United States, but to attempt it under circumstances where the chances of victory were higher. Under these pressures Japan's leaders conceived what they considered to be a *preemptive* surprise attack on Pearl Harbor and seizure of the Philippines. In its military-industrial potential and its fleet in the Pacific the United States had a very powerful

---

[24] Ibid., p. 304. Cf. the statement of the Japanese Minister of War at the cabinet meeting of October 12, 1941: "The problem of the stationing of the troops in China in itself means the life of the Army, and we shall not be able to make any concessions at all." Quoted in the memoirs of Prince Konoye, U.S. Congress, Joint Committee on the Investigation of Pearl Harbor Attack, *Pearl Harbor Attack: Hearings before the Joint Committee*, 79th Congress, 1st Session (Washington, D.C.: U.S. Government Printing Office, 1946), part 20, p. 4009.

[25] Cf. Butow, op. cit., p. 237. This assessment, incidentally, was fully shared by the Americans, who believed that "by mid-December [1941] U.S. air and submarine strength in the Philippines will have become a positive threat to any Japanese operations south of Formosa." *Hearings*, part 14, p. 1061.

deterrent, but in terms of more recent terminology the latter was also highly *vulnerable*. Its vulnerability presented a third option with higher expected utilities.

For all the audacity of the strike at Hawaii, its aims were modest: to destroy, by tactical surprise, the United States' existing offensive capabilities in the Pacific. The Japanese High Command hoped only to give its forces time to occupy the islands of the Southwest Pacific, to extract those islands' raw materials, and to turn the whole area into a virtually impregnable line of defense which could long delay an American counteroffensive and mete out heavy casualties when the counterattack did come. As a result of their early success the Japanese naval and military chiefs extended this line a little farther than they had first meant to do, but their original intentions were not grandiose.

In deciding to attack Pearl Harbor the Japanese took what they fully recognized to be a great risk. There is no doubt but that the Imperial government realized it could not win a long war with the United States *if the Americans chose to fight such a war*. Japanese strategists calculated that America's war potential was seven to eight times greater than their own; they knew that Japan could not hope to carry the war to the continental United States. Admiral Yamamoto, the brilliant inventor of the Pearl Harbor attack plan, warned:

> In the first six months to a year of war against the U.S. and England I will run wild, and I will show you an uninterrupted succession of victories; I must also tell you that, should the war be prolonged for two or three years, I have no confidence in our ultimate victory.[26]

Without examination of the alternatives that the Japanese leaders seem to have perceived, this would appear to be a singularly foolish gamble. Certainly the element of wishful thinking was strong, and possibly the pressures of the situation were such that a limited element of "irrationality," in the sense of a failure properly to examine the consequences of their act, was indeed present. (Though even here the "irrationality" label is not very helpful, and we are forced immediately to look for specific explanations. One might involve some careful hypotheses about the ways in which information may be distorted or its intake limited under duress. For example, a reduction in the number of facts considered seems to be a fairly common reaction to conditions of stress.) Because the proposed attack seemed an escape from the dilemma it was grasped with more enthusiasm than it deserved. The Japanese never seriously considered exactly what would cause the United States to forgo crushing Japan, or how Japan might best create the proper conditions for a negotiated peace. Certain key elements, such as the probable effect of the Pearl Harbor attack on the American will to win, were left completely

---

[26] Quoted in Wohlstetter, op. cit., p. 350. General Suzuki, chairman of the Planning Board, had reported that Japan's stockpile of resources was not adequate to support a long war.

unanalyzed.[27] Japan's sole strategy involved dealing maximum losses to the United States at the outset, making the prospects of a prolonged war as grim as possible, and counting, in an extremely vague and ill-defined way, on the American people's "softness" to end the war.

A MORE ADEQUATE THEORY OF DETERRENCE

Examined in the light of this general theory of deterrence, the Japanese decision to attack Pearl Harbor is quite explicable. Given the high probability they attached to America's readiness to defend the Indies, their implicit calculations about the utility of attacking the islands worked out to a most unattractive future. But the status quo was also highly unpalatable. Whichever of these options had the greatest utility (or least negative utility), however, became an academic question once the strategy of attacking the defender's vulnerable deterrent was conceived. Despite the great risks they doubtless saw in that strategy, it seemed to promise more gain or less loss than either of the former alternatives. Thus, once diplomatic negotiations revealed that the United States was not prepared to withdraw its demands for the Japanese withdrawal from China and Indochina, it became the clear and unanimous choice of the responsible Japanese officials. While they were well aware of America's potential strength and that the United States *could* win any war, they decided it might not *choose* to win a *long* war, and therefore picked the least unattractive course of action from a set of options few men would relish.

A general theory of deterrence must, therefore, very explicitly include all *three* (no attack; attack the pawn; attack the defender directly) of these gross options whenever it attempts to deal with deterrence of an attack on a third party rather than simply deterrence in a purely bilateral situation. Anything less is inadequate for theory and dangerous for policy. In assessing utilities and subjective probabilities, the crucial variables will include the nature and strength of the *ties* between defender and pawn; the *strength* of the defender's deterrent, both in a local and a strategic sense, and the *vulnerability* of that deterrent to surprise attack. And excessive attention by the defender to deterring an attack on an ally or client state can result merely in failing to deter, or rather in encouraging, an attack upon itself. If the attacker is also very dissatisfied with the status quo a lesson for modern policy bears remembrance —one should avoid presenting an opponent with options which are *all* highly unpalatable to him.[28]

---

[27] These seemingly obvious questions simply seem not to have been asked. See for example, General Suzuki's report of his meeting with the former premiers on November 29, 1941, IMTFE, *Transcript*, p. 35223. See also the material presented by Stephen S. Large, *The Japanese Decision for War: How Rational?* (Ann Arbor: University of Michigan, M.A. Thesis, 1965), pp. 46–48.

[28] As, for example, President Kennedy was careful to do both during the Cuban missile crisis and in his later praise of Khrushchev's "statesmanlike decision."

In terms of the general definition suggested at the beginning of the chapter, the *utilities* or preference schedules of decision makers cannot themselves be termed either rational or irrational; the absence of rationality would apply only if utilities not consciously considered nevertheless played a role in the decision. Subjective probabilities of course need not correspond to objective ones (and in any case it is incorrect to speak of the probability of a unique event). Some decision makers may indeed arrive at estimates quite different from those most other decision makers would specify, but it is more useful to ask what elements are peculiarly evaluated, and why, than simply to debate whether it is "rational." We have suggested an abstract model employing a limited number of variables; the analyst must then fill in its empirical content before it is of any use for prediction in concrete instances.

Some further tentative refinements may help point out how one can go about putting in the empirical content. Our notion of utilities attached by decision makers to various possible outcomes is conceptually clear enough, but is perhaps too oversimplified, obscuring some factors that an adequate theory ought to consider. Psychologists recently have employed a set of concepts, brought together in a motivational theory, that help to build a more complete model. Essentially they continue to employ the idea of subjective probability, but break down the utility variable into two elements, *motivational disposition* and *incentive*. In this formulation an incentive is the magnitude of the specific reward offered for performing a specific act, and motivational disposition represents a set of attitudes or personality traits to value certain incentives.[29] Thus we can separate out the incentives (or disincentives) entailed by Japanese pursuit of the various courses of action: loss of China; exhaustion of fuel supplies and loss of the possibility for independent military action in the future; military defeat at the hands of the United States. These incentives can then be matched with the apparent motivations of individuals at various loci in the Japanese decision-making system. The virtue of this formulation is that it explicitly forces us to look both at the possible outcomes and at the varying subjective values different decision makers might attach to them.

Such an analysis can be carried out either on the level of the *roles* of the decision makers, or of their particular *personality* characteristics.[30] Although there was surely substantial variation among individuals, it seems clear that all high Japanese army officials had strong motivational dispositions to retain

---

[29] J. W. Atkinson sets forth this scheme in "Motivational Determinants of Risk-Taking Behavior," *Psychological Review*, 64 (1947), pp. 359–72, and "Toward an Experimental Analysis of Human Motivation in Terms of Motives, Expectations, and Incentives," in J. W. Atkinson, editor, *Motives in Fantasy, Action and Society* (Princeton: Van Nostrand, 1958). Martin Patchen applied the concepts to my original deterrence model in his "Decision Theory in the Study of National Action: Problems and a Proposal," *Journal of Conflict Resolution*, 9, 2, (June 1965), pp. 164–76.

[30] For a fruitful analytical use of such a distinction see James N. Rosenau, "Senators and the Secretary: The Relative Potency of Individual and Role Variables," in *Quantitative International Politics: Insights and Evidence: International Yearbook of Political Behavior Research VI*, J. David Singer, editor, (New York: The Free Press, 1967).

their position in China. Again despite individual variation, all high Navy officials had strong motivations not to find themselves with insufficient oil to mount a naval campaign. Whether other personalities would have acted in a markedly different fashion in these roles, or whether they would have abhorred much more strongly the possibility of a defeat in war, is a subject still open to research, though it seems to me that it is unlikely. The men in those roles were not perceived by their fellow Japanese, nor since by Western political analysts, to be notably deviant in their motivations from other military, naval, and civilian personnel who might have held their formal positions. Yet in some circumstances personality characteristics may be crucial, and it is important to have a conceptual scheme which pinpoints rather than obscures the possibility. National character or other generalized explanations of personality type can also be employed here.

But perhaps most important of all is simply to have a scheme which penetrates below the aggregate level of "Japanese government." In terms of the labels used by political scientists, it must be a decision-making (to be distinguished from a decision-theory) approach which looks at the loci, formal and informal, of influence in the system. The man formally charged with making the final decision, such as the Prime Minister, is the focus of many forces pressing him with different motives, perceptions, and information. All must be potentially within the analyst's ken in a disciplined and explicit manner. But in these respects a theory of deterrence demands no more than any general theory of foreign policy making.

In at least one other respect more general theories of foreign policy making are of special relevance to a deterrence theory and to its particular application in the Pearl Harbor case; most major political decisions are reached incrementally. Great sudden departures from past policy are rare; momentous decisions are likely to be made by a successive closing-off of alternatives. The United States commitment to a large-scale land war in Vietnam in the 1960s, involving a half-million troops and annual expenditures in the tens of billions, was almost not an option that would have been freely chosen by American decision makers in the beginning. But successive decisions taken at various points of choice—to commit American troops as combatants rather than as advisors; to bomb North Vietnam; to bomb in the South; not to be satisfied with securing and over the long run slowly expanding some coastal enclaves—incrementally led to the commitment.

A similar process is painfully evident in the case of Japan in the 1930s and early 1940s. David Lu traces the Japanese road to immolation back to the Washington Naval Conference of 1922.[31] Without going that far into the past, the steps are nevertheless quite clear. They include all the acts which led deeper into the morass of China; signature of the Tripartite Pact with Germany and Italy; the invasion of Northern Indochina in September 1940; the occupation of bases in Southern Indochina, which provoked the American

---

[31] Lu, op. cit., pp. 1–2.

embargo; and the repeated steps within the government by which the actual decision to attack the United States was taken and confirmed. Possibly the clincher—a warning against a technician's approach to international politics— was the perfection of the attack plan itself. Originally thought by both the Japanese and the Americans to be impossible, the final project ranks as one of the most brilliant tactical strokes in history. In solving many formidable problems, such as the last-minute improvisation of aerial torpedoes capable of running in the shallow waters of the Pearl Harbor docks, Japanese naval officials seem to have experienced a justifiable but expensive sense of exhilaration, confusing the feasibility of the plan with its desirability.[32]

When applying a theory of deterrence to actual events one must scrutinize each of the relevant points for choice. Especially critical in the political steps of 1941 was the Imperial Conference of September 6, at which it was decided that unless a satisfactory diplomatic settlement was reached by mid-October preparations would be made for war. Just because of the difficulty in agreeing upon decisions in prewar Japan's very loosely coordinated policy-making system, the Imperial Conference, with decisions taken in the presence of Emperor Hirohito, was employed to freeze policy and prevent reconsideration. Afterward anyone advocating another course could be accused of disobeying the commands of the Emperor—though of course the Emperor's presence merely legitimized decisions and he rarely took an active role. Various further meetings of October and November followed the precedent of this step, and, as the plan of attack was developed and the rigidities of American and Japanese policy unfolded, severely limited the Japanese leaders' freedom of maneuver. As one option after another was foreclosed, the choice of war, however unattractive it might have been initially, came to look better than any of the shrinking set of other choices that remained. America's deterrent policy failed not because Japan's leaders really expected to win, but because they saw no alternative to war.[33]

---

[32] Some of the ingenious technical aspects of the plan were reported by Robert E. Ward, "The Inside Story of the Pearl Harbor Plan," *United States Naval Institute Proceedings*, 77 (1951), pp. 1271–83.

[33] In a paper that appeared after this was written Nobutaka Ike came to much the same conclusion. He did not, however, discuss the choice of attacking Southeast Asia alone vs. a direct attack on the United States. See his "Foreign Policy and Decision-Making in Japan 1941," *Transactions of the International Conference of Orientalists in Japan*, 19 (1965), pp. 42–60. Our theoretical position also differs from that of Dina Zinnes, Robert North, and Howard Koch regarding the 1914 crisis, in "Capability, Threat, and the Outbreak of War," in *International Politics and Foreign Policy*, James N. Rosenau, editor (New York: The Free Press, 1961), pp. 469–91. Despite our mutual conclusion that simple perceptions of one's great military inferiority do not always suffice for deterrence, they direct more attention to the Germans' "irrational" action in response to their perceptions of intense hostility, and less to the Germans' visions of their apparent alternatives.

14

A Countercombatant Deterrent?
Feasibility, Morality,
and Arms Control

AN ALTERNATIVE TO CITY BUSTING?

Since the beginning of the Cold War, the keystone of American strategic planning has been the principle that the ultimate deterrent to a Russian attack had to be the certainty of American retaliation against Russian cities. The Russians seemingly have adopted the same position vis-à-vis the United States, usually to the point of denying vigorously any possibility of limiting central war to counterforce strikes alone. A typical relatively recent formulation was expressed by former Defense Secretary McNamara in his 1968 "posture statement" to Congress:

> [It is] the clear and present ability to destroy the attacker as a viable twentieth century nation and an unwavering will to use those [assured destruction] forces in retaliation to a nuclear attack upon ourselves or our allies that provides the deterrent, and not the ability partially to limit damage to ourselves.[1]

Several points about this statement must be noted. One is the implicit precept of retaliation—the eye for an eye principle found in international law

Reprinted from *The Military-Industrial Complex: A Reassessment*, Sam Sarkesian, editor (Beverly Hills, Calif.: Sage Publications, Inc., 1972).

[1] *Statement of Secretary of Defense Robert S. McNamara before the Senate Armed Services Committee on the Fiscal Years 1969–73 Defense Program and 1969 Defense Budget* (Washington, D.C.: U.S. Government Printing Office, 1968), p. 73.

as well as in private behavior. Even so, this particular application, that one will retaliate against *civilians* for the acts of a *government* which we widely assume does not accurately reflect their wishes (to be sure, perhaps for acts committed against one's own civilians), might give us pause. Second, the deterrent umbrella is extended also to cover America's allies. This is quite in accord with generally accepted ideas of the right of the strong to protect the weak, and the international principle of collective defense. Finally, there is the clear implication, never completely disowned by American leaders, that even a counterforce strike initiated by the enemy might be met with a counter-city attack in "retaliation." The problem is one of retaining an "assured destruction" capability; if the enemy were too successful in his counterforce attack, what residual American missiles were left might be turned against Russian cities even though American cities had so far been left unscathed. This threat, of if "necessary" doing very great damage in response to *any* kind of large nuclear attack on the United States, is at the heart of the "assured destruction" principle. Despite all the doctrine and preparations for controlled tit-for-tat strikes against the enemy, the threat of initiating counter-city warfare, under dire circumstances, remains in the background.

In this chapter I want to challenge the idea that deterrence must rest on an assured capability of destroying an enemy's cities and noncombatant populace. I want to do so on the grounds that what I shall call a countercombatant strategy is militarily feasible, and also is preferable on widely accepted moral grounds. In short, I want to present a case that Americans could adopt a new deterrent policy that would ease the moral qualms many of them have about current strategy, without leaving them less secure than at present. I candidly admit that my search for an alternative deterrent strategy is rooted in a moral revulsion against plans deliberately to kill large numbers of civilians in case of central war, but I would not impose that view on others, nor would I trouble to pursue the question in public at all if I were not coming to the conclusion that there *is* a viable alternative short of pacifism.

I am somewhat diffident about making my proposal. It is not based on any new computations or empirical evidence, merely on what I think is a different perspective on familiar matters, possibly made more appropriate by some developments in weapons acquisition in recent years. By many tests it is not a radically new proposal. For example, it does not in itself challenge the widely— but increasingly less universally—accepted belief that in contemporary super-power politics *some* capability to inflict vast damage on the other remains a necessary ingredient of a war-deterring posture. It is not addressed to, nor does it anticipate, a great reduction in the number of nuclear delivery vehicles the United States must maintain. Nor will it in itself lead to major arms control agreements about numbers and types of weapons. It would be consistent with many such agreements, but not with others. While these things are important, they should not always be dominant. In bypassing them my proposal is perhaps a conservative one. But what it does do is require us to think less about deterrence as simply an ability to inflict casualties, and more about what kind of casualties might achieve politically significant results. Such a rethinking might have radical and highly desirable consequences.[2]

RESTRAINTS AND THEIR EROSION

It is not easy to draw a clear, unambiguous line between combatants and non-combatants. Nor have warriors always tried very hard to make the distinction; no precise codification of rules was ever fully accepted. But in the years following the enormous civilian suffering of the Thirty Years War various limits were generally respected. Wars were fought for restricted objectives, and a combination of self-interest, humanitarianism, technological incapacity, and the inability of aristocratic regimes to motivate their soldiery for long or intensive wars provided important restraints.

Some of these limits were eroded during World War I, with a partial failure of the international law of war, especially at sea in Germany's submarine warfare and Britain's embargo. International law on the matter of bombing non-combatants was vague; the strictures on the conduct of war evolved long ago and even now apply primarily to land warfare.[3] Whatever legal restraints might have been appropriate to aerial warfare were substantially loosened. In this first major conflict fought with aircraft and dirigibles, aerial warfare was conducted against civilians as well as against military targets. Subsequently, military theorists of various nations, such as Giulio Douhet, Billy Mitchell, and Air Marshal Sir Hugh Trenchard all advocated the use of air forces against civilian populations. Their doctrine, plus the World War I precedents and then such actions of the 1930s as those of the Italians in Ethiopia, the Spanish Civil War experience, and Japanese bombing of Chinese civilians prepared the governments of Europe for the worst in 1939. Although military people especially in England objected to Trenchard's plans for population attacks, it came to be considered inevitable that such methods would be turned on Britain and France once the war actually was begun. Elaborate civil defense preparations were made, and an exaggerated fear of air attacks on their cities seems to have been a significant factor in those governments' unwillingness to stand up to Hitler at Munich.

But they were pleasantly surprised by what actually did and did not happen in the first part of the war, known because of the restraints as the period of

---

[2] When I first drafted this paper I thought its proposal was quite new, though not without partial precedents. Since then, however, I discovered an important paper by Arthur Lee Burns that, though differing in a number of major respects, is strikingly similar in others and in basic outlook. See his "Ethics and Deterrence: A Nuclear Balance Without Hostage Cities," *Adelphi Papers*, No. 69 (London: Institute for Strategic Studies, July 1970).

[3] Although, see the Fourth Hague Convention of 1907 which, though still concerned essentially with land warfare, clearly forbade the bombardment of "undefended places."

"phoney" war. For almost a year Hitler carefully avoided making attacks on civilian areas in France and England, limiting the Luftwaffe to strictly military targets. He was less restrained in the Blitzkreig on Poland, but even there civilian deaths occurred largely as a result of tactical air support of ground forces. Since Hitler was no great humanitarian, his motives were governed by self-interest—he feared the effect that allied bombing of Berlin and other German cities might have on German morale, and so wanted to avoid initiating an exchange of city strikes. Furthermore, he hoped for an early compromise peace, and by withholding his air arm could both avoid antagonizing his enemies unnecessarily and also retain an implicit threat to initiate something worse if they did not cease fighting. Britain and France, for their part, recognized their inferiority in aircraft and knew that if anyone did start attacking cities they themselves would suffer more damage than they could return to the Germans.

These limits deteriorated somewhat during the first half of 1940, notably with the German bombing of Rotterdam in May. The ultimate collapse of restraints during and after the Battle of Britain and Blitz is well described by George Quester; apparently the breakdown ought not be to blamed entirely on the Germans, as is commonly believed.[4]

In any case, during the rest of the war saturation terror attacks became routine. On the Axis side they included the V-1 and V-2 bombs late in the war. As for the Allies, the British habitually attacked at night when precision bombing was impossible, deliberately directing many of their strikes against residential areas so as to undermine popular morale. By comparison, air raids by the United States were largely conducted during daylight hours and directed to industrial targets, which blows were thought to damage the German war effort more than terror attacks could. But the Americans too, as in the attack on Dresden, occasionally went after civilians deliberately. And if Americans can claim a few credits for restraint in the air war over Europe, the firebomb raids on Japanese cities (in which a ring of fire was carefully built to trap people inside), not to mention Hiroshima and Nagasaki, remove much virtue from the account.

The point is not that most of World War II was fought with little restraint on bombing civilian areas—that is obvious. Rather, it is equally important that for quite some time each side did limit its actions and was aware that the other side was doing the same. Neither moral nor self-interest restraints were entirely put aside at the outset. The former were still sufficiently in many peoples' minds that President Roosevelt could characterize the earliest, mildest German air attacks in Poland as "inhuman barbarism which has profoundly shocked the conscience of humanity."[5] The limits as observed, for whatever reasons,

---

[4] George Quester, *Deterrence before Hiroshima* (New York: Wiley, 1966).
[5] Quoted in Robert E. Osgood and Robert W. Tucker, *Force, Order, and Justice* (Baltimore: The Johns Hopkins University Press, 1967), p. 217.

should be remembered as well as the unrestricted bombing of the later years.

After World War II the original restraints were forgotten. On the basis of their own precedent in Japan, American military planners simply assumed that in future wars nuclear weapons would be used against cities to destroy the enemy's economy, society, and popular morale. In addition, the threat of such usage was to constitute the primary deterrent to war. In the 1948–1949 controversy over the B-36 a number of United States Navy officers argued that countercity war was immoral, but their objections were largely dismissed as rationalizations to further their Service's interests. The basic countercity strategy then remained essentially unquestioned until the late 1950s, in other countries as well as in the United States. Since World War II every major power, either in that conflict or in colonial wars thereafter (for example, the French in Algeria and against Tunisia), made deliberate air attacks on civilians.

Some very important and promising steps toward redefining limits on aerial warfare were nevertheless taken in the past decade or so. They began with the idea of tactical nuclear warfare. While the dream of confining nuclear weapons to tactical uses has by now been pretty thoroughly abandoned, it helped in defining the idea of limited strategic or central war. To some strategists it became not just something to be pursued if the opportunity to avoid general destruction should present itself, but even a feasible policy. In 1962 Secretary McNamara reached the point of making his now famous Ann Arbor statement: "Principal military objectives, in the event of a nuclear war stemming from a major attack on the Alliance, should be the destruction of the enemy's military forces, not of his civilian population."[6] Thus massive retaliation was to give way, even in response to "a major attack on the Alliance," to controlled graduated response and the hope of reciprocation from the enemy.

While the distinction between counterforce and countercity targeting remains important in American strategic doctrine, McNamara's attempted annunciation of a "no cities" strategy as a viable retaliatory policy has largely been rebuffed and withdrawn. His own 1968 statement witnesses an apparent return to "assured destruction" of civilian population centers as the perceived *sine qua non* for a credible deterrent. McNamara's Ann Arbor policy was widely attacked for many reasons. Primary among them, however, was the fear that the Russians would interpret it, and the weapons procurement to implement it, as indicating an American attempt to secure a high level of "damage limitation"—an emphasis on counterforce so strong as to seem to permit the United States to engage in a preemptive or even a preventive nuclear strike against the Soviet Union. That could be profoundly destabilizing, and might well bring on the horrible war McNamara hoped to avoid. It became widely assumed that if a counterforce capability was good enough to be "worth" having for damage

---

[6] Speech delivered at the commencement exercises of the University of Michigan at Ann Arbor, June 16, 1962.

limitation, it would bring too great a temptation, or too great an apparent temptation as seen by the opponent, to use it in a first strike capacity. McNamara's argument for counterforce retaliation was seen as not capable of being distinguished, in practice, from the ability to initiate war at what might, in extremis, be considered a politically acceptable cost. If not that, a damage-limiting policy might at least lead to an accelerated arms race with no ultimate gains; the Russians would take the necessary steps to counteract it.

The strategy embodied in McNamara's Ann Arbor speech was supported by many strategic analysts, perhaps most notably by Thomas Schelling in a model of clear thinking. Schelling noted that nuclear war was not a shooting gallery where one had to shoot at something. A doctrine of *not* attacking cities did not *necessarily* mean that the opponent's nuclear delivery vehicles therefore had to be attacked en masse. On the contrary, one might choose substantially, at least in the early stages of a war, *not to fire at anything*. The opponent's cities could be left for a while as hostages to his good behavior; so long as he avoided deliberately striking our civilians we would reciprocate. "The basic reason for not destroying the cities is to keep them at our mercy."[7] Schelling then went on to show why a city avoidance strategy was appropriate for adoption not only by a power with nuclear superiority (then the United States) but at least equally by a power with only equivalent or even inferior nuclear strength. He demonstrated that its desirability did not depend on being able actually to *disarm* the opponent, since the intention was to bargain away his willingness to use capabilities he might still retain. Nor, he argued, did it depend on the Russians following the substantial American lead of locating missile sites outside the boundaries of populous cities. While the latter might be a desirable condition from the Russian as well as the American point of view, once the shooting gallery notion was disposed of such location was not essential to an American pursuit of city avoidance.

Schelling's argument was subtle and not widely accepted. At the time of McNamara's speech much of the Russian nuclear retaliatory force was in fact vulnerable to an American first strike, and discussion of a city avoidance strategy, especially one so subtle, was feared to be unsettling.[8] Most important perhaps was the apparent lack of reciprocation by the Russians. Schelling's strategy, and McNamara's, did depend for its acceptability on Russian willingness also to consider avoiding cities, and to be capable of receiving the tacit or explicit bargaining messages in war. Virtually all public statements by Soviet

---

[7] Thomas C. Schelling, *Arms and Influence* (New Haven: Yale University Press, 1967), pp. 193, passim.

[8] Another reason—and one that would have to be taken into account in any effort to implement the strategy offered in this chapter—is simple organizational inertia and bureaucratic routine. In the Cuban missile crisis SAC bombers were dispersed to 40 civilian airports near cities around the United States because that is what the standard operating procedures called for. Thus, without the intention of Kennedy or McNamara, "the 'no cities' doctrine was laid to rest" for the duration of the crisis, when it was needed most. See Graham T. Allison, *Essence of Decision* (Boston: Little, Brown, 1971), p. 139.

military analysts dismissed the possibility of a city-avoiding nuclear war. A more relevant answer might have been contained in Soviet weapons procurement policy, had they clearly moved toward the acquisition of missiles of high accuracy and low yield. But in fact the procurement messages were at best ambiguous. One does not hear much about it today.

HOW MUCH IS ENOUGH?

Nevertheless, I intend here in part to revive the notion of counterforce strategy as plausible, in the form of what I call a countercombatant strategy. The strategy does not imply a first strike capability or anything resembling it; indeed it assumes that, given prudent vigilance on both sides, such a capability is not a realistic possibility for either superpower. Nor does it imply an ability to "win" a nuclear war, whatever that means—on the countrary it assumes that even in "losing" a countercombatant war the United States still could inflict such a level of damage on the Russians as to make the war's initiation unprofitable. Nor finally—and here it differs markedly from the Schelling-McNamara strategy— does it *depend* for success upon using the enemy's cities as hostages, on bargaining, or on reciprocation. While bargaining might well be attempted during its execution, it is nevertheless conceivable that an American government *might* want to hold to a countercombatant policy even if the enemy did not.

Again, the standard assumption of contemporary strategic theory has been that deterrence rests upon a capability of wreaking "assured destruction" which would "destroy the attacker as a viable twentieth century nation." One sees different figures, but under Secretary McNamara the operational measure of such destruction seems to have been on the order of 20–25 percent of the Russian population and half of Russian industry.[9] Anything less was thought to constitute a temptation to aggressive or reckless Soviet leaders.

It is not entirely clear just what was the basis of these estimates. In part, doubtless they represent an estimate of a level of destruction that would make it impossible to reconstitute anything like the present social and political system in the Soviet Union, a level which would move beyond just very great loss to something approaching chaos among the survivors, considerable number though they might be. It surely represents an understanding that, as Herman Kahn put it, the Russians lost about 20 million people in World War II (10 percent of the population) and doubtless considered it a good bargain, hence the level of assured destruction must be significantly higher.[10] For technical reasons it probably was approximately the level of damage beyond which it

---

[9] See McNamara's 1968 *Statement*, op. cit., p. 50. Earlier statements had set the figures somewhat higher.

[10] Herman Kahn, *On Thermonuclear War* (Princeton: Princeton University Press, 1960), pp. 142–3.

became increasingly costly to go. Because of diminishing marginal returns and the ability to achieve it with relatively few surviving weapons, the difference between Russian casualties from a first strike and a second strike was minimized—a crucial deterrent criterion. In any case, it assumes that the surest means of deterring Russian leaders is through a threat to their populace and industry. Given some of the folklore that all Bolsheviks are as callous toward their people as Stalin seemed to be this may seem a bit curious, though perhaps less so if we consider that a good Bolshevik presumably would be properly solicitous about his power base—populace and industry.

The reasoning is in fact highly questionable. Despite all the computations of megatonnage, defensive weapons, and population densities, it is composed of as much mythology as science. We simply cannot *know* what destructive capability is required to constitute effective deterrence. It may be that a very large assured destruction capability is necessary, or it may be that "merely" the collateral damage to civilian, industrial, and other military targets incurred from a counterforce strike would suffice. Furthermore, concern for his more narrowly military power base might weigh as heavily with a "rational" Russian leader who was contemplating an attack on the West. Severe damage to the armed forces of the Soviet Union, which are strongly relied upon for the maintenance of internal security as well as bloc cohesion, might be as unacceptable as the loss of cities.

Moreover, the level of retaliatory damage that a nation contemplating a first strike will accept is a *variable, not a constant.* The prospect of incurring great damage will be acceptable to a government if all other courses of action seem to lead to extremely undesirable outcomes. On the other hand, if "peace" offers halfway decent prospects the government will not follow a course of action promising anywhere near the level of probable war damage that it would accept if its back were against the wall. Thus in considering whether our nation has "enough" deterrent capability, we must always consider the policy context—what options are presented to the government one wants to deter. For example, imagine that in the Cuban missile crisis President Kennedy, instead of leaving Premier Khrushchev a relatively graceful exit, had tried to humiliate him and publicly to expose Soviet weakness in a way that would greatly have diminished Soviet influence in the world. Under conditions such as these, continued "peace" would have looked less desirable, and at least relatively speaking nuclear war would have become more "thinkable." A level of deterrent capability that had previously been more than enough might no longer have sufficed, and the Russians might have become willing to launch a first strike attack on the United States even in the knowledge that they would suffer severe retaliation.

I blush to make once again so obvious a point, one that was long ago stated clearly by such strategic analysts as Kahn, Schelling, and Albert Wohlstetter and expressed formally by such a variety of observers as Daniel Ellsberg, Morton Kaplan, J. David Singer, Glenn Snyder, and myself. But for many would-be strategists it does seem necessary. Deterrence results from making peace look better as well as from making war look worse. And super-power politics is not a zero-sum game. Thus it is prudent for a would-be deterring power not to present its opponent with the prospect of very undesirable outcomes in return for forbearance from taking the first strike option. It becomes extremely dangerous to seek clearcut "victory" on crucial issues *even* by peaceful means, for fear of driving the other side to initiate war.

We cannot know, without getting inside the Soviet leaders' heads, what they will accept under various conditions. Certainly Western academic specialists do not agree as to the Russians' degree of aggressiveness or on what kind and degree of damage is necessary to deter them. But under "normal" circumstances of peaceful coexistence it would seem that the standard rule of thumb, 25 percent of the Russian population, is a higher-than-necessary level of assured destruction most of the time. Only under conditions of *very* grave threat to the country or to Communist rule would the Russian leaders be likely to launch an attack at that price. Kahn's example of the acceptable cost of resistance to German invasion is compelling precisely because the alternative seemed so ghastly—especially when the Soviet people got a good look at Nazi behavior. Providing that the United States pursues a policy of reasonable restraint it might be secure with a somewhat less awful threat capability.

MILITARY TARGETS ONLY: FEASIBILITY

I will now propose that the United States could, without increasing the likelihood of war, significantly reduce, though hardly eliminate, the severity of possible war by adopting a policy of using its nuclear weapons only in what I call a countercombatant capacity. By countercombatant I mean to include first all of those basic nuclear striking forces of the enemy that are *currently* targeted, and their immediate support facilities: missile silos, military airbases, submarine bases and nuclear submarines in port, air defense and ABM systems, and weapons-oriented atomic energy plants. More than that, it would include internal security forces, all military bases of any kind, and those transport facilities devoted primarily to the movement of troops and military supplies. Since the Russian leaders will be concerned about maintaining domestic order, and with regulating the behavior both of the states on their Eastern borders and of their Chinese neighbors, these "tactical" forces *will* matter in the context of a nuclear war that lasts more than a very few days and in the context of picking up the pieces later. So too, if not during the nuclear war itself, weapons and military equipment-manufacturing plants would matter, and I include them as appropriate targets for a retaliatory strike. It is for this reason that I use the term countercombatant rather than the more familiar counterforce—it implies something more extensive than retaliation against nuclear striking forces, but less than a countercity strike.[11] (Even

---

[11] It appears that the term "countervalue" was originally devised to cover whatever the enemy was assumed to value, and hence could have been applied to the targets I suggest here. Common usage now, however, is to use it synonymously with counterpopulation or countercity.

so the term is imprecise since many or most workers in weapons plants will not be combatants in the usual sense of the term, but so far I have been able to think of nothing better. They are at least adults who know what they are making and do so with at least some minimal degree of consent.)

Moreover, it might well be stated (and intended) American policy to attack these targets almost *wherever* they may be found, even near or within big cities. The United States would presumably develop a capability that gave it very high confidence of destroying those targets. But it would take great care to use *only* the amount of force necessary to destroy those targets. "Clean" weapons, of low yield and high accuracy, could be designed for the purpose of honestly striving to reduce destruction of population centers to whatever level is unavoidable in destroying what I have designated as military targets. "Bonus effects" would *not* be sought.

The extent of collateral damage incurred in a given instance depends upon the choice of targets, the megatonnage of the warheads, the amount of radiation released due to the composition and explosion height of the warheads, and the accuracy of the missiles. Thus collateral damage is considerably diminished if military installations in major population centers are avoided and small "clean" airburst nuclear weapons with high accuracies are used. To the extent that installations within population centers are hit, the need for small, clean, accurate weapons is magnified if collateral damage is to be minimized.

The accuracy of intercontinental missiles has improved tremendously in recent years. The details change constantly and are in any case classified. But if we conservatively assume missiles with an accuracy (Circular Error Probability) of about a quarter of a mile, quite low bomb yield, with comparatively low heat and blast damage to all but the surrounding areas, would suffice to knock out such targets providing the targets were not greatly hardened.[12] Collateral damage can, therefore, be limited, except for the many persons who will probably die from long-term radioactive fallout almost regardless of the location of the blast. Providing that force targets remain vulnerable and strategic emphasis is upon the development of low yield weapons with high accuracies, avoiding damage to civilians will depend more on the type of target selected than on target location. Thus it seems plausible that a countercombatant strategy *could* be implemented, indeed even to the extent of striking at a wide range of military facilities without much regard to their location, without inflicting nearly such a high level of civilian casualties as would be implied by a deliberate countercity strategy. But at the same time we must not deny that many civilian deaths would occur despite an American effort to keep them down.

Thus in the event of a Soviet attack on the United States or its allies, an event calling forth American nuclear retaliation, the following situation could

---

[12] A target hardened to withstand 60 psi in overpressure will be destroyed by a 20 kiloton bomb striking within a quarter of a mile of it; that same bomb can destroy frame houses up to about 1¾ miles away, but not much farther. United States Atomic Energy Commission, *The Effects of Nuclear Weapons* (Washington, D.C.: U.S. Government Printing Office, 1962).

be expected to emerge in the Soviet Union: The great majority of Russia's population, even the urban population, even of Russia's nonmilitary industrial capacity, would survive. But its war-fighting capacity, and its capability for using force to maintain internal order, most certainly would not. Its tactical military capability, as well as much of its strategic forces, would be substantially gone. The Soviet Union's ability to defend its territory from its revanchist neighbors, even the small and now much weaker states of Eastern Europe, would be destroyed. To make this particularly painful the United States might strike, with special care, Russian bases and armed forces along the Chinese border. In effect, the penalty for a Soviet attack on the West would be Soviet impotence vis-à-vis their Asian neighbor. It is not at all obvious to me that this would be a less effective deterrent against Russian adventurism than is the current threat to destroy many of the Russian people and the majority of their industry.[13]

Note once again, the proposed countercombatant strategy in *no* way implies developing a force capable of delivering a first strike, and is not therefore destabilizing to the nuclear balance. It is indeed unimportant that its damage-limiting capacity be great. The intent is not to reduce Soviet capacity of harming the United States, but to reduce to an unacceptable level Soviet capacity to defend themselves tactically, or strategically, or tactically *and* strategically. *For these purposes* it does not matter whether the Russian missiles are destroyed on the ground or whether they really are used up against the United States. Even if substantial Soviet nuclear forces remained, they would be useless against internal dissent, and of only marginal utility in holding Eastern Europe, where ground troops would be needed for occupation. In a world where China or other third powers had significant nuclear and conventional capabilities, the political potential of nuclear weapons alone would be sharply circumscribed. To destroy the effectiveness of Soviet conventional forces we do not have to kill all their troops. It would be enough to hit bases, supply centers, military administration centers, and marshalling centers—in short, to destroy their ability to *use* troops.

Finally, the strategy does not require symmetrical damage-inflicting capability between the two superpowers, nor would it necessarily allow the United States to "win" the war. Nuclear war is not a football game where the side which runs up the highest point total emerges with a victory worth having. It is patently absurd to insist that to be deterred the Russians must have more damage done to them than they are able to do to others; whatever the relative body count they would not in any meaningful sense win the exchange I have described.

---

[13] While critics on the left have frequently attacked the doctrine of assured destruction as calling for damage far in excess of deterrence requirements, several right-of-center critics have denounced its usual interpretation as insufficient for deterrence. They emphasize the Soviet government's presumed evacuation and civil defense capability and suggest that the actual casualty total would not be high enough. Such critics might well find a concentration on military targets as described here to be in fact more plausible as a restraint on Soviet aggressive acts. For doubts about the sufficiency of current targeting see Eugene P. Wigner, "The Myth of 'Assured Destruction'," *Congressional Record*, October 13, 1971, p. E10744.

Does a countercombatant strategy require Russian reciprocation? Insofar as protecting the lives of American civilians, should a nuclear war occur, is a major American goal—and I am sure it is—then clearly Russian reciprocation is highly desirable. But as a strategy for *deterring the outbreak* of such a war reciprocation is *not* necessary. It assumes, and I think plausibly, only that the Russian leaders would gain too little satisfaction from *anything* they might do by initiating war with the United States to compensate them for the military losses they could expect to suffer. On the other hand, in the *actual conduct of a war* it surely would be hard to maintain a purely countercombatant American strategy in the face of obvious Russian nonreciprocation. "Irrational" forces, including the demand for revenge, might well expand the retaliation into a countercity one. Furthermore, the advantages of making American restraint conditional upon Russian war-fighting conduct are obvious. It could provide a major, and perhaps crucial, bargaining counter to insure Russian restraint. I think I personally would prefer the complete abandonment of *any* American intention to strike civilians deliberately, on the ground that it is unjust to punish civilians (including children) for acts of their government. But many people would surely retort that it is immoral to throw away a bargaining counter that might protect our own civilians.

Many varieties of reciprocation or nonreciprocation are possible. As a deterrent strategy the Russians might accept it and work both actively and visibly to implement it, they might be much more cautious or ambiguous, or they might reject it and refuse to change their policies. There is some reason to hope they might accept it. The Russian leaders have repeatedly declared they are in a struggle with the American government and capitalism, not the American people. They have consistently pictured ABM systems as desirable for preserving human lives. Despite their failure to respond favorably to McNamara's no cities initiative, they focus their statements about targeting on "the economic base of war, government and military administration, and groupings of enemy troops"—but not countercity strategy per se.[14] While their definition of war-related industry probably would be more inclusive than the one I am suggesting, that still is not quite the same as pure counterpopulation strikes. I would rather see them hit the River Rouge Ford plant than hit Detroit.

Nevertheless, they might reject the American initiative, with an extreme form of rejection taking the form of an attempt to exploit it. After all, they *could* choose to put a large proportion of their military forces of all types in greatly hardened sites directly within cities. In doing so they might well force the United States government to consider those sites to be primary targets despite the perhaps tens of millions of civilian deaths that would follow their destruction. (A key element of a countercombatant strategy, unlike the Schelling-McNamara no cities strategy, is to reduce greatly the Russian ability to deter the Chinese and control their own citizens.) Or they might,

---

[14] See Johan J. Holst, "Missile Defense, the Soviet Union, and the Arms Race," in *Why ABM?*, Johan J. Holst and William J. Schneider, editors (New York: Pergamon, 1969), p. 175.

through a combination of dispersion and provision for high mobility, vastly increase the number of military targets we would have to hit. But the moral burden would then be clearly shifted to the Soviet leaders; if we then abandoned the effort to spare civilians we would at least know that we had tried. Frankly I find it hard to imagine why the Russians would think they could exploit the American countercombatant initiative successfully. The effort would lead back to an American policy of retaliation against weapons *and* cities, not to an abandonment of our reliance on the nuclear deterrent.

SOME MORAL CONSIDERATIONS

Men reason from a variety of moral premises, and for that matter simply try to avoid difficult moral choices whenever possible. To many it seems that the American government has no feasible alternative to its present policy. Few lines of thought are more painful than facing an evaluation that one's acts are immoral if there in fact seems nothing else one would do. But what I have argued above is that there may indeed be an alternative; hence even for one who on moral grounds rejected the idea of countercity deterrence it could become possible to have one's cake and eat it too. If a policy of countercity retaliation were truly not essential to national preservation, then a failure to discard that policy would be much more widely regarded as immoral. Let us then briefly review some standard judgments as to what constitute morally acceptable acts of warfare.

A completely pacifist position may result from a philosophical and moral predilection for nonviolence, a rejection in principle of force as an instrument of national policy, a belief in the spiritually regenerative effect of a nonviolent response to violence, or an overriding concern for the preservation of human life. Or, a position which is pacifist for all practical purposes may emerge from consideration of the principle of proportionality, a presumption that in a modern thermonuclear war the costs must inevitably outweigh the gains. At the other end of the spectrum is the view which says essentially that war, and any act in war, is justifiable if it seems to serve the "national interest," or that rightness depends solely upon the ends being sought rather than on the methods used to obtain them. Between these, a variety of positions still are available.

For those who accept the use of force as a legitimate instrument of state policy in many but not all circumstances, there are two principal moral foci for viewing its limitations. One is concerned with the norms that govern *recourse* to war, and the second adds to them some norms to govern the *conduct* of war.[15] The first, which concentrates on what conditions justify an initial resort to physical violence, is typically less concerned with the manner in which the conflict is conducted, once begun. In the American philosophical tradition

---

[15] See Lynn H. Miller, "The Contemporary Significance of the Doctrine of the Just War," *World Politics*, 16, 2 (January 1964), pp. 254–86.

a "just war" often is considered only to be one undertaken in self-defense.[16] Self-defense by this definition includes defense of one's allies in keeping with a formal commitment, assistance to a small power under the principle of collective security when authorized by an international organization such as the United Nations even if there is no treaty commitment, or assistance to another government in response to its request for aid. Furthermore, the self to be defended is generally construed broadly to include not merely the physical territory but also the values and way of life which are believed to characterize the state. No grievances, however severe, would by this definition in themselves justify the initiation of war; grievances should always be subject only to negotiation or arbitration, or ultimately lived with in the hope they will become more tolerable through the evolution of circumstances.

On the other hand, once a war in self-defense is undertaken, limits on both the political objectives to be achieved and the means to be used in pursuit of them become hard to establish. The erosion of such limits helps destroy the opponent's incentive to make peace. The view emphasizing the justice of our recourse to war may have played a role in the breakdown of restraints on American conduct of air war in World War II, though as I noted above the breakdown was universal and by no means solely or initially the responsibility of this nation. I do suspect, however, that this view combined with the World War II precedents to make it easy for the doctrine of countercity deterrence to be accepted after the war, during the period of American nuclear monopoly.

We should also note the most common Communist view, according to which a war need not be undertaken in self-defense to be justifiable, but may be perfectly right if its purpose is to redress certain grievances, namely class oppression or national subjugation. In this respect it differs widely from the classical American doctrine. Even for the Communists, however, to be just the war must not have a reactionary effect. Specifically, a nuclear war which would result in the annihilation of capitalist *and* socialist civilizations would not be initiated. Not just any hypothetical war undertaken by a Communist or third-world country would be permissible. Differing interpretations of the likely result of nuclear war underlay some aspects of the public differences between Russian and Chinese leaders during the past decade.

The second and quite different position stems from the tradition of Christian moralists.[17] It takes off from a recognition that attempts only to limit the *resort* to war are subject to abuse, and seeks to supplement them with rules for the *conduct* of war. Relevant elements of this tradition regarding the conditions under which a war may be "just" include the following six points.

---

[16] Robert W. Tucker, *The Just War* (Baltimore: The Johns Hopkins University Press, 1960).

[17] Some version of this position is still typical of most "mainstream" thinkers in both Protestant and Catholic churches. See, for example, Joseph McKenna, "Ethics and War: A Catholic Viewpoint," *American Political Science Review*, 54, 3 (September 1960), pp. 647–58; William V. O'Brien, *War and/or Survival* (Garden City: Doubleday, 1969); Paul Ramsey, *War and the Christian Conscience* (Durham, N.C.: Duke University Press, 1961), and *The Just War* (New York: Scribner's, 1968), and Robert Tucker's sections in Osgood and Tucker, op. cit.

1. Those who resort to war must have a "right intention"; this means substantially that they must do so in self-defense or to correct a legitimate grievance (the definition of which varies).
2. The injury the war is intended to prevent must be real and "certain." (Obviously this last is elastic.)
3. War must be undertaken only as a last resort.
4. The measures employed in the war must themselves be moral. (Prisoners must be fairly treated; the inviolability of noncombatants respected, etc.)
5. The seriousness of the injury to be prevented must be proportional to the damages that are inflicted.
6. There must be reasonable hope of success; i.e., hopeless resistance cannot be justified.

The principle of double effect is frequently applied to the evaluation of particular courses of action during the war. That is, the evil done by any act must not be *willed*, but only tolerated. This criterion obviously is subject to casuistic abuse, but it does still offer the potential for important restraints. By precisely this principle it would be permissible to bomb missile sites near cities, even though some civilians would be killed by the bombing, provided that the above conditions were met (especially the principle of proportionality, point 5). But saturation bombing, deliberate aerial bombardment of residential areas, or use of larger bombs than were strictly necessary to destroy the military target would be condemned.

So would the deliberate initiation of attack on predominantly civilian targets. In a further elaboration of the "double effect" argument, any good achieved must follow directly from the *act*, not from the evil effect. This may really sound convoluted, but it is clear enough, for instance, regarding use of the atomic bomb against Hiroshima and Nagasaki. Though it may well have shortened the war and avoided hundreds of thousands of civilian casualties in savage ground combat, that would not be enough. The war presumably ended as a direct result of the intended civilian deaths in those cities (the evil effect), not from destruction of any traditionally legitimate military target or even of unavoidable civilian deaths in connection with the destruction of a military target.

Now certainly these criteria for just conduct in war are not capable of precise measurement by the objective observer. Some deal with interior motives; others concern estimates of the probability of various outcomes about which there may always be disagreement. But their purpose is to provide not a basis for judgment on others' acts, but some standards for internalized restraint that might be more effective than the situation arising where wars are judged solely by their causes and ends, when it is so easy to consider oneself wronged.

Using the preceding criteria, let us suppose that nuclear weapons per se are not branded as immoral even though many of their potential uses might be so characterized. The *initial* use of nuclear weapons seems imprudent to me under most circumstances, given the substantial, though not universal, consensus on the difficulty of maintaining limits in their use once the first have been used. Most analysts of limited tactical or central war now agree that the nuclear versus nonnuclear threshold is a terribly important and salient one; that given the general absence in the world of either the experience of limited nuclear war or a fully articulated military and political doctrine it is hard to have much confidence in the stability of limits above that threshold.[18] Hence the threshold should be crossed only with great reluctance.

Furthermore, the *initial* use of nuclear weapons may, by the above criteria, be immoral because the uncertain consequences make calculation of the rule of proportionality into almost sheer guesswork. One possible exception concerns the hypothetical circumstances when a nation's political leaders obtained information, with very high confidence, that their enemy was about to attack them with nuclear weapons. Perhaps then a preemptive strike would be proper if there were no alternative, such as negotiation or delivery of warning. But the conditions for such a strike—very high confidence in one's intelligence, and the absence of alternatives, are so stringent as to make the scenario border on fantasy. A somewhat more plausible situation applies to the defense of Western Europe. It is possible that European conventional defense is or could become so weak as to offer no reasonable prospect for success against a full Eastern attack, thus posing a very ugly dilemma. But despite the arguments either way, it still is not clear to me that the rich Atlantic nations *need* allow themselves to become so inferior in conventional forces that they would be faced with such a choice.

The first use of nuclear weapons, when that first use was directed deliberately against civilian targets, would pretty clearly be ruled out by the above criteria. Thus a Soviet conventional attack on Western Europe could not be met directly with an American countercity retaliatory strike. But of course that is not very likely anyway. By a fairly clear extension of the criteria enumerated above, it would also seem that being the first to escalate use of nuclear weapons onto civilian targets would also be ruled out. That is, neither a tactical nuclear attack in Europe nor a counterforce attack on the United States could be met with countercity retaliation. The hardest question is whether nuclear weapons may be used against cities even in retaliation for an attack against cities. The above criteria would seem to rule no on that too, except perhaps in a restrained bargaining fashion. Certainly a merely vengeful retaliation—to insure that, if one's own society cannot survive their's won't *either*—would be indefensible.

Some observers say that the American government need not really *intend* to carry out such an act of retaliation, that it would be enough to threaten it. Thus a President might say loudly and boldly that he would order retaliation on enemy cities while quietly inside himself rejecting the idea. Bluffs may work in some kinds of interpersonal and international behavior, but in this instance

---

[18] The principal recent dissenting voice is probably that of Bernard Brodie, *Escalation and the Nuclear Option* (Princeton: Princeton University Press, 1966).

how would a leader convey such a threat, in a credible manner, to the enemy? He would have to repeat it over and over (as both American and Russian leaders have done), and his subordinates would have to be kept completely in the dark as to his real intentions. He could never confide to anyone his unwillingness to carry out the threat because of the extreme importance of keeping his hesitations secret from the enemy. He would have to make the threat a firm national declaratory policy, and so would be responsible for the political climate that would influence his successor, if not himself, to mean the threat as well as to state it. Furthermore, he would have to take all the preliminary steps for carrying out the threat just as though he intended to do it. It would be extremely difficult to keep full control over the decision so that should the country ever actually be attacked, no subordinate would give the firing signal in the protracted absence of the expected word from his Commander-in-Chief. Thus this particular kind of bluff just does not seem available to the head of a government.

The moral evaluation of strategic postures poses innumerable difficult and divisive issues. I would not want an American president to impose his own moral values (even if they were also mine) on a populace that did not share them. While there are serious difficulties with the concept, the notion that in some sense a democratic leader must remain an "agent" of his people seems persuasive.

In any case, the proposal for a countercombatant strategy need not rest solely on an argument that it is immoral deliberately to kill civilians. One might simply agree that there is something brutal about the readiness with which most of us have accepted a countercity retaliatory posture up to now. It would be still more brutalizing to fight, and even to win, such a war. We cannot completely forget to ask what kind of people we would be in the end. Or at bottom, utilization in war of such a rule of restraint as I have suggested should make it likely that antagonisms would escalate more slowly, and hence less readily destroy a climate conducive to making peace. If accepted also by the Russians, and ultimately by the Chinese, it would offer the prospect, quite aside from moral considerations, of saving a great many civilian lives on the American side.

A COUNTERCOMBATANT STRATEGY
AND ARMS CONTROL

In conclusion, consider briefly some implications of an American countercombatant strategy for weapons procurement, arms control, and international politics generally.

1. Some readers may believe that in the present—and foreseeable—balance of terror the probability of central nuclear war is really almost zero. They may thus oppose any suggestion that modes of controlling nuclear war be developed, for fear that leaders would then become readier to resort to it.

But I fear that the chances of nuclear war over the next decades, whether from inadvertence, crisis desperation, third party catalyzation, technological break-through for one side, in fact are not trivial whatever we do. Nor do I think that implementing my strategy would make nuclear war attractive. If it did lead to any small increase in the chances of war at all, that liability would be more than offset by markedly reducing the chances that any nuclear exchange would lead to the death of hundreds of millions of civilians.

2. The strategy would not in itself exacerbate American relations with our European allies. Indeed, insofar as it would eliminate Russian capabilities to expand in Europe in any postwar world, our allies might well welcome the change.

3. It is fully compatible with improved American relations with China or Eastern Europe. For obvious reasons the Eastern European states might wel-come it even more than would those of Western Europe. Not only is it com-patible with better Sino-American relations, an American distinction between China and Russia as military enemies is critical to it. There could be no auto-matic American strike against China in the event of a Soviet attack on us; a militarily powerful China must be left unharmed to constitute the threat it can suggest most plausibly—against the state with which it shares thousands of miles of border.

4. It is not incompatible with further efforts to develop invulnerable de-terrents on both sides. While there could be some advantages to having a real counterforce capability in the traditional sense, such advantages would surely be cancelled out by the instabilities that would be threatened, and any way strategic retaliatory vehicles are not necessarily the primary targets under a countercombatant strategy. Insofar as a countercombatant strategy might be perceived as additionally destabilizing in a world of vulnerable deterrents, the development of secure retaliatory forces, for example submarine launched missiles, is to be welcomed. Probably the absence of such capabilities, on the Russian side, contributed seriously to the nonacceptance of McNamara's Ann Arbor version of "no cities."

5. On the above reasoning, it is basically not incompatible with ABM sys-tems designed to protect missile-launching sites. It is, however, incompatible with good area-defense ABM systems for protecting vast territories. Attempted Soviet acquisition of ABMs of such broad capability would require strenuous American counterefforts, or a negotiated and verifiable agreement to refrain.

6. Similarly, the strategy is not incompatible with civil defense systems designed to reduce civilian deaths from heat, blast, or fallout, since civilian deaths are assumed to be essentially superfluous to Russian leaders' calcula-tions of first strike attractiveness so long as destruction of their military capa-bility is assured. But any widespread Russian effort to put military bases (other than missile sites) or armament plants in secure underground locations would be entirely incompatible. Arms control agreements designed to prohibit such steps might well become of high priority.

7. It is not incompatible with the further development of small, clean, high accuracy weapons which would cause less collateral damage. It is important that it not require such new weapons as to bring a new round of arms acquisition or pressure on the nuclear test ban.

8. For implementing a countercombatant strategy, MIRV is neither a particular threat nor a "no MIRV" agreement particularly desirable. Insofar as it was necessary for penetrating an ABM system MIRV could be desirable, though an inaccurate MIRV system, capable of penetrating but not discriminating in its targets, would be highly undesirable.

9. A countercombatant strategy would not particularly benefit from a Soviet-American freeze on the number of nuclear delivery vehicles acquired by each side, nor from a negotiated reduction in the number of vehicles. While such action might be beneficial on other grounds, it would be undesirable if it diminished American or Soviet confidence in the ability of the United States very greatly to reduce Soviet war-fighting ability.

10. Because the strategy contemplates striking relatively many targets, it might require the United States to have more missiles capable of surviving a Soviet first strike than does the present assured destruction strategy. This could raise problems of risk, expense, and arms race phenomena. The gravity of this reservation depends partly on technical computations of requirements, and partly on decisions about just how much countercombatant destruction would be required for a satisfactory deterrent. No answer is possible here, but the mix of weapons and countermeasures is important. For example, with MIRV but not area ABMs, the existing number of missiles could hit a great many targets. MIRVs with small warheads might indeed be much more effective in this role than if used solely against hardened missile sites. Moreover, even if a countercombatant strategy should not be practicable now, it may become so in the future, especially if we want it. Later technology, if we try to develop in this direction, might make feasible certain kinds of offense and defense that would favor the strategy.

11. A countercombatant strategy does not intrinsically require Soviet reciprocation, though there would be major advantages, perhaps to both sides, if the Russians should indicate both receipt of our message of intent and a willingness to do likewise.

12. The strategy is fully compatible with a declaratory American policy of no first use of nuclear weapons.

13. It assumes some continued restraint in general American behavior in international politics, avoiding situations where a Soviet failure to initiate nuclear war in response to American acts would result in a really major shift in the status quo against the USSR or its rulers. In this context, of the phrase "peaceful coexistence" the second half needs to be emphasized as much as the first.

PART III

Influence and Integration

15

The Instruments of Influence
and the Limits of Power

METHODS OF INFLUENCE

How do nations influence each other? In a violence-prone world, perhaps initially we think of the *application of force*; specifically, the leaders of one nation make it physically impossible for those of another nation to do whatever it was they had been doing or intended to do. Through violent conflict the opponent's physical facilities may be destroyed, or his soldiers or civilians killed to eliminate his war potential. But despite the fact that nations do sometimes resort to the violent application of force, this crude form of influence is relatively rare and probably the least important means by which nations induce other nations to obey their will.

Much more important is *bargaining*. Bargaining implies the use or potential use of one or both of two elements: *punishment* and *reward*. Punishment of course includes the application of force, but may also take the form of withdrawal of some privilege, favor, or mutual contact that already exists. And in bargaining, punishment may actually be meted out, or it may merely be *threatened*. If meted out, it may be with the intent to persuade the opponent that the punishment will occur whenever he performs the act one dislikes, or it may be applied as a "sample" of further punishment, to be given in greater dosage if he continues or expands the disliked act. Thus one may simply threaten punishment without applying it, or one may apply some punishment

Adapted from a lecture delivered at the National War College, August 26, 1971.

as an implicit threat of further punishment. But the emphasis here is on punishment as a means of persuasion in bargaining, not in the initial sense of making certain acts physically impossible.

Even many applications of force properly belong in this category. For example, the American rationale behind bombing North Vietnam from 1965 to 1968 was less to destroy Hanoi's ability to carry on the war—it was generally recognized that strategic bombing of a poor, basically agricultural nation could not have that effect—but rather to persuade the North Vietnamese government that the war was too expensive to any goals it might hope to achieve, and to call it off even though Hanoi might still retain the purely physical capacity to fight. The Americans knew they could not make it impossible for Ho Chi Minh's government to infiltrate men and supplies into the South, but hoped to make the effort too costly. Also, at times the bombing was used in such a way as to convey an implicit threat that unless the North Vietnamese made peace aerial bombardment might be extended to initially off-limits targets such as urban areas. Thus force became an instrument of persuasion in attempted bargaining. Other more successful examples could be cited from earlier international history.

Punishment may be extended or threatened either to persuade someone else *to do* something, or *not to do* it or to cease doing it. In the latter case we often speak of deterrence; the United States and Russia attempt to persuade each other not to launch a nuclear attack by threatening dire retaliatory punishment of any attack. Deterrence through threatened punishment is usually a good deal easier than is a comparable effort at persuading someone to perform a specific act. This more positive persuasion we call coercion, or in the apt term of Thomas Schelling, *compellence*.[1] It may take the form either of threatened punishment if a given act is not performed, or the application of punishment until he does perform the act. For example, the American government made some small attempts, in the late 1950s, to deter the North Vietnamese government from assisting Communist guerillas in the South. Later on, when the assistance was in fact being extended, the task became one of trying to compel the North to stop.

Compellence is usually harder to do successfully because when it is applied one must try to persuade the opponent to change his mind and change his acts, whereas with deterrence one only needs to persuade him to keep on not doing whatever it is that one wants him not to do. If he is already performing an act, in modern governmental bureaucracies it presumably is the result of a deliberate decision arrived at after much discussion, intrabureaucratic and extrabureaucratic influence, and the commitment of substantial prestige and other resources by those who have accepted the policy. A reversal will be costly to them, so the inertia of their already adopted policy is likely to sustain it against the outside efforts of the would-be compelling agent.

There are many possible means of threatening or applying punishment in

---

[1] *Arms and Influence* (New Haven: Yale University Press, 1967).

bargaining situations. Physical (military) force is obvious, but others are far more common. A developed nation may withhold foreign aid from a poor one; an underdeveloped state may nationalize investment of the citizens of a rich nation; either may cut off trading relations with the other. Ambassadors may be withdrawn or diplomatic relations entirely severed or, much more mildly, one may withdraw support from another's position on a pet issue at the United Nations. A great many other forms of punishment can be imagined and are used at one time or another, but it is important to notice that in so many cases the punishment (or threat of punishment) consists in withdrawing something that had previously been available; it cannot be withdrawn unless it was there in the first place. One cannot cut off trade or sever diplomatic relations unless they already exist. Thus in refusing over a long period of time to carry on these normal channels of intercourse with another nation, both sides in the pair deprive themselves of possible instruments of influence over each other's policies. This is likely to be a special loss for the larger, more powerful state in the pair since, if the normal ties existed, the smaller and weaker state would be likely to be more dependent on them.

It may often be useful to establish a rewarding relationship with another party if only to provide a potential means of punishment. And of course a far more common use of *rewards* in bargaining situations is for their immediate influence potential. The would-be influencer must ask what he can do for the other side (other than simply stop punishing him). Consider a situation which quickly came to be considered one appropriate for the predominant use of threat and punishment, but perhaps need not have been: American policy in Southeast Asia in the middle and late 1950s. As it turned out, attempts to influence North Vietnam almost entirely took the form of punishments; in the context of actual developments over the following years it may be hard to imagine anything else. Attempts at the large-scale offer of rewards now seem preposterous. President Johnson's proposal, in 1965, of massive economic aid to the whole Mekong Valley area—which was particularly meant to include North Vietnam—was quickly brushed aside by the Communists. The offer to bring the North Vietnamese into development programs, and to provide substantial assistance for development of all Southeast Asian countries, was dismissed as just an imperialist bribe or an empty public relations gesture. But such an offer, a decade earlier and before the war, might not have been perceived quite that way.

Imagine a scenario rather like this: After the French evacuated Indochina and signed the Geneva agreements calling, at least temporarily, for separate governments in North and South Vietnam, the United States could have recognized the North Vietnamese government in Hanoi (in fact the American government did not do this). It really is not such a preposterous idea, considering, after all, that the United States had not been fighting in Indochina and so there was no question of recognizing a regime against which Americans had fought. At the same time, Washington might have encouraged trade with the new regime. Thus North Vietnam would not have been put on the

strategic embargo list that forbade or sharply limited American trade with
China, North Korea, the Soviet Union, and Eastern Europe. So long as the
North Vietnamese did not break the embargo by shipping Western goods on
to China, the United States might not only have permitted but actually have
encouraged trade with Hanoi. Furthermore, some economic aid for recon-
structing the economy might have been extended. In public statements the
American government might have managed to say some complimentary
things about "nationalist" Ho Chi Minh, de-emphasizing the fact that he
also happened to be a Communist. The United States might have stressed,
as it did, the fact of important differences between North and South Vietnam
and the need for the government of the South to be independent of the North,
but the tone could have been quite different. Instead of emphasizing anti-
communism and the ideological differences, it might instead have stressed the
cultural, religious, and ethnic differences between the two halves, and how they
had never really formed a unified nation.

The purpose of this strategy would have been to convey to the governments
of both parts of Vietnam a desire to see South Vietnam remain independent,
without directing strong condemnatory statements against the North. Instead
of cutting virtually all the normal ties among nations, a rather substantial
carrot would have been dangled before Hanoi to encourage peaceful relations
with the South. The threat to withdraw the carrot in case of a Northern inspired or assisted effort to overthrow the Saigon government could have been
made clear enough implicitly, as could the ultimate intention to oppose any
such effort militarily. But the primary effort would have been to soft-pedal
threats and to build, over time, substantial positive incentives for the behavior
desired by the American government.

Perhaps this policy seems too neoimperialist in style, or would have been
applied that way. Nor of course can one say in hindsight whether it would
have worked, or even whether it was better than some other possibility, such
as accepting unification of the country from the beginning. But certainly the
punishment-oriented policy that was tried was no great success, and it is
intriguing to speculate about the possibilities of a reward-oriented effort.
Within nations most people obey most laws less from fearful anticipation of
punishment than from habit, convenience, and a conviction that the law is
basically just. It is odd that so many conceptions of international politics
concentrate on coercion, deterrence, and punishment.

Our discussion of a possible strategy for influencing North Vietnam leads
us to another category of means of influence, one that is closely related to
bargaining but deserves separate treatment. Influence may come as a result of
improving one's asset position, of acquiring new resources and wider options.
The would-be influencer obtains more—in quantity and variety—of the instruments of bargaining; in effect it *invests* its power in order to obtain a base
of greater influence. The most obvious and perhaps the commonest strategy
is a rather straightforward type of material investment, such as trying to
foster economic growth, or encouraging scientific research, or improving the

level of education of the population. Toward the end of this chapter we will discuss the ease and difficulties of investing one base of influence to build another.

A kind of political investment is to do favors, establishing political credits that can be cashed later. Or a nation may try to see that its own citizens, or those of its allies, occupy key positions in an international organization. This kind of political activity is an important instance where one spends influence in order to create a greater influence base. But like most investments, there is always a chance of failure. Too obvious an effort to seize key political posts may breed counteraction that leaves the would-be influencer weaker than before. Despite the intention to invest one may merely consume.

In international politics, the establishment of trade and aid relations with another country—so that if necessary one may have something to withdraw— is a more subtle kind of investment. Much the same can be said for various kinds of military assistance or cultural and educational exchanges. A small country might quite deliberately allow a big one to establish a military base on its territory, so that the big power will become dependent on the base and later make concessions to the small one in order to retain the facilities. Spain seems to have done something of the sort with the United States; American retention of air and naval bases in Spain became a quid pro quo, many years after their establishment, for hundreds of millions of dollars of weapons and at least a vague security commitment that the American govern-ment was reluctant to extend. It may even be helpful for the small country to encourage a moderate amount of discontent with the bases among its own populace; it can then point to popular pressures for ending the basing agree-ment as evidence that it needs special concessions to mollify its people.

Again, the above shades into the bargaining strategy, but the emphasis is not on overt bargaining but on creating a situation where, *without* overt threats, the other partner comes to realize that you have acquired a more favorable position. Because he recognizes that you have strengthened your hand and obtained a better set of the tools of influence a hard bargaining situation may never arise; he may become ready to accede to requests without any bargaining having to occur. By avoiding the bargaining situation, where he is likely to have to give in anyway, he avoids acrimony and the spending of resources (time, attention) that the bargaining process would require. In-fluence is likely to be greatest when its instruments do not have to be utilized openly or even in veiled threats, where the other side knows you have a certain capability and it is unnecessary to threaten or perhaps even to promise. It may even become an occasion of anticipated reactions—where I know what you want me to do, and do it, without even a request being made. The "ideal servant" was thought to be a person who knew what his master would want even before his master became aware of the desire.

One further means of influence arises in the *building of a community*: a sense of kinship, common loyalties and values, a feeling of belonging together. Indi-viduals' perceptions of their self-interest can be greatly widened; if they no longer think only in terms of their own very narrow self-image, they will be willing to make certain sacrifices whether or not those sacrifices are directly reciprocated.[2] Within the family group, husband and wife, father and mother, and even—occasionally—brother and sister will give up for the common welfare, or for the welfare of another member. The identification and affection may be so strong that on some matters a husband or wife comes to prefer to do what the spouse wants rather than what he had originally intended.

Community building in this sense involves a tacit agreement—tacit because if you have to state it openly it is a very fragile affair—not to coerce, and to limit the scope of bargaining. In effect you give up certain bargaining options, without having to say so explicitly. One example is marriage between people who don't believe in divorce and remarriage. The partners in such a case are stuck with each other; they have little choice but to stick out the relationship, make it last, and make the best of it. They may occasionally threaten to break off the relationship, but not to marry someone else (which would otherwise be a more credible threat). They have given up this option, and the very fact that they have done so often predisposes each party to try harder to build trust, to meet each other's requests without having to get into the kind of situation of open bargaining and coercion. Naturally everyone does bargain somewhat within marriage, but in a reasonably good relationship both partners recognize both their common interest in keeping the bargaining limited and an altruistic desire not to coerce.

This sort of relationship is most common and usually strongest within the family group, or perhaps between very close friends. Some of this sense of mutual identification nevertheless applies more widely: to more distant relatives, friends, neighbors, colleagues at work, fellow inhabitants of a city, state, and even nation in a series of largely concentric circles. Obviously the strength of these relationships is very much weaker in the wide circles and, especially in politics, there is a great deal of bargaining within a city or nation. Still, within the United States for most of its history, for instance, along with the bargaining there was a degree of mutual identification, if not strong affection, among bargainers who recognized the joint interest to be served in reaching agreements without resorting to threats, especially to the threat of violence. There were limits to the degree that religious, occupational, or regional minorities were coerced (racial minorities gained the fewest benefits from these limits) not just out of the desire to avoid unpleasantness, but also from a recognition that the minorities had certain rights to have things their way too. In recognition of those rights, and more selfishly in recognition of everyone's interest in keeping the whole enterprise going, majorities sometimes limited themselves. Citizens of one part of the country were ready to defend in war, at the risk of their lives, citizens of other parts. Now, of course, it seems that all aspects of this sense of mutual identification and mutual fate have been breaking down in the United States, as the community has weakened.

---

[2] For further discussion and references, see the two final chapters in this volume.

Again, this kind of influence within a community is much weaker even in a tightly knot nation-state than in small groups, and it is usually even weaker between nations. But it still does happen. We speak, not entirely emptily, of an Atlantic community or a European community; the relationship is stronger within some segments of the wider area, for instance Scandinavia, or the United States and Britain and Canada. Certainly not all is love and affection between the United States and Canada, but there is something qualitatively different between that relationship and the United States-China relationship. How such conditions come about and are maintained is a matter that will occupy us in a later chapter, but we may note now that strong bonds of communication and attention are essential. We said above that a state might want to establish commercial relations or educational and cultural exchanges with another nation so as to have direct means of influence (rewards to offer, or to threaten to withdraw as punishment). Some of the most important functions of trade or other exchanges, however, may be in their contribution to building and maintaining a sense of community between nations. In this last means of influence we thus have reached the opposite end of the coercion spectrum from which we began.

AN INVENTORY OF INFLUENCE BASES

At this point it becomes necessary to make some further analytical distinctions. When we speak of power we speak of the ability to make someone else do something you want him to do and that he would not otherwise do.[3] Many writers limit the term "power" to exercises of coercion, leaving the term "influence" to cover the entire spectrum of coercive and noncoercive means that we have just discussed. This seems to be a useful distinction, and we shall continue it here. We may then, after Lasswell and Kaplan, speak of the *bases* of influence; that is, the resource we use to persuade someone else to do something. In the emphasis on persuasion we explicitly avoid any limitation to situations of conflict. We persuade someone else to do something he would not otherwise do in cooperative situations as well; we often exercise influence in situations where both parties may gain. In teaching, for instance, teacher and students learn from each other and influence each other; both act differently, and presumably more productively, as a result of the encounter.

We will employ a simple checklist of the bases of influence, a list that is intended to be exhaustive, on which any specific instrument of influence could be placed. Whether the reader likes all the words or adopts the scheme in exactly the form it is given here is less important than that he have some such system of scanning the universe of possible influence bases. Without a

---

[3] The basic discussions on which we draw throughout much of the chapter are Robert A. Dahl, "The Concept of Power," *Behavioral Science*, 2, 3 (July 1957), pp. 201–15, and Harold Lasswell and Abraham Kaplan, *Power and Society* (New Haven: Yale University Press, 1950).

systematic and semiconscious checklist he is likely to pay far too much attention to certain bases and to forget utterly about others.[4]

In international politics, *military power* is typically the influence base that most people think of first. (In fact, it is often precisely the lack of a systematic checklist that leads to an overemphasis on such obvious instruments as those of coercion.) There are a variety of possible measures, each tapping different aspects and concerned with elements that will be important in different circumstances.

In the world since 1945 we might first of all think about nuclear weapons: how many bombs does a nation have; how many weapons deliverable under what kinds of conditions? (Already we move beyond a simple count of bombs, and may wonder about whether they can be delivered only in a first strike attack on another nation, or whether their delivery vehicles are relatively invulnerable to attack and so are useful as potential retaliation.) What other kinds and numbers of weapons does the nation possess? How many men does it have under arms; in the regular army and in reserves?

As a rather crude but still quite useful summary measure one might compare the total military budgets of various nations. There are great difficulties in comparing expenditures in different national currencies, in obtaining reasonably full and accurate disclosure, and in seeing that the same kinds of expenditure are counted in each case (for instance, border guards and internal security forces, or expenditure for research and development on projects that may have both civilian and military uses). Still, the rough overall measure has great use if employed carefully. It is a better and more valid indicator than the number of men under arms, for instance, because soldiers in an underdeveloped country may be poorly equipped and less effective in battle than the highly trained and splendidly armed soldiers of some industrial nations. Table 15-1 gives some rather crude estimates for a selected 30 of the world's nations as of 1965. (The figure for the Soviet Union is probably a little low due to the difficulty of obtaining accurate information, but almost certainly its ranking—a clear second—is right.)[5]

Note the enormous differences between the two superpowers and all the rest of the world, even the other, much weaker, nuclear powers: China, Britain, and France. The United States outspends each of the last by almost ten times. Here we see the basis of military bipolarity so prominent in the world today, even ignoring the nuclear versus nonnuclear distinction among the smaller powers. And the median (middle) country is enormously weaker

---

[4] As first mentioned in Chapter 3 of this volume, the following list is adapted from Lasswell and Kaplan, op. cit.

[5] All data and fuller definitions for the following tables are from Charles L. Taylor and Michael C. Hudson, *World Handbook of Political and Social Indicators*, 2nd edition (New Haven: Yale University Press, 1972). While more recent data are now available for some variables, it seemed more useful to use data all for approximately the same time point, and in a single source which can readily be consulted by the reader.

Table 15-1
Military Expenditures (Millions of U.S. Dollars), 1965

United States	51,844
Soviet Union	28,170
China	6,000
United Kingdom	5,855
France	5,125
West Germany	4,979
India	2,077
Italy	1,939
Poland	1,700
Canada	1,535
East Germany	1,000
Indonesia	1,000
Sweden	843
Japan	781
Brazil	641
Spain	587
Turkey	425
Israel	413
Yugoslavia	396
United Arab Republic	392
South Africa	320
Argentina	272
Cuba	213
Mexico	153
Chile	102
Thailand	84
Philippines	76
WORLD MEDIAN	67
Nigeria	66
Senegal	15
Tanzania	6

militarily, spending hardly more than a thousandth as much as the United States.

Before going on, however, it is important to note that such a rank order as that in Table 15-1 is not necessarily a predictive ranking for the outcome of any particular war. As in sports, sometimes a weak team will beat one much higher up on the rankings. Various factors, such as morale or even chance, come into play. One of special importance is often *distance*; the effectiveness of military power declines with distance. The decline over distance is, however, not simple and certainly not linear. Cost and effectiveness vary greatly with topography. Because much of the cost of ocean transport is in the loading and unloading rather than the carrying, a great seapower like the United States can deliver conventional forces to the coastline of Asia at a cost that is actually not enormously greater than that of putting them onto an island in the Caribbean. And the United States is better able than the People's Republic of China to put forces on Taiwan not because it is cheaper to ship from San Francisco to Taiwan than from the China coast to Taiwan (it isn't), but because only the United States has the transportation capability to get large numbers of troops and supplies there. Thus you have to discount severely the effectiveness of the millions of Chinese troops for action anywhere outside the Chinese mainland.[6]

The qualifications about distance and topography, and how their effects may be overcome, lead naturally into quite another element of national influence: *wealth*. Various measures are available, such as a nation's total consumption of energy from fossil fuels (coal, oil, natural gas) and electric power, but gross national product (GNP) is as good a measure as any. As before there are difficulties with the indicator, chiefly here in converting the value of production in national currencies (pounds, francs, rubles, yen, rupees) into a single comparable currency like United States dollars. Still, so long as the figures are not treated as precise reports capable of showing very fine gradations, they are generally useful. Analytically the money measure is a good one because it emphasizes the flexibility, over time, of most resources. Resources may be shifted from consumption to the production of military goods to space boosters to investment, as the need for different kinds of goods becomes apparent. GNP, as an aggregate measure of the production of an economy, captures this. Also, money itself is valuable as a fluid (or fungible, as the economists say) resource; for instance it can be lent or given away in the form of foreign aid. Table 15-2 shows the ranking of the same nations as in Table 15-1 by total GNP in 1965. The figures are now a number of years old, but as with most of the figures in this chapter the basic relationships have not changed much.[7] Most nations fall within an average growth rate of two to five percent per year so that with a few exceptions (notably the very high growth rate of Japan in recent years) it takes more than ten years for the rankings to shift very drastically.

----

[6] An important theoretical discussion of the effect of distance is in Kenneth Boulding, *Conflict and Defense* (New York: Harper and Row, 1962). John Herz, *International Politics in the Atomic Age* (New York: Columbia University Press, 1965), emphasizes the decreasing protection provided by distance, and a sophisticated discussion showing that sheer distance is much less important than topography and physical capabilities is Albert Wohlstetter, "Theory and Opposed Systems Design," *Journal of Conflict Resolution*, 12, 3 (September 1968), pp. 302–31.

[7] These data and those in Tables 15-1 and 15-5 employ the exchange rates current in 1965; contemporary rates would reduce the figure for the United States by over ten percent, and even more with respect to West Germany and Japan.

Table 15-2
Gross National Product (Millions of
U.S. Dollars), 1965

United States	695,500
Soviet Union	313,000
West Germany	112,232
United Kingdom	99,260
France	94,125
Japan	84,347
China	76,000
Italy	56,947
India	49,220
Canada	48,473
Poland	30,800
Brazil	21,970
East Germany	21,546
Sweden	19,714
Mexico	19,432
Spain	17,443
Argentina	17,204
Indonesia	10,450
South Africa	10,911
Yugoslavia	8,800
Turkey	8,776
Philippines	5,172
Nigeria	4,852
Chile	4,482
United Arab Republic	4,700
Thailand	3,930
Israel	3,645
Cuba	3,000
WORLD MEDIAN	1,360
Tanzania	751
Senegal	680

The rankings of wealth are similar to but not the same as those for military expenditure. As in the previous list, the United States and then the Soviet Union lead, but Japan, which was only fourteenth on military spending, ranks sixth and China here drops to seventh position. Again, however, there is a tremendous spread between the great and the small, with the United States economy about 500 times as great as the median country in the whole world. And once more we see the basis of bipolarity, with a difference of about two to one between even the second and third place powers. Therefore, the typical country of the world has, by American, Russian, or even Japanese or

European standards, a small influence base and also a very small market, unable to exploit many of the economies of scale which citizens of the giants take for granted. Furthermore, such a small economy is seldom diversified, and is likely to be dependent on foreign markets for only two or three big exports and thus subject to potential coercion by purchasing nations.[8] The very big economies can, by contrast, boycott a small nation's products without suffering much damage.

Also, it is worth remarking how slight a difference in this national influence base—wealth—the acquisition or loss of a single small ally can make to a superpower. South Vietnam's total gross national product, for instance, is roughly .35 percent of that of the United States—approximately equivalent to one month's normal *growth* of the American economy or one month's conduct of the Vietnam War during the late 1960s.

For some purposes, however, it would be useful to know about a country's wealth in particular resources or other assets. Oil is of very special importance in the contemporary world, as are certain industrial metals like chromium or copper. No matter how wealthy a nation is it cannot be a nuclear power unless it has access to uranium; France has had to make special efforts to cultivate good relationships with a few independent uranium-producing states of Africa. At other times it may be necessary to take into account the foreign investments a nation controls. When Britain was at war in 1914 to 1918, the British were able greatly to magnify their war effort by selling many of their foreign investments. With the foreign currency thus earned, they could buy war materiel abroad, critically supplementing what could be produced at home. Their GNP, under those circumstances, would have been a deceptively low measure of the resources they could pour into the war—in a one-shot expenditure of their overseas assets.[9]

It is important to be aware how weak the relationship is between wealth as GNP (or for that matter energy production) and some other commonly employed measures of wealth, or at least size. Table 15-3 for instance shows the rankings of the world's nations by total population in the year 1965, and Table 15-4, page 268, gives the rankings for total area in square kilometers.

Here the United States ranks but fourth, behind the Soviet Union, and a number of poor countries are larger or not very much smaller. There is little or no support here for the previously apparent bipolarity, except that a superpower must be large, but certainly not the biggest, in terms of human resources.

As for the distribution from great to small, once again we see a tremendous spread. About half the world lives in one of the four biggest countries. The median country, however, is very small, only about five million or less than one percent the size of China. Even with great economic growth it would

---

[8] Using data in Taylor and Hudson, op. cit, the correlation of GNP with concentration of export commodities is −.49 and with concentration of export receiving countries is −.39.

[9] For example, see Charles J. Hitch and Dayton McKean, *The Economics of Defense in the Nuclear Age* (Cambridge: Harvard University Press, 1960), Chapter 1, and Klaus Knorr, *Military Power and Potential* (Lexington, Mass.: D. C. Heath, 1970).

Table 15-3
Population (Thousands), 1965

China	700,000
India	486,729
Soviet Union	230,600
United States	194,572
Indonesia	105,300
Japan	97,960
Brazil	82,222
West Germany	59,041
Nigeria	57,500
United Kingdom	54,595
Italy	51,576
France	48,922
Mexico	42,689
Philippines	32,345
Spain	31,604
Poland	31,496
Turkey	31,086
Thailand	30,591
United Arab Republic	29,600
Argentina	22,352
Canada	19,604
Yugoslavia	19,508
South Africa	17,867
East Germany	17,100
Tanzania	10,515
Chile	8,567
Sweden	7,734
Cuba	7,631
WORLD MEDIAN	5,300
Senegal	3,490
Israel	2,563

therefore never escape, by itself, having a small market and a small base of influence on this dimension. On the other hand, the average country is small enough to have a relatively homogeneous population ethnically and linguistically, which may serve as a great asset for national unity and political stability. Furthermore, the country is small enough to avoid many of the dilemmas of local option and potential chaos versus centralization in a distant bureaucratic capital, which so often plague big countries like China, India, the Soviet Union, and the United States.

Like mere numbers of people, sheer physical area does not alone suffice as a major influence base for a superpower, though it would appear difficult

Table 15-4
Area (Thousand Square Kilometers),
1965

Soviet Union	22,402
Canada	9,976
China	9,561
United States	9,363
Brazil	8,512
India	3,184
Argentina	2,777
Mexico	1,973
Indonesia	1,492
South Africa	1,221
United Arab Republic	1,000
Tanzania	940
Nigeria	924
Turkey	781
Chile	757
France	547
Thailand	514
Spain	505
Sweden	450
Japan	370
Italy	301
Philippines	300
Poland	313
Yugoslavia	256
WORLD MEDIAN	256
West Germany	249
United Kingdom	244
Senegal	196
Cuba	115
East Germany	108
Israel	21

to reach the top without quite a substantial territory. Japan nevertheless ranks very far down the list (twentieth), making clear how deceptive this index is when taken alone.

As with all the previous measures, the range is very wide. The median country is relatively small: about 256,000 square kilometers, or under 100,000 square miles—about the same as the State of Colorado. Hence the average nation is physically vulnerable to attack; it has little depth for military defense or isolation from its neighbors. Unlike the United States, China, or Russia during much of the history of those countries, the average country of the world

Table 15-5
Gross National Product per Capita
(U.S. Dollars), 1965

United States	3,575
Sweden	2,549
Canada	2,473
France	1,924
West Germany	1,901
United Kingdom	1,818
Israel	1,422
Soviet Union	1,357
East Germany	1,260
Italy	1,104
Poland	978
Japan	861
Argentina	770
South Africa	611
Chile	565
Spain	561
Mexico	455
Yugoslavia	451
Cuba	393
Turkey	282
Brazil	267
WORLD MEDIAN	256
Senegal	195
Philippines	160
United Arab Republic	159
Thailand	129
China	109
India	101
Indonesia	99
Nigeria	84
Tanzania	71

is deeply involved in international politics simply because of where it is and how big it is, or rather, isn't.

Another set of figures helps to tell us not how wealthy is the nation, but how rich are the nation's people. That is the GNP per capita (an average figure that may of course hide great inequalities between rich and poor *within* any one nation), shown in Table 15-5.

Once more there is a very great difference between the top and the bottom of the list, amounting to a tremendous difference in life-styles even allowing for problems of comparing the value of different national currencies. Even the low median is deceptive here, since many of the big countries are found at the bottom with average annual incomes of barely more than $100, or even less. Over half the world's population lives in such countries. In other words, the median *person* is much poorer than the average inhabitant of the median *country*.

These differences in living styles by income level are superimposed on differences associated with race and region of the world. Notice, for instance, that all the countries with per capita incomes of more than $1,000 a year are in Europe or are settled predominantly by citizens of European origin. Almost all the nations of Western Europe have average incomes exceeding $1,000, as do many of the Eastern European states. The average for Eastern Europe is around $1,000. Most of Latin America, by contrast, falls in the $200 to $600 range, and Asia and Africa, except Japan, usually below $300— and often much below that figure.

Three other categories concern the quality of human resources available to a nation—not, of course, inherent human ability, but the degree to which a people's capabilities have been developed so that they can make a contribution to the nation. One we may call *enlightenment* to try to indicate the extent of high education and access to specialized knowledge in science, engineering, and the professions. Obviously a nation's military strength depends in large part on access to scientific knowledge; building modern weapons requires a body of scientific manpower that is unavailable to small and poor nations, and is not uniformly available to big rich ones. More broadly, a nation needs physicians, architects, social scientists, lawyers, and administrators to run a bureaucracy, and many others with advanced training and ability. Many possible measures that tap aspects of this can be found, such as the number of students in higher education, the number of individuals in all age groups who have completed higher education, or the number of scientists. The one we shall look at in Table 15-6 is also a partial measure, but useful because it is not so well known as some: the number of scientific and technical journals published in a nation. This serves as a rough indicator of the size of the scientific base, and is more comparable across nations than are attempts to count the number of scientists. Specialized studies have shown that, given the need for all scientists to use journals as a means of communication among themselves, there is a fairly constant relationship between the number of scientists in a country and the number of technical journals published. The association with total wealth (GNP) is strong, but by no means perfect.

Other aspects too are relevant, and not necessarily closely correlated with the number of scientists. One would be the reservoir of political, social, and organizational knowledge so as to make the most efficient use of their specialized abilities. A further aspect of enlightenment is almost impossible to measure but cannot be ignored—the capacity for originality and creativity, the ability to design new instruments for achieving one's goals as new challenges arise. The political system of a country—whether dissent is encouraged

Table 15-6
Scientific Journals, 1961

United States	6,000
Japan	2,820
France	2,780
West Germany	2,560
Soviet Union	2,100
United Kingdom	2,090
Italy	1,530
Poland	750
Sweden	710
India	670
China	660
Brazil	650
East Germany	550
Canada	540
Yugoslavia	400
Spain	320
Argentina	310
South Africa	295
Mexico	225
Chile	150
Philippines	110
Cuba	100
Indonesia	90
Turkey	90
United Arab Republic	70
Thailand	50
Israel	30
WORLD MEDIAN	10
Nigeria	<5
Senegal	<5
Tanzania	<5

and competing ideologies are permitted to develop—greatly affects the health of the social sciences.

We should recognize the scarcity, in all countries, of a higher and much more difficult kind of flexibility and creativity—the ability to challenge and change not only one's means, but also one's *goals*; the ability to recognize that a previously sought goal is no longer attainable or, if attainable, no longer worth the cost of getting there. This is a special problem in recognizing the changes in society that will be required to deal with pollution and human interdependence, the reorientation of needs in an affluent society, and maybe especially changes in foreign policy when old conflicts become no longer worth the candle. In this aspect of enlightenment neither economic development nor great size may be much of an advantage. Individual and cultural adaptivity (note Japan) does not necessarily follow either pattern. In heavy traffic a bicycle is far more maneuverable than is a Cadillac.

At least many aspects of enlightenment are related to wealth and material development; scientists are expensive to train and equip. The same is true, with less force, for a more basic kind of knowledge we shall call *skill*. Here we refer to knowledge necessary to get along in modern life even at a rather low level of sophistication, such as simple literacy, or familiarity with machinery, or what one learns in primary and secondary education. Literacy is perhaps especially important as it serves as the basis for acquiring so many other skills and kinds of enlightenment; widespread literacy is both directly a resource base for a government and a means whereby the government can communicate information or propaganda quickly to its people through the printed word. But universal education, even at the rather low levels required to produce simple literacy, is costly and difficult for a poor nation to achieve. One can also turn the argument around and say that only a literate and educated nation can become rich. Table 15-7 shows the proportion of the adult population in the major countries that can read and write.

This index appears to correlate fairly highly with the development or per capita GNP index, though there are a number of interesting exceptions which suggest the cultural differences or variations in the priorities of national governments. Eastern Europe, though much poorer, ranks with North America and Western Europe at virtually complete literacy. So too does Japan. Italy and Spain do less well. Some Latin American countries are quite high, but most fall in the range of 40 to 65 percent. Many Asian countries, the homes of very ancient civilizations, do about as well. China's place at 50 percent is notable, especially as its per capita GNP is not significantly higher than India's. Virtually all of Africa falls in the 5 to 35 percent range.

The spread between the highest countries and those about midway on the list is much less severe than is the spread normally found in other development-related indices. About a quarter of the world's population lives in countries with virtually complete literacy. The median country is 60 percent literate. On the other hand, there still are very many countries where less than a quarter of the population is literate; there technology is necessarily very backward and it is very difficult to introduce new methods and ideas.

One more aspect of population "quality" is the *health* and well-being of the people. What access do they have to good medical care? How long do they typically live? How free is the country from various contagious diseases that are now in principle preventable? Does the nation possess really first class centers of medical treatment where the latest knowledge is available? How equally is good health distributed throughout the population? Are there substantial minorities with markedly poorer-than-average facilities?

Table 15-7
Percentage of Adults Literate, 1965

Sweden	100
Canada	99
East Germany	99
France	99
Soviet Union	99
United Kingdom	99
United States	99
West Germany	99
Japan	98
Poland	98
Italy	92
Argentina	91
Israel	90
Spain	87
Chile	84
Yugoslavia	77
Cuba	75
Philippines	72
Thailand	70
Mexico	65
Brazil	61
WORLD MEDIAN	60
China	50
Turkey	46
Indonesia	43
South Africa	35
Nigeria	33
United Arab Republic	30
India	28
Tanzania	18
Senegal	8

The availability of specialized, advanced treatment and diagnostic centers may provide the possessing nation with an important instrument of influence over the elites of other countries. Access to these facilities can be used covertly as a bargaining instrument, or merely the ability to offer it selectively may make others well disposed. It is not unlikely that more than one national leader right now is indebted to government doctors in a superpower for his life or good health.

In quite a different way the health of a nation's own population is an important base of influence. Military power depends in part on having a healthy population of young males. Here it is important that access to good medical facilities be spread well across the entire population regardless of income. At the simplest, most crass level, poor distribution of health will result in physical of mental handicaps and, consequently many military rejects. One quite good measure that combines an average with the equality of distribution within a population is the infant mortality rate. In almost all poor countries many babies will die in their first year of life simply because there is not enough good medical care to go around and because public health (clean water and food) standards are low. But in developed economies the infant mortality rate could be very low; they have the wealth and basic knowledge to bring it near to the level of only ten deaths per thousand births. Where this does not happen it is virtually conclusive evidence that certain segments of the populace do not have adequate medical care in general, and that their health conditions are markedly worse than average for the country. Table 15-8 shows very approximately how some countries rank on this index.

In many underdeveloped countries the infant mortality rate is extremely high, so high that, combined with high mortality rates throughout childhood, only about one baby in two ever reaches maturity. But perhaps the most striking aspect of this table is the relatively low rank of the United States—the country with the world's highest average standard of living. Most of Western Europe, Canada, and even Japan do better; East Germany does as well. This pinpoints some of the inequalities in American society that, much more broadly than the considerations listed immediately above, threaten the basic cohesion of the nation and reduce its potential influence in the world.

So far we have been dealing with influence bases that are fairly easy to identify with objective characteristics of a nation or its people so that one can say, with some measurement error to be sure, how much is possessed. They are influence bases susceptible to tactics of giving away or withholding, as elements in a bargaining process or sometimes coercion. There is another category of influence bases, however, that appear less in the holder than in the eye of the beholder. These *deference* values affect people's behavior when they do something you wish not because of what you can give them but because they respect you or like you or think you are right. We may call these respect, affection, and rectitude or "rightness." Influence derived from deference values depends on concepts of legitimacy; we may call it *authority*.

Respect is perhaps the most difficult to specify precisely, because it usually includes elements of affection and a sense of rightness as well. Normally we respect others because of their achievements, because they occupy positions of legitimate authority, or in more traditional societies, because of their age or special roles in society. Respect goes to persons who may be said to have status, which in turn may be built upon elements of power, wealth, enlightenment, skill or other values. The word prestige also taps many of the connotations important here. Nations too have prestige and are accorded respect—not necessarily affection or moral esteem, but at least a recognition of their particular roles in the international system. One attempt to measure, albeit

Table 15-8
Infant Mortality Rate
(per Thousand), 1965

Sweden	13
Japan	19
United Kingdom	20
France	22
Canada	24
West Germany	24
East Germany	25
United States	25
Israel	26
Soviet Union	27
Cuba	36
Italy	36
Spain	37
Thailand	38
Poland	42
WORLD MEDIAN	53
Argentina	60
Mexico	61
Philippines	71
Yugoslavia	72
Indonesia	75
Senegal	93
Chile	107
United Arab Republic	119
India	139
Turkey	165
Tanzania	170
Brazil	?
China	?
Nigeria	?
South Africa	?

crudely, a nation's relative status on respect has been to count the number of diplomats sent to them by other nations. The more prestigious the state, the more important it will be to other countries that they be amply represented in its capital city. Table 15-9, page 276, presents this information.

This ranking resembles those for military power or GNP, but there are some important differences. The Soviet Union is two notches lower than would be predicted by those other two listings, reflecting the suspicion and lack of esteem many countries still felt, even in the 1960s, for the chief Communist power. China is a rather surprisingly low eleventh, barely ahead of

Table 15-9
Diplomats Received from Abroad, 1964

United States	1,418
United Kingdom	1,305
West Germany	778
Soviet Union	732
France	716
Italy	707
United Arab Republic	559
India	530
Japan	494
Brazil	431
China	389†
Canada	383
Turkey	353
Spain	342
Indonesia	339
Yugoslavia	324
Mexico	315
Argentina	301†
Poland	301
Sweden	287
Thailand	286
Israel	229
Nigeria	223
Chile	214
Cuba	201
East Germany	186
Philippines	180
WORLD MEDIAN	172
Senegal	163
Tanzania	104
South Africa	98

†No data on diplomats received; data refer to
diplomats *sent*.

Canada. Japan is also unexpectedly low considering its wealth and population. Overall we can see that *as seen by most nations*, having a Communist government lowers a country's status, as does being populated by Asians or, more generally, by non-Europeans. Some of the European nations doing surprisingly well, considering their rather lower standings on other scales, are Italy and Spain, the latter fairly high because of numerous ties to its former empire in the western hemisphere. The international system still is a place where whites have disproportionately high status. The most impressive performance by a non-European state is recorded by the United Arab Republic, the major Arab nation and a leader among the nonaligned.

Affection is another dimension, perhaps in rather short supply in international affairs but still of more than negligible importance. The bonds of community that we discussed earlier—sense of kinship, common loyalties, a feeling of belonging together—in large part reflect the affection that individuals of one nation often really do feel for another country or is inhabitants. It is much less appropriate to try to establish worldwide rankings for this influence base since different peoples will have quite different perspectives on the matter, depending on such factors as common language, cultural similarities, and where their own bonds of community lie. Great Britain is well regarded in much of the English-speaking world but not in all her former colonies. Israel holds a place of special affection for many Americans, but hardly among Arab nations or in the Moslem world more broadly. Some few nations, however, hold almost universally low positions in international affection. South Africa, a pariah, is the most obvious example now, and Nazi Germany was certainly not popular a generation ago.

"Rightness" is the last of these deference values; like affection, patterns of valuation vary around the world, so it is difficult to establish any clear ranking that most nationals would agree upon. We refer here to rightness in a moral, religious, or ethical sense; it is what people often mean by the phrase "world opinion." Stalin once contemptuously asked, "How many divisions does the Pope have?" in deprecating the significance of all but material bases of influence. Nevertheless nations or leaders who are widely regarded as following "right" norms of behavior can sometimes exert important influence as a result. A would-be mediator, for example, has to be considered fair-minded. The image of some Scandinavian leaders as relatively unbiased neutrals allows them to play roles in the United Nations political process that far exceed what one would expect from an inventory of their countries' material assets.

In times past even the United States was able to exert greater influence because of its good reputation. The Cuban missile crisis of 1962 marks one such instance. The United States had taken aerial photographs of Soviet missile emplacements in Cuba; the Russians had denied putting missiles there; and the American government took the evidence to the United Nations and presented the pictures to the assembled delegates. Ambassador Adlai Stevenson—a man widely respected and regarded as honest—showed the photographs (which of course *could* have been faked) and made the charges. Delegates were ready to believe that the United States government would not lie on such an important matter and especially that Adlai Stevenson would not lend himself to any such deception.

The exercise of coercion, therefore, is likely to cause him who coerces to lose deference, especially affection and an aura of rightness. Flagrant disregard of treaty commitments, or violation of international law, or indifference to a nearly unanimous resolution of the United Nations, will have some costs. How important the losses will be is a very difficult matter to predict or measure; doubtless they are often exaggerated by those who appeal to world opinion or worry exceedingly about the national image. But still the costs are there, and consistently ignoring them will cause a nation, or an individual, to lose *some* influence. In fact most national governments recognize this even though they may not accord it very great importance. They do spend money on cultural exchange, propaganda, overseas radio service like the Voice of America and the BBC, or on promoting a compatible brand of ideology. Ideological attractiveness combines important elements of affection and rightness.

The deference values are likely to be of special importance to small and weak nations; it may require a certain degree of skill or enlightenment to obtain affection, but size and riches are a dubious advantage. Because of the great variation among nations in what they love and consider right we will not present any attempted rankings for these influence bases.

EXCHANGE AND INVESTMENT OF INFLUENCE BASES

These various instruments of influence can in some degree be converted into each other. Some assets, like money, are especially capable of exchange for something else. Wealth can be used to obtain military power, or turned into enlightenment by funneling resources into research and education, or used to build a healthier population. By coercing others to give up territory, military power may often be used to acquire wealth. Virtually all bases of influence have some utility for obtaining other forms, but the exchange rates vary greatly. Sometimes one can in fact buy an imitation of affection, but few people really love the powerful. Affection is probably the most difficult value to accumulate directly; surely the conversion of military power into affection is one of the hardest tasks. (In Vietnam the American forces had a program for rebuilding villages and befriending peasants, with an unfortunate acronym: *W*inning *H*earts *a*nd *M*inds.)

Without carefully specifying what it is that we want to obtain (the *scope* of influence) it is impossible to measure the amount of *weight* of influence. For example, if I confine my requests within a certain scope I may seem to have great influence over an airline stewardess: she will bring me a newspaper, a drink, or a pillow. But some other requests she is less likely to grant. In international politics we need to know a great deal more about the likely results of investing one base of influence to build another.

It is true, nevertheless, that the bases of influence are somewhat interdependent. It probably requires some fairly notable amount of several bases to obtain a very high ranking on any one. Great differences between an individual or nation's position on one scale as compared with other scales are likely to be very frustrating, especially if a single rating is particularly low.

This may especially be true where the low rating is on a deference value, where the nation has achieved great size and power, for instance, but is still denied high status by others.[10]

The general fact of moderate interdependence among the bases of influence can be demonstrated with the measures we looked at in the preceding section. We can take the full worldwide distribution (not just the countries listed above) on each of the measures presented and correlate them with one another. From the correlations we obtain a figure (r^2) for the percentage of variation in one distribution that is "accounted for" by another distribution. Table 15-10, page 280, presents the results.

Two quite distinct dimensions, or separate clusters of measures, emerge. One is related to gross size, with the closest correlation among military expenditure and total GNP, with slightly lesser correlations of those two with population, science journals, and diplomats received. The other concerns development, with GNP per capita, literacy, and low infant deaths closely related. Science journals and diplomats also bear some relation to this cluster, showing the combined importance of size and development in their achievement.

The relationship among these sources of influence means that a nation can indeed invest some current resources in the hope of obtaining more of the same or different kinds of resources in later years. The present can be used to provide for the future; alternatively, the future of one kind of influence base can easily be *squandered* by a too ready exhaustion of a source of influence in the present. We noted that power may be exercised at the cost of affection. More clearly, military power may be bought now at the cost of future wealth, well-being, and enlightenment. Resources are scarce, and every time a government buys more armaments it gives up something, whether or not it knows or intends the sacrifice. In earlier research, for instance, I discovered that there were rather regular patterns of tradeoffs on the ups and downs of defense spending in the United States.[11] Typically, an extra dollar of military expenditure was obtained by taking 71 cents from consumption or other government spending programs, but 29 cents came from investment (fixed capital formation). Furthermore, the civilian government spending programs included 8 cents for education and another 2 cents for health and hospitals. Thus almost 40 percent of current military spending was borne by programs intended to build a wealthier, healthier, better-educated population. In politics too, a form of cost-benefit analysis is required. As a general and Republican President once put it, "Every gun that is made, every warship launched,

---

[10] Much of the recent interest in this phenomenon stems from the very stimulating work of John Galtung, notably his "A Structural Theory of Aggression," *Journal of Peace Research*, 2, 1964, pp. 95–119.

[11] See Bruce M. Russett, *What Price Vigilance? The Burdens of National Defense* (New Haven: Yale University Press, 1970), Chapter 5. On opportunity costs see also John C. Harsanyi, "Measurement of Social Power, Opportunity Costs, and the Theory of Two-Person Bargaining Games," *Behavioral Science*, 7, 1 (January 1962), pp. 67–80.

Table 15-10
Correlations among Some Influence-Base Indicators

	Size of nation			Richness of life in nation				Deference measure
	GNP	*Area*	*Popula-tion*	*GNP per capita*	*Science journals*	*Literacy*	*Infant deaths*	*Diplomats received*
Military expenditures	**.94**	.38	**.77**	.57	**.81**	.60	−.45	**.86**
GNP		.37	**.81**	**.63**	**.87**	.60	−.42	**.85**
Area			**.62**	−.14	.23	−.26	.25	.43
Population				.05	**.61**	.11	−.05	**.79**
GNP per capita					**.67**	**.84**	−**.73**	.36
Science journals						**.73**	−.53	**.72**
Literacy							−**.78**	.39
Infant death rate								−.24

Note: For technical reasons skewed distributions were normalized by logarithmic transformations before correlating. Correlations greater than .60 are printed in bold face for emphasis.

every rocket fired signifies, in the final sense, a theft from those who hunger and are not fed, those who are cold and are not clothed. This world in arms is not spending money alone. It is spending the sweat of its laborers, the genius of its scientists, the hopes of its children."[12]

We began the chapter with some comments about the application of force. With military power, especially nuclear weapons but also the heavy firepower of conventional bombing and artillery, a nation may be able to exercise a great deal of force, inflicting tremendous physical damage. But there is an essential distinction between force and control. If it is to function usefully as a means of political influence, force usually must be subject to control; he who would apply it must be able to do so selectively, with discrimination. This is true even with nuclear force in the context of central or general war. Strategists long ago realized that the mere possession of hydrogen bombs and missiles did not satisfy even the requirements of military deterrence. An acceptable system had to be one that the political leaders could control even under warfare conditions, so that bombs might be unleashed or withheld according to some political purpose.

Even conventional weapons form a blunt instrument. In bombing North Vietnam in the 1960s, for instance, the United States government attempted not so much to inflict a lot of damage—that would have been easy—but to inflict it selectively against military targets while sparing civilians and areas such as ports where foreign (especially Chinese and Russian) citizens might be. As the situation developed, it became clear that the need to use the force selectively was so great that it was impossible to apply enough force to be militarily and politically effective. Nevertheless it required more than three years to reach the 1968 decision to stop (for a while) bombing North Vietnam.

Finally, therefore, we return to the aspect of enlightenment, the ability to *learn*, as the key element in the exercise of influence. Nations like individuals, must ultimately be able to change their methods, and even their goals, when earlier ones have outlived their usefulness.

---

[12] President Eisenhower, Speech to the American Society of Newspaper Editors, April 16, 1953.

16

Components of an Operational Theory
of International Alliance Formation

Explaining or predicting patterns of alliance among nations has long been a central concern in the study of international politics and organization. There is, however, no satisfactory theory to indicate what nations will ally with what others in the system. This chapter is intended to outline an approach to the construction of such a comprehensive theory, suggesting some of the definitions and propositions that would be central to the effort, as well as some of the research obstacles that would be faced.

First, we shall indicate the context of the problem:

1. There are three or more nations.
2. The situation is at least partly competitive; i.e., there is no single outcome that will maximize the gains of each of the participants.
3. No single nation is either in a dominant position—it can win without allying itself with any other nation—or in a position of potential veto—it must be included in any winning coalition.
4. There is the possibility of a *decision*, usually a war, that would result in major and notable different gains or losses to the various nations in the system.

Consistent with point 4 we will limit our attention to alliances formed in response to the threat or actuality of military conflict; that is, to alliances formed during wartime, in anticipation of war, or for the purpose of deterring war. Certainly these are not the only reasons for concluding something that

Reprinted from *Journal of Conflict Resolution*, XII, 3 (September 1968).

may be labelled an alliance—for example, one government may ally with another as a means of legitimizing itself with its own population, or to obtain foreign aid for economic development or for perfecting its military and police instruments of control over its populace. The different partners to an alliance very often have *complementary* interests without many *common* ones, and where one partner is not seriously concerned with military security the approach I shall suggest below is not likely to be as productive. We shall discuss ways of distinguishing among alliances according to their function so as to concentrate analytical efforts on those that the theory is intended to confront.

PREFERENCES AND THE SIZE PRINCIPLE

Two seemingly contradictory theoretical perspectives have been brought to bear on the question of what it is that determines alliance patterns. Much of the traditional literature, perhaps in part influenced by the Cold War, stresses the various bonds of community among nations, suggesting that countries ally with others that share certain common interests. Frequently ties of common ideology, similar political or economic institutions, language, culture, and religion are mentioned, as sometimes are bonds of economic interest such as trade.[1] Certainly the observer can find many examples in the history of past decades when nations sharing such characteristics did indeed ally with one another and there have been numerous studies of particular cases, but no study of the frequencies and conditions of such alliances has ever been done on a comparative basis. The lack of such a study is serious because the prima facie case for common interests so defined as the determining factor of alliances is not at all strong; on the contrary, the most casual recall brings to mind many instances where these bonds failed to produce joint action or to prevent the states concerned from joining opposing alliances. It seems likely that such factors explain some of the variance in alliance formation, but that they are not of equal importance, and that the role of each varies with some other circumstances. Accordingly, some other principle must also be at work.

George Liska summarizes another point of view which has gained currency and refinement in a variety of recent studies: "Alliances are against, and only derivatively for, someone or something. The sense of community may consolidate alliances; it rarely brings them about."[2] This point of view is manifested most rigorously in various formulations derived from the theory of

---

[1] An example is Raymond Dawson, and Richard Rosecrance, "Theory and Reality in the Anglo-American Alliance," *World Politics*, 19, 1 (1966), 21–53, who purport to show that in the post-World War II period the ties of sentiment between Britain and the United States have prevailed where other interests pointed against continuing the alliance. My own past work, Bruce M. Russett, *Community and Contention: Britain and America in the Twentieth Century* (Cambridge, Mass.: M.I.T. Press, 1963), *International Regions and the International System* (Chicago: Rand McNally, 1967) and Chapter 12, this volume, on alliances has also stressed this kind of determinant.

[2] See George Liska, *Nations in Alliance* (Baltimore: The Johns Hopkins University Press, 1962), p. 12.

games as applied to more than two players. Most influential for political scientists is certainly that of William Riker.[3] It is built around the size principle; that is, the principle that the players will form that grouping which is the smallest winning coalition, that contains just enough power to gain the decision, but no more than is necessary for the purpose (allowing for lumpiness or indivisibilities due to the size of various actors). This is attributed to a desire on the part of the potential winners not to spread the winnings out among superfluous partners—the fewer the actors who must be rewarded, the greater the payoff to those who are rewarded.

While the theory rests upon an impressive piece of deductive reasoning, and some bits of empirical evidence as well, its limitations are severe. It is very nearly impossible to get a determinate solution when there are more than a few actors; with only five or six the complexities already become great. Most historical international systems of much interest, even those which are to a large degree bipolar, have had several middle level states whose adherence to one side or another exerted significant effects on the distribution of power in the system. In addition, the problems of measurement are substantial; Riker does not indicate how the weight of different states would be calculated for the purpose of assessing what would be the smallest winning coalition in *international* politics. If there is imprecision in an actor's perceptions of other actors' resources, the indeterminacies are compounded. (This is not, of course, to imply that this is a fault in Riker's work, which achieved enough else so as not to make this further demand appropriate.) And what happens when the two sides are, or appear to be, equally powerful? Then one would expect bonds of community to determine where the wavering state went.

Some other work has attempted to combine these two perspectives, the concern with common interests and the size principle, into a single theory. None of these has been applied to international politics, and the difficulties in so doing promise to be serious indeed. The basic work is by William Gamson, who has developed a formal model and tested it in small-group experiments and with historical data on coalitions in American party nominating conventions.[4] It too posits that a player will prefer the smallest winning coalition. He qualifies this, however, with the assumption that players will distinguish among such coalitions only within payoff *classes*, and not make very fine distinctions. That is, there may be two or more "smallest" winning coalitions of approximately the same total resources, between which a prospective member will, on those grounds, be indifferent. In such a case, predicting which coalition the player will join depends upon what Gamson calls his "nonutilitarian strategy preferences," which he measures as similarity of ideology

---

[3] See William Riker, *The Theory of Political Coalitions* (New Haven: Yale University Press, 1962). The classic nonmathematical statement in international relations is of course Hans J. Morgenthau, *Politics among Nations* (New York: Knopf, 1960) 3rd edition, Part 4.

[4] See William A. Gamson, "A Theory of Coalition Formation," *American Sociological Review*, 26, 3 (1961), pp. 373–82; "An Experimental Test of a Theory of Coalition Formation," *American Sociological Review*, 36, 4 (1961), pp. 565–73; and "Coalition Formation at Presidential Nomination Conventions," *American Journal of Sociology*, 58, 2 (1962), pp. 157–71.

and policy preference.[5] These "nonutilitarian" strategy preferences correspond to what we earlier called "ties of common interest" because they are not directly part of the *power* interests objectively resulting from winning or losing. They are important as they help to *define* the payoffs—more generally, the reward to a player is greater when the coalition is ideologically comfortable than when it is not. Though not mentioned by Gamson, it is also possible that the payoff might be increased by the defeat of certain ideologically anti-pathetic players. Nevertheless, in Gamson's formulation ideology remains a subordinate influence. Given total payoffs within the same class, the player will prefer the partner with the more similar ideology or who otherwise has the highest rank on his scale of nonutilitarian preferences. But ideological leanings will not cause him to go outside this payoff class to form a larger-than-winning coalition.

Thus the payoff for the *individual member* of a coalition varies with his share of the total payoff of the coalition and, to a degree, according to his non-utilitarian preferences for the coalition's composition. The payoff to the winning *coalition*, however, is constant regardless of the composition of the alliance—the value of winning does not depend, for the alliance as a whole, on *who* belongs to it, though it may under some circumstances vary with the relative *size* of the aggregate. This theory has been refined further and tested both in experimental situations and on the behavior of parties in parliamentary coalitions in Western Europe, by Michael Leiserson.[6] If applicable to international situations it would, for example, rule out for a very long time to come any possibility of a Soviet-American alliance against China. In addition to the ideological differences that would make such an alliance difficult, it would violate the size principle so long as China was notably weaker than the other two.

SOME SUGGESTIONS FROM HISTORICAL DATA

The evidence for the predictive power of a theory composed essentially of these elements is strong. In a variety of domains it seems to indicate the true outcome more frequently than could be expected by chance alone, and its

---

[5] Gamson, ibid., ably reviews the earlier work. On the role of ideology in a theory for national conventions, see also Frank Munger and James Blackhurst, "Factionalism in the National Convention, 1940–1960: An Analysis of Ideological Consistency in State Delegation Voting," *Journal of Politics*, 27, 2 (1965), pp. 375–94.

[6] Michael Leiserson, *Coalitions in Politics: A Theoretical and Empirical Study* (New Haven: Yale University, doctoral dissertation, 1966). John Harsanyi, "A Simplified Bargaining Model for the *n*-Person Cooperative Game," *International Economic Review*, 4 (May 1963), pp. 194–220, and "A General Theory of Rational Behavior in Game Situations," *Econometrica*, 34, 3 (July 1966), pp. 613–34, has provided a theory that explains the formation of coalitions as a function of communication bias. He says that if communication is free and unbiased all possible coalitions in the system will form at the same time, as specified in the ideal cross-pressures model of pluralism, but that where communication is hindered more permanent alliances, applying over many subissues, will form. In this context ideology and other non-utilitarian strategy preferences can be seen as communications biasers.

elements are found throughout the literature of international relations. It may, for example, explain much of the action of major states during World War II. The French government left its alliance and *surrendered* to Hitler in 1940 not only because it knew France to be beaten, but because it was confident Germany would win the rest of the war, defeating England. Italy entered the war against France for the same reason, expecting Germany to win and not wanting to be left on the sidelines. At the same time, its ideological ties to Germany were not especially strong. Italian fascism was not the same as nazism, and there were numerous antifascists prepared to form a government given the opportunity. Italy had no *defensive* common cause with Germany. Hence when Axis superiority was no longer apparent, the Italians had a strong motivation to switch sides whenever the opportunity presented itself, as it did after allied troops had landed.[7]

Furthermore, this perspective makes better sense of Hitler's decision to attack the Soviet Union than does any competing formulation of which I am aware. The Nazi-Soviet neutrality pact of August 1939 gave Germany a free hand against Poland and the Western allies without having to fear Russian attack, presenting the possibility of a quick German victory over France and Britain. (Whether Hitler expected that he actually would have to fight France and Britain is a controversial question.) But when, despite the defeat of France and the entry of Italy, the prospect of an immediate victory over Britain receded, the situation changed. Russia at this point became the critical component of any winning coalition. (I am assuming the Axis and Britain—by then receiving active American help short of war—were sufficiently well balanced that neither could be sure that it had achieved a smallest winning coalition except in the most marginal sense, requiring a very extended war of attrition which each would prefer if possible to avoid.) Since there were no notable ideological ties between Russia and either Britain or the Axis powers, nonutilitarian strategy preferences were essentially neutralized. Russia was thus presented with the opportunity of forming a coalition which, because of Russian entry, would decide the outcome of the war. This put each of the major belligerents into a dilemma. To win, they would have to enlist Russia on their own side, and thus share the winnings with the Soviets. But a failure to enlist the Soviets presented the other side with an opportunity to do so. "Winnings" in this context partly included booty such as reparations and territory (explicitly demanded by the Russians in conversation with Hitler), as well as predominant influence in the postwar world.

For the British the choice of the lesser evil was obvious, and they had to hope for Russian entry on their own side, though there was little they could do actively to encourage it. Hitler, however, did have a real choice. Rather than pay the high price implied by Russian support, a price that might have left Germany dangerously weak relative to the Soviets in the postwar world,

---

[7] See Paul Kecskemeti, *Strategic Surrender* (Stanford, Calif.: Stanford University Press, 1958).

Hitler could attack Russia himself. By doing so he could remove the possibility that Russia would later come into the war against him, and obtain Russian resources for use in prosecuting the war against Britain. The particular strategic situation of the time, which greatly diminished Britain's ability to bring its power to bear in a militarily effective way against a *defensive* Germany, raised the possibility of a successful German attack on the Soviet Union, which might be isolated and defeated before Britain could do anything to prevent its collapse.[8] Hence, given this situation and an inability to conclude a peace with Britain, Hitler's attack on Russia may well have been the most "rational" thing for him to have done. It was surely a gamble, and Hitler's own personality, rather than "rational" strategic calculation, may have accounted for his decision. But that decision may well be fully compatible with a theory which does not *require* any assumptions about peculiar personality characteristics.

Before we can test this theory rigorously, however, severe problems of conceptualization and measurement must be overcome. Furthermore, there are several variants of the theory that give somewhat different predictions under particular circumstances, and these must be spelled out.

SOME ALTERNATIVES TO THE SIZE PRINCIPLE

The basic assumption of the game-theoretic approach is that the distribution of benefits accruing to the members of the winning coalition will be some function of the relative contribution each member makes to the resources of the coalition. (Usually this function is assumed to be directly *proportional* to their relative contributions, but it would not change the outcomes if some other transformation, such as a distribution proportional to the square or the logarithm of their contributions, were assumed.) It is not clear, however, the degree to which this assumption is empirically rather than normatively based and, if empirically based, the precise conditions under which it applies. Riker developed his theory for zero-sum situations, and is unclear about the degree to which he thinks it applicable to non-zero-sum games. Despite the final chapter of his book, neither he nor many other observers would regard most international politics situations as strictly zero-sum. And most of the empirical work so far done on coalitions has been in small-group laboratory situations, certainly not in international politics. Several alternative assumptions are plausible under certain circumstances.

---

[8] It seems to me likely that, by most indices, the combination of Germany and Italy would actually appear as slightly *more* powerful than Britain, but that they were prevented by geography from bringing this power to bear for a clear-cut victory. If so, the above case fits the Riker theory even better, since Russia-Britain would be a smaller winning coalition than Russia-Germany-Italy. By this theory Russia would eventually have come in against Hitler anyway, and the best Hitler could do was to hope by surprise attack to defeat Russia before its power potential could be brought fully into play. Operation Barbarossa may not have been promising, but the alternative—waiting—was even worse.

1. If the game is perceived as terminal, or episodic and unrelated to further plays of related games, it seems reasonable to hypothesize that the players' relative resources will *not* enter into their calculations. Suppose we have an experimental situation where A is assigned a constant weight half again as great as B and twice as great as C, and the players are university students who are unacquainted with each other. After all plays the winners are allowed to divide the modest winnings as they see fit, but then they go back to their classes. The "weights" assigned are in fact irrelevant to the outcome of each game since a coalition must be formed (no single player can win) and the size of the payoff is constant whatever the particular coalition happens to be. In no further play of this or any other game is the relative strength of the players affected by the distribution of winnings within a coalition. Thus, regardless of the assigned weights, each player can make an equal contribution to forming the winning alliance—there is no advantage or disadvantage in winning by a big margin, e.g., AB versus C. All three possible combinations "should" be equally likely according to assumptions of rationality.

It happens, however, that even under these limiting assumptions all coalitions are *not* equally likely. The experimental evidence is mixed, but even with rather careful attempts to allow the episodic nature of plays to become apparent, the smallest winning coalition is *somewhat* more likely to form than are the others. It becomes less likely with repeated plays, and it seems eventually to become apparent to the players that the "power" distribution is not relevant to winning the game.[9] But in the early stages at least, the weights do affect the players' behavior even though normatively such behavior may in some ways be "irrational." Possibly the weights contribute to a prominent solution for the players.

International politics is of course a continuous game, not an episodic one. Resources are redistributed, incrementally or substantially, at frequent intervals. Accordingly it appears reasonable to expect that the relative power positions of the members *will* affect their coalition-forming behavor. Implicit or explicit bargaining must go on, and the distribution of winnings from one decision will affect the relative power positions of the players in the rest. Even in the most extreme zero-sum case, a war in which the loser is annihilated, the members of the winning coalition still must continue the political process among themselves after the war is concluded.

2. There are several theories that take the relative sizes of the players into effect, not all of which give quite the same results as Riker's. Theodore Caplow, for instance, assumes merely that each player wishes to control the others, including the other members of his coalition.[10] Hence with the weights

[9] See H. H. Kelley, and A. J. Arrowood, "Coalitions in the Triad: Critique and Experiment," *Sociometry*, 23 (1960), pp. 231–44. The review by Dina Zinnes, "Coalition Theories and the Balance of Power" (Bloomington, Ind.: Indiana University, 1967, mimeo.), is helpful on some of the experimental literature.

[10] Theodore Caplow, "A Theory of Coalitions in the Triad," *American Sociological Review*, 21 (1956), pp. 489–93, and "Further Development of a Theory of Coalitions in the Triad," *American Journal of Sociology*, 64 (1959), pp. 488–93.

in the example specified above, each actor will prefer to ally with an actor weaker than himself. *B* will prefer a winning alliance with *C* rather than one with *A* where, though victorious, he would still be weaker than *A*. But without the size principle operating as specified by Riker, *A* will be indifferent between *B* and *C* as partners, since both are weaker, and *C* will be indifferent between *A* and *B* as partners. Thus *AC* or *BC* can form, and will be equally likely, but *AB* will be rejected by *B*. Riker of course predicts only *BC* for this situation because, unlike Caplow, he assumes that *C* will be able to bargain for a larger share of the joint rewards when he is in a position of moderate inferiority to his partner rather than one of great inferiority.

3. Yet another version is offered by Jerome Chertkoff,[11] whose probabilistic theory says that since

A prefers *B* and *C* equally

and

C prefers *A* and *B* equally,

but

B prefers *C*,

BC is more likely than *AC*, but *AC* will occur half as often as a result of their indifference for each between *B* and the other (*AB* never happens since it is actively rejected by *B*). The limited experimental evidence regarding these theories is ambiguous since some relevant conditions are not always well controlled by the experimenters. On the whole Caplow's theory is supported least, but there is as yet no firm basis for choosing between the Riker and Chertkoff versions.

The experimental evidence is of only limited relevance to international relations situations, except to induce a certain skepticism about the empirical basis of Riker's assumptions. Despite the obviously continuous nature of the game, it is possible to specify a number of international situations, especially under non-zero-sum conditions, where the size principle would not work as hypothesized.

4. One is the *deterrent* situation, where a status quo alliance is formed for the purpose of *avoiding* a "decision," or war, that might shift the distribution of resources and in any case would be costly to fight. Here a very large coalition would be attractive if each member made *some* contribution and had confidence in the efficiency of deterrence. Here, as in some other international politics situations, *avoidance* of a "decision" constitutes the payoff, and comes to each member equally regardless of the size of its contributions.[12]

---

[11] Jerome Chertkoff, "The Effects of Probability of Future Success on Coalition Formation," *Journal of Experimental and Social Psychology*, 2, 3 (July 1966), pp. 265–77, and "A Revision of Caplow's Coalition Theory," *Journal of Experimental and Social Psychology*, 3 (1967).

[12] See Mancur Olson, Jr., *The Logic of Collective Action* (Cambridge, Mass.: Harvard University Press, 1966) and Olson and Richard Zeckhauser, "An Economic Theory of Alliances," *Review of Economics and Statistics*, 48, 3 (August 1966), pp. 266–79.

5. A variant of the deterrent situation is one where an actor is concerned primarily with the stability of his domestic political system and uses an external threat to enforce domestic unity. Within limits he may prefer an apparently *large* external threat, and may not wish to join a potentially winning coalition. This will probably not be a common situation, but it is possible, and shades over into the consideration that alliances often serve functions other than military security alone.

6. The deterrent situation, where a large coalition is sought for the sake of security, is a subset of a larger class of coalitions influenced by the completeness and accuracy of *information*. If information is poor the coalition members cannot be sure they will win, but can only estimate some subjective *probability* of victory. They may well form what seems in the most likely event to be a *larger*-than-winning coalition just to minimize the chance that their coalition will turn out to be less than winning. Wayne Francis has found in American state legislatures that the *proportion* of the total number of legislators sought as allies by other representatives varies with the size of the legislature.[13] His original hypothesis was deduced from the assumption that the proportion of relevant information they possessed about the membership would vary inversely with the size of the legislative chamber. In international relations, estimates of relative national power are notoriously hard to make, especially where fine calibration is required, so we would expect this aspect to be an important influence. We would expect larger-than-winning international coalitions where (*a*) the system is composed of many states, and (*b*) where intelligence gathering is poor or effectively hindered by border control and internal security.

7. Under some conditions more than a prospective majority of the resources of the system may be required to entice a state to enter the war, since if the balance is close the expected costs of fighting the war may well exceed any expected gains. In this case the total payoffs to the coalition are *not* invariant with its size. Empirically we must discover when nations will prefer to have a small share of a big net payoff from a quick, easy war (e.g., the Polish partitions, or the de facto alliance of powers to coerce China in the Boxer Rebellion) and when they will prefer a bigger share of a smaller payoff obtained by a smallest winning coalition through a war of attrition.

8. Another consideration involves the greater complexity of a world larger than three powers. If *A*, *B*, *C*, *D* equal 4, 2, 2, 1 respectively, there are two general possibilities. Either *A* can combine with any one of the smaller players or the three small ones together can win over *A*. Both *AD* and *BCD* are smallest winning coalitions. Experimental evidence shows, however, that *AD*

---

[13] Wayne L. Francis, "Coalitions in American State Legislatures," in *The Study of Coalition Behavior*, Sven Groennings, E. W. Kelley, and Michael Leiserson, editors (New York: Holt, Rinehart and Winston, 1970).

is more frequent, and even *AB* and *AC* are not uncommon. The reason, it seems, is that the one step (*A* plus *B*, *C*, or *D*) coalition is easier to form than is the two step combination of *B*, *C*, and *D*, which requires more complex bargaining.[14] Here the *costs of bargaining* become an important variable.

Hence the focus of research must be on the *conditions* under which the size principle will be operative. It may be useful to approach the study with a kind of *marginal utility analysis*, asking what the tradeoffs of cost and benefit are for violating the size principle under different circumstances. While the laboratory work has been useful for generating alternative hypotheses and identifying some of the key variables, an unavoidable step, and probably the next one, must be hypothesis testing with actual international relations data, in a variety of systems and on many alliance decisions.

NATIONAL POWER AND OTHER MEASUREMENT PROBLEMS

Perhaps the most critical challenge to an operational theory stems from an old bogy—the measurement of national power or resources. We will not have the advantage of the laboratory experiments where the weights are simply assigned. And we are handicapped far more than in attempts to apply these theories to legislatures or party conventions, where the resources of each member or delegate are equal—one vote (excluding, of course particular advantages some delegates have for persuading others to go along with them). No single index can ever identify all the subtleties involved in national power, but it may be possible to identify at least the gross differences, to the point where the theory acquires some predictive power.

A comparison of existing military establishments, as measured by expenditures or force levels, is attractive, especially for wartime alliances. They are limited by power base (resources) but indicate a regime's willingness to allocate resources to the war. They would help to distinguish between the resource endowment and that proportion of the endowment that is allocated to foreign policy pursuits.[15] Such a focus, however, ignores the commensurability problems between grossly different military establishments, as between a land power and a sea power, or one heavily dependent upon nuclear deterrence as against one utilizing large but poorly equipped conventional armies. No common index like total number of military personnel or size of military budget would control this satisfactorily. More seriously, a comparison of existing military establishments would omit proper consideration of the mobilization

---

[14] See Lloyda M. Shears, "Patterns of Coalition Formation in Two Games Played by Male Tetrads," *Behavioral Science*, 12, 2 (1967), pp. 130–7.

[15] A good discussion making this point is that of George Modelski, *A Theory of Foreign Policy* (New York: Praeger, 1960), Chapter 2. Much of his discussion of power can be operationalized by comparative national budget analysis.

base so critical in sustained conflict, as the United States demonstrated in two wars despite the initial unimpressive character of its defense forces.

A *power base* index or indices thus seems more appropriate. One of the best single summary indices would be gross national product (GNP), except for the difficulties inherent in conversion to a common currency unit.[16] Probably even better, especially as it avoids the latter problem, would be total fuel and electric energy consumption for each nation. Energy consumption figures have been found to be highly correlated with GNP data,[17] and also are already expressed in a common unit which has more meaning in cross-national comparision. Furthermore, the data are relatively comparable and reliable, and extend back in time into periods where for most countries adequate GNP figures are nonexistent.

While it is not sensitive to the efficiency and organization of the economy, this is probably as good an index as can be devised, especially for situations where a mobilization base can be brought to bear. But a serious difficulty remaining is associated with the need to control any index for the distance between the nation in question and the point where its power is to be exerted. Thus the United States is a member both of the global international system and of virtually any regional subsystem imaginable; Italy and Indonesia are surely part of their regional subsystems but even they might not critically affect alliance patterns in the global system, and for many such worldwide analyses they could be ignored. Conceptually the measurement of declining power as a function of distance is the same as Boulding's[18] loss-of-strength gradient, though empirically it is very difficult to measure and doubtless is not a smooth function—terrain and transportation facilities would be highly salient. Some relevant work is being done by Albert Wohlstetter, stemming originally from his work on the relation of distance to the cost and effectiveness of strategic air bases in the 1950s.[19] Because of the loss-of-strength gradient or other strategic conditions the value of a state to one coalition may exceed

[16] See A. F. K. Organski, *World Politics* (New York: Knopf, 1958), Charles Hitch, and Dayton McKean, *The Economics of Defense in the Nuclear Age* (Cambridge, Mass.: Harvard University Press, 1960), and B. M. Russett, *Trends in World Politics* (New York: Macmillan, 1965), Chapter 1, for discussion of these complexities, with an argument that total GNP is nevertheless still a useful summary index. For some of the subtleties, Klaus Knorr, *The War Potential of Nations* (Princeton, N. J.: Princeton University Press, 1956) remains excellent.

[17] See Norton Ginsburg, *Atlas of Economic Development* (Chicago: University of Chicago Press, 1961) and Theodore Caplow and Kurt Finsterbusch, "A Matrix of Modernization," Paper presented at the annual meeting of the American Sociological Association, 1964.

[18] K. E. Boulding, *Conflict and Defense* (New York: Harper, 1962).

[19] See Albert Wohlstetter, "Distant Wars and Far-Out Estimates." Paper presented to the annual meeting of the American Political Science Association, New York, 1966, and Wohlstetter, et al. *Selection and Use of Strategic Airbases*, R-266 (Santa Monica, Calif.: RAND Corporation, 1954). See also the important if still incomplete work, being done in geography, discussed for example in Gunnar Olsson, *Distance and Human Interaction: A Review and Bibliography* (Pennsylvania, Regional Science Research Institute, Bibliography Series No. 2, 1965), and William Warntz, *Macrogeography and Income Fronts* (Pennsylvania, Regional Science Research Institute, Monograph Series No. 3, 1965.)

its value to another (e.g., because of geography it cannot as effectively bring its resources to bear).

Clearly the resources of the United States for action in the Caribbean are somewhat greater than in Asia. Probably the index can be modified in such a way as to make any loss of explanatory power tolerable. It is essential, in any case, to avoid an index so subtle, supple, and sophisticated as not to correspond well with the general image that would be possessed by national decision makers with reasonable intelligence capabilities.

This leads to yet another difficulty. We are, after all, working toward a theory that will explain the actions of nation-states in the past; when we are considering the resources various states might contribute to a coalition, the theory must address itself to the *perceptions* of resources that were available to decision makers at the time, not to some perfect objective measure. In principle it might be possible to comb national archives for the actual intelligence estimates; in practice it may be necessary to assume (*a*) that all decision makers have the same information on the resources of various actors, and (*b*) that said information agrees with the indices.[20] Singer and Small's ranking of countries by diplomatic status (i.e., attributed diplomatic importance)[21] might be a useful first step in checking *perceptions* in a peacetime international system, but there are some obvious anomalies (e.g., the high apparent status of Spain in the twentieth century) that would keep this from being more than a preliminary measure. Possibly in a late stage of refinement the theory can incorporate an element for the confidence with which an actor holds a given power estimate; that is, the *subjective probability* he assigns to a given coalition's victory.

One final difficulty has to do with the aggregation of power in an alliance. It should be intuitively obvious, and our recent experience with NATO provides a wealth of empirical confirmation, that the power of an alliance is not equal to the sum of the power of its individual members. Especially in the context of modern weapons systems, national military establishments are subject to substantial economies of scale. A small nation, spending one-fifth as much on aircraft as a large one, will not be able to maintain one-fifth as large an air force of the same caliber as its major power ally's. Even if it bought equipment

---

[20] I am well aware that perceptions of other states' resources often vary from "objective truth" and that two different states may reach different estimates of the resources of a third party. (See for example Samuel P. Huntington, "Arms Races: Prerequisites and Results," in *Public Policy*, Carl J. Friedrich and Seymour E. Harris, editors [Cambridge, Mass.: Harvard University Press, 1958], pp. 41–86). It may be hypothesized, however, that where the formation of an alliance is at stake decision makers' "motivation" and ability to secure adequate intelligence will keep the error small enough so as not seriously to degrade attempts to test the theory. This whole discussion may seem more deterministic than it is intended to be. I mean merely that it should be possible to measure resources with enough precision so as to predict with results much better than chance. Failures of prediction will doubtless occur, stemming both from poor measurement and from exogenous variables.

[21] J. David Singer and Melvin Small, "The Composition and Status Ordering of the International System, 1815–1940," *World Politics*, 18, 2 (January 1966), pp. 236–82.

from its ally, and so did not have the diseconomies of a short production run, the unit cost of logistics and maintaining spare parts is very great for a small force.[22]

Probably much of this could be controlled with care. It would be more serious for current alliances than for pre-World War II ones, when technology was simpler and economies of scale probably smaller. It is less serious for comparing large and middle level powers (e.g., the United States and France or Britain) than when applied to differences as great as between the United States and Greece or Norway, and the theoretical focus of the effect should be primarily on explaining the alliance decisions of the larger powers. For the modern alliances a fair degree of control could probably be achieved by discounting the power index (energy consumption, or defense expenditures, or military personnel) by a coefficient for the relation of that index to the total number of modern weapons (such as first-line combat aircraft). Or the number of military personnel could be weighted by an index of firepower capability. Ideally, still greater refinement could be provided by a weight for aircraft airtime or days of operation to allow for the effect of poor logistics.[23]

A more disturbing aspect, however, stems from the fact that not all the military expenditure of alliance members, even if economically efficient, contributes to the joint strength of the alliance. Approximately one-third of British and French defense spending goes to their nuclear deterrent forces, which, though they *may* be worthwhile to the British and French, provide only a very small increment to the collective power of NATO. Other examples for different countries would include ground forces that cannot be deployed to areas of alliance interest though they serve an internal security function for the particular nation. Proper discounting coefficients for these effects would be hard to create, but a failure to take them into account would exaggerate the alliance's total strength.

This list of caveats for the measurement of power seems formidable indeed, though imaginative research may make it manageable. A substantial inductive component would be essential to any analysis in which the investigator was willing to try several different approaches with a good deal of flexibility, keeping an open mind about which one would have more explanatory power. Certainly the precise techniques and weighting factors would vary over historical time-periods and probably over geographical areas or economic systems. It should be far easier to obtain measures that would *rank order* nations by power than ones that would produce a precise calibration for an internal measure. In the end, at least a rough interval measure will be necessary, but

---

[22] Andrew Marshall, *Determinants of NATO Force Posture*, P-3280 (Santa Monica, Calif.: RAND Corporation, 1966).

[23] This kind of procedure would take into account the fact that the proportionate (to GNP) military expenditures of alliance members seem to decline directly with total GNP, an effect explained by economists with the theory of collective goods. See Mancur Olson, Jr. and Richard Zeckhauser, "An Economic Theory of Alliances," *Review of Economics and Statistics*, 48, 3 (August 1966), pp. 266–79.

some recent computational advances suggest ways in which rank order measures, giving judgments of more or less for all pairs in a set, can be converted into approximate interval scales.[24]

Should the Caplow or Chertkoff versions of the theory specified in points 2 and 3 of the third section of this chapter ("Some Alternatives to the Size Principle") prove to have good explanatory power, a number of these measurement problems would be greatly eased. According to those versions, we need only rank order information on power (plus whether the power of A is less than B and C combined) to predict the alliance pattern. The only size assumption retained would be that a nation will never ally with a stronger power (or alliance) against a power (or alliance) that is weaker than itself. If *both* the alternative powers or alliances were weaker (or stronger) than itself, then the choice would be determined by the middle power's preference or by nonutilitarian preferences. Thus we could avoid having to measure the relative size of possible partners within broad classes, as compared with any state; we could reduce the classes to two (those larger and those smaller); and for the entire system we could be satisfied with the ranks.

The international *system* to be studied may be the global system for the twentieth century or, in earlier periods, a regional subsystem if "sufficiently" closed. Latin America in the nineteenth century would almost certainly be such a case; the ancient Greek city-state system might also be. (It is not clear whether Persia would be included in the Greek system.) For purposes of the theory the states concerned would include any nation that could, with some possible combination of one or more of the more powerful states, determine which of two opposing coalitions would win.

The kinds of nonutilitarian strategy preferences, or bonds of common interest, that may operate to affect choices probably vary considerably over time. Ideology has not always been as important a variable as it may be today. In any research effort covering a long time period, one would have to be alert for surrogates—dynastic ties, perhaps, or bonds of economic interest.[25] The hypothesis is that there would be some kind of preference that would play an important though subordinate role in the choice of alliance partners; the precise nature of those preferences might vary substantially between systems.

---

[24] See Roger Shepard, "The Analysis of Proximities with an Unknown Distance Function," *Psychometrika*, 28, 2 (June 1963), pp. 125–39 and "The Analysis of Proximities with an Unknown Distance Function," *Psychometrika*, 28, 3 (September 1963), pp. 219–46; J. B. Kruskal, "Multidimensional Scaling by Optimizing Goodness of Fit to a Nonmetric Hypothesis," *Psychometrika*, 29, 1 (March 1964), pp. 115–29; and James C. Lingoes, "An IBM-7090 Program for Guttman-Lingoes Smallest Space Analysis," *Behavioral Science*, 10, 2 (April 1965), pp. 183–4, "An IBM-7090 Program for Guttman-Lingoes Smallest Space Analysis," *Behavioral Science*, 10, 4 (October 1965) p. 487, and "An IBM-7090 Program for Guttman-Lingoes Smallest Space Analysis," *Behavioral Science*, 11, 1 (January 1966), pp. 75–6.

[25] In the current international system, at least, many of these bonds are highly correlated with one another. For evidence that ties of cultural similarity, political outlook, economic interest, and intergovernmental institutions tend strongly to coincide, see Bruce M. Russett, *International Regions and the International System* (Chicago: Rand McNally, 1967). Ideology per se was probably quite unimportant to alliance patterns in Europe during 1871–1918.

In the case of ideology-cum-political system types, some adaptation of the Almond and Coleman[26] typology probably would be adequate for a rank order of classes, though not initially for an interval scale with fine distinctions. In any case, this would not be a simple spectrum or one-dimensional ordering. The "distance" between Communist and Fascist states, for instance, would have to be specified as equivalent to one or more categories on the basis of consultations with experts. The coding of countries into categories would also depend to some extent on expert judgment, though certain objective indicators, such as those concerning the presence and characteristics of elections, would be satisfactory for the majority of classificatory decisions.

DISTRIBUTING PAYOFFS WITHIN THE COALITION

The problem of side payments must be faced. Most theories assume that the distribution of benefits within an alliance is some function of the relative size of the partners; a function that may or may not be constant over time and in different systems. Sometimes, however, a prospective partner may be able, by the criticality and timing of his contribution, to demand a special *side payment* for adherence to an alliance, and the prospect of such a side payment may determine with which of two potential cheapest winning coalitions a state may line up (instead of ideology or similar nonutilitarian strategy preferences). This was an extremely relevant consideration for Italy in 1915, and perhaps for other states in periods when ideological or constitutional differences were not great. Side payments may also be offered as a means of "buying" neutrality. In the present state of mathematical theory, side payments can only be handled with the assumption of "transferable utility," which requires that the utility of the good in which payment is made (e.g., a piece of territory) have the same utility to A, who gives it up, as to B, who receives it as his reward for entering the alliance.[27] In international politics such as assumption would be extremely hard to justify, and in many instances manifestly false. It is not credible, for example, that some Italian ethnic areas in Austria-Hungary, which in 1915 France and Britain could promise to Italy if Austria were defeated, had the same utility to each of the allies. But without such an assumption the side payment refinement may be unmanageable, and in existing game-theoretic models one cannot properly consider anything else as a side payment.

A working hypothesis, always subject to disproof, would be that the failure to incorporate side payments in the theory would not seriously degrade its explanatory power. Certainly, for the offer of a side payment to be accepted by a wooed coalition partner, there must be reasonable prospect that the coali-

---

[26] Gabriel Almond and James Coleman, editors, *The Politics of the Developing Areas* (Princeton, N.J.: Princeton University Press, 1960).

[27] Leiserson, op. cit.

tion indeed has the strength to be a winning one. And if there is some other potential coalition that is cheaper, the wooer may have no incentive to offer a side payment to a state whose power is larger than necessary to gain the decision.

PEACETIME AND WARTIME ALLIANCES

It will be necessary to distinguish between alliances formed in relative peacetime and wartime alliances, probably including in the latter case those concluded when war seemed imminent. The distinction in international politics concretizes some of the conditions that we listed earlier, under which the size principle might not hold. The outcome of a war is a *decision*, and where a decision is highly probable it becomes necessary for nations to take positions with reference to that decision. For example, it seems plausible to assume that there would be heavy pressures to be on the winning side. (Obviously it is better to be on the winning than on the losing side, yet it may also be important not to have been merely a neutral bystander, but to be able to claim, as the rights of an active participant, a share in the winnings.) Coalition formation in wartime does not always require reciprocation, since it is hard to prevent another power from declaring war on your enemy. There will also, however, be incentives to remaining neutral. The positive incentives include the benefits from being able, under some circumstances, to sell to both belligerents. The negative ones include the expected costs (costs times subjective probabilities) of fighting the war.

Once a greater-than-winning coalition has been produced, the question as between entrance and neutrality is not relevant to this theory. But before then it is relevant, and will not always be an easy prediction to make. It should be far easier to say which side a state will ally with *if* it chooses to enter into an alliance than to say *when and if* it will join any alliance at all. Probably some reference to the proportion of the resources of the total system that will be available to the prospective winners would help, on the assumption that the pressures to join some coalition are directly related to the potential dominating position of the prospective winners. Whether there is some fairly clear step level, as for example 50 percent or even less, would be the subject of investigation. These problems are less serious with legislatures or conventions, where the decision for or against a particular measure or candidate is usually clear-cut and will affect all participants. Even there, however, there may be benefits to be gained from abstention or ambiguity.

This question involves the *decision point* more generally. In legislatures or nominating conventions the problem is somewhat more manageable, since there are rules governing the size of the majority (simple, two-thirds, etc.) that will be required. (Although Gamson noticed that no coalition in a presidential nominating convention ever exceeded 40 percent—or 59 percent where the two-thirds rule was in operation—and still failed to nominate its candidate. At a point near but still short of a majority the bandwagon begins to roll inexorably.) Possibly in international alliances *more* than a simple majority of resources will always form the effective decision point. In a peacetime deterrent alliance a high decision point may be typical so that there will be as little doubt as possible, on the part of those in the smaller alliance, that the others do indeed have a winning coalition. We suggested earlier that the margin insisted on would vary inversely with the quality and completeness of information available. Another key variable will surely be the above-mentioned expected cost of fighting a prospective war. A peacetime alliance may also be constructed to gain the benefits of war without fighting it; i.e., to coerce a smaller alliance with the threat of overwhelming force.[28] It will be important to establish empirically what the conditions are under which the decision point will vary.

In wartime the competitive (zero-sum) elements of the situation are predominant; in peacetime the cooperative non-zero-sum elements play a greater role than in war, because of the common interest many or all states may have in avoiding the costs of conducting a war. Under these circumstances the role of ideology, political system, and other nonutilitarian preferences are likely to be more important, and the size principle may be violated more freely (or perhaps simply the effective decision point will change). Even here, however, it is unlikely that size will be ignored for long, despite ideological and other ties. Over extended periods, the utilitarian gains to be achieved from deserting a larger-than-smallest coalition (not necessarily deserting it with the intention of waging war) will be apparent and may chip away at the strength of the large alliance. A series of small decisions on relatively minor issues may change the distribution of resources within the system, but only as a result of great informational inadequacies would a larger-than-smallest winning coalition actually be so deserted as to lose a major decision with consequences equivalent to war.

In peacetime alliances it is obvious that states may *change coalitions*, and this is allowed for also in the theories of Gamson, Riker, etc., cited previously. Under some circumstances it may be useful to treat certain coalitions (or subsets of coalitions) as fixed—no member will change sides or leave the war without the others. Such a situation might possibly apply to highly integrated areas like present-day Benelux, in which case the entire subcoalition could be treated as an actor, rather than considering the separate nations individually.

In the real world, however, this situation is not likely often to apply, and it will usually be necessary to treat each nation as an actor, with the expectation that even in wartime alliances may shift. Certainly during World Wars I and

---

[28] Note Robert L. Rothstein, "Alignment, and Small Powers," *International Organization*, 20, 3 (1966), pp. 397–418: "In the past the influence of Small Powers rose only when they were sought as allies on the eve of a great-power conflict. But now, with great-power military conflict limited, they are still sought as allies or friends—but *in place of* not *because of* an imminent great-power war."

II a number of small states changed sides, as did Italy in World War II. Both Japan and Germany, in the latter conflict, prolonged their resistance to a clearly superior coalition in the hope of a split between the major alliance partners. In each case they expected not merely neutrality, but active assistance from one part of the existing alliance. (Hitler, of course, hoped the Americans and British would go to war against Russia; many Japanese leaders, more incredibly, seemed to think there was a prospect of Russian military help against the United States.[29] One major question that may be very hard to answer rigorously is why the breakup of a coalition is delayed beyond the conclusion of the war. According to the size principle as usually enunciated, the mere achievement of imminent victory would require a new cheapest winning coalition. Empirically it would appear that such shifts usually do occur, but *after*, not so often *during* the prosecution of the war.

If the determinants of wartime and peacetime alliances are different, other distinctions are likely also to matter. We suggested at the beginning that some arrangements that went by the label "alliance" were likely in fact to be unrelated to military considerations or to any potentially system-changing decision. Governments' goals in joining alliances are varied and not necessarily oriented to security from external threat. Will it be essential to search in great detail for the particular government's *motivations* to know which variant of our alliance theory to apply, or even whether the arrangement falls into a class where our theory is applicable at all? Possibly such extreme "preanalysis" will be required, but there should be some useful shortcuts. Very probably the difference will be manifested in visible characteristics of the arrangement itself —the mere presence of side payments is a clue to the presence of other interests, and particular kinds of side payments (e.g., foreign aid) may turn out to be closely associated with certain behavioral patterns. A systematic coding of all 137 "alliances" concluded in the international system since 1920 constitutes a beginning. In the following chapter I derive an empirically based typology of alliances according to institutional structures for consultation, planning, or coordinated military operations; the presence of side payments; the temporal proximity to war; the kind and degree of military contribution made by each partner; and so on. When this information is examined by powerful inductive techniques for identifying common patterns among large numbers of partly associated variables (e.g., factor analysis) it is almost certain that some interesting regularities will emerge.

More important, it is very likely that there will emerge certain *behavioral* regularities involving the size and composition of the alliances formed, and that the behavioral regularities will be correlated with particular institutional patterns or other attributes. Such inductive procedures hardly preclude the need for careful deductive theory formulation, but they may help us decide which kinds of "alliances" are likely to be most amenable to particular variants

---

[29] See Paul Keckskemeti, op. cit., and Robert J. C. Butow, *Japan's Decision to Surrender* (Stanford, Calif.; Stanford University Press, 1964).

of the deductive theory. And while they hardly preclude—in fact they *demand*—the need for careful and detailed coding rules for distinguishing alliances, they would free us from the need to specify *a priori* precisely what the uses of the typology were to be.

This chapter not only has discussed in some detail the principal components of a promising theory of international alliances, but has outlined some of the major theoretical and empirical problems in the way of its formulation and testing as an adequate explanation of events. There is at present *no* general theory of international alliance formation capable of being tested; creating such a theory will require the combination of many elements, with eventual refinement and parsimony. The challenges are so varied and extensive that they will require contributions by a number of researchers over a period of years. The immediate need is *not* for work in the mathematical theory of coalitions, but for the adaptation of existing theories, by appropriate assumptions, to a form that is useful for explaining international politics empirically.

17

An Empirical Typology of
International Military Alliances

This chapter offers an empirically based classification of international military alliances, a classification relevant to the development of theory about alliance formation, operation, and disintegration. Alliance is a widely and often imprecisely used term in international politics. Some writers use it to cover any agreement to cooperate; others employ it much as a synonym for alignment, as for example voting "allies" in the United Nations. The predominant usage is restricted to military matters, but even there ambiguity exists. For some an alliance is defined as a formal agreement to cooperate militarily; others would broaden the term to include cases of cooperation and protection even without a formal military commitment, such as the contemporary arrangements between the United States and Spain; still others would include any two powers who happen to be fighting on the same side in a war, whether or not there is any formal agreement or overt coordination.

While there may be good reason to employ the term alliance in any of these ways, providing one is precise in doing so, we will use a fairly limited definition here: *a formal agreement among a limited number of countries concerning the conditions under which they will or will not employ military force.* By this definition we explicitly exclude both nonmilitary alignments and informal or implicit military constellations. However important these phenomena may be, their differences make a narrower focus appropriate. Even so, quite a

---

Reprinted from *Midwest Journal of Political Science*, XV, 2 (May 1971), by permission of Wayne State University Press.

variety of arrangements are still covered, ranging from agreements to consult in the event of external attack, through pledges *not* to use force against one another (nonaggression or neutrality pacts), to promises to defend each other militarily or even to fight on the same side regardless of a war's origin (defensive and offensive alliances). The qualificaton "limited number of countries" is inserted only to exclude quasi-global collective security arrangements like the League of Nations Covenant, which bind all members to coalesce against any aggressor, even one of their own number. On the other hand, it does not require an alliance to make a specific identification of the threatening country;[1] it would seem more useful to use the presence or absence of such identification as one of the characteristics by which alliances may vary.

For theoretical purposes it is indeed necessary to subdivide the general category of alliance, even as that category is defined in a relatively limited way here. States enter into alliances for a variety of purposes, of which the pursuit of military security is but one. Sometimes the members' goals may be ones they hold in common, and in other instances their goals may be merely complementary. Even where military security is the central aim, it may be seen primarily as a result of *mutual* assistance, or alternatively a large state may in fact offer protection and a small state accept it even though the alliance may formally be written as a mutual commitment. Or the smaller state may accept alliance in anticipation of being able to reduce drastically its own defense efforts as a consequence of coming under the big power's umbrella. Under many circumstances a state may conclude an alliance not for military security at all, but rather for such "side payments" from its ally as territorial concessions, economic assistance, or legitimacy in the eyes of its own citizens. Or it may demand military advisors or arms shipments not to promote its external security, but in order better to restrain its own populace. If one wishes to study the formation, cohesion, maintenance, disintegration, wartime behavior, etc. of alliances, it would be foolish not to differentiate alliances according to their apparent purposes.[2]

Certainly there have been a number of efforts to distinguish alliances by function, behavior, degree of integration, or other criteria. Alliances concluded in wartime or immediately before war in anticipation of conflict may differ radically from those signed in peacetime. Singer and Small decided to discuss only alliances formed more than six months before the outbreak of major war.[3] They also limited themselves to mutual agreements, excluding unilateral guarantees. Among those pacts they did examine, they made a threefold distinction according to the character and strength of the military commitment incurred: ententes, neutrality or nonaggression pacts, and defensive alliances.

---

[1] E.g., the Rio Pact. See Jerome Slater, *A Revaluaton of Collective Security: The OAS in Action* (Columbus, Ohio: Mershon Social Science Program, Ohio State University Press, 1965).

[2] See Bruce M. Russett, *What Price Vigilance? The Burdens of National Defense* (New Haven: Yale University Press, 1970), Chapter 4, and Chapter 16, this volume.

[3] J. David Singer and Melvin Small, "Formal Alliances, 1815–1965: An Extension of the Basic Data," *Journal of Peace Research*, VI (August 1969), pp. 257–82.

John Herz distinguishes many modern alliances from more traditional undertakings by their implementation clauses, which lead to standardized equipment, unified commands, networks of military bases, and infrastructures which make a "hard shell" around the bloc.[4]

Hans J. Morgenthau offers a classification of alliances according to whether they are (1) mutual or unilateral, (2) temporary or permanent, (3) operative or inoperative, depending on their ability to coordinate members' policies, (4) general or limited in their distribution of benefits, and (5) complementary, identical, or ideological in their scope of interest.[5] K. J. Holsti identifies (1) the situation in which commitments are to become operational, (2) the type of commitments undertaken, (3) the degree of military cooperation or integration, and (4) the geographic scope of the treaty.[6] And Edwin Fedder gives a typology based upon the (1) number of states, (2) geographical limitations, (3) duration, (4) relative distribution of power among the members, (5) active or passive orientation, (6) unilateral or mutual nature of the guarantee, and (7) the security mechanism (i.e., joint forces-in-being versus a mere guarantee).[7]

None of these authors, however, has established systematically how many alliances fall in each category, or the degree to which the various criteria overlap and are redundant. Nor has there been any attempt to relate characteristics of membership, institutionalization, or terms of agreement, to behavior such as war-fighting alignments. Given the strong probability that there are such relationships it seems essential to make the effort. A preliminary classification is required just on the basis of the theoretically justified assumption that not all alliances can be explained in the same terms and that knowledge of their purposes should precede efforts to generalize about their consequences.[8] This discussion will differ from most previous efforts in that the alliance is the unit of analysis—a level between the sovereign state and the international system as a whole.

ALLIANCE CHARACTERISTICS

I have identified 137 international alliances in the period 1920–1957, drawing on and extending the list of Singer and Small.[9] The definition is the same as theirs except for addition of unilateral guarantees and wartime pacts, both of which they omitted. In order to see the development and consequences of alliances we take none signed later than 1957. We shall use that "universe" of

---

[4] *International Politics in the Atomic Age* (New York: Columbia University Press, 1965), p. 124.
[5] *Politics Among Nations* (3rd edition; New York: Knopf, 1960), p. 87.
[6] *International Politics* (Englewood Cliffs: Prentice-Hall, 1967), p. 12.
[7] *Theory and Process of Alliance*, forthcoming, Chapter 2.
[8] See Chapter 16, this volume.
[9] Op. cit.

recent alliances to try to derive an empirically based typology. All 137 alliances have been coded according to 44 variables derived from the above typologies and others, including both input and output characteristics, wherever the characteristics seemed important and capable of expression in operational terms. Neither unilateral guarantees nor wartime alliances are sufficiently numerous to deserve special treatment within the group. The complete list of alliances, codings, and qualifications is available,[10] but it is summarized under various general headings below.

I. Background and formation.
    A. Relation to international system.
        1. Year of signature.
        2. Number of members of the alliance who were major powers (major powers pre-1945: Britain, France, Germany, Russia, U.S., Japan, Italy; post-1945: U.S. and Russia only).
        3. Ratio of total population of the alliance to the world's population.
        4. Were all members European states?
        5. Did the text mention a specific threat from a particular region or country?
    B. Nature of commitment.
        1. Defense pact.
        2. Neutrality pact.
        3. Entente.[11]
    C. Intended duration.
        1. Were there specific provisions concerning the length of time the treaty was to last?
        2. If provisions present, for low long?
    D. Equality relations among members.
        1. Bilateral or multilateral?
        2. Ratio of the armed forces of the largest member to the total armed forces of the alliance.

---

[10] From the Inter-university Consortum for Political Research, Ann Arbor, Michigan, 48106.

[11] These classifications are essentially those of Singer and Small, except that entente and neutrality pact are not here considered to be mutually exclusive categories since some instruments contain the essential features of both. In an entente the signatories pledge themselves to consult or cooperate, or to do both, concerning political matters. In a defensive pact they commit themselves to lend direct military assistance to a treaty member subjected to armed aggression. The commitment need not require automatic intervention, but some phrase equivalent to that in NATO, ". . . an armed attack against . . . one member . . . shall be considered an attack against them all" must be present. Both NATO and the Warsaw Pact are thus coded as defensive alliances. SEATO, with a somewhat weaker and more qualified clause, is as an entente. A few readers may object to inclusion of neutrality pacts (agreements not to use force against a partner) in a study where the other pacts consider conditions when force *will* be used against others. Historically, however, contemporary observers have often treated neutrality pacts as at least implying further commitments regarding nonmembers (e.g., the Hitler-Stalin pact of 1939). In any case, if neutrality pacts really are different in important ways from the other type, that fact will emerge from the following analysis.

     3. Same ratio for domestic energy consumption.
  E. Prealliance bonds among members.
     1. Language, race, and religion.
       a. Some members have same principal or official languages?
       b. All members predominantly of the same race?
       c. Relative frequency with which the majority religion of one member of the alliance same as that of another member (religions: Christian, Moslem, Buddhist, Confucian).
     2. Geographical dispersion.
       a. Average distance between members' capitals.
       b. Average distance at nearest point between borders of members.
       c. Average distance at nearest point between members' borders, counting colonies as part of members' territory.
     3. Had most members of the alliance been allied at any time during previous 25 years?
     4. If any member of the alliance was at war during the previous 25 years, did half or more of the members of the current alliance fight on the same side? (If no war, coded blank.)[12]
     5. If any member was at war during the previous 25 years, did half or more members fight on opposite sides? (If no war, coded blank.)
II. Integration, duration, and termination.
  A. Kind and degree of cooperation and integration.
     1. Was there evidence of official contact between general officers or civilians in the defense ministry or related ministries of the members?
     2. Military aid (loan or grant for purchase of arms, not just outright purchase by one member from another).
     3. Was there either an integrated military command, or the military establishment of one member subordinated to another member through such procedures as one member's nationals holding positions in another's general staff?
     4. Military bases of one member on another's territory.
     5. Economic aid.
     6. Did the alliance establish any institutions, not including integrated military commands?
  B. Duration.
     1. Duration of alliance in years. (Blank if still in effect.)
     2. Actual duration as percentage of intended duration. (Blank if still in effect or no intended duration specified.)

---

[12] J. David Singer and Melvin Small, *The Wages of War: International War, 1815–1965, A Statistical Handbook* (New York: Wiley, 1971) was the basis of our list of war participants. To this we added the Vietnam War and the Six Days War in 1967 in the Middle East, using Singer and Small's criteria. Several instances, not in the Singer-Small list, of forced direct transfer of territory were also coded as war for our purposes.

3. Did the treaty last 100 percent of the time intended, *or*, was it replaced by a new treaty of at least equal commitment, *or*, if no intended duration specified, did it last at least 12 years? Treaties still in force will have lasted more than 12 years (no treaties signed since 1957 being analyzed) so they too are coded as positive on this item, regardless of intended duration.

C. Mode of termination.
   1. New alliance.
   2. Denunciation.
   3. War between members.
   4. One member ceased to be independent (not as a result of absorption by another member, which is coded as war).
   5. Expiration.
   6. Termination sanctioned by terms of treaty? (Items 1, 4, and 5, or 2 if denunciation permitted by terms of treaty and done under permitted terms.)
   7. Alliance still in effect.

D. Future war and alliance behavior.
   1. Did most members become parties to another alliance within 12 years of formation of this one?
   2. If no member of the alliance was at war when the alliance took effect, how many months elapsed before any member was at war?
   3. Did any member of the alliance enter a war while the alliance was still operative?
   4. If war (other than one existing at time alliance took effect) did occur while alliance was operative, did half or more of the members fight on the same side? (If no war, coded blank.)
   5. If any member was at war during the 12 years following formation of the alliance, did half or more of the members fight on the same side? (If no war, coded blank.)
   6. If any member was at war during the 12 years following formation of the alliance, did half or more of the members fight on opposite sides? (If no war, coded blank.)

A CLASSIFICATION OF ALL ALLIANCES

We shall analyze the data in several different ways to derive an empirically based typology. There are a variety of available clustering procedures; as is well known, each will produce somewhat different results, and none should be treated as definitive. In some preliminary analysis I used a hierarchical clustering procedure, but will rely solely on factor analysis here. The virtues and limitations of factor analysis have been discussed in great detail elsewhere; the applications here will be the same as those in my previous work, to which the reader is referred.[13] We shall use both the basic R-analysis, for finding variables that cluster together, and then proceed to employ Q-analysis for an understanding of what alliances are in important ways similar to one another. The R-analysis will be performed first for the entire data set of 137 alliances, and then separately for the periods 1920–1941 and 1941–1957, to isolate the effect of changes in the international system.[14] It would surely be neat, and highly desirable, if we could identify a hierarchical set of variables with very high discriminating power, on the order of a biological taxonomy—for example, vertebrates; warm-blooded vertebrates; warm-blooded vertebrates whose young are born alive, etc. Unfortunately, the regularities of international politics are not quite so strong or simple, but nevertheless we will find some important consistent associations. The distinct dimensions—uncorrelated factors—will constitute the basis of a typology. During the course of this analysis we will tentatively consider a variety of propositions about the relations among input and output variables, but the detailed testing of specific hypotheses will be taken up in other studies.

First, the analysis of the entire set. Table 17-1 shows all the variables with correlations, or factor loadings, greater than .30. With respect to each factor, correlations are listed in descending order with the loadings to the *right*. The top variables more accurately characterize the factor than those toward the bottom. For variables not listed the factor accounts for less than 10 percent of the variance, and so the relationship can safely be ignored. Down the *left*-hand column is the variable identification number from the preceding scheme. The percentage of the total variance in all the data that is accounted for by each factor is given at the top; the four factors together account for nearly 43 percent of the total variance. If two variables each load highly on different factors, they are essentially *un*related (not negatively related) to each other.

The first factor I have labelled "Dominance"; it characterizes alliances between a major power and one or more smaller states, where the big state

---

[13] Bruce M. Russett, *International Regions and the International System* (Chicago: Rand McNally, 1967), Chapters 2 and 3, and citations there. As there, the method here is principal components, with unities inserted in the diagonal, and orthogonal rotation. The one difference is in the criterion of how many factors to rotate. The criterion of all factors with eigenvalues equal to or exceeding 1.0 would here give 14, which is clearly excessive for 44 variables, and I have usually used the scree test instead. For the first analysis below, and in all but one of the others, that gave four factors. An alternative rotation of seven attenuated the factors somewhat, but to no great effect. Skewed distributions were normalized before the correlations were computed. There are no missing data except where the category is not applicable to a particular alliance (e.g., the variable labelled I.C.1). Some variables are dichotomous, but coding categories were chosen so that no split would be more extreme than 90–10. For the Q-analysis below, all variables were first transformed to a range of 0 to 1.0.

[14] For example, Robert E. Osgood argues that pre-World War II alliances, very unlike the typical postwar one, were for war-fighting purposes or initiated by a big power to limit the options of an ally, not for deterrence. See Robert E. Osgood and Robert W. Tucker, *Force, Order, and Justice* (Baltimore: The Johns Hopkins University Press, 1967), p. 87. See also Robert E. Osgood, *Alliances and American Foreign Policy* (Baltimore: The Johns Hopkins University Press, 1968), p. 18.

extends various forms of assistance. The predominance of a big power within an alliance is clear from the importance of three variables in the cluster: number of major powers (variable I.A.2, loading only at .53 since some of these alliances in the pre-World War II period included more than one big power),

Table 17-1
Factors (Groups of Variables) Characterizing International Alliances Signed 1920–1957

Factor 1: *"Dominance"* (11 percent of variance)		Loadings	Factor 2: *"Amicability and duration"* (12 percent of variance)		Loadings
I.E.2.a	Distance between capitals	.76	I.C.6	Termination sanctioned	.78
II.A.4	Military bases	.66	II.B.2	Actual/intended duration	.77
I.E.1.b	Common race	−.66	II.B.3	Lasted long	.77
II.A.2	Military aid	.65	II.D.2	Months before war	.76
I.A.3	Percent of world population	.63	II.B.1	Actual duration	.67
I.A.4	All members European	−.62	I.E.3	Allies past 25 years	−.55
I.D.3	Energy consumption ratio	.53	II.C.3	Termination war between members	−.46
I.A.2	Number of major powers	.53	I.C.2	Intended duration	−.46
I.E.1.c	Common religion	−.47	I.A.1	Year signed	−.46
I.D.2	Armed forces ratio	.44	II.D.6	Fight opposite next 12 years	−.45
II.A.5	Economic aid	.40	II.C.2	Termination denunciation	−.41
II.A.1	Official contacts	.36	I.B.1	Defensive pact	−.35
I.A.5	Specific threat	−.35	II.C.5	Termination expiration	.35
II.C.4	Terminated by loss of member's independence	−.34	II.D.1	New alliance next 12 years	.31
II.D.3	Entry into war	.33			
I.E.2.b	Miles between borders	.32			

Factor 3: *"Multilateral equality and voluntarism"* (9 percent of variance)		Loadings	Factor 4: *"Integrated defense"* (11 percent of variance)		Loadings
I.D.1	Multilateral	.69	I.C.2	Intended duration	.75
I.E.2.c	Distance between territories	.60	I.B.2	Neutrality pact	−.65
I.D.2	Armed forces ratio	−.56	I.B.1	Defensive pact	.63
I.E.2.b	Distance between borders	.54	I.A.1	Year signed	.62
I.C.1	Length specified	−.53	I.A.5	Specific threat	.61
I.A.3	Entente	.52	II.C.7	Still in effect	.61
II.D.4	Fight same side while allied	.52	II.D.6	Fight opposite next 12 years	−.56
I.E.1.a	Common language	.49	II.C.3	Termination war between members	−.54
II.D.5	Fight same side next 12 years	.49	II.B.5	Economic aid	.53
I.D.3	Energy consumption ratio	−.40	II.A.1	Official contact	.51
I.A.4	All members European	−.35	I.A.2	Number of major powers	−.37
II.D.2	Months before war	−.34	II.A.6	Institutions	.36
I.E.1.b	Common race	−.32	II.A.3	Integrated military command	.36
			II.A.4	Military bases	.34

and the dominance of one power in terms of the alliance total of energy (I.D.3) and armed forces (I.D.2). Similarly, the presence of at least one major power is attested by the fact that the alliance as a whole is likely to account for a substantial portion of the world's population (I.A.3).

Just as these are alliances between states of unequal power, they are between states that are culturally dissimilar. The members are unlikely to share common racial stock (I.E.1.b) or a common major religion (I.E.1.c). Often at least some members are non-European states (I.A.4). Physically, their capitals and metropolitan territories are likely to be far apart (I.E.2.a and I.E.2.b), though the importance of distance washes out when the land of colonies is counted as part of a state's territory (I.E.2.c does not load on the factor), suggesting that many of these pacts incorporate colonial powers who retain colonial possessions in the neighborhood of the small-state members. Frequently the big power extended military assistance (II.A.2), less often, economic aid (II.A.5), and frequently both. In return, it was allowed to establish one or more military bases on the small state's territory (II.A.4). While there were typically official contacts at high governmental levels (II.A.1), institution building was avoided.

It is clear that one big power usually dominates this type of alliance; one might be tempted to label such pacts protective or deterrent alliances, but several elements prescribe caution. Members are moderately likely to find themselves at war while the alliance remains operative (II.D.3), though the war may be in a theatre where the alliance was not intended to apply. Nor do alliances dominated by one big power seem to have been notably successful as deterrents, at least in the sense of being of particularly long duration (no loadings for the II.B variables), and they seldom refer in writing to any specific threat (I.A.5). Earlier work using the theory of collective goods has established that when big powers succeed in extending deterrent umbrellas over smaller states, the big powers typically have disproportionately large armies.[15] From that, we should expect that in these data the military dominance measure for armed forces should load more highly on the factor than should the dominance ratio based on energy consumption. In fact the opposite happens. And if Osgood is correct about deterrent alliances being largely a post-World War II phenomenon and these all were deterrent alliances, year of signature (I.A.1) should load on the factor—but it does not. Thus it seems likely that while deterrence may be the major purpose of some of these arrangements, big power control over smaller states is also often a principal goal.

Skipping next to the *third* factor, it identifies a set of variables in many substantive respects quite opposed to those of the first.[16] I have called it "Multilateral equality and voluntarism"; somewhat facetiously it might be "Hands across the sea." The variables characterize multilateral pacts (I.D.1.)

---

[15] Russett, *What Price Vigilance?*, loc. cit.

[16] Mathematically, of course, the use of orthogonal rotation means that the factors overall will be completely uncorrelated—though single variables may load moderately on more than one factor.

among states not greatly disparate in economic or military strength (negative loadings for variables I.D.2 and I.D.3). Members of such alliances tend to be quite distant from one another (I.E.2.c and I.E.2.b), as was true with the first factor, but here the high loading is for distance between territories including *colonies*; since allowing for the nearness of any extant colonies does not make the members "closer," we must conclude that they do not include states which, at the time of signature, retained substantial colonial holdings. Like the Factor 1 set, there is a tendency (though here much weaker) for the members to be racially dissimilar (I.E.1.b) and to include non-European states (I.A.4), but, unlike Factor 1, to share a common language (I.E.1.a). Typically these alliances entail only entente commitments rather than anything stronger (I.A.3), and no specific duration is indicated (I.C.1). They seem not to be very successful in preventing or deterring war (II.D.2) but to be quite effective in insuring that the members will *fight side-by-side when war does occur* (II.D.4 and II.D.5). Perhaps deterrence was not the intention of the signatories, who may rather have wished to acquire alliance commitments from one another at a time when violent conflict with a mutual enemy seemed probable. The fact that these alliances did lead to wartime cooperation even though common belligerency usually was not required (most often they were ententes) strengthens the view that these are agreements freely accepted among relative equals, entered into under the influence of cultural and perhaps ideological similarity, and reflecting or leading to a degree of commitment greater than was legalistically specified.

As is well known, there are two major conflicting theories about the determinants of a nation's choice of alliance partners. One is the traditional power theory, with a formal version derived from game theory by William Riker and others, that a nation will choose sides so as to form a coalition large enough to win a given contest, but not so large as unnecessarily to dilute the distribution of winnings. By this principle, bonds of ideology or common culture are virtually irrelevant to the choice of partners; by far the most important influence is the relative size of the members. The opposite view, which some have described as particularly applicable to the post-1945 international system, stresses the preference for ideological partnerships when they conflict with the choice that might be dictated by purely "objective" power-maximizing considerations.[17] There is a suggestion, in the two factors identified above, that both of these theories can in fact meet substantial confirmation in the international politics of the years since 1920. Factor 1 may represent alliances based largely on power considerations, and Factor 3 the set of variables associated with alliances rooted partly in ideological or other similarities. This point can only be offered tentatively from the analysis of this chapter, but it may help to prevent adoption of an exclusive viewpoint that seeks to explain all alliances in terms of either theory alone. The failure of the year of signature (I.A.1) variable to correlate with either of the factors suggests in addition that neither is it correct simply to assert that one theory is appropriate for the inter-

---

[17] See the previous chapter.

war period and the other for the post-1945 years.[18] Furthermore, the clustering together, in two separate factors, of a variety of variables may help indicate the circumstances under which the considerations of one theory may prevail over the other. Finally, they suggest some important implications for the output of different alliances. For example, the Factor 1 or, tentatively, "power-oriented" alliances may provide some deterrence, but the Factor 3 or "similarity-oriented" alliances are better at holding their coalitions together once war does occur.

The *second* factor groups together a set of variables relevant to matters of "Amicability and duration." This factor picks out treaties which lasted a long time (II.B.1), especially relative to the period originally specified (II.B.2 and II.B.3). When and if the alliance was terminated, it was frequently replaced by a new one or at least ended in some manner sanctioned by the terms of the treaty (II.C.6). Such alliances frequently led to later alliances, perhaps usually temporal extensions of the first ones but often different pacts either with fewer members or casting a wider net (II.D.1). While some of these pacts simply were allowed to expire (II.C.5), they were unlikely to terminate by denunciation (II.C.2) or war between the members (II.C.3). The members were unlikely to fight each other in any case (II.D.6). Despite the fact that these alliances did indeed tend to last quite a few years, the initial duration called for was typically rather short (I.C.2) and they were not likely to be defensive (I.B.1). Perhaps this linking of durability with limitation of commitment in time and quality buttresses the argument that avoidance of strain, by not accepting a higher level of institutional integration than can be supported by underlying bonds of community, is a major requirement for the success of international organizations. Or, one may more simply view these as alliances concluded in long-term low-stress situations; external threats neither demanded high commitment nor soon strained what was done. The strong relationship between these variables and a long elapse of time before any member became involved in war (II.D.2) supports the latter argument, but the point needs further investigation. These are largely alliances formed well in advance of World War II, as shown by the substantial negative correlation with year of signature (I.A.1).

What is surprising about this cluster of variables is how little relationship they bear, either positively or negatively, to bonds of similarity or any of the standard predictors to integration that are included in our list of variables. Nor is there any relation to the measures of institution building or such indicators of cooperation as aid or contact between high officials. The only strong correlation appearing is a *negative* one with a history of alliance during the preceding 25 years (I.E.3).

Factor 4, however, brings together most of the variables we can put under the rubric "Integrated defense." These describe pacts with extended and strong

---

[18] This point will be checked further below when we analyze the two sets of alliances separately. One example of the argument that the determinants of post-World War II alliances are fundamentally different from previous periods is Herbert Dinerstein, "The Transformation of Alliance Systems," *American Political Science Review*, LIX (September 1965), pp. 589–601.

commitments. They envisage long duration (I.C.2), and typically are defensive pacts (I.B.1), rarely neutrality pacts (I.B.2). They usually were signed with a specific threat in mind and identified in the text of the treaty (I.A.5). These too are alliances of long duration, since most are still in effect (II.C.7) and this means, with a sample limited to the pre-1958 period, that they have lasted at least 13 years. Unlike the last two clusters of variables, this one is also associated with a moderate probability of assistance and integration among the members. Loading on the factor are official contact between high functionaries (II.A.1), economic aid (II.A.5), the creation of common institutions (II.A.6), and the establishment of an integrated military command (II.A.3) and military bases on one another's territory (II.A.4). Members are very unlikely to fight against each other subsequently (II.D.6 and II.C.3), though the causal relation is uncertain. Rather surprising in this light, however, is the fact that these variables do not predict to fighting on the *same* side. While members are not likely to have fought each other, they often seem to have sat out each other's violent conflicts.

It is important to note that these are relatively recent and hence usually post-World War II alliances (I.A.1). Perhaps for this reason we see a mild negative correlation with the presence of major powers (I.A.2). That variable was coded to reflect the change from a multipolar system before World War II to a bipolar world thereafter; given the American-Soviet hostility, by definition no post-1945 alliance could include more than one major power, whereas before World War II quite a few alliances numbered two major power members and one, among the Axis states, included three. Since these are alliances concluded in a bipolar world, one must, as noted above, be especially careful in explaining their apparent permanence. It may be a result of the integration and bond creation noted, or it may merely reflect the frozen character of international alignments in recent decades.

These last two factors show that time, or more plausibly, time-associated change in the international system, is indeed a major discriminating variable in characterizing international alliances. The prewar alliances characterized by high scores on the Factor 2 variables were durable and did not end in war among the members, but not as the result of specially created bonds or institutions. Postwar alliances typically also have been durable and war among members has been very rare; in addition postwar alliances often show the "hard shell" of infrastructure noted by Herz.[19] In light of these differences it becomes necessary to analyze the two sets separately.

PREWAR ALLIANCES

We shall do so with an R-analysis and a Q-analysis for each set dividing the alliances between those preceding and following the entry of the United States

---

[19] Herz, loc. cit.

into the war at the end of 1941.[20] The R-analysis merely repeats on a subset what we did in Table 17-1; the Q-analysis treats *alliances* as *variables* and provides a way of discovering not which characteristics of alliances are associated, but which particular alliances are, in most of the respects measured, like each other.[21] Although there is not necessarily any simple relationship between the patterns uncovered in the two types of analyses, we will in fact find that each group of alliances found to be similar in the Q-analysis can in useful ways be characterized by a group of variables, or factor, from the R-analysis.[22] Thus we shall proceed first with the R- and Q-analyses together of the prewar set, and then move to the analyses of the postwar set.

The first grouping in the R-analysis of Table 17-2 is quite similar to that which began Table 17-1 for the entire 1920–1957 period. We again may identify it with the label "Dominance." Common race was deleted for lack of variation (few interracial alliances in the prewar era), and the military assistance and cooperation measures loom a little more prominent. Again these are pacts between a major power and one or more smaller ones; military cooperation and economic assistance are important, especially by pre-World War II standards. The big powers seem to have been motivated by some mixture of desire to control their allies and a wish to protect them from attack. The former purpose, however, appears to be rather more common. First, we see the much higher position of the energy consumption ratio than the armed forces ratio, meaning that the discrepancy of the members' economic size is greater than that of their military establishments. As noted earlier, the theory of collective goods predicts that where deterrence really is provided, the small state will usually seize the opportunity to reduce its military burdens below the level that would be "expected" according to its economic size. The opposite happens with these pacts. Furthermore, often these are alliances between states that have not fought side-by-side in the recent past; hence the inference of big

---

[20] This may seem a rather Americanocentric dividing point. I chose it so as to keep in the later set only those alliances that seem to have been concluded at least as much with postwar international politics in mind as for fighting World War II. In fact, at least two of those I did put in the "postwar" group, were war-fighting alliances, but this was forced by a technical consideration—the inability of the Q-analysis procedure to accommodate more than 80 variables, a limitation which would have been exceeded if the cut were made later than 1941. However, any cut would be arbitrary. Two or three alliances either way will make little difference, and it can be effectively argued that American entry into World War II did indeed mark the end of a Europe-centered international system.

[21] As in Table 17-1 the numbers on the right of the entries in each column give the factor loadings; numbers to the left in Table 17-3 are the last two digits of year of signature.

[22] Ideally we might group alliances by their factor scores from the R-analysis, but the presence of many blanks (not applicable) in a number of variables makes it impossible to compute the factor scores. Some variables have had to be dropped due to lack of variation in one of the periods, i.e., for prewar: integrated military command, common language, common race, and still in effect; for postwar: neutrality pact (and also entente, since all non-ententes are defensive pacts), official contact, fight opposite next 12 years, termination war between members, termination member loses independence, and expiration. It should also be noted that the four sets of factor loadings from the Q-analysis can be used as new variables in further studies of the characteristics of alliances.

power control to see that such omissions are not repeated. This characterization is generally borne out if we match the *variables* in Factor 1 of Table 17-2 with the *alliances* in Factor 1 of the Q-analysis in Table 17-3; the latter factor is named "Dominated and integrated pacts" for that reason.

Factor 2 in Table 17-2 is labeled "Amicability and duration"; its corre-

Table 17-2

Factors (Groups of Variables) Characterizing Pre-World War II Alliances

Factor 1: "Dominance" (11 percent of variance)	Loadings	Factor 2: "Amicability and duration" (16 percent of variance)	Loadings
Military aid	.78	Months before war	.89
Official contact	.72	Actual/intended duration	.79
Economic aid	.62	Year signed	−.78
Termination new alliance	.55	Lasted long	.76
Energy consumption ratio	.52	Actual duration	.72
Number of major powers	.51	Termination sanctioned	.65
Distance between capitals	.50	Allies past 25 years	−.55
Fought same side past 25 years	−.49	Termination war between members	.55
Military bases	.45	Number of major powers	−.53
Percent of world population	.43	Fight opposite next 12 years	−.50
All members European	−.42	Intended duration	−.47
Armed forces ratio	.42	Percent of world population	−.47
Defensive pact	.35	Military bases	−.39
		Termination expiration	.35
		Fought same side next 12 years	−.32
		Entry into war	−.32

Factor 3: "Neighborly hostility" (10 percent of variance)	Loadings	Factor 4: "Common defense" (7 percent of variance)	Loadings
Multilateral	−.67	Fight opposite past 25 years	−.53
Armed forces ratio	.65	Defensive pact	.53
Distance between borders	−.65	Termination by loss by member's independence	.50
Distance between territories	−.64	Specific threat	.49
Neutrality pact	.54	Common religion	.48
Fight same side next 12 years	−.53	Termination war between members	−.45
Fight same side while allied	−.53	Institutions	−.41
Energy consumption ratio	.52	All members European	.40
Length specified	.43	Distance between capitals	−.38
Fight opposite next 12 years	.42	Termination sanctioned	.38
Defensive pact	−.34	Neutrality pact	−.36
New alliance next 12 years	−.33		
Allies past 25 years	−.31		
Distance between capitals	−.31		

spondence with the factor of the same name and number in Table 17-1 is extraordinarily close. Nine of the top ten variables in each are to be found among the top ten of the other. Those variables show up prominently in the group of alliances under Factor 2 in Table 17-3, "Small-power neutrality pacts." As is apparent from the list of variables in Table 17-2, the alliances with high loadings on this factor do not in fact include major powers. More often than not it is impossible to identify one member as clearly dominant, and rarely is it the kind of relationship where the right to establish military bases on another's territory is obtained in a bargain for military or economic assistance. Rather, the primary purpose often seems to be *mutual* assurance that the partner will stay neutral in the event that one goes to war, and they are largely successful in this quest. The pacts last, and though the members are unlikely to fight side-by-side in later wars, they are even more unlikely to fight against each other. Neutrality pact does not appear in the Table 17-2 list of variables loading on the factor, but there is nevertheless some relation (.25) below the arbitrary cutoff mark for inclusion in the table.

The third factor in Table 17-2 also matches extremely well with factor 3 in Table 17-1, but as its *mirror image*. Negative loadings on the one become positive on the other, and vice-versa. Whereas in Table 17-1 I named the cluster "Multilateral equality and voluntarism," here I chose "Neighborly hostility." Proximity, size dominance, and bilateralism are all closely associated. Alliances with these characteristics tend, however, to include past and, especially, future enemies. The members are moderately unlikely to have been allies in the previous 25 years, do not fight side-by-side thereafter, and in fact often fight against each other in future years.[23] A look at the list of alliances loading highly on Factor 3 in Table 17-3 shows how appropriate these characterizations are. That factor is labeled "Alliances ending in war between members." It particularly includes the pacts formed by Germany and Russia with their weak neighbors; pacts that ended with the neighbors' invasion or absorption at the beginning of World War II. *These* neutrality pacts were a peculiar feature of the interwar system, and were systematically violated by the larger signatory whenever it seemed expedient. For a small power, accepting such a pact was a far better index of fear than of security.

Factor 4 of Table 17-2, finally, I have called "Common defense." It is related, but does not correspond precisely to the "Integrated defense," Factor 4 of Table 17-1. The difference, obviously, is primarily the absence of the integration variables that were moderately important for the factor that spanned the entire four decades. Yet defensive pact, a specified threat, and termination by cause other than war between members trace the similarity. In Table 17-2,

---

[23] The presentation of this factor as the mirror image of Factor 3 in Table 17-1 should not obscure the very strong basic continuity between them. If one simply reversed all the signs— as is a perfectly legitimate procedure—their similarity would be even more apparent. I have chosen to present it this way, however, so as better to illuminate the associated grouping of alliances in Table 17-3.

Table 17-3

Factors Designating Groups of Pre-World War II Alliances

Factor 1: "Dominated and and integrated pacts" (13 percent of variance)		Loadings†	Factor 2: "Small-power neutrality pacts" (19 percent of variance)		Loadings
27	Iran-Russia	.77	29	Hungary-Turkey	.82
26	Afghanistan-Russia	.76	33	Turkey-Romania	.80
36	Mongolia-Russia	.72	30	Turkey-Greece	.80
37	China-Russia	.72	33	Turkey-Yugoslavia	.80
26	Germany-Russia	.70	29	Bulgaria-Turkey	.80
26	Albania-Italy	.63	34	Greece-Romania-Turkey-	
30	France-Turkey	.62		Yugoslavia	.78
32	U.K.-Iraq	.60	28	Greece-Italy	.76
28	Italy-Turkey	.60	24	Italy-Yugoslavia	.74
36	U.K.-Egypt	.58	27	Afghanistan-Iran	.70
36	Pan American	.54	28	Greece-Romania	.69
27	Hungary-Italy	.52	26	Turkey-Iran	.66
25	Russia-Turkey	.48	23	Estonia-Latvia	.65
40	U.S.-Canada	.47	39	Portugal-Spain	.63
32	Estonia-Russia	.47	41	Russia-Yugoslavia	.63
32	Latvia-Russia	.47	21	Austria-Czechoslovakia	.62
32	France-Russia	.47	27	France-Yugoslavia	.60
26	France-Romania	.46	24	Czechoslovakia-Italy	.60
24	Czechoslovakia-France	.45	32	Latvia-Italy	.59
26	Italy-Romania	.45	21	Romania-Yugoslavia	.59
21	Afghanistan-Turkey	.45	32	Estonia-Romania	.58
20	Belgium-France	.44	39	Latvia-Germany	.58
39	France-Turkey	.44	39	Estonia-Germany	.58
26	Iran-Turkey	.43	21	Czechoslovakia-Yugoslavia	.57
39	Portugal-Spain	.42	34	Estonia-Latvia-Lithuania	.54
34	Greece-Romania-Turkey-		36	Iraq-Arabia-Yemen	.53
	Yugoslavia	.41			

†Loadings below .40 are not shown.

this factor pulls out characteristics peculiar to pre-World War II conditions: alignment of states together around the periphery of Germany in an effort to contain the former Central Power and prevent German territorial revision. The attempt was of course in vain, culminating in at least the temporary loss of independence of many of the small states. Factor 4 of Table 17-3 identifies these "Defensive pacts."[24]

---

[24] It should be noted that for technical reasons a three-factor solution in Table 17-2 might well be preferable to the four-factor solution shown. Three factors, accounting for 37 percent of the variance, instead of four and 44 percent, might have been a better choice for rotation. I nevertheless used the four-factor solution because it matched so nicely with that of Table 17-1 and particularly with all the subsequent tables, where the choice of a four-factor solution was really not in question. The reader might nonetheless remember that it is just as accurate to think of only three clusters of variables for Table 2 prewar alliances. In such a case Factor 4 dissolves essentially without affecting the loadings on the first three factors.

Factor 3: "Alliances ending in war between members" (13 percent of variance)		Loadings
39	Denmark-Germany	.80
37	Italy-Yugoslavia	.80
39	Germany-Russia	.77
38	France-Germany	.76
39	Russia-Latvia	.75
39	Russia-Estonia	.75
32	Russia-Finland	.75
41	Russia-Japan	.68
26	Russia-Lithuania	.68
33	Italy-Russia	.68
32	Russia-Poland	.68
27	Italy-Albania	.62
39	Germany-Italy	.56
34	Germany-Poland	.55
33	U.K.-France-Germany-Italy	.55
35	France-Italy	.53
38	Five Balkans	.52
21	Poland-Romania	.51
32	Finland-Russia	.51
37	Afghanistan-Iran-Iraq-Turkey	.46
30	France-Turkey	.46
26	Italy-Romania	.45
26	France-Romania	.45
28	Afghanistan-Turkey	.44
40	Six Axis	.44
21	Czechoslovakia-Romania	.43
28	Italy-Turkey	.42
33	Italy-Russia	.40

Factor 4: "Defensive pacts" (10 percent of variance)		Loadings
39	U.K.-France-Poland	.79
39	U.K.-France-Greece	.74
25	France-Czechoslovakia	.73
21	France-Poland	.71
39	U.K.-Poland	.69
33	Czechoslovakia-Romania-Yugoslavia	.64
21	Poland-Romania	.59
35	France-Russia	.55
21	Czechoslovakia-Romania	.55
39	U.K.-France-Romania	.55
35	Czechoslovakia-Romania	.54
20	Czechoslovakia-Yugoslavia	.53
21	Romania-Yugoslavia	.50
23	Estonia-Latvia	.45
39	France-Turkey	.43
21	Afghanistan-Turkey	.42

POSTWAR ALLIANCES

Tables 17-4 and 17-5 repeat the above procedures for the post-World War II era. The first grouping is one which we may still identify as characterized by dominance. Factor 1 in the R-analysis of the postwar years corresponds extremely closely to Factor 1 in the 137 alliance R-analysis, and also to Factor 1 in the prewar analysis (Table 17-2). In fact, all of the top eight variables of Factor 1 in Table 17-4 are among the top ten of Factor 1 in Table 17-1. Here are alliances between a big power and one or more much smaller states which are usually geographically distant and racially different from their protector, again with exchange of military facilities (the big power providing military assistance in return for basing rights). These are predominantly, but not exclusively, alliances in the American global system of collective defense.

Table 17-4

Factors (Groups of Variables) Characterizing Post-World War II Alliances

Factor 1: "Dominance" (15 percent of variance)	Loadings	Factor 2: "Short duration" (11 percent of variance)	Loadings
Number of major powers	.80	Lasted long	−.89
Percent of world population	.76	Termination denunciation	.77
Distance between capitals	.73	Fought opposite past 25 year	−.72
Military aid	.70	Termination sanctioned	−.71
Military bases	.68	New alliance next 12 years	−.66
Common race	−.65	Still in effect	−.64
Armed forces ratio	.51	Months before war	−.41
Entry into war	.44	Fight same side next 12 years	.34
Energy consumption ratio	.44	Economic aid	−.33
Termination new alliance	−.35	Alliance past 25 years	.31
Length specified	−.36		
All members European	−.35		
Actual duration	.34		
New alliance next 12 years	−.33		
Distance between borders	.32		
Fight same side next 12 years	.31		

Factor 3: "Equality and voluntarism" (10 percent of variance)	Loadings	Factor 4: "Common defense" (17 percent of variance)	Loadings
Actual/intended duration	.94	Specific threat	.83
Fight same side next 12 years	.76	All members European	.73
Actual duration	.72	Defensive pact	.72
Entry into war	.56	Termination sanctioned	−.68
Common language	.54	Distance between borders	−.67
Fight same side while allied	.51	Length specified	.62
Integrated military command	.40	Common religion	.59
Fought same side past 25 years	.34	Distance between territories	−.54
		Year signed	−.53
		Distance between capitals	−.52
		Multilateral	−.50
		Intended duration	.48
		Termination new alliance	−.47
		Common race	.44
		Common language	−.41
		Termination denunciation	.37
		Fought opposite past 25 years	.35
		Military bases	−.33
		Lasted long	−.32

Factor 1 in Table 17-5, the Q-analysis, lists a group of similar alliances that generally seems to correspond to the characteristics identified in Factor 1 of Table 17-4. The word "dominated" in the label for that factor should not be taken pejoratively; it is meant merely to point out the gross power discrepancies within the membership of each pact. As we might expect for postwar alliances, there is more suggestion than earlier that deterrence, rather than control over the small ally, is a major concern of the dominant power. The armed forces ratio is likely to be a little more one-sided than the energy ratio, as predicted by collective goods theory for successful deterrent alliances. Though it is common for one member to go to war at some time after the alliance is concluded, it is usually the protecting power fighting in some other theatre, not any attack on the protégé.

The second factor in Table 17-4 also corresponds well with that in Table 17-1 for the entire period and in Table 17-2 for the prewar years. I have used the label "Short duration" because this factor is another case of a mirror image, the negative of "Amicability and duration" in Table 17-1. Note the high loadings in each case (but negative here) for such variables as lasted long, termination sanctioned, new alliance within 12 years (not in Table 17-2), and here, the positive high loading for termination by denunciation. Viewed in this negative way, the factor matches nicely with a group of short-term alliances identified by Factor 2 in the Q-analysis of Table 17-5. These are preeminently the immediate postwar alliances of the new Communist governments of Eastern Europe with Yugoslavia, denounced when Tito was expelled from the Cominform. In provisions and outcome they share much the same features as the British and French wartime alliances with Russia, and even the Japanese-Siamese wartime alliance and the much later pacts between Egypt and Saudi Arabia which ended in the Yemen war. These pacts were signed by states which had not been at war with each other in the recent past. If no member was currently at war then they rarely fought anyone soon thereafter; however, if war did occur or if a war was going on at the time of signature, they were somewhat likely to fight side-by-side.

The third cluster of alliance characteristics in Table 17-4 is labeled "Equality and voluntarism" to point out its continuity with the "Multilateral equality and voluntarism" factor from Table 17-1, and with its mirror image, Factor 3 of Table 17-2. Appearing on both Tables 17-1 and 17-4 are such items as sharing a common language, negative relationships to dominance in armed forces, and two output measures showing that they tend to fight on the same side in wars fought during the years after the pact was concluded. These variables are prominent in the pacts identified in the Q-analysis of Table 17-5 by the third factor named "Small-power pacts." Should the appearance of durability (in the R-analysis, the ratio of actual to intended duration and the number of years of actual duration) for these alliances seem strange, remember again that these variables apply only to alliances which have in fact *been terminated*. Of the larger set of postwar alliances which have gone by the board (largely those of Yugoslavia with the other Communist countries as well as Britain

Table 17-5

Factors Designating Groups of Post-World War II Alliances

Factor 1: "Dominated and integrated pacts" (14 percent of variance)		Loadings†	Factor 2: "Denounced defense pacts" (15 percent of variance)		Loadings
54	SEATO	.88	45	Russia-Yugoslavia	.80
54	U.S.-Taiwan	.88	42	Britain-Russia	.80
47	Rio Pact	.80	46	Czechoslovakia-Yugoslavia	.78
51	Australia-New Zealand-U.S.	.80	47	Romania-Yugoslavia	.76
53	U.S.-Korea	.76	47	Bulgaria-Yugoslavia	.75
55	CENTO	.68	48	Jordan-Britain	.71
57	U.K.-Malaya	.68	44	Russia-France	.69
51	U.S.-Philippines	.67	46	Yugoslavia-Poland	.69
50	Arab League II	.66	46	Yugoslavia-Albania	.67
51	U.S.-Japan	.64	41	Japan-Siam	.64
50	Russia-China	.61	47	Hungary-Yugoslavia	.63
49	NATO	.60	45	Russia-Nationalist China	.54
53	U.K.-Libya	.60	56	Egypt-Saudi Arabia-Yemen	.50
46	Russia-Mongolia	.57	55	Egypt-Saudia Arabia	.45
42	U.K.-Russia-Iran	.51	43	Russia-Czechoslovakia	.41
			55	Warsaw Treaty	.40
			50	Russia-China	.40

Factor 3: "Small-power pacts" (11 percent of variance)		Loadings	Factor 4: "Bilateral defense in Eastern Europe" (22 percent of variance)		Loadings
44	Australia-New Zealand	.69	49	Czechoslovakia-Hungary	.94
53	Turkey-Yugoslavia-Greece I	.65	48	Poland-Hungary	.93
47	Jordan-Iraq	.61	47	Czechoslovakia-Poland	.89
55	Egypt-Syria	.59	48	Russia-Romania	.86
56	Egypt-Saudi Arabia-Yemen	.55	48	Russia-Hungary	.84
45	Arab League I	.54	48	Hungary-Romania	.83
54	Turkey-Yugoslavia-Greece II	.53	48	Russia-Bulgaria	.82
55	Egypt-Saudi Arabia	.48	48	Bulgaria-Hungary	.81
48	Romania-Bulgaria	.47	48	Bulgaria-Czechoslovakia	.76
48	Bulgaria-Poland	.45	49	Poland-Romania	.74
48	Czechoslovakia-Romania	.44	48	Czechoslovakia-Romania	.74
49	Poland-Romania	.44	45	Russia-Poland	.72
54	Pakistan-Turkey	.41	48	Bulgaria-Poland	.69
			48	Romania-Bulgaria	.68
			48	Russia-Finland	.63
			43	Russia-Czechoslovakia	.61
			48	Bulgaria-Albania	.59
			47	France-Britain	.57
			47	Hungary-Yugoslavia	.54
			55	Warsaw Treaty	.42
			46	Yugoslavia-Poland	.41

†Loadings below .40 are not shown.

and France with Russia) many of those in Factor 3 did rather well. The Jordan-Iraq alliance, for instance, lasted more than ten years, and the two involving Egypt and Saudi Arabia more than five years. Also, they were established with only modest expectations; for example the latter two were only intended initially for five years, as compared with ten for all those in Eastern Europe. Thus they most often did last out their intended length and so show a comparatively favorable duration ratio.

Finally, there is a cluster of variables only moderately well related to factors in the entire 137 alliance set and the R-analysis of the prewar years. It is close enough to deserve the same name as the one in Table 17-2 ("Common defense"). Certain variables, especially defensive pact and specific threat, appear prominently in all three. As will be apparent, these alliances in the 1940s and 1950s were between culturally fairly similar European states not greatly distant from each other, and tend to have been signed relatively early in the period. Typically they were bilateral, intended as long-term alliances directed against a specific threat, and extracted the firm commitment of a defensive pact. They seem best to match the final factor in the Q-analysis results of Table 17-5. That factor has been named "Bilateral defense in Eastern Europe." It includes all the successful Eastern European pacts (that is, excluding those with Yugoslavia) and almost no others.

Note that hardly any of the integration variables are associated with this cluster of characteristics called "Common defense,"[25] and that too is appropriate. Bilateral integration among the East European countries in the form of military and economic aid or establishment of military bases has not been terribly common, though it is much more so between each of them and the Soviet Union. The result has been to wash those variables out as important discriminators either way for these alliances. In nearly all other respects the strong similarities among all these Eastern pacts is striking. Only in one respect does it seem odd to match the "Common defense" characteristics with the cluster of Eastern European defense pacts, and that concerns termination. The problem, however, is only an artifact of the coding and the fact that very few of these alliances have been terminated at all. Of the very few that *have* terminated (two Yugoslav treaties and the one between Albania and Bulgaria), denunciation has been the most common method.

CONTRASTS AND CONTINUITIES

To sum up our findings about alliances in the postwar period, it is notable first that, if we exclude the bilateral ones among the Communist states of Eastern Europe, *few* are among relative equals. There are some, appearing largely in Factor 3 in Table 17-5, but this is a very small group as compared

---

[25] Interestingly, that is not true for the all-period factor "Integrated defense" which it otherwise resembles.

with the large number of small-power pacts in the prewar period (see Factor 2 in Table 17-3). (It seems fair to ignore the East European postwar pacts because they were concluded in a regional system that was imposed by the Soviet Union, and the important political ties in that area in the 1940s were really between each of these states and the Russians, not among the "satellites.") This reflects the changed international system where small states, caught between the bipolar colossi, could no longer hope to find security by banding together in small groups of two or three. Most of them felt, in the 1940s and 1950s, that their defense required the guarantee of a superpower, and they rarely bothered to conclude alliances limited in composition solely to other small states. Small states were linked together by means of common bonds to the superpowers rather than directly with one another. Although this phenomenon is in a sense well known, the extent of the contrast is impressive.

Drawing on the sociological literature, Johan Galtung has termed this pattern of relationships essentially a "feudal" system, and if not pressed too far, the image of warring lords, with each lord owed fealty by his retainers, has some merit here.[26] Probably in very large degree such a pattern has always been typical of the interstate system, and perhaps will be as long as states remain sovereign. The question of trends in "feudalism" over time is nevertheless an intriguing one. By measures other than those of political ties (as with alliances) the evidence is sketchy and contradictory. In some previous research on international trading links, I found patterns that were fully as "feudal" in the 1950s as in the 1930s, though the old colonial trade bonds had *begun* to loosen by the early 1960s.[27] Gleditsch, on the other hand, found evidence of *increasing* "feudalism" in the international airline network over the period from 1930 to 1958.[28] He, too, found that "feudalism" was declining in the 1960s. This agrees both with our impressions of the general situation of world politics and with the evidence from military pacts. Though more than a dozen new international alliances (that is, pacts between states not previously allied) have been concluded since 1955, most are solely within the third world and only one (North Korea and Russia, 1961) includes a superpower.

A related matter concerns an important continuity over the entire four-decade span: integration and dominance have tended to go together in the same alliances.[29] Few small-state alliances ever have shown much political or military integration. One must of course remember that some of the modern behavioral phenomena subsumed under these particular measures of inter-

---

[26] "East-West Interaction Patterns," *Journal of Peace Research*, III (May 1966), pp. 146–76.

[27] Bruce M. Russett, *International Regions and the International System* (Chicago: Rand McNally, 1967), Chapters 8 and 9; and Chapter 5, this volume.

[28] Nils Petter Gleditsch, "Trends in World Airline Patterns," *Journal of Peace Research*, IV (December 1967), pp. 366–407.

[29] This squares with the inductive findings of Karl Deutsch, et al., *Political Community and the North Atlantic Area* (Princeton: Princeton University Press, 1957), and Amitai Etzioni, *Political Unification* (New York: Holt, Rinehart, and Winston, 1965), that integration was promoted by the presence of a large "core-area." This can more usefully be understood, I believe, by the theory of collective goods. See Chapter 19 of this volume.

national cooperation and integration, most notably integrated military commands, are themselves postwar phenomena and were less widespread before 1939. But many were also fairly common in the 1920s and 1930s in the alliances that joined big and small states.

Even so, the relative success of superpower "pactomania" in the 1940s and 1950s must not be exaggerated. While the big powers were associated with most of the alliances and much of the integration of the period, their pact involvement was not closely related to war-fighting patterns. Neither the dominance variables nor the integration ones predict well to countries fighting on the same side in subsequent wars. Partly this is because no small power explicitly and formally under the protection of a superpower has in fact been subject to a full scale attack; thus, the protector has not had to fight beside its client. But in addition, the big powers have not been notably successful in getting their small allies to help them fight wars that have arisen in theatres far from the small allies' homelands. While some of America's NATO allies did participate in the Korean War, United States pleas in Europe and Latin America for help in Vietnam met with icy indifference.

A typology of alliances should reflect these four separate dimensions: Alliances characterized by *dominance* and its association with close military cooperation are common in both periods. The apparent relative shift of the big powers' concern from control to deterrence must not obscure the continuity. Similarly, throughout the period *duration* remains stubbornly separate as a feature of alliances. It is independent of most forms of structural integration, and dominant alliances are not necessarily durable. Still other alliances are characterized by *equality and voluntarism*; dominance is absent from the relationship and such alliances vary greatly in their typical duration. One final type of alliance is that typified by the features associated with *integrated defense* or "common defense."

We may compare this empirically based typological effort with the analytical ones cited at the beginning of the chapter. In general, the previous classifications do not predict well from initial characteristics of alliances to their outputs; that is, to integration, duration, and wartime behavior of members. For instance, the defensive pact–neutrality pact–entente classification has only moderate power. The neutrality pact does indeed prove to be a peculiar sort of alliance, or perhaps nonalliance is more accurate. It virtually disappeared from contemporary international politics. Defensive pacts are far more likely than ententes to show the paraphernalia of cooperation and integration. Defensive pacts, however, have not been notably more successful than ententes in ensuring long duration or cobelligerency in wartime. Possibly elements of Fedder's classificatory scheme might prove most useful, if instead of taking each of his variables as independent, we try to predict to duration with the others. But actually, we find that number of states, relative distribution of power among the members, and the security mechanisms employed all have very limited utility in this role.

This exercise has been a preliminary one, introductory both to further taxonomic exercises with different methods and other variables and to specific bivariate and multivariate hypothesis testing. We have, nevertheless, found important *regularities* both within each of two different international systems analyzed separately—multipolar before World War II, and bipolar afterwards —and *across the entire period* regardless of system changes. This last regularity is extremely important and argues strongly against views that stress the differences of alliances in each. The four basic clusters of variables that appear in the prewar analysis remain in the postwar era, and in two cases the similarities are remarkable. Equally important is the inability of the dominance and military cooperation variables to explain members' subsequent war-fighting behavior. That failure amply illustrates the limits of big-power dominance, and as a general phenomenon brings poignant thoughts about the problems of contemporary NATO. Similarly, throughout the period, duration remains stubbornly separate, independent both of dominance and of most forms of structural integration. As we must beware of interpretations that contrast alliances before and after World War II, we must be equally critical when those interpretations homogenize all alliances within either period. Our findings affirm the continuing differences underlying the very general label of international military alliance.

18
Transactions, Community, and International Political Integration

DEFINITIONS OF POLITICAL INTEGRATION

One of the most confused issues in the theory of international political integration remains that of the role of transactions—whether community bonds among peoples can be used as indicators or predictors of political integration. The proponents of transaction analysis are perhaps as much to blame for the confusion as are the approach's critics; it seems to me that someone basically sympathetic to transaction analysis ought to make the attempt to clear away some of the confusion. Although I have largely ceased to write on integration theory, a year in Brussels, where it is impossible not to be interested in political integration, convinced me that I should try. The writing that resulted forms the basis of this chapter. In it I suggest some new directions for research and theory. We will try to integrate some of the integration literature.

The beginning of any discussion of this issue must be with a clarification of various meanings attached to the term "political integration," since much of the difficulty stems simply from a failure to be precise on that matter. At least four basic and quite different meanings can be distinguished among the principal theorists. First there is the "classical" concern for political unification through the construction of supranational *institutions*, on the assumption that with a bare minimum of cultural and political homogeneity

Reprinted from *Journal of Common Market Studies*, IX, 3 (March 1971).

among the peoples concerned, institutionalization offered a feasible and effective means for maintaining unity. There was little concern for the matter of common loyalties, assuming rather that these would more or less autonomously grow up once the institutions were established. Most of the advocates of Atlantic Union, and more extremely of World Federalism, could fairly reasonably be classed among these institutionalists.

A second group owes its most influential work to the very innovative thought of Ernst Haas. Perhaps Haas's greatest contribution has been to focus attention on the political process of transferring *loyalities to new institutions*, rather than simply on institution building *per se*. Two quotations from his classic study, *The Uniting of Europe* make this clear: "Political community, therefore, is a condition in which specific groups and individuals show more loyalty to their central political institutions than to any other political authority." Political integration is defined as a process leading to the above condition. "The scheme here used by contrast [to Deutsch, see below] makes the existence of political institutions capable of translating ideologies into law the cornerstone of the definition."[1] This focus on loyalties, nevertheless, is limited to a concern with elite attitudes and behavior; Haas explicitly rejects much attention to popular attitudes because of mass ignorance about, and lack of sustained interest in, matters of political integration and other aspects of foreign affairs.[2] Furthermore, the concern remains with loyalties to institutions. For Haas the "ideal type" condition of political integration toward which members presumably strive is that of unification, possibly confederation but more probably federation. Much the same position can be attributed to Amitai Etzioni, who looks for a "center of decision making that is able to affect the allocation of resources and rewards throughout the community."[3] Leon Lindberg also requires "central institutions and central policies must develop," though he does not postulate as centralized an ideal type as does Haas.[4]

The perspective of Karl Deutsch is quite different. Probably his most important contribution to integration theory was to shift the focus of attention to institutions, even loyalties to institutions, from that of an end to a means. Deutsch's goal, as a theoretical dependent variable and for policy, is *the*

---

[1] Stanford: Stanford University Press, 1958, pp. 4, 7. By citing this early work I do not mean to imply that Haas's thought has not evolved further. In fact it has, and in directions that tend toward convergence with that of less institutionally oriented theorists to be cited below. The enormous influence of this particular book, however, requires us to treat it as a critical point of reference.

[2] Ibid., pp. 17–18.

[3] "A Paradigm for the Study of Political Unification," *World Politics*, 15, 1 (1962), p. 45.

[4] *The Political Dynamics of European Integration* (Stanford: Stanford University Press, 1963), pp. 7–9. See also Lindberg's more recent statement, "The essence of political integration is the emergence or creation over time of collective decision-making processes; i.e., *political institutions* to which governments delegate decision-making authority and/or through which they decide jointly via more familiar intergovernmental negotiation." In "Political Integration as a Multidimensional Phenomenon Requiring Multivariate Measurement," *International Organization*, 24, 4 (autumn 1970). (Italics mine.)

avoidance of war under conditions of continued voluntary association. The basic set of definitions at the beginning of *Political Community and the North Atlantic Area* reads:

> A *security community* is a group of people which has become "integrated." By *integration* we mean the attainment, within a territory, of a "sense of community" and of institutions and practices strong enough and widespread enough to assure . . . dependable expectations of "peaceful change" among its population. By *sense of community* we mean a belief . . . that common social problems must and can be resolved by process of "peaceful change."[5]

"Peace" maintained largely by repression or deterrence would not fit these requirements.

For Deutsch and his colleagues institutions are merely a possible means to the end of war avoidance without coercion; whether and when strong central institutions help in the achievement of a security community becomes a prime candidate for empirical investigation, not *a priori* assumption. Therefore they distinguish between amalgamation, involving a formal merger of previously independent units, and pluralistic security communities where the legal independence of the separate governments is maintained. Even here there may be some, perhaps very loose, institutionalization, but the emphasis is elsewhere. The point is that amalgamation—whether voluntary or imposed —may lead to formation or consolidation of a security community, but may also lead to empire or to provoking new strains and in fact the breakdown of a preexisting security community. The insight represents a fundamental break with earlier institution-oriented theories of integration.

Equally important as a distinctive feature of the Deutsch approach is the emphasis on people-to-people loyalties:

> The kind of sense of community that is relevant for integration . . . turned out to be rather a matter of mutual sympathy and loyalties; of "we feeling," trust, and mutual consideration; of partial identification in terms of self-images and interests; of mutually successful predictions of behavior . . . in short, a matter of a perpetual dynamic process of mutual attention, communication, perception of needs, and responsiveness in the process of decision making.[6]

For Deutsch, these loyalties are relevant not just among the elites, but for all the "politically relevant strata." Not only does he not rule out mass attitudes as irrelevant, "it is important to note that the enlisting of popular

---

[5] K. W. Deutsch, et al., *Political Community and the North Atlantic Area* (Princeton: Princeton University Press, 1957), p. 5.

[6] Ibid., p. 36. Because of these two features it seems appropriate to regard Deutsch's approach as an essentially new paradigm, addressed to questions unanswered and even unasked previously. The difficulty in relating it to previous efforts is therefore understandable. See Thomas F. Kuhn, *The Structure of Scientific Revolutions* (Chicago: University of Chicago Press, 1962).

participation was one of the most successful methods used to promote successfully a movement for amalgamation."[7] This stress on ties between the two communities is complemented by his declaration of the need for community ties on the vertical dimension, between the elite and masses of each nation. Without such bonds the two elites may be integrated but the masses alienated both from them and from their counterparts in the other nation. It becomes an empirical question as to how long, and under what circumstances, elites can ignore contrary popular preferences. It would appear that the development of community ties at the mass level is a longer and slower process than the elite transfer of loyalties that interests Haas; Deutsch would perhaps add that once achieved it is more secure.

It is useful to consider Deutsch's perspective as an essentially sociological one, on creating the bonds of community that must underlie continued peaceful interaction. In the grand sociological tradition, it is an emphasis on *gemeinschaft*: kinship, common loyalties and values, a feeling of belonging together, as contrasted with the *gesellschaft* focus on society as competitiveness and contract.[8] As Donald Puchala expresses it, community bonds "dampen international conflict by relieving domestic pressures for adamance, consequently defusing questions of 'face,' and making compromise and accommodation feasible."[9] Psychological-sociological community building must be attended to because institutions alone are (a) inadequate; (b) dangerous because they may provoke strains among people not yet ready to submit to coercion; (c) dangerous because if the community is lacking the union, if sustained, will be held together by force; and (d) largely irrelevant for modern political integration anyway, since the days of empires, or of *blut und boden* German unification, are substantially over. To quote Puchala again, "The initiative toward amalgamation remains an act of elite or governmental will, probably influenced but certainly not determined by community ties between peoples."[10] I would state the case more strongly: social community is a necessary, though not sufficient, condition for voluntary amalgamation. I do not dispute the analytical distinction between political community and social community, for example as used by Lindberg derived from David Easton.[11] However, I do propose, as a hypothesis that has been partially tested, that in noncoercive political communities social community must develop first or simultaneously. Note that community, as used here, is not to be equated with love.

One further meaning of integration for our inventory is that used by this

---

[7] Ibid., p. 93. Etzioni, in *Political Unification* (New York: Holt, Rinehart and Winston, 1965) also distinguishes between elitist and egalitarian unions and notes the advantages of the latter.

[8] I owe this distinction to Paul Taylor, "The Concept of Community and the European Integration Process," *Journal of Common Market Studies*, 7, 2 (December 1968), pp. 83–101.

[9] Integration and Disintegration in Franco-German Relations, 1954–1965," *International Organization*, 24, 2 (spring 1970), p. 199.

[10] Ibid., p. 200.

[11] See Leon N. Lindberg, "The European Community as a Political System," *Journal of Common Market Studies*, 5, 4 (June 1967) pp. 344–87.

author, the notion of *responsiveness,* or the probability that requests emanating from one state to the other will be met favorably.[12] Responsiveness in turn is the behavioral consequence of a ratio of capabilities to loads or burdens in a relationship, and the process of integration may be considered the process of building capabilities for responsiveness relative to the loads put on the capabilities. The degree of integration at any one time would be the current ratio of capabilities to loads. Thus we are concerned with behavior, and with the community ties underlying behavior. Integration may therefore be identified either in terms of behavior (responsiveness) or by the underlying capabilities-to-loads ratio; it is presumed that the two aspects would be extremely highly correlated, though there are very difficult measurement problems with both—see below—and *firm* proof of their close correlation is not yet available. At the moment the formulation is analytically akin to that which postulates a link between a ratio of achievement to aspiration and aggressive behavior, recognizing in each case that a complete inventory of the numerator and denominator of the ratio will not be easy, and that anyway there is probably another element (presumably small) in the determination of behavior that may best be termed a random element.

Whatever its difficulties, the purpose and supposed virtue of this formulation is to extend interest beyond the "mere" question of war avoidance (obviously I do not mean to deprecate concern with the war problem or the contribution that its solution would make to mankind's welfare) to a much broader spectrum of cooperative behavior. The concern becomes one of mutual problem solving, seeking a "higher" level of integration and a level that, with nations who are closely involved in one another's affairs, demands tighter and more numerous community bonds. War avoidance is a necessary but elementary aspect of responsiveness. Two nations, for example the United States and Great Britain, long ago achieved a security community. Depending on how one reads the evidence, and how slight an expectation of war one requires for the application of the term "security community," the two powers' achievement of that state can probably be dated from the turn of this century and certainly from the Washington Naval Conference of 1922. Yet within the no-war expectations one can point to various quite drastic ups and downs in relations between them. At times they have cooperated very closely to reach important goals, even at the cost of serious sacrifices by one or the other in the interest of maintaining the basic relationship. At other times, most dramatically in recent years the Suez crisis of 1956, they have worked at cross-purposes to each other's severe deprivation.

> Responsiveness of course implies a *mutual* relationship, it . . . does not insist that
> for a state to be considered "responsive" it must always give in to the demands of

---

[12] Bruce M. Russett, *Community and Contention: Britain and America in the Twentieth Century* (Cambridge: M.I.T. Press, 1963), especially Chapter 2, and *International Regions and the International System* (Chicago: Rand McNally, 1967), pp. 94–98.

the other. If so, the demanding state would be acting in a manner highly unresponsive to the needs of its jellyfish partner. Between nations as between individuals in primary groups interests will not always coincide, and the interaction of the partners will insure that some conflicts of interest become salient. When this happens there must be explicit or tacit negotiation, resulting perhaps in compromise, an exchange of concessions on one issue for some on another, or an "upgrading of common interests" to a new solution. Sometimes two governments' interests will be nearly identical, sometimes they will merely converge on the same goal for different reasons. But very often they will indeed conflict, and it is a relationship or pattern of behavior, the ability to work out that conflict with a minimum of violence and without one party always making the important concessions, that marks the condition of successful political integration.[13]

Again, responsiveness is the probability with which requests will be met favorably; any *particular* request may be met sympathetically or not. And in so far as we are concerned with *political* integration we are interested in the responsiveness of governments, of individual members of the political elite, of private individuals' attitudes toward the policy of their governments. Purely private acts (such as earthquake assistance provided by a private relief agency) are not part of the dependent variable of political integration, though they may well contribute to a growth in capabilities. As with Deutsch, I consider institutionalization *per se* not the focus of attention, though it may be a highly relevant independent variable affecting responsiveness.

> Where serious conflicts of interest exist between nations that can affect each others' destinies, some institutional structures must exist to facilitate negotiation, compromise, and coordination to produce common or compatible policies. Institutions provide important capabilities for attention and communication. An institution can be described as essentially a set of channels for processing information, solving problems, and transmitting communications. Along with less formal channels, they are vital capabilities in any effort to produce a high level of responsiveness between political units, even though by themselves they cannot guarantee the nonviolent resolution of conflict.[14]

There are also some important latent effects of institutions in changing the perspectives of those who participate in them.[15] Nevertheless, institutions alone are not enough, and may even put great strains on the relationship. In any particular case it may be difficult to know how to evaluate institutionalization; the best general statement is probably that if other capabilities are high, institutions also are likely to serve that function, but if other capabilities

---

[13] Russett, *International Regions*, p. 96.
[14] Ibid., p. 98.
[15] See Lindberg, *Political Dynamics*, p. 19, and Chadwick Alger, "Nonresolution Consequences of the United Nations and Their Effect on International Conflict," *Journal of Conflict Reseolution*, 5 (1961), pp. 128–45, and "Personal Contact in Intergovernmental Organization," in *International Behavior: A Social-Psychological Analysis*, Herbert C. Kelman, editor (New York: Holt, Rinehart and Winston, 1965).

are low, institutions may belong on the burdens side of the ratio in aggravating the situation. Nongovernmental and intergovernmental organizations are less likely to be seen as burdens than are supranational ones; they also are much more limited in their potential effectiveness.

By capabilities I mean facilities for attention, communication, and mutual identification. The first two are essential but clearly insufficient. One may keep close watch on an enemy and even maintain frequent communication with him. On the other hand, one cannot repeatedly respond favorably to another's requests without some current means of knowing those requests and their basis, without a large continuous exchange of information. Essential bonds of the social fabric between groups or especially nations are such ties as trade, migration, tourism, communication facilities like mail and telephone, and cultural and educational exchange. These ties serve as channels of communication whereby the needs and perspectives of one group of people are made known to others; they serve to strengthen the sense of mutual identification within the entire collectivity, and to promote a readiness to respond sympathetically to the needs of others within the collectivity. They contribute to mutual *predictability* of behavior and the accurate communication of wishes, without which cooperative efforts are hazardous. I have discussed the evidence for this in detail elsewhere and will not repeat most of it here, but to illustrate the general proposition I will cite once again two pieces of evidence about the relation of trade to politics. In a study of French businessmen's attitudes toward the European Defense Community (EDC) in 1954, Daniel Lerner found that businessmen who engage in no foreign trade whatever tended to favor establishment of EDC by a margin of 2 to 1, but that individuals whose firms did at least half their business in foreign trade favored EDC 6 to 1. Similarly, in my own work on British and American legislators I found that American Senators with personal ties or constituency economic ties to Britain were twice as likely to take a "pro-British" position on political issues than were Senators with no known ties. Correspondingly, British M.P.s with ties to the United States were twice as likely to be pro-American than were those who lacked discernible ties; those with two or more ties were three times as likely to be responsive as were those with none.[16]

In both these studies the issues at stake were broad and diverse, going well beyond anything that can be labelled a direct economic interest of the individuals involved. All these contacts become general channels of communication, opening individuals up to information and viewpoints they would not otherwise receive. In reviewing the literature on international exchange and attitude change Herbert Kelman concluded,

---

[16] Lerner, "French Business Leaders Look at EDC," *Public Opinion Quarterly*, XX, 1 (1956), p. 220, and Russett, *Community and Contention*, Chapter 9. The evidence on other kinds of ties is considered at length in ibid., Chapters 3, 6, 7. Similarly, see the view of J. S. Nye, "Comparative Regional Integration: Concept and Measurement," *International Organization*, 22, 4 (autumn 1968), p. 863, of transactions as indicators of *social* integration.

These are not necessarily changes in general favorableness toward the host country, but rather changes in the cognitive structure—for example in the complexity and differentiation of images of the host country. Such changes are probably more meaningful in the long run than total approval of the country would be; they indicate a greater richness and refinement of images and a greater understanding of the other society in its own terms.[17]

Puchala ties the argument to learning theory: "Learning during regional integration is a direct result of mutually rewarding actions among regional partners."[18]

Of course, trade, tourism, migration, and the rest *can* serve as irritants, though on the average they seem to bind nations or social groups together. The most important qualification—and that is a serious one—is that the exchanges must be *mutual* and on a basis of *relative equality*. Ties perceived as exploitative or "colonial," however strong, do not seem to have this beneficial quality. Contacts that are for one party involuntary (an extreme case being the payment of reparations) would not fit, nor would highly status-conscious relations such as those between employer and employee be good candidates. Contacts between highly disparate cultures are also very likely to carry conflict as much as to serve as capabilities. Tourists from "northern" to "southern" countries, for instance, may create animosities among their hosts and distress in their own minds. Thus the nature of the contacts must be examined for the particular case before any firm conclusions about their capability value can be proferred. A theory that ignored this necessity might be simpler, but would surely be misleading. Fortunately some very general observations can be made, indicating that ties between nations that are already culturally rather similar, and perhaps geographically proximate, carry a certain presumption of capability. Again, the presence of the ties themselves does not *prove* anything, but as Lijphart notes about relationships within a common government, a high level of political contacts requires a high level of social contacts for the relationship to be mutually rewarding.[19] In my emphasis on responsiveness and the ability to solve mutual problems I typically demand a higher level of capabilities than would Deutsch's concern with establishing a security community, but less than the successful functioning of Haas's institutional ideal type would require.

We can summarize this section with a simple fourfold table (Table 18-1) placing various schools or authors according to the importance their definitions of political integration assign to institutionalization and the establishment of loyalties.

---

[17] Kelman, editor, *International Behavior* (New York: Holt, Rinehart and Winston, 1965), p. 573.
[18] "The Pattern of Contemporary Regional Integration," *International Studies Quarterly*, 22, 1 (March 1958), p. 51.
[19] Arend Lijphart, "Consociational Democracy," *World Politics*, 21, 2 (January 1969), pp. 207–25.

Table 18-1
Some Definitions of Political Integration, and Their Definers

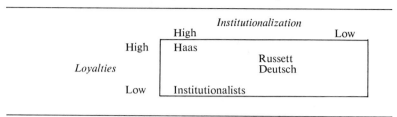

WHY MEASURE TRANSACTION FLOWS?

Carrying on from the preceding discussion we can further clarify the role of communication and transaction measures as related to political integration. Much of the literature on the topic, even as written by some of the principal theorists, is confused and confusing. Part of the difficulty is in a lack of precision about the definition of political integration being employed, and part stems from a failure to state precisely what the function of the transaction data is supposed to be. Often the question is "Why measure transactions instead of measuring integration directly?" Even where there is a specifiable role for transactions data, a failure to define the function of transaction data clearly has led to confusion as to which of several possible indices is appropriate. This point too needs elaboration, since the choice of indices is by no means self-evident even where the relevance of transactions in general is clear.

An analyst may have several roles for transaction data in mind. First, he may hope to use data on transaction flows to *describe* the state of political integration at any one time, or changes over time. According to Hayward Alker and Donald Puchala, the level of trade between nations "can serve as a reliable indicator of their degree of political integration";[20] Haas, on the other hand, flatly asserts that trade is not equal to political integration. A second question is whether transactions indicators can be used to *predict* political integration, in a sense to describe, with a high probability of accuracy, the future. Yet another is whether they are in effect necessary conditions without which there can be no integration—or, properly speaking, without which the probability of successful integration is "very low" since we do not want to be deterministic. Finally, can we say that in some sense heavy transaction flows "*cause*" political integration in the sense that they are sufficient conditions, or nearly so, bringing a "very high" probability of integration?

In turn, these must be related to various meanings of "political integration." We shall deal with the definitions of institutions without concern for the transfer of loyalties, of a security community as in Deutsch's work (leaving institutionalization aside), and my own concern with responsiveness. In so doing we omit Haas's interest in transfer of loyalties to institutions, largely because of Haas's own insistence that popular attitudes are relatively unimportant. While transaction flows are certainly not irrelevant to elite attitudes, few of the usual transaction data directly concern high politics at the governmental elite level and the case for the relevance to that variety of "political integration" is probably the least convincing.[21] A summary of the answers is given in Table 18-2: many of the items, especially all the "yeses," however, need careful qualification and will be subject to discussion below. The answers, it is important to note, are often tentative, *hypotheses* about what would appear given much more very careful research than now exists.

First we shall review the entire table, and then list the qualifications for the final two columns systematically. Clearly transaction data do not serve for *describing* the degree of institutionalization achieved between two states. If one wants to know about institutionalization it is much better to measure it directly, according to the number, powers, functional area covered, etc., of various institutions. Transaction flows are not sufficiently relevant to institutionalization alone—again remember that we are *not* in this first column concerned with the attachment of popular loyalties to these institutions— that it makes any sense to use transaction data as substitutes for direct measurement. There may be enough correlation at the very high and low extremes of transaction flows (if transactions are very high some institutionalization is almost certain to be present, and extremely unlikely if transactions are nil) but for most interesting cases the correlations are not likely to be strong enough to use the transaction data for descriptive purposes.

For the creation of a security community, however, the relationship may be a good deal stronger, subject to the qualifications to be listed. By definition, when transaction levels are very low nations are not relevant to each other (e.g., Burma and Bolivia) so although peace is of course expected, "peaceful change" is not at issue and it seems inappropriate to think in terms of a security community. On the other hand, there is good reason, in part from Deutsch's own work on the North Atlantic area, to think that security communities will evidence a high level of exchange in transactions (note the affirmative responses in the rows directly below). Nevertheless, the correlation may not be extremely high, and for areas where one thinks the security community has been established for some time here too it is best to measure the presence or absence of violence, expectations of peaceful change, and the absence of preparations for war directly. For areas where one may suspect the very recent establishment of a security community, however, transactions flows may provide valuable descriptive assistance if the direct measurements are ambiguous.

As for integration defined as responsiveness, the reasoning and evidence

---

[21] However, some of the typical indicators refer to elite transactions, and others could doubtless be devised should the theoretical basis warrant it.

Table 18-2

Transactions as Relevant to Meanings of Political Integration

	Definitions of integration		
Transaction flows	*As institutions (loyalties aside)*	*As security communities (institutions aside)*	*As responsiveness*
Do they describe integration?	No (except at extremes). Much better to measure directly	Yes. For long-term, measure directly	Yes. Maybe easier than measuring directly
Do they predict integration?	No (except at extremes)	Yes	Yes
Do they make possible integration?	Probably not	Yes	Yes
Do they cause integration?	Perhaps, at high levels	Probably, at least at high levels	Yes

discussed in the preceding section seem strong enough for us to believe that transaction flows may indeed provide a quite serviceable descriptive measure, in so far as they constitute capabilities. This is particularly so because of some very serious difficulties in efforts to measure responsiveness directly that have become apparent. Responsiveness may be sufficiently harder to measure than institutionalization or establishment of a security community that here the case for a surrogate transactions measure may be quite strong. We shall discuss some of these problems below. Even so, the need to establish qualifications to deal with the loads aspects of the relations must be considered, and will be dealt with. Research is badly needed to tell us how often, and with what qualifications, transaction data will do as a surrogate.

Transactions data do not *predict* institutionalization any better than they describe it, except again at the extremes. If transactions flows are now nil, institutionalization in the "near" future is most unlikely; if they are very high, future deinstitutionalization is also unlikely; but in the great middle range there is less to be said. On the other hand, transactions flows probably will predict to the other two varieties of political integration. Observed *changes* in transaction levels give a pretty good idea of the trends of war expectations and responsiveness, and in any case international transaction levels change at quite a slow, even glacial, pace. There is good evidence that barring unusual and drastic political change the year-to-year or even decade-to-decade transaction changes will be small.[22] Hence, if one has current data, especially on

---

[22] Russett, *International Regions*, and Chapter 5, this volume. Note that the relationship between transactions and war expectation may be curvilinear: starting at the zero level, increased transactions may lead to increased conflict, with the relationship reversing at high levels. At any rate a complex interaction with other variables is at issue. See below, and *International Regions*, pp. 196–202.

whatever trend does exist, one can make some reasonably confident mid-term predictions about political integration.

Transactions do not seem a necessary condition to make institutionalization *possible*, either, though here it seems desirable to hedge the answer just a little. Even coercive institutionalization requires some flow of transactions to carry intelligence to the rulers.[23] For the other two varieties of integration, however, the answer is quite a flat yes; neither security community nor responsiveness seems possible without "substantial" transaction flows.

Finally, do transaction flows in any sense *cause* political integration, in the sense of being a sufficient condition? The notion of cause is an ambiguous one, carrying much philosophical baggage, and perhaps it would be just as well to avoid it. And it would not be right to say that institutionalization must occur if transactions are high. But it may not be very inaccurate to say that institutionalization must occur if transactions *remain* at a high level, or at least that a high level of transactions, in the absence of institutionalization, will very quickly force a hard decision either in favor of institutionalization or of cutting back the transaction level. This seems to be what has recently happened among the nations of the European Economic Community concerning political integration in the financial domain. Trade, and to a lesser degree investment flows, have become so high among the Six that their economies are highly interdependent; all members are extremely sensitive to exchange rate fluctuations, price changes, and interest rate changes in each other's national economy. The resulting sensitivities appear to be so great as to impel them toward financial integration—initially mutual access to a community stabilization fund, but ultimately leading to a common currency. This seems to be the meaning of the decisions reached at and immediately following the Hague conference in autumn 1969.[24] Without such integration

---

[23] It should also be noted that according to Donald Puchala, "Mutual attentiveness, responsiveness, relevance, and the like, predate the launching of the EEC by nearly a decade. These transactional phenomena predate strong and widespread support for political federation by almost a decade and a half." ("Patterns in West European Integration," paper presented to the annual meeting of the American Political Science Association, Los Angeles, September 1970, p. 41.) Also, Lindberg, "Political Integration as a Multidimensional Phenomenon," does recognize that "the development of horizontal, identitive, ties among elites, and perhaps mass publics, is likely to be an important political resource, especially if the system is to handle stressful issues." He looks at survey and trade data, and his category of "resources of collective decision makers" includes many of what I call capabilities. I suspect further that my capabilities-to-loads ratio is in fact close to what Lindberg urges with his plea for attention to "stress response capability." Neither of these authors, however, goes so far as to regard these particular items as necessary for institutionalization.

[24] In a personal communication, Ernst Haas made it clear that he sees this phenomenon as a manifestation of spillover—evidence that there is indeed a good deal of convergence in our theoretical conceptions. For economists' views that economic integration does not *necessarily* bring political institutionalization see, among others, Lawrence B. Krause, *European Integration and the United States* (Washington: Brookings Institution, 1967), Bela Balassa, *The Theory of Economic Integration* (Homewood, Ill.: Dorsey, 1961), and Roger D. Hansen, "Regional Integration: Reflections on a Decade of Theoretical Efforts," *World Politics*, 21, 2 (January 1969), pp. 242–71. It seems to me, however, that these views essentially deal with situations of lower levels of transaction flows than are now emerging in the EEC. For support of my argument see Hans Schmitt, "Capital Markets and the Unification of Europe," *World Politics*, 20, 1 (January 1968), pp. 228–44.

purely national steps to deal with the instabilities, steps intended to diminish the economic interdependence of the members, would seem required. Something on this same order, of a less drastic nature, also may be occurring more generally among the OECD nations.[25]

Transactions, at least if carried on at high levels, may also be considered a cause of security community, in so far as they provide capabilities. To say that they cause integration, however, does not excuse us also from asking what may cause transaction flows to be high—they certainly are not a "prime cause." Similarly we may expect that high levels of transactions will virtually always result in substantial responsiveness, though in neither case do we ignore some fundamental qualifications.

CONDITIONS FOR TRANSACTIONS AS CAPABILITIES

What are these qualifications that have been attached to all the affirmative answers in the second and third columns? "Yes" always depends upon the following conditions being met:

1. The level of transactions must be high *relative to transactions within each subsystem*. The problem at issue is essentially one of competition for the attention of busy individuals often suffering from information overload. This is especially true at the elite level, but to a lesser degree also among the attentive public and even the mass. There are only 24 hours in the day; a man can read only so much, have so many briefings, make so many decisions. Various administrative and technical procedures may be devised to condense information or delegate responsibility, but there are limits to their value. Multiplying levels of information processing means increasing the probability of willful or inadvertent information distortion as it comes up the chain.[26] Ultimately, and particularly for busy elites, the *ratio* of messages from one source to the number of messages from all sources is a more important determinant of attention and understanding than is the total *number* of messages from any particular source.[27] Operationally, we may measure this with a ratio of messages originating externally to those originating within the domestic system, or for the relations of two particular nations, the number of messages originating in the partner to all other messages, external and domestic combined. The result gives a measure of the *weight* of the partner in decision-making processes. A typical empirical index, for example, is X_{ij}/GNP_i, where X is exports, GNP is gross national product, i a subscript for the exporting country, and j for the importing country.

---

[25] See Richard N. Cooper, *The Economics of Interdependence* (New York: McGraw-Hill, 1968). Interestingly, Cooper sees other capabilities within the wider OECD area as too slight to support successful voluntary institutionalization, so he in fact advocates certain very careful and limited national steps to limit the destabilizing effect of financial movements.

[26] See Anthony Downs, *Inside Bureaucracy* (Boston: Little, Brown, 1967).

[27] I have developed this point in more detail in *Community and Contention*, pp. 28–29.

It is essential to note that this index should be fairly high for *both* partners. If it is high for one and not the other, then instead of *inter*dependence there is a case of dependence one on the other. One country exerts important weight on the system of the other, but not vice versa. This is always a risk in the relation between a very large and very small country, or one where the economic system of one is very much more developed than that of the other. The danger is that the relationship will be, or will be perceived as being, exploitative or colonial. Even with the best of intentions the big country will, though inadvertently, exert great influence on the small one but it may be very hard for the little one to make itself felt in the big one to evoke responsiveness even if the predispositions in the big one are favorable.

2. The level of transactions must be high *relative specifically to other systems*, they must show a level that is appreciably greater than would be expected by random probability. To measure this Deutsch devised his well-known index of relative acceptance (RA) to control for size and measure the degree to which observed exchanges differ from random expectation. This becomes an index of one nation's *preference* for another. Like the weight index it is important, though perhaps less so, that the preferences be reciprocated. The preference index is certainly not a substitute for the weight index; empirically they are only moderately correlated in the world, they have different political effects; and each is essential to effective capabilities. Good evidence on their relative importance to political integration is lacking at the moment. This is very serious, and when the two indices point in different directions it is hard to draw convincing conclusions. In his more recent study of European integration Deutsch noted that the RAs among the Common Market countries, though generally positive, had risen but little since the mid-1950s. From this he drew his well-known conclusion about a plateau in European integration. On the other hand, I have noted approximately a doubling in the trade-to-GNP ratios for the same nations, and suggested that this pointed toward continued progress in political integration.[28] Part of the difficulty stems from

---

[28] Karl W. Deutsch, et al., *France, Germany, and the Western Alliance* (New York: Scribner's, 1967), Chapter 13, and Russett, *Trends in World Politics* (New York: Macmillan, 1965), pp. 36–37; later data in my "Interdependence and Capabilities for European Cooperation," *Journal of Common Market Studies*, 9, 2 (December 1970), pp. 143–50. Incidentally, this is extremely relevant to the criticism many have made of the recent Deutsch book, that it shows an alleged plateau in European integration when some specifically political indicators suggest continued progress. (For example, William E. Fisher, "An Analysis of the Deutsch Sociocausal Paradigm of Political Integration," *International Organization*, 23, 2 (spring 1969), pp. 254–90). From this, those who see continued political progress often conclude that transaction measurement should be discarded. Perhaps it means only that Deutsch's transaction data should have been interpreted from a slightly different theoretical viewpoint, and hence different indices formed of the same data. This is a theoretical rather than a methodological distinction. The point may be, to use a much overworked expression, that the very promising baby of transaction analysis should not be thrown out even if one does regard Deutsch's analysis as bathwater. (The Fisher critique's utility is compromised still further because his methods for measuring institutional decision making are so poorly described that his interpretation of political trends is equally questionable.)

the typicality of this as a situation where indicators conflict or are ambiguous; another part stems from the lack of evidence on past cases of integration as to which is the more relevant measure. Still another source of confusion stems from our apparent different usages of "political integration." My conclusions were meant to apply to capabilities for responsiveness. Deutsch, despite his earlier interest in security communities, seems in the more recent study to have focused on institution building or perhaps on the transfer of loyalties to institutions, since the achievement of a security community seems clear. One tentative hypothesis is that the preference index may be the more relevant to institution building or the creation of a security community, but the weight index more relevant to responsiveness.

It must be admitted that there is a certain zero-sum flavor to this emphasis on *relative* transactions. If transactions between two nations are high relative to domestic ones, and to transactions with other nations, somewhere the relative level of transactions has to be low. In short, one must give up capabilities in one geographic area to build them in others. I suspect this is a somewhat extreme formulation, and that by careful and knowledgeable acts the total supply of capabilities can be expanded. But there are limits to the rate and extent of that expansion, just as there are limits to a nation's ability to expand its economy. Moderate new demands on the economy or a national budget can be financed out of annual economic growth, but great demands will require the sacrifice of one or more former activities. This is unfortunate, but part of the human dilemma. We always have to make difficult choices, and at best we only can hope to sacrifice what is least important to achieve something more valuable. In making decisions that will affect the allocation of their capabilities for dealing with other nations, and with their own system, leaders must decide where the greatest burdens lie and try to direct their capabilities accordingly. It may not be possible to have the entire world integrated at once, by anyone's definition of integration. But political actors can attempt to build integration among nations where the potential rewards are greatest or to avert the most serious dangers.

3. The transactions must be *balanced*, truly an exchange. This is already suggested by the above statements that both preferences and weight should be mutual. Deutsch refers to the importance of "role reversal." It is surely not necessary that every particular class of transaction be in balance, but only that some overall balance among all major transaction categories be achieved. A flow of persons through migration, for example, may be balanced by flows of money or goods. Some cultural products may emanate from a new metropolitan center but be balanced by a flow of ideological or religious symbols from an older center. The important factor is that there be some sort of balance, especially in the perceptions of the citizens themselves.[29]

---

[29] To some degree the balance may be achieved by political processes—coalition formation, bargaining, and side payments.

4. Finally, transactions, as capabilities, must be high *relative to loads or burdens*. Only with reference to the level of burdens can one make any statement about how many capabilities are required to produce a desired level of responsiveness. In large part this point has already been made, with the insistence that transactions must be (1) high relative to intrasystemic transactions for both parties, (2) high relative to transactions with other systems for both parties, and (3) balanced. Imbalance is itself a serious burden on the relationship. Also, one must be aware of the particular political demands posed by other relationships. In the late nineteenth century, for example, there was substantial migration both from Great Britain and from Ireland to the United States. In both cases the immigrants already spoke English, came in at higher levels in the social order than did many immigrants from other countries, and could have been expected to contribute to capabilities in the relationship of the United States with the United Kingdom. However, this coincided with the Irish struggle for freedom from Britain. As a result, the Irish immigration made it substantially harder for the American government to establish good relations with the British government until Irish independence was achieved in 1923. Had the same level of Irish immigration come instead from almost any other country, it would have been, instead of a burden on the American-British relationship, essentially irrelevant. Similarly, heavy British exports to North America at the same time, which in principle should have served overwhelmingly as a capability, happened to be concentrated especially in certain products (woolen textiles, band and hoop iron, tin plate) whose American manufacturers were demanding heavy tariff protection. This coincidence of trade with domestic antitrade political pressures made the transactions into substantial carriers of burdens as well as capabilities, as they would not have been had British exports been of some product not made in America. An analogous problem exists with present-day United States imports from Japan.

A final example is from contemporary international politics. In a major triangular relationship with the Soviet Union, both English-speaking countries still see most of their contacts with the Soviet Union as threatening and burdensome. Given the hostility on both legs of the triangle connected with the Soviet Union, cognitive dissonance theory would lead us to expect that each of the other two countries would tend to perceive its relationship with the other in the most favorable possible light.[30] Also, coalition and alliance theory would lead us to expect them to make special efforts to emphasize the capabilities and suppress or resolve the burdens in their mutual relationship. And considering just the American-Soviet pair alone, clearly whatever transactions are carried on between them carry the special burden of inevitable

---

[30] An interesting application of this to Sino-Soviet-American relations is P. Terrence Hopmann, "International Conflict and Cohesion in The Communist System," *International Studies Quarterly*, 11, 3 (September 1967), pp. 212–36.

strains between the two greatest world powers in a bipolar system. Transactions must certainly be interpreted in light of the structure of the international system in which they occur.

Thus, transaction flows can never be counted mechanically and simply automatically assigned to capabilities. One must look for balance, for their relationship to level of transactions with others, and for special political burdens. These points have been made often in print before, but apparently they cannot be made often enough. While one may reasonably make certain presumptions about the capability of transaction flows in many circumstances, one must do so consciously and be alert for particular evidence which would contradict or reinforce the initial assumption.

NEXT STEPS IN THE DEVELOPMENT OF INTEGRATION THEORY

It is clear that much remains to be done in refining theory about political integration. These efforts must attend both to deductive theory building and to empirical testing; neither so far has been remotely adequate. There still are relatively few cases that have been subjected to intensive empirical analysis, and for many of those the theory employed was either insufficiently precise, or insufficiently comparable with other scholars' work, that the cumulative value of work so far is not great. More seriously, however, are some intrinsic limits to the quantity of empirical research on specifically international integration that can be done. If we are concerned with responsiveness between pairs of countries, then for recent international politics with approximately 130 nations there are more than 8000 pairwise relationships. Even leaving out relationships between countries that are essentially irrelevant to each other, we have potentially more than a thousand cases for examination. Perhaps much the same is true if the establishment of security communities is our concern.

If the creation of supranational institutions, and the transfer of loyalties to those institutions, is the phenomenon of most interest, the problem is much more difficult. There are few cases available for examination during recent decades, particularly if we restrict ourselves to cases of integration between states that are reasonably economically developed. And while we cannot yet be sure, there seems to be fairly good reason to suspect that the integrative process is very different for developed states; Nye noted that in East Africa one may readily concentrate on elite perceptions and behavior while almost ignoring those of the general populace, but that cannot be done in Western Europe with anywhere near such confidence.[31] If we insist on a

---

[31] See J. S. Nye, *Pan-Africanism and East African Integration* (Cambridge: Harvard University Press, 1965).

strong criterion of institution building—political union—there are at most only two cases of previously separate economically developed national entities uniting in this century: Canada-Newfoundland, and Yugoslavia after 1918. In the latter case, furthermore, we have to stretch our definition of economic development. Even if we lower the institutional criterion to include such half cases as the Belgian-Luxembourg Economic Union and the European Community, the available universe is not large. Extending it back into the nineteenth century might get us a few more cases—Sweden-Norway, Germany, Italy—but at the cost of losing control of some important political variables in systems where mass participation was much more limited than it is now. There are enough cases to sharpen our insights, refine existing hypotheses, generate new ones, and discard some old ones, but hardly enough for proper hypothesis testing. Hence, the case some writers make for a "configurational" approach to integration.

There are various ways in which the universe of cases for analysis might be expanded, but each exacts a price. I have already mentioned the use of historical material from previous eras. A great deal of information may be available in studies of subnational integration—the unification of metropolitan areas, or provinces or regional units of government, or the transfer of functions and loyalties from provincial to national institutions. There is much to be said for studies at the *very* subnational level, that is controlled laboratory experiments with small groups, perhaps somewhat on the order of Harold Guetzkow's Inter-Nation Simulation. But analytical and theoretical problems are certainly not avoided there either; one must worry about all the inevitably uncontrolled variables and the confidence with which small-group findings can be extended to the international level.

The need for analytical refinement of existing theory is just as great and as demanding as is empirical work. I consider my own focus on responsiveness to be substantively and theoretically very important, but fraught with difficulties that may make the effort sometimes seem of questionable worth. There are serious questions as to the degree it can be made rigorously operational. One is looking essentially for the probability of favorable response within the time desired by the party making the request (e.g., American blacks: "We can't want another hundred years."). In my book on Anglo-American relations I attempted to measure these through a combination of relatively "soft" analysis using the more or less traditional materials of diplomatic history with harder, more quantitative counts of treaty signatures and content analysis of elite communications. Basically, this is, I think, the approach that must be continued, but I feel my results there were only moderately successful and the intrinsic difficulties are great. For example, how about the *scope* of responsiveness? A party may be reasonably responsive to the other in certain cases of concern, such as trade and economic relations, but terribly dense and unmoving on security or cultural matters. If this is the case, how does one *weight* responsiveness in one area against unresponsiveness in the other to create any kind of overall index?[32] Or how weight responsiveness to elites rather than to mass demands, or to one interest group rather than another? Or what does one do about the problem of anticipated response; where a "responsive" act is taken before the request is even made overtly? Such a case might be the ultimate in responsiveness but might utterly elude our data-gathering net. In short, we are likely to have here most of the problems of "national interest" theory, and even more so those of the analysis and measurement of power. The relation to power theory is especially striking because in fact what we may have in responsiveness is mutual power, power over *each other*. As the problems with power theory are formidable, so are those with responsiveness.

Some help, especially at the international level, can and must come from efforts to develop refined measures of specifically political integration and community directly, as for example in the recent work of Lindberg and Scheingold, and Nye.[33] These efforts, however—notably the Lindberg scheme—often are extremely complex and empirically forbidding. For many purposes survey research on mass attitudes is very important.[34] It will be useful to know attitudes on directly political questions, such as readiness to delegate authority to institutions or, on responsiveness, approval of specific policies. Furthermore, survey data provide a direct measure of mutual identification. We must of course recognize the difference between elite and popular attitudes, since for the latter matters of integration are felt far less salient. In the end, neither direct measurement of political acts nor survey research will solve all our problems, given the difficulties mentioned above.

Instead, it may be worth while to contemplate adding yet another definition to our compendium of meanings for "political integration." I hesitate to suggest such a step given the level of confusion that already exists over the term, but I think there is substantial potential utility in a definition of political integration as *unity of action in relation to the external system*. We thus treat the relevant international or supranational organization as a subsystem of the superordinate global system, itself composed of national subsystems. We would look at various political acts by those national governments within the allegedly "integrating" system to see the degree to which they adopted a

---

[32] In this case I tend to agree with the argument of Lindberg, "Political Integration as a Multidimensional Phenomenon," rather than with Ernst Haas in "The Study of Regional Integration: Reflections on the Joy and Anguish of Pre-Theorizing," *International Organization*, 24, 4 (autumn 1970) on the difficulties of aggregating integrative processes across properties and issue-areas, and the multi-dimensionality of most.

[33] Leon N. Lindberg and Stuart A. Scheingold, *Europe's Would-Be Polity* (Englewood Cliffs: Prentice-Hall, 1970), and J. S. Nye, "Comparative Regional Integration: Concept and Measurement," *International Organization*, 22, 4 (autumn 1968), pp. 855–80.

[34] See particularly Ronald Inglehart, "Public Opinion and Regional Integration," *International Organization*, 24, 4 (autumn 1970), pp. 764–95, and David Handley and Dusan Sidjanski, "Aperçu des sondages d'opinion sur l'intégration européenne, 1945–1969," in *Methodes quantitatives et intégration européenne*, Dusan Sidjanski, editor (Geneva: Institut universitaire d'etudes européennes, 1970).

common policy. Various kinds of political acts in international politics are readily measurable and would be appropriate: signing trade agreements and customs unions, voting behavior in the United Nations, conclusion of military alliances, cobelligerency in war, comembership in international organizations. Clearly there are problems with this approach too; for example it is most useful for subsystems and thus it is not easily applicable to universal or quasi-universal integration. Also, it requires clearly identifiable political subsystems within the integrating unit, and hence might not prove valuable in those cases where "integration" had gone so far as to erase the demarcation lines around political subsystems.

The problem of scope remains also, since we might have to balance close cooperation in one policy area (e.g., trade) against serious divergence in another (military alignment). There is the possibility, nevertheless, that this handicap may not be so serious as it sounds, and there is some evidence that nations' policies in the international arena are in fact scalable. That is, one could predict with high if not perfect confidence that if several nations pursued a common policy on one matter that they also would be pursuing a common policy on certain other matters. For example there are no current cases of nations forming a common market without also being militarily allied. If this is approximately true over several different items the set of items together is said to form a Guttman scale; such scales are common in many areas of political research, including national behavior in international organizations. If with some regularity expansion of common action into a particular new functional area implies a higher level of integration, the scope problem is much alleviated.[35]

A perhaps more serious difficulty is how to control for apparent coercion; this is, how to deal with a case where a set of nations maintain a common policy toward the external world but where this common policy is *imposed* by one member on the rest, rather than freely chosen. Specifically in the contemporary world, how do we treat the apparent circumstances of Eastern Europe? The common action criterion might call those highly integrated, but that does too much violence (literally) to our other meanings of integration.[36] Of course we can define integration any way we wish, but this seems not to be a very useful or intuitively satisfying result.

One possible way of dealing with this might be to insist that the group of nations in question *also* meet all the transaction criteria, for level and balance. This would reestablish the requirements for voluntarism and mutual reward, while still leaving us with a measurable and important political output. If

---

[35] The evidence that many national actions of this sort are in fact scalable is contained in Robert A. Bernstein, *International Integration* (Ithaca, N.Y.: Cornell University Ph.D. dissertation, 1969). I am fundamentally indebted to Bernstein's study for suggesting common action as an operational definition of integration.

[36] Actually this may not be as serious a problem as it appears, since in Bernstein's coding on a six-point scale the satellites alone rank only 4 and the Communist system as a whole ranks 3.

both dimensions, of transaction and common action, are required, Eastern Europe's level of integration comes out much lower, and we perhaps have a definition that is intuitively satisfying but empirically workable. It is not empirically easy, because some of the measurement demands, when we check the transaction in depth to ascertain their capability content, are difficult. Nor is it intuitively perfect, for we still would be interested in institutionalization, transfer of loyalties, security communities, and responsiveness—all of which essentially deal with actions or perceptions internal in the "integrating" system. But it just might be a way to break out of some other shackles that at present threaten seriously to slow progress in the development and application of political integration theory.

19

Collective Goods and International Organization

IN COLLABORATION WITH John D. Sullivan

COLLECTIVE GOODS AMONG STATES

As they pursue their goals, actors—whether individuals, groups, or states—attempt to consume goods and services of various types. Generally they try to obtain such goods through private action. Thus, individuals clothe and entertain themselves by means of their individual actions in various marketplaces. Similarly, states will attempt to achieve goals and put policies into effect through their own actions. They will trade with other countries, develop defensive capabilities, and produce scientific knowledge substantially through their own efforts. States behave, then, as if they were private consumers in a market economy.

It frequently happens, however, that individuals and states discover they cannot produce a desired or needed good or cannot produce it in sufficient quantity. The realization that a desired good cannot be efficiently produced by individual actions may lead actors to consider development of a collectivity whose primary purpose will be the generation of the desired good. For example, members of a community will jointly support a fire department and a police department. Similarly, states may collectively support defense systems, scientific investigations, and environmental conservation and restoration programs. Forming a collectivity may permit them to produce the desired good for less than it would cost if provided through private action.

This chapter explores the problem of collective action through an analytical

Reprinted from *International Organization*, XXV, 4 (autumn 1971). Copyright © 1967 by the Regents of the University of Wisconsin. Written in collaboration with John D. Sullivan.

perspective derived in large part from the theory of collective goods. Collective goods theory promises to be of central importance in the understanding of many political phenomena. It deals with the conditions under which individuals or groups, often joined together in voluntary organizations, can coordinate their actions to achieve common benefits. The theory is most relevant in systems characterized by a low level of organized or institutionalized coercion: Individuals or states may try to coerce each other directly but cannot effectively appeal to a higher authority to enforce compliance with agreements, sharing of burdens, or collection of taxes. In short, it is made to order for the student who wants to know why *nation-states* behave as they do. Furthermore, unless the theory's implications are understood, many attempts to achieve collective benefits at the international level will be futile.[1]

First we must say what we mean by a *collective* (also called *public*) good. According to the standard distinctions collective goods are defined by two properties, one of which is "nonexclusiveness." As individuals pursue their interests independently, they frequently create external economies (or externalities) for other actors. That is, they provide benefits for other actors even though those actors may not pay all or even part of the costs involved. External economies are considered public goods when the benefits are made available to all members of a group; it is not possible or economically feasible to exclude nonpurchasers from the benefits. The other essential property is called "nonrivalness" or "jointness" of supply, meaning that each individual's consumption leads to no reduction in the supply available to others; this implies that the additional cost to others, if the good is provided to one, is small or actually zero. Private goods lack both these properties.

It is important to stress that the term "public" does not mean that the good must be produced by some governmental body. Rather, in perhaps confusing but nonetheless standard economic usage public here implies only that no one in the group can be excluded from access to the good, or that one person's consumption of the good does not hinder another's consumption, or both. This may well mean that the actors involved will seek some nonmarket solution to the problem, such as the development of some political mechanism.[2]

---

[1] The theory of collective goods has been developed in detail by economists. Its application to political problems stems from the work of Mancur Olson, Jr., in *The Logic of Collective Action: Political Goods and the Theory of Groups* (Cambridge: Harvard University Press, 1965); and to international politics from Mancur Olson, Jr., and Richard Zeckhauser in "An Economic Theory of Alliances," *Review of Economics and Statistics*, 48, 3 (August 1966), pp. 266–79, reprinted in *Economic Theories of International Politics*, Bruce M. Russett, editor (Chicago: Markham Publishing Co., 1968), Chapter 2. The present authors have also made substantial use of the theory, notably Bruce M. Russett in *What Price Vigilance? The Burdens of National Defense* (New Haven: Yale University Press, 1970), Chapter 4; and John D. Sullivan, "Cooperation in International Politics: Quantitative Perspectives on Formal Alliances," in *Behavioral International Relations*, Michael Haas, editor (San Francisco: Chandler Publishing Co., forthcoming).

[2] A number of writers have emphasized the development of political mechanisms in the supply of public goods. See James M. Buchanan and Gordon Tullock, *The Calculus of Consent: Logical Foundations of Constitutional Democracy* (Ann Arbor: University of Michigan Press, 1962); and Paul A. Samuelson, "Aspects of Public Expenditure Theories," *Review of Economics and Statistics*, 40, 4 (November 1958), pp. 332–8.

The private production of public goods need not lead to some form of political action, but political action is likely to result in production of more of the good —with more stable expectations and more nearly optimal supply—than is purely private action.

Most of what we buy as individual consumers—food, clothing, housing—are private goods. If a man buys a house, for example, its use is henceforth exclusively under his control. Similarly, the purchase (consumption) of the house takes it off the real estate market, and the supply of houses available to other potential buyers is diminished by one. Nevertheless, some purchases do not fit this description.

Production or consumption frequently has effects on other people in the form of positive or negative externalities. In the former case someone gets a free ride. In the latter case an actor has a burden imposed on him whose removal will require him to expend additional resources of his own. In the presence of such externalities actors are led to consider the possibility of ceasing their individual actions and of exploring instead the formation of a collectivity to apportion in some equitable manner the costs or benefits of the externalities being produced.

The control of air pollution is an excellent case of positive externalities in a public good which removes previous negative externalities. Take, for example, a factory, a "dark satanic mill" that produces, in addition to its intended manufacture, a great deal of smoke. For some reason, perhaps because the pollution is interfering with productivity, the owner decides that the smoke has to be reduced, and he goes to some expense to buy air pollution control devices for the chimney. Having done so, he realizes that not only his factory but also all the residents of the surrounding area benefit from the reduction in air pollution—though the factory owner has paid all the cost. Therefore he decides to take up a collection among the townspeople to defray his expenses.

Some residents contribute, but others ignore his pleas. In the immediate context, however, there is nothing he can do about the shirkers or free riders. Pollution control is nonexclusive; that is, it is impossible for the factory owner to make the air clean for contributors but dirty over the homes of those who paid nothing. Furthermore, nonrivalness of supply applies; the mere fact that the noncontributors breathe and enjoy the clear air does not diminish in any measureable degree the supply available to everyone else.[3] Thus, it will be very difficult for the owner to obtain voluntary contributions from others. Therefore, even though the total benefits, to him and others, may be very much higher than the costs, the factory owner will undertake the expense only if (1) the benefits to him alone are higher than the costs or (2) by some means, such as bargaining or organized coercion or tax collection, others can be induced to pay a share.

In most formulations of the theory of collective goods it is assumed that the good under discussion is "pure," i.e., it conforms completely to the two

---

[3] Of course, they may be actively polluting the air, but that is another matter.

criteria of nonexclusivity and jointness of supply. As Paul Samuelson has noted, this is one extreme point on the purely public to purely private good continuum. He suggests that a model of a mixed public-private good could be developed although he himself has not proposed one. James Buchanan has discussed such a model, and Morton Kamien and Nancy Schwartz have formally analyzed one aspect of the impure public good problem.[4] Any theory of public goods will ultimately have to deal with the consequences of departure from pure publicness. But for the purposes of this chapter we assume that the public goods produced by states are relatively pure public goods.

Most government purchases are of goods and services which largely fit the collective good characterization. Not only pollution control but also crime prevention, external defense, even public health and education (in the sense that the individual benefits when those around him are healthy and literate) meet the criteria. Governments purchase the goods and collect taxes to pay for them. Most individuals if left to themselves would not buy the goods or at least would not buy them in "sufficient" quantity because the benefits would be diffused to others; yet they are willing to pay taxes to cover the cost of those goods when they know that others are similarly required to pay. Still, some collective goods cannot be purchased effectively even at the level of municipal or state governments. For example, welfare benefits are distributed not only for humanitarian reasons but also for alleviation of the even more costly crime- and disease-breeding conditions of poverty. But if the benefits are set "too high" in a single city, poor people from other areas may move in and both they and the permanent residents elsewhere (who are relieved of any burden) benefit at the cost of the city's taxpayers. Hence the pressure for national welfare standards. This is also true of pollution control when the filth one area produces may travel hundreds of miles.

The same goods may appear as public or private goods depending on one's perspective. From the viewpoint of an individual within a state, military deterrence is clearly a public good. The state's deterrent forces, if necessary and effective, protect all citizens of the country; no member of the state can plausibly be excluded. For the state's opponents, however, its deterrence will appear as a private good (or "bad") since it is purchased at their expense, a case of rivalness. But the first state's deterrent forces may again provide a public good to the ally that takes shelter under its protector's umbrella. Thus, countries' purchases may constitute public goods for their own citizens and private or public goods for the citizens of other states.

One of the meanings of living in a "smaller," more interdependent world is that increasingly even the nation-state can no longer provide desired benefits because more and more goods are becoming collective at the international

---

[4] Samuelson, *Review of Economics and Statistics*, 40, 4 (November 1958). See also James M. Buchanan, *The Demand and Supply of Public Goods* (Chicago: Rand McNally, 1968), Chapter 4; and Morton I. Kamien and Nancy L. Schwartz, "Revelation of Preference for a Public Good with Imperfect Exclusion," *Public Choice*, 9 (fall 1970), pp. 19–30.

level. The present authors have shown, in their works cited previously, how military deterrence in international alliances, if provided at all, is such a collective good. As a consequence it becomes extraordinarily difficult to apportion the costs "equitably" within a voluntary organization such as the typical alliance or other international organization. Unless some form of coercion is applied, usually either the level of deterrence is lower than if some form of taxation could be enforced or the largest member or members pay(s) a notably disproportionate share of the costs. Often both phenomena occur.

Nation-states seek to form a collectivity to produce a collective good, then, when they are faced with external diseconomies which they cannot handle as individual actors. In economic terms, when they are unable to "purchase" a desired capability, such as an effective deterrent, in the international marketplace, they are forced to seek an alternative arrangement to generate that resource. This predicament presents states with a political problem. How can a situation best be structured to facilitate optimal production of the desired good at lowest cost? How can other states be induced to share the costs of producing the good? What strategies can be employed to ensure maximum participation with the lowest potential for conflict?

In this chapter we explore a number of implications of this principle for international politics in general, extending it beyond the current applications to deterrence and alliance theory. Problems of arms control, economic development, and international control of pollution illustrate the scope of the principle. We begin with a discussion of the conditions which may make possible the provision of a collective good; when available, empirical evidence will be given. These conditions may be brought into play through the adoption of appropriate strategies. In later sections we discuss some implications for the theory of international integration and conclude with a consideration of other collective goods among states.

Before leaving this general discussion, however, we should note one kind of problem which states or other types of actors may encounter. To what extent can an actor actually consume a collective good once it is created? As we noted above, a collective good is indivisible in that consumption of that good by one member of a group does not prohibit another member from consuming it. But the creation of a good does not guarantee that all members of the group will be able to consume that good. Frequently actors will find that certain additional resources are necessary to enable them to consume the good created by the collectivity. For example, a ghetto family pays taxes to the state in which it resides. Part of the state's tax dollar goes toward the development and maintenance of state parks. The family living in an urban ghetto may find, however, that it lacks the necessary means of transportation to get to a state park and benefit from that good. Similarly, a country may join with other countries in a collective effort to develop an industrial process only to find that its economy cannot support the industrial factors necessary for manufacture of the product involved. Scientific knowledge is a kind of collective good since, once it is published, all states can share it. But many countries will find that they do not have a resource base sufficient to permit them to consume such knowledge whether or not they contributed to its development. In general states will sometimes find that the existence of a collective good is, in one sense, not "public" as far as they are concerned since they are unable to consume that good for reasons unrelated to the good itself.

CONDITIONS FOR THE ACHIEVEMENT OF COLLECTIVE GOODS

Realization that a desired or needed good cannot be produced by individual action does not alone ensure that collective action will result or that the collective good will be produced. It is necessary for the actors to coordinate their behavior and to make decisions regarding the amounts of the good to be produced and the share of the burden to be assumed by each actor. Mancur Olson has suggested a numbef of circumstances in which the collective good can be provided to members of an organization. Using his discussion as a point of departure, in this section we consider various influences on the development of cost-sharing mechanisms for collective goods; alternatively those influences can be viewed as strategies that can be employed by states in deliberate attempts to generate a collective good.

1. At one extreme the collective good can be provided when members are *coerced* to pay their share of the costs. By coercion we do not necessarily mean brute force applied to unwilling subjects; on the contrary, most cases probably involve situations in which the members delegate to some authority the right to coerce them, freely accepting the coercion on the condition that it be applied equally to all members. Thus, citizens of a political system delegate tax-collecting power (under the principle of taxation *and* representation) in a democracy and are then able to obtain the standard collective goods that are the purpose of most governments. In private organizations, too, members may delegate coercive authority. The union shop, that in which all workers in a factory must join the labor union in order to retain their jobs, is such an example. Without coercion many workers would not join the union, but they would expect to obtain the benefit of higher wages negotiated by the bargaining agent. Yet, if very many workers did not join, the bargaining power of the union would be gravely weakened, and it would not be able to obtain higher wages for anyone.

In international organizations this delegation of authority is typically resisted. Any power of taxation is likely to be limited to nearly nominal amounts (as in the share of tariff receipts paid into a fund whose use is at present controlled by the Commission of the European Community, or the budget of the United Nations), or the authority to collect "taxes" may not in fact be backed up with the power to enforce payment (e.g., the United Nations after the Article 19 crisis). Delegation of coercive tax-collecting power is of course recognized as a key element in supranationalism and so marks a more advanced stage than has been reached by almost any international organization.

Given national preferences for independence, the cost of accepting coercion will often seem to exceed its probable benefits.[5] It is precisely the lack of overarching organizations with power to enforce agreements that creates an international problem when a nation-state produces something that becomes a collective good for other states. There is usually no coercive mechanism to which that state may appeal in an effort to make beneficiaries of the good share the burden. One of the classic concerns of international integration theory has therefore been the problem of how such institutions can be created and made acceptable. It has become apparent how difficult the process is.

2. A quite different perspective, which often stresses the undesirability or at least the irrelevance of coercive institutions, is that strand of political integration theory directed to ways in which *individuals' perceptions of their self-interest* can be greatly *widened*. If individuals no longer think only in terms of their own very narrow self-interest but include also the interests of others in their self-image, they will be willing to make certain sacrifices whether or not those sacrifices are directly reciprocated. The collective good may then be provided in adequate quantity. Beyond the family group the strength of such attachments is not likely to be great enough to produce very great sacrifices except among saints. Some of this does happen, however, in charity collections and within well-integrated nation-states generally. Within limits citizens of a rich area are usually willing to see some of their tax money go to help poorer areas without expectation of an immediate return. As noted in the previous chapter, a number of writers discuss the foundations of political integration in just these terms: a widening of mutual identification, a shift in loyalties whereby other peoples become involved in the individual's broader sense of self and the individual therefore becomes willing to listen sympathetically and often respond favorably to their requests.[6] Such a shift in loyalties does not occur quickly; typically it is a slow, often uneven process of change in social ties. At best it does have limits, even within the best-integrated nation-state—which makes substantial use of taxation and other coercion. So this means of achieving the collective good is not very dependable, particularly in the short run.

When the alternatives are posed in terms of probably unachievable or undesirable coercive mechanisms or an equally unachievable broadening of self-interest, one may be tempted to despair. Collective goods theory has alerted us to the importance of achieving many collective goods among states but has not yet offered a practical means of obtaining them. Yet there are in fact quite

---

[5] See John Gerard Ruggie, "Strategies and Structures of International Organization," paper presented at the Sixty-sixth Annual Meeting of the American Political Science Association, Los Angeles, California, September 1970.

[6] Karl W. Deutsch, et al., *Political Community and the North Atlantic Area: International Organization in the Light of Historical Experence* (Princeton: Princeton University Press, 1957), Chapter 1; and Bruce M. Russett, *Community and Contention: Britain and America in the Twentieth Century* (Cambridge: M.I.T. Press, 1963), Chapter 2.

a number of other strategies whereby states can provide incentives to one another, and it is essential, both for the formulation of policy and for the development of international politics theory, to examine them. We must shift our focus to methods which neither depend on selflessness nor require the delegation of coercive powers to a central authority.

Three related problems will be discussed. First, it is necessary to identify strategies designed to lead to a collectivity capable of producing the collective good. This requires that states or other types of actors coordinate their behavior and establish a group where none existed previously. Second, we will discuss strategies designed to bring into an existing group a country which is not presently a member but which benefits from the collective good. Third, some of the strategies considered below can be employed by a state attempting to alter the burden-sharing arrangements in a collectivity to make them more advantageous or to increase production of the collective good. Many of the strategies are applicable to all three problems while some are limited to one problem.

In any actual international situation many influences will of course apply; some will favor achievement of the collective good and others will hinder it. No one strategy or influence is likely to be decisive if many others point in the opposite direction. In any case, it is extremely rare anywhere in social science to find an interesting variable that always produces the same result. Hence we phrase all the following propositions in probability terms—the influence presumably raises the probability of the desired outcome—without being able to specify just what the probability is. At the current stage of research we are usually unable to cite systematic evidence for our theoretical propositions and often have to rely on examples to support our statements. The reader will, of course, frequently be able to think of counterexamples. For instance, we suggest that, ceteris paribus, a collective good will more readily be achieved in small groups than in large ones. But surely there are cases, including cases of international organizations, in which larger groups have been more successful in obtaining the good thanks to the intervention of other influences. Further research must involve careful study of such interactions. Similarly, with so many influences or potential strategies we cannot at this stage suggest what is likely to be the most successful mix of strategies, either in general or in any particular situation.

3. The collective good may be provided to an almost "optimal" degree in a group in which *one member* is very much *larger* than all the other members; Olson labels this a "privileged" group. In such a group the big member may find it worthwhile to provide all of the good regardless of whether the others contribute anything. By bigger we mean wealthier, richer in resources. The argument is an extension of the principle of marginal cost. For a rich member the proportionate sacrifice of $100 is less than for a poor member: For a state with 10,000 taxpayers the per person cost is one cent while for a state with 100 taxpayers the per person cost is one dollar. Hence the big member will

feel it is forgoing less to take up a particular burden than will the smaller member. Similarly, if the good at issue is truly a collective one, the small member will gain proportionately far more benefit from the big member's exertions than vice versa. Thus, the costs seem much lighter to the big member, and the benefits can be obtained so easily by the small member without any sacrifice that the burdens actually borne are very disproportionate. In his book Olson calls this "the 'exploitation' of the large by the small."[7]

This is not just a deductive theoretical statement. In circumstances in which the conditions are really met (i.e., the good is truly collective and no coercion is involved) there is a great deal of empirical evidence for the proposition. Enough evidence exists in international organizations to satisfy us of the theory's relevance for the behavior of states (e.g., United Nations special assessments, and military pacts such as the North Atlantic Treaty Organization [NATO], the Warsaw Treaty Organization [WTO], the Inter-American Treaty of Reciprocal Assistance [Rio treaty], the Central Treaty Organization [CENTO], the Southeast Asia Treaty Organization [SEATO], etc.).[8] What is not at all clear, however, is how big the disproportionality in size must be for the group to be "privileged," i.e., to be a group in which the big member pays *all* the cost. One can make purely deductive arguments that are not very helpful; in international affairs there is evidence to suggest that the membership of the Rio treaty for defense of the Western Hemisphere may constitute such a group, but probably NATO, which contains a number of middle-sized European members, does not. As a strategy deliberate inclusion of a larger state among several small ones may be an effective means to ensure provision of the collective good, but it is unlikely to promote proportionate sharing of the costs.

It is important to stress that it is not just largeness as such but also the value of the good to a state which will have an impact on the amount it is willing

---

[7] Olson, p. 29.

[8] Olson and Zeckhauser, in Russett, *Economic Theories;* and Russett, *What Price Vigilance?* and references in that volume. More recently Robert Angell has compiled data on the ratio of national voluntary contributions to agencies of the United Nations system to the same states' assessments. See Robert Angell, "National Support for World Order: A Research Report," *Journal of Conflict Resolution*, 17, 3 (September 1973). The numerator is composed of the contributions made by each state to the Expanded Program of Technical Assistance (EPTA), the UN Special Fund, the United Nations Children's Fund (UNICEF), and the United Nations–Food and Agricultural Organization (FAO) World Food Program during 1961–1968. The denominator is composed of assessments for the United Nations, FAO, the United Nations Educational, Scientific and Cultural Organization (UNESCO), the World Health Organization (WHO), and the International Civil Aeronautics Organization (ICAO) for the same years. States with high voluntary-to-assessed ratios tend to be large states. The rank orders on the contribution scale correlate positively with an r^2 of .10 with the rank orders for gross national product (GNP) in 1965. It may be contended that the Union of Soviet Socialist Republics and its military allies should be excluded from this computation on the grounds that they have consistently been a minority within the UN which gains disproportionately few benefits from it and hence have little incentive to make voluntary contributions to UN activities. If this is done, the r^2 for the ranks of the remaining states on the two indices rises to .21. There is also a small but statistically significant correlation ($r^2 = .12$) between states' sizes and their contributions to the International Red Cross (IRC) as a percentage of GNP. We are grateful to Angell for sending us his data.

to share. The evidence cited above supports the hypothesis that largeness has an impact and assumes that each state values the good equally. One can, however, construct situations in which a small state would be willing to assume more than a proportionate share of the burden because it valued the collective good more highly than did other states. For example, two small allies may both take shelter under the deterrent umbrella of great power. One may be geographically very close to a potential aggressor while the other is very distant. Presumably the former will value the major power's deterrence more highly than will the latter and will thus be more likely to make some contribution of its own to a collective deterrent effort. Or, two countries may equally contribute to international water pollution and may each border on the polluted river. But if one has an alternative supply of clean water and the other does not, presumably the one without the alternative supply will value the collective good, pollution control, more highly and will pay more to obtain it. In these circumstances countries which value a collective good especially highly must find additional incentives, valuable to other states, if they are to induce the others to cooperate and share the burden.

4. There is some evidence that free riders, those that attempt to benefit from a collective good without contributing to the costs of achieving it, are especially common in very large groups. The problem seems to be one of visibility, and the *size of the group* producing the collective good is likely to be an important factor both in the procurement of the good and in the arrangements for sharing the burden.

Olson describes an "intermediate group" as an entity in which no single member has enough incentive to pay the entire cost of obtaining the collective good, but the membership is nevertheless small enough that one member will notice whether the others are paying any of the costs and will be able to see the effect of its own contribution. Olson is not entirely clear which of these factors (the ability to see what others are doing or the ability to see the effect of one's own actions) is likely to be more important, but in any case there is reason to think that small groups will be more effective than larger ones. According to this principle bilateral international organizations ought to be more successful in providing collective goods to their members than multilateral organizations would be, and three-member organizations should be more successful than larger ones.[9] Hence a strategy for producing collective goods

---

[9] This assumes, of course, that the membership is large enough to command the resources needed to provide the good and that the good is not importantly a collective good provided at no cost to nonmembers as well. A recent article points out that the apparent effect of size cannot be deduced merely from the principles of rationality and self-interest as has sometimes been assumed. The authors nevertheless "admit that with regard to the supply of many collective goods, the problems of coordination necessary to overcome the free rider tendencies in the group could increase as the group gets larger. . . . We would expect that most of the relations between size and free riders stem from changes in the costs of the goods and the costs of communication among the individuals who would receive the goods." (Norman Frohlich and Joe A. Oppenheimer, "I Get By with a Little Help from My Friends," *World Politics*, 23, 1 [October 1970], p. 108, footnote 10.)

might involve keeping the group small or at least focusing attention on members' contributions (see proposition 6 below).

It is not at all obvious what the interaction between propositions 3 and 4 is —for instance, whether more of the good will be provided in a three member group in which one member is very large or in a two member group in which both are the same size. The matter needs to be investigated empirically and probably cannot be settled deductively.

5. The collective good may be obtained if the group can use the *provision of private goods to members* as an inducement to states to join and to bear their share of the burdens in achieving collective goods. That is, in addition to providing collective goods that go to contributors and noncontributors, or even to members and nonmembers alike, the group may also provide something whose distribution it can control. The typical labor union, for example, is able to obtain for its members seniority rights, procedures for processing grievances against the management, and special insurance schemes. Some of these may not go to nonunion workers at all, others such as grievance processing may be formally available to all but may not always be prosecuted vigorously. Hence even when union membership is not required and nonmembers will benefit from the higher wages negotiated, most workers still have strong incentives to join. In coalition theory these particular individual or private benefits are often referred to as side payments. The use of such incentives is common in international organizations such as military alliances. A small member of an alliance may be able to shelter under the deterrent umbrella of a big state without making any significant military effort of its own; however, for their own reasons the leaders of the small state may want access to the big partner's sophisticated military equipment. Supersonic aircraft become a prestige symbol in return for which a government may make budgetary and manpower contributions to the alliance's military forces.

In the water pollution example discussed above it may be the case that the technology for ending pollution exists and all that is required is the expenditure of resources to put the technology to work. In such a case a state may attempt to "buy" the support of other countries by offering a purely private good. For example, the state downstream may offer the other state a favorable trade arrangement in return for support in sharing the burden of cleaning up the river.

In other cases, however, participation in production of the collective good may itself provide private benefits. Research and development necessary for producing pollution control equipment, or for producing an effective military deterrent, have technological side effects which may yield payoffs in developing the capacity of a country to produce other kinds of goods. While such private benefits cannot always be anticipated or planned for, they do serve as inducements to join the activity and hence to share the burden of the collective good. We discuss this further under proposition 7 below.

6. The collective good may also be provided when *social pressure* can be

used to encourage members to make contributions. In charity collections it is common to use neighbors or coworkers to solicit contributions; university alumni groups often publicize not only the names of all their members who contributed to the alma mater but the amounts as well. Similar procedures may be used in international organizations. The NATO annual review and its secretariat's annual publication of members' national income and military budget figures according to standardized definitions are attempts to put the spotlight on laggard member states. Analytically this may be only a subset of proposition 5: Prestige and social standing in the group become a private good for which members are willing to pay some share of the costs of collective goods. This influence is worth distinguishing, nevertheless, for there is a real question as to how effectively it may work in international organizations. Olson suggests social pressure can be effective only in small face-to-face groups, and sociologically this seems sound. In large degree the NATO annual review and the periodic meeting of foreign or defense ministers constitute such face-to-face groups, but the issue is the source of their prestige, social standing, and especially political power. A political leader may be much more willing to face the scorn of counterparts from other states than to make demands of his countrymen. While this chapter largely considers the nation-state as the basic unit of analysis, that is, of course, a dangerous simplification if its obvious limitations are forgotten.

7. The collective good can often be achieved largely as a *by-product of* members' expenditures undertaken solely to obtain *private goods*. As has been noted in previous research small states that would prefer to rely on their big allies rather than build their own military forces for deterrent purposes may nevertheless have a large army for purposes of internal security and coercion of their native populations. As a by-product such an army may also have deterrent value, and so the common deterrent force will be larger than it would be if the functions of an army could be kept nearly segmented. Some United Nations members may earmark military forces for international peacekeeping when they would be unwilling to pay for the upkeep of troops permanently under the UN. Earmarked forces can always be used to serve the state's private needs, UN troops cannot.

8. Sometimes a collective good may be provided by breaking a large group down into several smaller ones after which the *small groups* would be *federated*, at a higher level, into a more comprehensive unit. Then the effects of propositions 4 and perhaps 6 pertaining to the greater success of smaller groups can be brought into play. Also, by judicious distribution of small members and big ones proposition 3 about the value of having some members very much bigger than others can be applied.

9. The collective good may be provided in more nearly optimal quantities as a result of *education or propaganda*. Two aspects of this proposition deserve mention. The first involves the nature of the appeal made to the other state.

Messages may either be attempts to shift the perceptions of another actor or attempts to alter the other actor's preferences. A state may directly attempt to convince a free rider that it is benefiting from a collective good and should assume some of its cost. Or, states may duplicate each other's efforts and by their independent actions "overproduce" certain goods. In an alliance the smaller power may feel that the larger's deterrent umbrella is not in fact protecting it adequately and may, as France and the United Kingdom have done, build its own nuclear forces. If the big-power defender (e.g., the United States) could persuade its allies they were indeed covered, they would not need their own deterrents. Instead of then asking them to make a direct contribution toward the cost of the common deterrent the major power might urge them to put their newly freed resources into some other endeavor of common interest such as economic aid to less developed countries. Whether to induce another state to assume a share of an existing burden or to remove the inefficiencies associated with duplicated efforts, states can use education to change perceptions.

Alternatively, a country may try to convince another that its current policy in some area is not in its own best interests. Such a strategy is designed to shift the preferences of the target state. The United States government for some time tried (with little success, which is probably fortunate) to convince the Europeans that the Indochina war affected them and that they should become involved in the conflict. These appeals were attempts to alter the preferences of the European states and induce them to convert the military conflict into a collective action. In general such an approach is designed to increase the marginal utility of a good so that other states will sacrifice more alternative goods to get the one in question. The strategy may focus directly on the collective good itself in an effort to persuade all members and especially the larger ones to spend more for it (see particularly proposition 3), or it may focus on certain private goods whose provision indirectly contributes to achievement of the collective good (proposition 7).

The second aspect of this strategy concerns the target of the educational appeal. Most often it will be directed toward the relevant ruling elite in the target country, the intent being to shift preferences or alter perceptions of those responsible for existing policies. In some instances, however, the educational strategy may be directed toward the citizens of the target country in the hope that they in turn will put the appropriate demands on their own political system. Given the difficulties of propagandizing the citizens of another country and moving them to action, the probability of success in this strategy is usually low.

Most efforts to "sell" collective goods across national boundaries are likely to be problematic. Typically the product is an intangible one. It may be relatively easy to recognize that external economies and diseconomies are created internationally but very difficult to put a value on them. There is no clear market price internationally for goods such as health or military security.

Perhaps more important, the vast majority of communications reaching people still originate from within their own countries; cross-national propaganda will probably be only a drop in the ocean of messages competing for most individuals' attention and hence will not be very effective. A shift from material to moral incentives, which may be possible within small revolutionary countries like Cuba or Tanzania, is much less likely to be effective globally.

10. As a supplement to some of the other strategies, it may be possible to increase to a modest extent the amount of the collective good provided by using Thomas Schelling's famous tactic of focusing on a *prominent solution*. If some level of contribution can be identified as in some way obvious and perhaps fair, members may respect it. This is often the practical virtue of equal assessments, or assessments proportionate to size, provided that the amounts in question are not large enough to make evasion worthwhile. International law serves to some degree as a normative system to strengthen incentives. If other guidelines are lacking and if the costs are not too high, the behavior prescribed by law will be followed.

Some potential division of labor may emerge to provide a prominent solution whereby each actor has a different task in the achievement of the collective good. If nonperformance of the task is obvious, one actor may retaliate against a shirker by shirking its responsibilities until the other's efforts are resumed. One clear example would be two neighboring states, each of which is to blame for some pollution extending beyond its boundaries. If one is downwind but upstream from the other, there is a potential for individual but coordinated action to relieve both kinds of pollution. Similarly, burden sharing in a military alliance may be encouraged if there is a very powerful technological or logistic basis for a division of labor. Both land and sea forces might be essential for effective deterrence, but one state may have a clear comparative advantage in producing the former and the other the latter. By itself, however, the tactic of identifying a prominent solution among states is not likely to be very effective, and it needs to be combined with the effect attributable to one or more of the preceding propositions.

SOME IMPLICATIONS FOR POLITICAL INTEGRATION THEORY

These strategies, then, can be utilized by states as they attempt to coordinate their behavior. Frequently the states involved develop institutions to facilitate cooperation, and the countries' elites and citizens alter their perceptions of each other and extend the area of cooperation to many different problems. Since collective goods are so often at issue, it is important to look at existing political integration theory in light of collective goods theory and the above strategies. In the following discussion we can only make some illustrative connections between the two sets of theory rather than attempt a full discussion of the political integration literature.[10]

Proposition 4, and perhaps also proposition 6, would explain the apparent greater success of many small, especially regional, international organizations as compared with big ones. The evidence for the advantage of smaller international organizations is incomplete, but there is some. Robert Bernstein has developed a six point scale for measuring the effectiveness of twenty multilateral international organizations. This scale correlates negatively with the number of states in the organization, showing a Kendall's tau of $-.23$.[11] Of course, the virtue of regional organization may not be due entirely to rather small size. The greater degree of interaction and of cultural similarity, which are highly correlated with geographic propinquity,[12] makes the members much more susceptible to social pressures (proposition 6) than would be the case with the same number of highly disparate members. Proposition 2 also applies.

From this apparent advantage conveyed by small size and the suggestion that large groups be broken down into federations of smaller groups (proposition 8), we have support for some traditional theories of international organization which stress a role for regional units as "constituent and permanent elements of a World Government structure."[13] Such units become "building blocks" in images of a multilevel wider union, sharing the burdens of such a union and handling issues of a restricted scope. Collective goods theory thus strengthens the theoretical basis for this viewpoint.

Proposition 3, furthermore, provides a deductive basis for explaining the well-known finding of Karl Deutsch et al about the value of a predominant large "core area" in promoting integration.[14] The value of a core area may stem

---

[10] In their discussion of "coalition formation mechanisms," Leon N. Lindberg and Stuart A. Scheingold identify a set of factors which include several of the strategies discussed above. In analyzing integration in the European Community they discuss functional spillover, side payment, actor socialization, and feedback as mechanisms actors can employ in forming coalitions. See their *Europe's Would-Be Policy: Patterns of Change in the European Community* (Englewood Cliffs: Princtice Hall, 1970), Chapter 4 and pp. 155-7. See also the special issue of *International Organization* that they edited, 24, 4, (autumn 1970); and the previous chapter.

[11] See especially Robert Bernstein, *International Integration* (Ithaca, N.Y.: Cornell University Ph.D. dissertation, 1969).

[12] Bruce M. Russett, *International Regions and the International System: A Study in Political Ecology* (Chicago: Rand McNally, 1967), Chapter 2.

[13] See Alan de Rusett, *Strengthening the Framework of Peace: A Study of Current Proposals for Amending, Developing, or Replacing Present International Instituions for the Maintenance of Peace* (London: Royal Institute of International Affairs, 1950), p. 159. For reference to other representatives of this school see Russett, *International Regions*, p. 12.

[14] Deutsch, et al. See also Amitai Etzioni, *Political Unification: A Comparative Study of Leaders and Forces* (New York: Holt, Rinehart, and Winston, 1965). The desirability of having one member large enough to constitute a core area has been challenged by Ernst B. Haas and Philippe C. Schmitter in "Economics and Differential Patterns of Political Integration: Projections about Unity in Latin America," *International Organization*, 18, 4 (autumn 1964), pp. 705-37. Joseph S. Nye, "Comparative Regional Integration: Concept and Measurement," *International Organization*, 22, 4 (autumn 1968), especially pp. 877-9, shows that among sets of less developed countries economic integration is likely to be greater when the members are more or less of *equal* size. In fact, the proposition about a core area may apply least to common markets in which the mix of goods is relatively nearer the private end of the public-private spectrum.

much less from its potential coercive power than from the likely willingness of its political leaders to accept for their country a disproportionate share of the burdens of providing the collective good. When the total costs are spread over a large populace, the marginal costs to each individual, even for obtaining a substantial amount of the collective good, may be small enough be make the effort appear worthwhile to them.

The Deutsch et al findings about the need for a generally high rate of economic growth within the area to be integrated, and for mutual balance of rewards accruing to different members, can also be understood in the light of collective goods theory, specifically proposition 5. Members may be induced to bear the burdens of providing the collective good if private goods can be generated by the integrative process and withheld from noncooperative members. The "balance of rewards" seems to be a matter of observing the wide exchange of these goods in the cases of successful integration. A high rate of economic growth is important in generating resources that can be distributed mainly as private goods to those groups or individuals (such as farmers, or workers in declining industries, or groups in less developed areas) that do not benefit automatically from, or may even seem to be damaged by, the immediate effects of integration. In general the exchange of private goods is likely to involve one party surrendering something it does not regard too highly to another party that wants it more. Such processes can establish trust and an apparatus for continual exchange.

The European Community seems to present a case of highly successful economic integration and moderately successful, if still incomplete, political unification. It has achieved a very high rate of economic growth and does appear to show a good mutual balance of rewards. It does not, however, have a core area. The largest national unit, the Federal Republic of Germany (West Germany), has a gross national product (GNP) only a little over 25 percent larger than France's and its margin in population is even smaller. Normally this difference would not be enough to evoke the benefits of proposition 3. Nevertheless, an impressionistic view of the situation suggests that West Germany does take over a major function of a core area for the European Community since it is willing to bear a more than proportionate share of the cost of providing the collective goods. This shows up most clearly in agricultural price supports through which the West Germans have long subsidized French agriculture at very costly levels. Yet, this has been a worthwhile investment for West Germany since in return it has received a private good for great value following the Hitler years: respectability and stable ties to Europe. Now, however, these goals have largely been achieved, and West German citizens may be less willing to continue to make disproportionate economic sacrifices in order to sustain the momentum of European unification.

Several writers have maintained the position that if successful political unification is not to be based excessively on coercion, it must be grounded on high levels of mutual responsiveness, loyalties, and identification between the members—in short, upon the kind of social base discussed in proposition 2. This kind of base can be built up between states, but it is dependent on a slow accretion of transactions, communications, and institution building. Noncoercive or pluralistic integration requires fewer preconditions, and imposes fewer strains on the relationship, than do efforts to create institutions capable of supranational coercion.[15] From the perspective of this chapter, nevertheless, there is a major difficulty with the emphasis on pluralistic integration: If it demands less, it also is likely to achieve less. When collective goods are at stake, as they are so often, it may seem possible to achieve them in adequate amounts only with institutions capable of enforcing the collection of contributions toward their cost. But, if coercive mechanisms are undesirable or unattainable, how can states obtain benefits they very greatly desire: peace, security, control of pollution, etc.? Simple exhortation is rarely successful. The alternative is to explore, more carefully and with a greater sense of urgency than before, possible applications of the noncoercive mechanisms we have suggested above.[16]

COLLECTIVE GOODS AS A GENERAL PHENOMENON

The problem of collective goods is acute in many areas of international politics and is certainly not limited to the most obviously economic questions of costs and "tax" collection. One example is the relative efforts made by various industrialized states to promote scientific research and development. It could well be argued that whereas research and development can provide very important private goods for states—e.g., development of special strains of wheat resistant to local diseases or military research especially when kept secret by security measures—much research and development produces collective goods for all countries. That is, the product of science comes quickly into the public domain and can be exploited by technicians anywhere regardless of whether they made any contribution to its production. To the degree that this is correct collective goods theory predicts that big states will bear a more than proportionate share of the costs of world science. This is in fact precisely what happens. Data on research and development as a proportion of GNP for sixteen members of the Organization for European Cooperation and Development (OECD) in 1963 and 1964 show a correlation of $r^2 = .60$ with total GNP. For a big state the monetary cost of any given scientific project is much

---

[15] Deutsch, et al. See also, inter alia, Russett, *Community and Contention;* and, most recently, by Russett, "Interdependence and Capabilities for European Cooperation," *Journal of Common Market Studies*, 9, 2 (December 1970), pp. 143–50.

[16] We would like to point out the many basic similarities between the problem identified by collective goods theory and that known in game theory as the prisoners' dilemma. It seems likely that a deliberate effort to bring these two literatures together, especially drawing on the experimental material on conditions favoring cooperative behavior in the prisoners' dilemma, would be very valuable.

less painful than it is for a small one, and ultimately all states share most of the benefits in a world in which science is international.[17]

The whole area of control of international pollution is one which has received little attention but which has potentially significant consequences for international politics. Observers who have noted that nation-states in the mid-twentieth century are highly penetrated anticipate even more such penetration. In the not-so-distant future states will be forced to sign treaties which not only require that they regulate their relations with other states but also stipulate that they must regulate the activities of their citizens in order to prevent pollution. States may have to agree, for instance, to prohibit the production of types of consumer goods for which it is impossible or too costly to institute pollution control measures. Such developments would obviously create extremely difficult political problems for the leaders of many countries and would constitute a potential source of domestic conflict and disruption. Such activities would raise serious questions about individual freedom in democracies and about national sovereignty.

Problems of pollution control interact with concerns for global economic development and political stability. All states have an interest in reducing international pollution, but rich states can most easily bear the cost of introducing low-polluting but expensive technologies. Poor countries, however, will find it difficult or impossible to do so. For example, in order to feed their people they may need to continue to use cheap DDT despite its domestic and global polluting effects. If so, rich states may have to assume some of the poor states' costs as well as their own. This conflict of public and private goods has profound implications for a potential global redistribution of income. Collective goods theory also has enormous implications for population control. For some countries, at least, a large population may still appear as a plausible route to national power—even if it damages the global environment. This is said to be the view of the current Brazilian government.

Elsewhere in international politics the application of sanctions against states violating international norms, the enforcement of arms embargoes, and the observation of agreements against the spread of nuclear weapons all illustrate the basic difficulty. It may appear to be in the general interest of all states, for instance, that economic sanctions succeed in disciplining a deviant govern-

---

[17] The data are from *The Overall Level and Structure of R and D Efforts in OECD Member Countries* (Paris: Organization for Economic Cooperation and Development, 1967), pp. 9, 14. The correlation is substantially unaffected by various transformations of the GNP data such as $\log_{10}$ and use only of rank orders. Note that these are all advanced countries. The least developed states might not have the private technological resources necessary to exploit the available collective good. See our discussion above. We should also note that technical objections are sometimes raised to correlations such as this in which one variable (e.g., GNP) appears in the denominator of the other (e.g., research and development to GNP). It can be shown, however, that in all such instances cited in this chapter the effect is in no way to inflate the apparent relationship between the variables and that the procedure is both theoretically and methodologically appropriate.

ment. Any one individual state, however, can reap very substantial commercial and political benefits by trading with the outlaw, benefits that may seem far to exceed the cost it would suffer by the breakdown in international order that violation of the sanctions would cause. Thus, even when there are no particular ideological or political incentives to maintain the violator's defiance (as there are for Portugal and the Republic of South Africa vis-à-vis Rhodesia), it may be very hard to obtain universal observance of the sanctions on a voluntary basis. Small states particularly—since they will gain proportionately more from a few million dollars worth of trade than large ones will— may see net benefits in ignoring the sanctions. Much the same is often true of arms embargoes.

Whether this will also be the fate of efforts to prevent the spread of nuclear weapons is still unclear. The incentives for nth countries to build atomic bombs may become very great if their immediate enemies seem to have them or to be about to get them. Any breakdown in international restraints, or any resulting general increase in the risk of nuclear war, may seem slight compared with the need for a counter to the direct menace to the threatened state's security. Again, the incentive to be "irresponsible" is probably greater for a small country than for a big one. Here, however, there are also important disincentives. The material cost of a nuclear weapons program is high, and this will bear most heavily on small countries. Furthermore, the immediate political costs of being the first to break the nonnuclear front are likely to be very high. If one state in a conflict pair acquires nuclear weapons first, it is likely to drive its opponent to do the same, resulting in a decline in the security of both. Thus, there is much less pressure to violate the nonnuclear norm until an opponent does; both Israel and the United Arab Republic, for instance, have continued so far to abstain despite the depth of their hostility toward each other. Finally, this is an instance in which the existing nuclear powers have tried fairly hard to offer special compensation to states that stay nonnuclear even in the face of a threat. By explicit alliances and implicit assurances some effort has been made to assure nonnuclear states that they will be sheltered from nuclear attack even if, and indeed perhaps only if, they stay nonnuclear.

This leads us to a last and very general observation about the possible means for achieving collective goods among states. Typically the focus of practitioners and even scholars is upon coercion in one form or another: States must be prevented from damaging the common good or forced to pay a fair share of the costs. But as we have argued, effective coercion, particularly among states, is often unachievable or manifestly unfair or at best risky and likely to provoke new strains. Given a world not yet ready to accept strong global coercive institutions, more attention should be paid to ways in which the rewards for cooperative behavior can be made stronger and more apparent. A rather old-fashioned legalist view is concerned with creating norms and ensuring their enforcement. Newer approaches to international law stress the creation of incentives for a desired behavior and disincentives for other behavior, an

approach which looks for the basic motivations behind acts and tries to reinforce those that lead to approved behavior. Learning theory in psychology
stresses rewards as well as punishments, and indeed for many situations rewards for desired behavior are more effective than is punishment for undesired
acts. Punishment, or threatened punishment, may raise a decision maker's
anxiety level and make it difficult for him to perceive alternatives or to weigh
calmly the consequences of his action. Punishment, deterrence, and coercion
have long been central foci for attention in international politics; greater concern with structuring rewards might now pay dividends.[18]

The focus on creating incentives and disincentives also points to a problem
implicit in collective goods theory and crucial for the development of successful collectivities in the international system. Such groups and organizations
will not form by happenstance, nor can one rely solely on "spillover" or other
more or less automatic mechanisms. Rather, national leaders must recognize
that frequently the only way an external diseconomy or economy can be handled is by some form of deliberate collective action. The question of the styles
of international leadership and of the prerequisites for successful collaboration between states becomes paramount.

In his discussion of the growth of international organizations Ernst Haas
has stressed the importance of the active role that the head of an international
bureaucracy must take to develop the organization's ideology so that the organization may grow. He argues that any organizational ideology which does
not meet his "desiderata" will fail to overcome certain obstacles to growth.[19]
We share his concern for effective leadership, whether by states or by international organizations, and have suggested some strategies for the noncoercive
achievement of collective goods by collective action. An appropriate ideology
will have to incorporate collective goods theory in some form.

---

[18] See, for example, Johan Galtung, "Two Approaches to Disarmement: The Legalist and the
Structuralist," *Journal of Peace Research*, 5, 2 (1967), pp. 161–94; John Raser, "Deterrence
Research: Past Progress and Future Needs," *Journal of Peace Research*, 4, 4 (1966), pp. 297–
327; and by the same author, "Learning and Affect in International Politics," *Journal of Peace
Research*, 3, 3 (1965), pp. 216–26.

[19] See Ernst B. Haas, *Beyond the Nation-State: Functionalism and International Organization*
(Stanford, Calif.: Stanford University Press, 1964), pp. 119ff.

Index